Hide-and-Seek with Angels

Hide-and-Seek
with Angels

A LIFE OF J. M. BARRIE

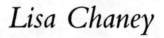

Lisa Chaney

ST. MARTIN'S PRESS

New York

Extracts from *Peter Pan Works* by J. M. Barrie © 1937 Great Ormond Street Hospital for Children, London

www.stmartins.com

Library of Congress Cataloging-in-Publication Data

Chaney, Lisa.
    Hide-and-seek with angels: a life of J. M. Barrie / Lisa Chaney.
        p. cm.
    Originally published: London: Hutchinson, 2005.
    Includes bibliographical references and index.
    ISBN-13: 978-0-312-35779-5
    ISBN-10: 0-312-35779-6
    1. Barrie, J. M. (James Matthew), 1860–1937. 2. Authors, Scottish—20th century—Biography. I. Title.

PR4076.C54 2006
828'.91209—dc22
[B]

                                                                                    2006042355

First published in Great Britain by Hutchinson

First Edition: July 2006

10 9 8 7 6 5 4 3 2 1

For Jessica and Olivia

'So singular in each particular'

and for Paul, James,
Anna and Kate

Contents

List of Illustrations

Every effort has been made to contact copyright holders. The publishers will be glad to make good in future editions any errors or omissions brought to their attention.

The Barrie and Ogilvy families

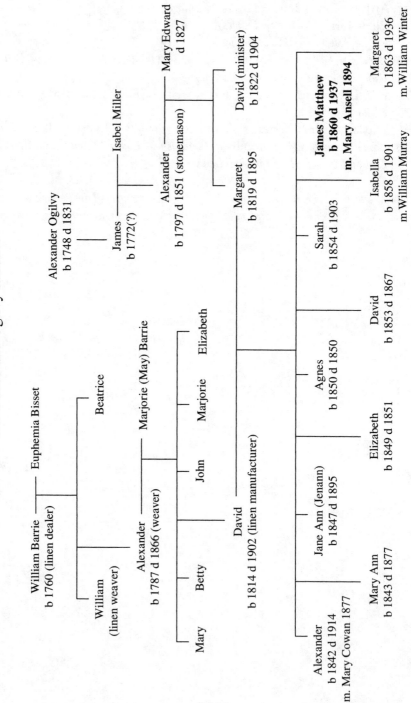

Acknowledgements

In a lightning strike my computer was destroyed – and with it apparently half this book – requiring hours of skilled effort way beyond my capabilities to recover the hard drive. On this and several other demanding occasions, Barrie's warning, 'May God blast any one who writes a biography of me,' came to mind. Without the patience, goodwill, and humour shown me by those involved in the book's making, I might have admitted superstition and abandoned the task.

Barrie's earlier biographers, in particular Mackail, Darlington, Hammerton, and Dunbar, and more recently writers such as Birkin, Ormond, and Jack, have looked at various aspects of his complex personality and writing. The works of Mackail, Birkin, Ormond and Jack have been of much value in the development of my own argument and are more fully acknowledged in the Bibliography. In addition, Cynthia Asquith's writings, Roger Lancelyn Green's study of *Peter Pan*, an article by Lynette Hunter, and the most recent bibliography of Barrie's work, by Carl Markgraf, have been of great help. These are described in the Bibliography.

I am grateful to the librarians of that ideal institution, the London Library, who provided numerous books with their customary acumen and courtesy, matched only by the librarians at the Beinecke Library, Yale University. In combination with the riches in their care, their efforts on my behalf made research at Yale a daily pleasure. I owe especial thanks to Taran Schindler, unfailingly gracious and capable, who organised for copies of Barrie's notebooks, then more manuscripts, and pictures, to be sent to England.

I thank those whose assistance, and enthusiasm for a project not their own, often proved crucial: Peter Burman, Director of Conservation, National Trust for Scotland; Desmond Banks; Madeleine Judd; Harry Burton, (*Peter Pan*, Birmingham Rep, 2002); David Crane; Maggie Jackson; Paul Taylor, Samuel French Ltd; Richard Ellis; Andy Kale; Julia Binns; Ben Armstrong; Nick Baldwin, Archivist, Great Ormond Street Hospital for Children; Janet Birkett, National Museum of Performing Arts; Roxanne Peters, V&A Picture Library; Philip Burnham-Richards, Hulton Getty; Sheila Philp, previously of the Barrie Birthplace (National Trust for Scotland); Robert Greenham; Brian Shaw of Kirriemuir; Fiona Guest,

Gateway to the Glens Museum; Christine Sharp, Kirriemuir Library; Malcolm Macbeath, Kirriemuir; Norman Atkinson, Angus Council Cultural Services and The Scott Polar Research Institute.

For welcoming hospitality and the variety of ways in which I have been helped to gain a better picture of J. M. Barrie, also for permitting me to look at their papers, Laura Ponsonby and Kate Russell (who have permitted me to quote from Lord and Lady Ponsonby's writings, and whose liberality made everything about research and staying at Shulbrede Priory memorable); Charles and Pippa Sweeton; Tanya Sweeton (who gave permission to quote from Margaret Ogilvy Sweeton's writings); Marjorie Barrie who lent many of her papers; John Richardson for Hazelshaw House; and Martin Sheehan, *Peter Pan* Development Officer, who has permitted quotation from *Peter Pan Works* by J. M. Barrie: copyright 1937 Great Ormond Street Hospital for Children, London, and also from Andrew Birkin's *J. M. Barrie and The Lost Boys*: copyright the Special Trustees of Great Ormond Street Hospital Children's Charity. I am also indebted to Anita Brookner for permission to quote the extract from her novel, *Latecomers*.

The friends and family who have discussed, encouraged, and sustained, despite the neglect on my part that immersion in Barrie's life has led to, include: my father Keith, whose conversation once again proved the cornerstone; my mother Elizabeth, who has been unfailingly solicitous; Saul and Vanessa Jacka; Sira Dermen; Roger Eland; Harlan and Delia Walker; Christianne Heal; Joe and Emma Roberts; Helena and David Alexander; Jo and Richard Baker (unerring facilitators); Nadia Cockayne; the late Stephen Warburton, and Phil Thomas; Peter and Esther Coates; Jane Moody; John and Mairi McCormick; Simon and Julie Mitchell, Bruce Wannell, Christine Roe and Alisdair Hood. I am deeply grateful to my sister Anna who, throughout the book's making, has read, commented, supported and, as always, given wise advice. To those friends who read the manuscript: Jane Moody speed-read and made useful corrections; Jo Baker, typically thoughtful and sensitive, recommended important changes; Phil Thomas, with customary verve, painstakingly trimmed and made it more transparent; and George Ramsden, with inimitable wit and humour, pointed out howlers and suggested numerous and subtle improvements. Although I haven't taken all their advice, and the responsibility for any omissions and mistakes is my own, they have all contributed to making this a better book, and I am tremendously grateful.

To my agent Clare Alexander, for her equanimity and encouragement in developing the idea, I owe much. For taking the book on, I am very grateful to Sue Freestone; I am most appreciative of James Nightingale's undeviating calmness and skilful management through the final stages.

Tony Whittome's shepherding of the book and its author with such enlightened conviction and constant discernment made him the perfect editor. He has my heartfelt thanks.

My daughter Jessica suggested characteristically ingenious alterations to the jacket design, while she and her sister, Olivia, have steadfastly amused, counselled, and been constant sources of strength. My final thanks are to Marcus, whose contribution has been paramount.

'When I was ten, I read fairy tales in secret and would have been ashamed if I had been found doing so. Now that I am fifty I read them openly. When I became a man I put away childish things, including the fear of childish things and the desire to be grown up.'

On Three Ways of Writing for Children, C. S. Lewis

'No dramatist has ever been more perilous to criticism than Barrie within a week of his death.'

'Barrie as Dramatist', TLS, 1937

'This all goes to show that there is more in me than meets your eye.'

Letters of J. M. Barrie, August 1919

Introduction

When James Matthew Barrie died, in 1937, there was national mourning. Crowds gathered; reporters and newsreel men came to record the day and well-known figures followed the coffin to its resting-place in the churchyard on the hill. A month later a memorial service led by the Archbishop of Canterbury was held in St Paul's Cathedral for the Scottish weaver's son, who died Britain's most famous playwright. With accolades that included a baronetcy, the Order of Merit, honorary doctorates from a string of universities, and friendship with some of the most eminent men and women of his time, Barrie was a world-famous author even before he wrote *Peter Pan*. And yet the life and work of the author of the greatest theatrical work for children ever written is today little known. Although at times he irritated them, the majority of his contemporaries considered him an exceptional artist whose reputation was assured. Robert Louis Stevenson, for example, was not alone when he wrote to Barrie: 'I am a capable artist; but it looks to me as if you are a man of genius'. Like that of many popular authors, Barrie's reputation was much reduced after his death, but with the exception of *Peter Pan*, the degree to which this has remained the case is extreme. Seventy years on, no more than a handful of perceptive modern critics have recognised that his essentially radical art, including a repeatedly spelt out belief in the superiority of women, has for too long gone unnoticed.

A succession of novels (including *Sentimental Tommy*, one of the most inspired on childhood yet written), followed by long-running plays of sophisticated political satire and subtle social comedy, brought Barrie great wealth and huge popular acclaim. By 1902, his name was such a draw that more than one of his plays was often on in London at the same time; in that year it was *Quality Street* and *The Admirable Crichton*. But his success wasn't only a popular one, and Barrie could boast the respect and friendship of older literary luminaries: George Meredith and Thomas Hardy, as well as many of those nearer to his own age.

His ability to write successes meant that Barrie attracted financial support, in turn permitting the highest-level productions. Underpinned by his consummate stagecraft, these were enhanced by elaborate sets and costumes, the most avant-garde lighting techniques, specially written music and the best actors of the day. Unhappily, his astounding success did little to modify the strains in Barrie's private life, and his divorce in 1910 – which then carried great social stigma – was followed by a series of bereavements which finally left him broken in spirit.

Savouring his tremendous public image, Barrie nonetheless gave almost no interviews, remaining an inscrutable, enigmatic figure and, to a greater degree than many writers, an outsider. He put doggedness on record as one of his foremost qualities. Once he had decided, for instance, that someone was to be his friend, there was little to be done in the face of the onslaught. Barrie was by turns entertaining, charming, funny, selfless and generous. His philanthropy went far beyond the valuable gift of *Peter Pan* to the Great Ormond Street Hospital. In addition to many anony-mous charitable gifts, he spent large amounts of time writing plays and sketches for fund-raising.

In person elusive, likewise in his art he was difficult to categorise. Much of the critical establishment has remained wary of him, chastising him for being popular, by implication no more than middle-brow. Critics' inability properly to explain the intangibly moving quality of the best of Barrie's plays has often been converted into hostility.

More often than not, Barrie camouflaged a serious purpose behind deliberately stylised and pleasant surfaces, with the result that the increas-ingly prevailing realist school of thought was antagonised. Apt to bury his demanding message too successfully beneath complex riddles and humour, Barrie laid himself open to misunderstanding. But he also persisted by making his point in many different ways, in the hope that his audience would eventually understand. He was by nature driven to make contact, and parts of his nature were intensely feeling and emotional. Although the charge is not unfounded, in his best work Barrie was not the whimsical sentimentalist he has so often been judged. If the true sentimentalist produces a falsity of emotion, a mismatch between feel-ings and what happens, and a wish to skate over the shadowy side of humanity, then much of Barrie's own self, and absolutely central to his art, was an acceptance of the darkest aspects of human existence putting him far beyond the realms of sentimentality.

His deepest personal and artistic preoccupation grew from an inescapable tension. While on the one hand it would not be an exag-geration to say that Barrie's whole being was devoted to escape – some-thing necessary as a mechanism to survive the reality of his earliest childhood experiences – on the other his greatest writing was a profound enquiry into the inescapable implications of time, and the idea of one's own end. As one learns more about the man it becomes clear that his work was an uncanny transfiguration of his preoccupations and experience. In *Peter Pan*, the distillation of years of thought, his immense artistic gift was displayed to its extraordinary best. In the play where 'all children except one grow up', Barrie unmasked himself and at the same time touched on a universal nerve, the *problem* of growing up. For him it wasn't simply that growing up was a passing difficulty that gradually one found ways of accommodating; to an unusual degree its implications touched all aspects of his life.

As the quintessential artist, who didn't simply investigate a problem, Barrie was so endlessly fascinated by it that he *lived* it. Time, with its implications of mortality, was an obsession and he wished that the universe were different. (Thus it was that he came up with one of the most inspired images of time and its attendant fears in modern literature: the crocodile who had swallowed a clock.) Why was it necessary to abandon childhood and a life of play? Why did one have to become adult and responsible? Why couldn't time stand still? Barrie's work was not a simple escapist fantasy but a mature investigation into childhood and its implications for the adult who must eventually grow old.

This was the central motivating force that drove his life and art. As an artist of real stature, he was able to transform and project his vision on the grandest scale; in this case he created a myth. *Peter Pan*, one of the greatest of twentieth-century myths, was a work of art quite unlike anything that had gone before. A century after his debut the eternal Boy continues to exert his mysterious appeal, long since a part of the common culture of the Western world. Peter Pan's story is an enduring myth of modernity. A modern child, he signifies a type, and is as relevant today as on his first appearance one hundred years ago.

As my research progressed, the complexity of Barrie's ideas and quite how significant he was became increasingly evident. This book is not, then, an exhaustive study. Rather, it is an attempt to give an overview of Barrie's life and work in the hope that the reader might discover, as I did, how remarkable an artist he was.

1

'It's no' him, it's just me . . .'

Cemetery Hill is long, rising almost three hundred feet above Kirriemuir's clutch of narrow closes, twisting wynds and steep braes. The grassy upland is crisp under last night's hard frost. A cricket ground on the summit looks out to the rugged grandeur of the Angus glens, a terrain renowned for its rivers, forests and remote lochs. Here, the first snows often leave the single-track roads impassable. Further on up the glens the hills grow craggier and wilder, while the streams narrow and become more precipitous, eventually leading back to the looming heights of the Grampians. In the early morning sun Glen Prosen and Glen Clova's snow-bound slopes look closer than their four miles' distance. This is a harsh terrain, beautiful but not kindly. It is a landscape marked with the past; one from which sprang myths, ghosts and the seductive, heartless fairies.

A few miles southwest the tiny settlement of Meigle was once a gathering place for the ancient Picts, one of the few peoples whom the Romans never managed to subdue. Nearby Forfar was their capital. At Meigle a collection of monumental stones is inscribed with those enigmatic Pictish characters, mythological beasts, and men. Other stones nearby are etched with the symbols of early Christianity. Under a slab beneath a great seven-foot-high cross, King Arthur's Queen, Guinevere, is said to lie.

With its back against the wildness of the glens Cemetery Hill looks out over quite another landscape; a landscape suggestive of the more disciplined and practical men and women who created it. To left and right as far as the eye can see lies a narrow band of fertile land, Strathmore, separated from the old port of Dundee and the Firth of Tay by the low-lying Sidlaw Hills. Punctuating the length of Strathmore's rolling farmland is a string of small market towns, whose staple forms of employment were the manufacture of jute and the weaving of linen cloth. During the nineteenth century the city of Dundee was so successful it became known as Juteopolis. In Kirriemuir, meanwhile, they wove linen.

If 'the Child is father of the Man', so, too, a place becomes location and milieu, making it both physical setting and social surround of people and artefacts. In this way the two starkly contrasting landscapes, each with its corresponding implicit vision, would infuse and inform everything that the man James Matthew Barrie was one day to write down.

During the course of the later eighteenth century, and the whole of the nineteenth, Scotland, like the rest of Britain, was subject to great waves of change. The population rose sharply and this rise was especially concentrated in the towns. In parallel and closely connected to these events, two revolutions were taking place: an agricultural revolution and an industrial one. Indeed, without the great advances in agricultural practice the industrial revolution could not have happened. A steady increase in food production – due mainly to 'enclosure', and a multitude of agricultural improvements – encouraged the growth in population. This in turn brought about the creation of a huge industrial labour force.

What had begun in the eighteenth century was set to continue and expand, so that throughout the nineteenth century Britain's population grew unceasingly. The nation gradually redefined itself, replacing its agrarian foundation, and was eventually transformed into the world's first industrial society. In 1801, when the first census was taken, four fifths of the population lived in the countryside and only one fifth in the towns. By 1901 these proportions had entirely reversed: four fifths of the nation lived in towns. Scotland's largest city, Glasgow, perfectly reflects this transformation. In 1801 its population numbered 77,000. A century later it had risen to almost 800,000 and was changed beyond recognition.

Already, before the middle of the eighteenth century, landlord farmers had begun responding to an increased demand for food. Thanks to the radical new ideas in farming, the progressive farmer was usually successful in his attempts to increase production. After 1750, when food prices also began to rise and it became more attractive to such farmers to put down land to crops and livestock, more and more people were forced off this land as greater areas of it were enclosed.

Enclosure was not a new phenomenon. The enterprising farmer had long since understood the advantage of hedging the old intermixed open fields and common meadows. What changed around the middle of the eighteenth century, and made enclosing such a deeply resented practice, was that it took on such a feverish pace, driving before it multitudes of beasts and men. Over the years countless despairing appeals were lodged. The pitiful wording of many of these petitions reveals how successfully many simple country people were manipulated by lawyers in the pay of landowners, who were quite heedless of the ancient customary rights of the poor.

The labourers were forbidden to grow crops on the old strip system of open fields. Equally importantly, they suffered the loss of traditional rights to graze their animals and to collect wood from the now shrinking acreage of open common land. With these new practices the economic simplicity of rural life was swept away, as many Scottish tenants were evicted from the land and the tied cottar's house that went with it. Without income and shelter, if they were not to starve or end in the poor house these people must collect up their belongings and children and make for the towns to find work. In one way or another there was almost no part of Scotland left untouched by these developments. Nor was the little town of Kirriemuir immune from their effects.

From the discovery of pre-Christian Pictish and Celtic burial stones in Kirriemuir we can be sure that for many centuries there has been some kind of habitation on this site. By 1201 the hamlet of Kirktoun is recorded, having grown up around the church of Kerimore. In 1660 the Kirktoun of Kerimore's population had still reached no more than 167. In 1748 this number had risen dramatically to 670, and by 1792 Kirriemuir, as it was now known, numbered 1,587 souls.

Spinning and weaving were traditionally the means by which Scotland's country people clothed their families, and whenever possible they earnt extra income by weaving surplus cloth to sell. As numbers of these people were forced off the land throughout the eighteenth century, Kirriemuir saw its population steadily rise, and weaving was the employment these incomers were most likely to take up.

In 1787 a son, Alexander, was born to the Kirriemuir linen weaver William Barrie and his wife Euphemia Bissett. While a young man Alexander was recorded as practising his father's craft of linen weaving. In due course he married a Kirriemuir girl, Marjorie Mitchell, and between 1808 and 1821 they had six children. One of these, born in 1814, they named David, and like so many of his forebears David, too, would become a linen weaver. It was this David who would one day become the father of the writer J. M. Barrie.

Hand-loom weavers were extremely skilled, kept long hours and, like all artisans of the period, were poorly paid. Many weavers, such as David Barrie, had been put to the loom while still children to help supplement the family income. From dawn till dusk, and sometimes beyond, the clatter and thump of the looms could be heard all along Kirriemuir's narrow streets. Most houses worked at least one loom, while other weavers came together in small workshops. In 1833 it was estimated that between 1,500 and 1,800 looms were at work in the town. A few years before this it was the town's proud boast that, with the exception of Forfar and Dundee, the quantity of cloth made here was more than in any other town in the county.

Unlike the city of Dundee and several other neighbouring towns, weaving in Kirriemuir remained a cottage industry for the greater part of the nineteenth century. The weavers were still out-workers, more often than not in their own cottages. As a result of the great industry and enterprise characteristic of weaving communities, in 1850 Kirriemuir was still managing to withstand the powerful national drive towards mechanisation of the trade. In many other towns the cottage industry of spinning and hand-loom weaving had already been overtaken and replaced by the steam-powered spinning machines and looms operated by workers in 'manufactories'. As an indication of the Kirriemuir weavers' particular enterprise, during a difficult period in the early nineteenth century, when the French wars prevented the export of cloth, the weavers discovered that they could sell their own wares at any market town in the country. Soon they were making a wider variety of linens, from shirting to sheeting to lining, and about eighty weavers regularly travelled far afield in search of new markets for their cloth.

In company with many artisans the weavers were a keenly political social group. Many belonged to the popular and temporarily powerful Chartist movement. Objecting to their exclusion from the franchise, for lack of the necessary property qualifications, the weavers were often vociferous exponents of their rights.

When a weaver had completed one or more 'webs', these were wheeled in barrows along the winding lanes to the Kirriemuir Town House. A web was a piece of cloth measuring 146 feet in length; the old word for a weaver was 'wobster'. At the Town House the cloth was weighed up, measured, and minutely checked for quality by the government inspector. Woe betide any weaver whose cloth fell below standard, particularly if he had tried to hide any blemish or fault. It had for long been the custom that webs of bad cloth were publicly burned on market days in Kirriemuir and neighbouring weaving towns. If, however, the cloth passed the test of quality it was stamped, the duty levied and the weaver paid forthwith.

In 1841 the linen weaver David Barrie, by now aged twenty-seven, married young Margaret Ogilvy, the twenty-one-year-old daughter of Alexander Ogilvy, a stonemason in the local sandstone quarry. (The Barries, and the families with whom they intermarried, were as thrifty with first names as they were with material goods. The resulting genealogies are often confusing.) In her childhood, when Margaret Ogilvy was only eight and her brother David was five, their mother had died. The children's father didn't remarry. It is unclear how much domestic support was forthcoming from the extended family, but, whatever the case, Alexander Ogilvy raised the two children himself. At the same time he had no choice but to continue working at the quarry beyond Cemetery Hill; there was no other financial support. As a consequence the eight-year-old Margaret became surrogate housewife and mother.

During this period, when child labour was widespread for the less well off, many worked in appalling conditions for the same hours each day as grown men and women. With childhood thus wrested from them they were prematurely charged with responsibilities far beyond their years. In this climate, Margaret Ogilvy's position in the Kirriemuir of 1827 probably gave no special cause for alarm. Her father was a kind, hard-working man and the community would no doubt have regarded his daughter as unfortunate in the loss of her mother, rather than exploited in her labours.

The extent to which Margaret managed the house on her own for her father and brother may have been exaggerated. Our only source here is the account of her childhood given many years later by her son, Jamie Barrie, a storyteller rather than a meticulous chronicler of facts. It appears that his mother was possessed of the same cast of mind, and in the telling either mother or son may have dramatised to heighten the story's appeal. As we shall see, many times over, for Margaret's son any fact that impeded the flow or that mitigated the efficacy of a good story was firmly and cheerfully ignored. It seems unlikely, though, that in a small, close community such as Kirriemuir there would have been no offers of help for Margaret, either from neighbours or female relations. Bearing these cautions in mind, the little girl nonetheless shouldered a large part of the domestic burden, which at times must have felt an onerous one.

After her marriage to David Barrie, Margaret lived with him in the little end house of a row of cottages on the Brechin Road. The Barrie cottage had four very small rooms: two up and two down, with a steep wooden staircase through the middle. There followed many years of child rearing and hard work for the couple. Pregnancy followed pregnancy in fairly rapid succession, so that by the time she was thirty-one Margaret had five children under the age of eight. Although only about five foot tall and of a slight build, Margaret was a determined young woman. After her successive pregnancies, however, the physical strain was beginning to tell and the birth of the fifth child initiated a period of great trial for the entire family.

Not only was the baby, Agnes, very frail, but shortly after her difficult delivery Margaret fell ill. Medically unrecognised at this time, she had probably contracted puerperal fever, the infection that carried off so many childbearing women before the principles of bacterial infection were understood. Margaret's brother commented at the time that there had recently been many cases of 'childbirth fever'.

Too ill to feed her baby, mother and child grew weaker and a wet nurse had to be found. After several weeks with virtually no improvement in Agnes's strength, she died. Her mother was hardly any better. The other children were looked after whenever possible by those neighbours and family who could spare time from their own families to come in and help. There were also three different paid 'helpers' who came to care for the ailing young mother. For David Barrie, the person upon whom the family depended for its financial support, it was a harsh struggle to carry on throughout those months.

At the time of Margaret's illness Alexander, the eldest child, was eight, Mary was seven, Jane Ann three and Elizabeth only one. An unexpected blessing emerging from this troubled period was the formation of a strong mutual bond between the children's maternal grandfather, Alexander Ogilvy, and Elizabeth, a most engaging little girl. As a consequence Alexander took it upon himself to take care of her a good deal of the time. He wrote, 'There is a sad confusion in the house and Margaret is very worried about the expense.'[1]

But fate had not done with the Barrie family yet. Elizabeth fell ill with whooping cough. With no known cure the illness often proved fatal, and she was not to be one of the lucky ones. Her death, coming only three months after that of baby Agnes, cast Margaret and David into even deeper mourning. For Margaret's father the loss of his granddaughter was a great blow. Meanwhile, Margaret was still too unwell to leave her bed, and now refused to eat.

With David's ailing wife in need of nursing, three small children to care for and the wet nurse for the baby who had died, the bills had mounted. In addition, there was the cost of two funerals within three months. David was increasingly concerned he would be unable financially to survive. In spite of his persistently hard work there was little enough money, even before this present accumulation of troubles. Now desperate, he overcame his pride and wrote to Margaret's brother asking for anything he might be able to spare. Then came the final blow: Margaret's father fell ill. His chest was weakened from the years of quarry dust, but more significantly his heart had been broken by the death of his granddaughter Elizabeth. In the end he simply gave up and in a short space of time, at fifty-four, he, too, had died. With Alexander's death, the third sombre family procession in less than six months wound its way to Cemetery Hill, up above the town.

Margaret was now close to despair. The doctor prescribed a 'sea bathing cure'. Instead, she remained at home while David Barrie's brother, John, took the children away to care for them on his farm. Finally Margaret grew better, and eventually made a complete recovery, enabling the young family to throw off the unhappy atmosphere of sickness and death that had lingered for so long over the cottage on Brechin Road.

Fifteen months after this dreadful winter Margaret was once again pregnant and in 1853 gave birth, this time to a healthy boy. He was named after his father and uncle, David Ogilvy, and soon proved to be a delightful and sympathetic child, who rapidly became his mother's favourite. The family continued to grow. The following year Sarah was born, and four years later another girl, Isabella, arrived.

In 1858, the year of Isabella's birth, the eldest Barrie, Alexander (the family called him Alick), had reached the age of sixteen. In that same year a decade of hard work was rewarded when he won the coveted Kirriemuir Bursary, given in order that studious poor boys might attend university. It may appear unusual that in the middle of the nineteenth century – in the days before state-subsidised education, when all instruction had to be paid for out of a family's own purse – the son of a humble weaver should be able to work his way to a place at university. This, however, would be to underestimate the prevailing spirit in much of Scottish life. Along with the Protestant work ethic, a fervent belief in education was a powerful force in Scotland and set the tone in many families such as David and Margaret Barrie's.

Their own education had been limited; nevertheless, they could both read fluently and David always remained earnestly devoted to his books. With the little spare time available to him he persisted throughout his life in trying to acquire some of the learning missed out on in his youth. The Barries were determined that they would rise. In particular they were determined that their children would not follow generations of their forebears, who had been tied to the loom for their living. David belonged to that eminently respectable sector of the Kirriemuir community, the hand-loom weavers, the stratum of the artisan class whose earnings, although modest, were adequate to support a large family. Unlike many weavers' wives, Margaret appears never to have been put to spinning or weaving herself. The Barrie family were not 'dirt poor', not constantly preoccupied with the search for the next meal. And, no matter how difficult the payments, the children were all sent to school. For David and Margaret a university education remained one of the pinnacles of social achievement.

In 1831 Dr Easton's *Statistical Account of the Parish of Kirriemuir* listed sixteen schools in the town and neighbourhood. Admittedly many of these were little more than dame schools where the children's education went no further than 'reading, writing and arithmetic'. None the less it is impressive that Dr Easton could write, 'The number of persons upward of fifteen years of age who cannot read or write is not one to a thousand.' Indeed there were at least half a dozen schools in the town whose standard was extremely high. Alexander Barrie, for example, studied Greek and Latin at Webster's Academy for several years and was to progress to a degree in Classics at Aberdeen University.

Following their eldest brother the younger Barrie children, including the girls, all attended school. Although the girls were not eligible for bursaries or a place at university, they were sent first to a dame school, then on to the Free Church School for more advanced studies. Three of Margaret and David's daughters would eventually become teachers.

This devotion to the idea of learning was combined in David and Margaret Barrie with a similar devotion to the Church. David was a devout follower of the Free Church, one of the stricter sects of Scottish Calvinism, while Margaret had been raised by her equally devout father in an even more aridly fundamentalist sect, the Auld Lichts.

Throughout its history the Church of Scotland has been riven with a sectarianism whose origins lay ultimately in the beginnings of the Scottish Reformation in the late sixteenth century. The Protestant reformer John Knox had returned from exile a follower of Calvin and, in 1561, declared to his appalled sovereign, Mary Queen of Scots, that subjects were not bound to obey an ungodly monarch such as her.

From Luther, Knox took over the belief that each individual's conscience was capable of discerning God's will and that therefore neither a hierarchy of priests nor even a monarch was necessary to interpret this will. In addition Knox argued, with Calvin, that as God was omnipotent he must know everything; this included knowledge of every human being's destiny. This doctrine of Predestination proclaimed that it is already 'written' before birth who are the Elect (who will achieve heavenly glory), and who are not. In practice the usual effect of this confusing doctrine was that it imposed great pressure on believers to demonstrate, through their godly behaviour, that they were of this Elect.

These beliefs were expanded, refined and fought over for the next two centuries and more. Out of the confusion two basic divisions transpired. The Episcopalians, like the Anglicans in the south, believed that bishops should rule the church. The Presbyterians, meanwhile, believed that the church should be run by assemblies, part elected and part appointed, and not by bishops. A series of ferocious battles led to the formation of an increasing number of Presbyterian sects.

The Auld Licht sect presumed that on marriage a woman would take on her husband's kirk, and this Margaret Barrie had done. In her heart, though, Margaret always remained loyal to the rigid precepts of her own sect. The Auld Lichts were fierce in their espousal of what they thought were the most fundamental Christian beliefs, referring back to the earliest Apostolic church. 'If any man have not the spirit of the Lord he is not one of His' was their creed. They held that true worship only occurred when there was nothing in it reflecting 'the carnal work of man'. As a result, in the barrenness of their vision they allowed neither instrumental music of any kind, nor the singing of hymns, nor written sermons or prayers. The Auld Lichts fervently believed that the spirit of the Lord was opposed to any manifestation of graciousness of living. Life on earth was to be stripped bare of all activity that did not reflect an earnest devotion.

Fear of God, great diligence and a reverence for education, these were the significant forces prevailing in the hearts of both David and Margaret Barrie. Fortunately this did not mean that the atmosphere in the Barrie home was entirely grim and dark. Nor did it censor that dry Scottish humour. Certainly, though, there was an underlying seriousness in the household, an intense, fervent attitude to life noticeable in all the Barrie children.

Into this household, on 9th May 1860, after nineteen years of marriage, Margaret – now a sober forty-one – gave birth to her ninth child and third son. As was the rule in the Free Church sect, before the first Sunday after the birth the couple had the child christened. This was duly performed in Kirriemuir's South Free Church. The boy was named James Matthew Barrie.

Of the seven surviving Barrie children, Alick, eighteen in 1860, had achieved his parents' ambition and was away studying at Aberdeen University. Next came Mary Ann, who was then seventeen and a novice teacher. Jane Ann was thirteen, David seven, Sarah six, little Isabella two, and finally there was the new baby, James. Even when we remember that both the size of the family and their cramped living quarters were typical of the period, maintaining any sense of order in the cottage on Brechin Road must have demanded of Margaret a steely discipline and a determined spirit.

In their very small cottage, somehow the Barrie's managed. The upstairs rooms alone were available for family use, because traditionally the weaver's loom virtually filled one of those downstairs, while the other was used to store yarn and the 'webs' of cloth. Two, sometimes three of the children slept in an extremely small box bed against the kitchen-cum-living-room wall, while a truckle bed was pulled out from underneath the box bed at night. David and Margaret were next door in another box bed with the baby in his wooden Angus rocking cradle, while the yarn room downstairs may have held another bed for one or more of the children.

Some time shortly after the birth of James Matthew his father moved his loom to another workshop nearby. David Barrie was a shrewd, practical man who had thoughtfully faced up to the great changes in the offing. He foresaw that mechanisation was inevitable, and decided that rather than being defeated by these great changes a man could carve out of them opportunities for himself and his family. Armed with this foresight, his savings and an immense capacity for hard work, David made the first steps that would ensure his livelihood for the future. He bought more looms and set about employing a small number of other weavers to work them.

The new workshop gave David the right to be referred to in the parish records as 'linen manufacturer' rather than the more humble title, 'weaver', he had held hitherto. He would first supervise and check the weavers' work, then take on the responsibility for selling the finished cloth, which often entailed travelling long distances. In those years when much of the country was not yet served by a rail system, travel for many people meant no more than going to the local market town on foot or by some form of horse transport. In contrast to this, David's trading sometimes took him to towns as far away as Manchester, or to remote parts of Scotland, such as the Hebridean Islands.

With her husband's move into another workshop, Margaret was at last able to convert the 'loom shop' on the ground floor into an additional room for the family, a *parlour*: a triumphant step up the social ladder. The parlour, so yearned after by every small aspiring Victorian home, was normally empty: a gesture of luxury, of wasted space, it was out of bounds for all but special occasions. This was the room reserved for visitors in their best clothes, and the ritual honouring of birth, marriage and death.

In build the eldest of the Barrie children, Alick, was his father's son, tall and broad. A pleasant, intelligent face reflected the hard-working and purposeful nature of a young man undeterred by setback and dogged in his will to succeed. His ambition was to become a teacher. Alick's parents were immensely proud of him. It was the younger brother, David, however, upon whom their mother's affections were most concentrated. His beautiful looks and pleasing disposition were combined with a natural poise and notable skill at games. Besides this, he was a gifted scholar. Like many of her contemporaries Margaret did nothing to hide her tendency to favour a particular child, and whatever their private feelings might have been the family outwardly accepted.

The Ogilvys, like the Barries, were high achievers. Throughout her life Margaret remained close to her only brother, David Ogilvy. Inspired by his father, the stonemason Alexander Ogilvy, and by his sister, Margaret, David had, after years of dedication and hard work, finally triumphed in his studies and progressed to become a Doctor of Divinity. He then became a minister in the Free Church in Lanarkshire. This precedent was clearly in Margaret's mind when she decided that her beloved second son would also become a minister. If the son of a poor quarryman could achieve this ambition, might not the son of a weaver follow his uncle and seek the very highest of social goals: to work for God? Margaret may have been physically slight, with a tendency to emotional frailty, but she was also strong-willed and tenacious. To see David as a minister became her most fervent wish.

Although the detail of the Barries' individual lives is obscure, we can decipher a picture of family life. We can make out the strength of religious feeling, a certain narrowness born of fundamentalism, and by contrast a genuine respect for those different from themselves. We can see the Barries' seriousness, the capacity for hard work, the canniness and the intense determination to succeed. We also catch glimpses of family life – and humour – that soften and modify what otherwise might have been an unrelentingly bleak regime. Much later Jamie Barrie would describe, and only slightly caricature, in his play *What Every Woman Knows*, the mental world his family inhabited. Here, the artisan family is settled, canny, ambitious and to a large degree inarticulate, both about themselves and the world they occupy.

Unlike his two strapping older brothers, who physically resembled their father, the third son, Jamie, inherited his mother's physique, making him a small and slight child. With time his lack of height became more apparent, and as the other boys continued to grow Jamie remained particularly fine-boned and slim. It was not until many years later that he filled out a little. During these early years, except for his smallness, Jamie appears to have been unexceptional, and cheerful enough. Added to his relative insignificance as almost the last in a large family, the growing boy showed no particular aptitude for school work and possessed unremarkable looks. None of the Barrie children was neglected by their mother. Nevertheless, as Jamie grew it was clear that Margaret found little in this third son, unlike his older brothers, to call forth in her that capacity for great commitment.

When Jamie was three and Isabella five, and now at school every day, Margaret gave birth to her tenth and final child, a girl, named after her mother. By the time the baby Margaret could walk she was often playfellow to Jamie, and these two fell quickly into the positions in which they would remain for the rest of their lives: adoring younger sister and protective older brother. Not that Jamie was short of companionship: there were always other children nearby, and neighbours were in all senses close. They probably attended the same kirk, worked as weavers, lived in similarly cramped conditions and managed – or sometimes didn't – on similarly poor wages. In such physical proximity it was almost impossible to keep secrets. Your neighbours were a party to most of what there was to know about you.

Like countless children before and after him, both clarifying the world and shielding themselves from it through fantasy, the boy Jamie constructed stories. He took this custom a step further, however, and was the clown, the one who kept his friends amused. The stories soon developed further and became little performances. Towards the end of his life the storyteller famously recorded how these playlets took place in the washhouse, shared with the other cottagers and standing just outside his parents' back door. For many years after he became famous, postcards of the washhouse were sold as 'J. M. Barrie's first theatre'.

Several small children regularly taking over a hard-used communal washhouse such as this seems improbable. However, it all makes for a good story, and little performances of some kind clearly did take place somewhere. Besides, factual accuracy was never of interest to James Barrie. At the end of his life he wrote: 'Facts were never pleasing to him. He acquired them with reluctance and got rid of them with relief.' Little Jamie's need to perform sprang from a natural response to his inconspicuous position within a large family. It was a means of making himself, however fleetingly, the centre of attention. In a photograph taken when he was about six years old, a grave and intense little boy looks out at us. We catch a hint of the dreamer in his eyes, but more persistent is a sense of apprehension in the mournful little face.

With David's ceaseless industry at the loom and Margaret's scrupulous care with housekeeping, the Barries made sure of money for their children's education. In this way, following all his older brothers and sisters, at five Jamie was sent to school. This was in Bank Street, just around the corner from the Barries' cottage, and run by the Misses Adam, the prototypes of the Misses Ailie in *Sentimental Tommy* and the Misses Throssel in *Quality Street*. Here the children were required to bring a clean handkerchief each day on which they knelt to say their prayers. Teaching was limited to the three Rs, and Jamie was soon sent on to the more advanced South Free Church School at Southmuir, on the hill beyond the burn and the gas works on the other side of town.

Meanwhile Alick had graduated with a First in Classics at Aberdeen. He then went on to complete an MA. Soon after graduating he continued in the family tradition of resourcefulness and enterprise by opening a small private school. The eldest Barrie daughter, Mary Ann, whose earnings as a pupil-teacher had been augmenting the family income, launched herself into a wider world by becoming Alick's housekeeper and teaching assistant. In a short time Alick's sense of goodwill and his desire for the family to progress inspired him to write to his parents from the school, at Bothwell in Lanarkshire, with a proposal. He encouraged them to send the boy David to live with him and Mary Ann in order to further his education beyond Kirriemuir's limited confines. While their father, David, was in wholehearted agreement at this point he and Alick had, surprisingly, underestimated a powerful factor in the Barrie family dynamic.

An implicit bar on any dramatic show of emotion in the household was unable of course to eradicate the family's ineluctable emotional life, and sometimes this life became more active. As his achievements revealed, David senior was tough, a man of decision and character, but at a deeper level Margaret ruled the Barrie home. She held a position of emotional pre-eminence apparently unchallenged by either her husband or her children. David was Margaret's favourite child; everyone knew this. And, despite her ambitions, despite the appeals from her husband and Alick that venturing further afield would ensure a better future for him, Margaret adamantly refused to let David go.

Out of respect for his mother Alick stepped back, but only for a time. His quiet self-assurance and determination, emanating from generations of independent-minded self-employed forebears, gave him conviction. Alick's feelings towards his father went beyond gratitude for the sacrifices he had made. Although not driven by the same religious zeal as many Kirriemuirians of his father's generation, there was always a natural bond of sympathy between father and son. Here they were at one in their desire for the family to better itself and enlarge its horizons.

David and Alick once again approached Margaret. Young David *must*, for his own good, go to his brother and sister in Lanarkshire. Margaret was eventually made to see that if David didn't leave Kirriemuir he might well fail in her ambition for him to become a minister. Finally, and with great reluctance, his mother let go of her boy. The emotional wrench was severe. How David himself felt we don't know. What we do know is that his happy disposition and his elder brother and sister's support enabled him to settle away from home in a new school without difficulty. Alick was soon writing home to his parents of David's swift progress.

Alick was an eminently sensible and capable young man. He was also kind, fiercely loyal and disposed to share some of the rewards of his hard work with the family. His earnings were not large, and everything was accounted for, but he was prospering and his interest in young David's future led him to waive any contribution from their father for the boy's board and lodging.

By 1866 Alick was able to write to his parents that he intended to sell up the little school and, in the autumn of 1867, was to move on with his sister Mary Ann. He had been appointed as the new Classics master at the prestigious Glasgow Academy. Once again he was happy to share his good fortune. If David went with them, the Academy would further his studies. The prospect before the three young Barries was of a more expansive and gracious life in Glasgow, Scotland's second city.

The January of 1867 was bitterly cold. Lakes and rivers froze over. Skating was a favourite winter pastime and David shared Alick's present of a pair of skates with a friend. The boys were out together on the ice; David had taken his turn and handed over the skates to his friend. Buckling them on, the boy tore off at great speed, careering into David as he went. David fell heavily and hit his head on the ice. So serious were his injuries that he was soon unconscious. Alick telegraphed his parents from Lanarkshire. David's skull was badly fractured, but while there was the slightest hope they must come at once. Years later, in *Margaret Ogilvy*, the story of his mother's life, Jamie Barrie recalled:

> when the terrible news came . . . I have been told the face of my mother was awful in its calmness as she set off to get between Death and her boy. We trooped with her down the brae to the wooden station, and I was envying her the journey in the mysterious wagons; I know we played around her, proud of our right to be there . . . Her ticket was taken, she had bidden us goodbye . . . and then my father came out of the telegraph office and said huskily, 'He's gone!' Then we turned very quietly and went home again up the little brae.[2]

In just two days' time the boy David would have been fourteen.

During the nineteenth century death may have lurked closer, been more familiar to everyone, and religious belief helped many towards its acceptance. None the less, there were few whose feelings ever became brutalised by the persistence of loss. The death of children in particular brought no less a sense of bereavement than in our own time. Its familiarity did little to reduce death's shocking power. For David and Margaret Barrie, their son David's death snuffed out a light, and the routine burdens of daily life became heavier to bear. Even so, the intensity of Margaret Barrie's feelings was to swamp, almost sweep aside, either the grieving of the dead boy's father or that of his elder brother and sister. In spite of a lifetime of religious observance, Margaret was unprepared. She appears also to have been unable to achieve that intense psychic discipline necessary to continue caring for the brothers and sisters of a recently dead child. Inconsolable, she could only turn inward, driven to an all-consuming emotional crisis.

In *Margaret Ogilvy* James Barrie recalled David's death and its devastating effect: 'She was always delicate from that hour, and for many months she was very ill . . . I peeped in many times at the door and then went to the stair and sat on it and sobbed.' After several days his older sister, Jane Ann, grew concerned for Jamie's well-being. 'She came to him . . . with a very anxious face . . . and told him to go to their mother and . . . say to her that she still had another boy.' Standing still in the dark of the bedroom the little boy felt that his breathing, or perhaps crying, alerted his mother so that, after a time,

> I heard a listless voice that had never been listless before say,
>   'Is that you?'
>   I think the tone hurt me, for I made no answer.[3]

His mother called out again, but, surmising it was his dead brother David she was speaking to, Jamie said, in what he called a lonely voice,

> 'No, it's no' him, it's just me.'
>   Then I heard a cry, and my mother turned in bed, and though it was dark I knew she was holding out her arms . . . After that I sat a great deal in her bed trying to make her forget him, which was my crafty way of playing physician . . . I suppose I was an odd little figure: I have been told that my anxiety to brighten her gave my face a strained look.[4]

Collecting jokes in his attempts to make his mother laugh, he said, 'I would stand on my head in the bed, my feet against the wall, and then cry excitedly, "Are you laughing, Mother?"'

In *Margaret Ogilvy* he remembered how Jane Ann told him not to sulk when his mother was clearly thinking of David. She told him that instead he should

> try and get her to talk about him . . . At first, they say, I was often jealous, stopping her fond memories with the cry, 'Do you mind nothing about me?' But that did not last; its place was taken by an

intense desire . . . to become so like him that even my mother
should not see the difference . . . Then I practised in secret, but after
a whole week had passed I was still rather like myself.[5]

The little boy practised his brother's mannerisms, learnt his whistle
from friends, the way he stood, even donning a suit of David's clothes
so as to carry off more successfully the impersonation for his mother. In
spite of Jamie's Herculean efforts at self-elimination the enterprise was,
of course, a failure, and his adult conclusion is pitiful. Without any rancour
he observes that despite sometimes cheering his mother in the months
after David's death – and regularly again during those successive years of
incessant devotion – at her death he knew he had never succeeded in
resuscitating that part of her which had died with her older son twenty-
nine years before.

The powerful and far-reaching impact on the boy Jamie Barrie of the
events surrounding his brother's death has long been acknowledged by
biographers and readers alike. And yet the story arises from one source
alone, and that source is James Barrie himself. It is his adult perception
of the events as he wrote them down in *Margaret Ogilvy*. In general this
adoring portrait of his mother is not in sympathy with the sensibilities
of our own time. None the less the book is invaluable, above all because
its underlying and most absorbing theme is not its subject but its author,
James Barrie. Written when he was thirty-six, it reviews crucial elements
of his past: his childhood and his relationship with his mother. The things
that he believed motivated him and his mother to act in the way they
did are at the core of his book. And, in the absence of any other perspective, James Barrie's description and interpretation of his crucial early life
has usually gone unchallenged. Yet, as we become more familiar with the
man and the ways in which, throughout his life, he approached anything
to do with fact or history, it becomes ever more clear that we must
proceed with caution.

While there is no reason to doubt the essential sincerity of his
story – he *believed* it had happened as he told it, and numerous passages
are essentially true – there is little doubt that in *Margaret Ogilvy* the adult
James Barrie subtly edited the episode of his mother's collapse subsequent to David's death. What is significant is his silence about his life
before his brother's death. He makes only one comment: 'It is all guesswork for [the first] six years . . .' But there is much more in those first
six years than guesswork.

We have seen Margaret Barrie's ambition for her sons. To her great
satisfaction Alexander had gained his degree in Classics and already
opened his own school. David's academic drive was equal to that of his

older brother, while his good looks and engaging personality made him the one upon whom Margaret Ogilvy pinned her hopes. Jamie, on the other hand, neither showed his brother's academic promise nor was he blessed with David's looks or physical prowess; even as a grown man Jamie never reached more than a little over five feet.

All the evidence suggests that the heart of the whole matter does not in fact lie with David's death, but somewhere else. Margaret's traumatic grief, her turning inward, away from all of her children including her youngest son, is best understood when we recognise that it was not, as James Barrie believed, through David's *death* that his mother's attention was wrested from him. The terrible, unbearable truth for Jamie was that it had always been absent. Margaret Barrie had never really *seen* her youngest son. Her eyes were befogged with her image of David. As a result, although the adult James Barrie found it too painful to admit, the little Jamie had always felt himself inferior, essentially rejected by his mother; the one person whose attention he craved above all else. In order to avoid reproaching her and facing the enormity of this realisation about his earliest years, James Barrie transfers his sense of rejection – as do his biographers – to the time of his brother's death. This alone, he believes, is the trigger for his rejection, and in this way he successfully rewrites the past.

If we accept that rejection wasn't a new experience for Jamie, then David's death did not precipitate his mother's rejection of her youngest son. What this death really triggered in this little boy's life was something altogether more constructive. It triggered an improvement in the way Jamie responded to his old problem of not being *seen*. In response to this unbearable situation, and no longer overshadowed by his older brother, the small boy devised a course of action which was extraordinarily creative. His earlier instinct to perform, to tell stories was, after his brother's death, to flourish with greater purpose. In this way he would make himself even more visible than before. And, as he unconsciously refined his methods, we see the anguish of Jamie Barrie's inheritance gradually transformed into something fertile and quite brilliant. Indeed, this desire to make himself visible would develop to such a degree that it was to become the driving force in James Barrie's strange and absorbing life.

2

The Happiest Years of His Life

As Margaret Barrie lay in the dark imprisonment of her suffering, days turned into weeks. Meanwhile, her solicitous daughter Jane Ann, determined to prevent little Jamie from keeping such nervously constant watch over his mother, sent him back to school. The longer hours now expected of him there, the obligatory two church services and a bible class on Sundays, kept Jamie's days busy with activity. Between periods of preoccupation, the cheerful and high-spirited side to him re-emerged.

The children of Kirriemuir may have grown up without luxuries, but they were in many ways fortunate in their surroundings. In the old stone-built town of busy comings and goings, amongst its up-and-down and winding streets and obscure corners and secrets, oases of green still remained. The Commonty, the Den, the Cuttle Well, the banks of the river Gairie; these soon became places much wilder still in the minds of the children who colonised them. Further afield, beyond the town there was Witch Knowe, the great Standing Stone and Caddam Wood. It was to Caddam Wood that the gypsies came with their horses and wagons to set up camp. And when the ubiquitous speculation about their strange otherness dried up, there was always fishing in the burns to be done. High above the town, on top of the hill by the Standing Stone, lay the cricket field. Here, undeterred by their lack of kit, the small boys of Kirriemuir played. With the grand mountains of the glens for backdrop, rolled-up jackets marking the pitch, a homemade bat and an upended boulder for wicket, with a joyful fierceness they battled it out. The seeds were sown early; Jamie Barrie never lost his love of cricket.

Returning again and again to these places, the children gradually invested them with inventive meaning and memory. For Jamie these memories would take on an almost magical significance. Talismans, they were a fruitful resource to be used over and again in his writing in the long years to come. Returning home from his travels he was

learning better how to draw his mother out of her wretchedness. As
the weeks passed she became more willing to listen to her small boy's
adventures. Besides, he had a way of telling that captured you, and
Margaret loved stories as much as did her small son. In this they were
discovering a bond that would bind them together as closely as anything
ever could.

After David's death, Margaret talked to Jamie about her own childhood spent around their little town. It eased the pain of loss to recall a
happier time. As a child not much older than Jamie now was himself,
Margaret, as surrogate mother to her small brother, had cheerfully scrubbed
and mended, baked and sewed. Then she had washed and ironed and
gossiped as if a grown woman. Now she told vivid stories of the past,
and James would eventually retell something like them. In *Margaret Ogilvy*
he says,

> My mother's father, the one hero of her life, died nine years before
> I was born, and I remember this with bewilderment, so familiarly
> does the weather beaten mason's figure rise before me from the old
> chair on which I was nursed and now write my books.
>
> I watch, as from a window, while she sets off through the long
> parks to the distant places where he is at work, in her hand a flagon
> which contains his dinner. She is singing to herself and gleefully
> . . . jumps the burn . . .[1]

Margaret's solace and escape in reliving her childhood with Jamie in turn
helped him to forget his own pain as he became absorbed in her past.
His mother was a gifted storyteller and Jamie was entranced.

> I see her frocks lengthening . . . and the games given reluctantly up
> . . . Those innumerable talks with her made her youth as vivid as
> my own, and so much more quaint, for, to a child, the oddest of
> things, and the most richly coloured picture book, is that his mother
> was once a child . . .[2]

Margaret's love for her father and her pride in her premature responsibilities transmitted another powerful and implicit message from mother
to son. There is something amiss with responsibility, something awry with
growing up; whatever Margaret's actual words, this was how the little
boy saw it. The adult James Barrie put it thus:

> The horror of my boyhood was that I knew a time would come
> when I also must give up the games . . . I felt that I must continue

playing in secret, and I took this shadow to her, when she told me her own experience, which convinced us both that we were very like each other inside.[3]

Interwoven with Margaret's reminiscences about her own past were other stories told to her as a child, about a time still further back. These were the tales of Kirriemuir's weaving community before her birth, and many of them revolved around the Auld Lichts of her upbringing.

We are told that Jamie entered so successfully into these stories that sometimes the differences between past and present would merge, so that momentarily he couldn't tell one from the other. Nor could he always tell the difference between himself and the central character. Earlier, when he had tried to convince Margaret that he was his brother David, he had in some sense attempted to efface himself. In almost becoming little Margaret, Jamie once again nearly disappeared. That chameleon quality, common to all artists to a greater or lesser degree, existed in James Barrie sometimes to a breathtaking extent. Describing his incorrigible, immensely likeable and deeply flawed protagonist Tommy Sandys in *Sentimental Tommy*, he would later say,

for most conspicuous of his traits was the faculty of stepping into other people's shoes and remaining there until he had become someone else; his individuality consisted in him having none.[4]

In the autumn of 1867 Alick and Mary Ann made their move to Glasgow, and Alick began teaching at the Academy. He was soon writing to his parents to say that Jamie's education would be improved if he went further afield than Kirriemuir. Nothing happened for a year but by August 1868, accompanied by a very small wooden trunk, Jamie boarded the train for Glasgow, a long eighty miles distant from the place of his birth. He was not yet eight and a half.

Though life with Jamie's older brother and sister seems to have been comfortable enough, he was disoriented, lonely and homesick. This must have been inevitable for a boy intimately familiar with his birthplace, whose playmates he had known for much of his life and who had at home an adoring younger sister and the comfort and sympathy of three older ones too. Transplanted to the anonymous atmosphere of the huge, bustling city, he spent many hours daydreaming and miserably longing for home.

Homesickness, relieved only by occasional journeys to Kirriemuir, gave intensity to Jamie's memories. Partially severed from his roots, as he grew so his love of his native place increased. Naturally, being the boy he was, it was an attachment that fed as much on imagination as on any real experience. For Jamie, Kirriemuir would come to represent the perfection of time past; and in particular the imaginary perfection of childhood.

In May 1870, at the age of fifty-five, David Barrie was bringing his days as a weaver to an end; he was embarking on a new life. Although there was now a power-loom factory in Kirriemuir, David secured for himself a post not as a weaver, but as a clerk in the counting house in Laird's, a new linen factory at Forfar, five miles down the road. He had understood for years that things must change, but unlike many others in Kirriemuir, who were unable to comprehend the future, he had acted upon his perception that soon the ancient craft of the hand-loom weaver would be gone. His son would write,

> before I reached my tenth year a giant entered my native place in the night, and we woke to find him in possession. He transformed it into a new town at a rate with which we boys only could keep up ... But though there were never circumstances to which boys could not adapt themselves in half an hour, older folk are slower in the uptake ...Where had been formerly but the click of the shuttle was soon the roar of 'power', handlooms were pushed into a corner as a room is cleared for a dance; every morning at half-past five the town was wakened with a yell, and from a chimney stack that rose high into our caller air the conqueror waved for evermore his flag of smoke. Another era had dawned, new customs, new fashions sprang into life ... the daughter, till now a knitter of stockings, became the breadwinner, he who had been the breadwinner sat down to the knitting of stockings: what had yesterday been a nest of weavers was to-day a town of girls.
>
> I am not one of those who would fling stones at the change; it is something, surely, that backs are no longer prematurely bent; you may no longer look ... at the aged poor weaving tremulously for their little bit of ground in the cemetery. Rather are their working years too few now because it is with youth that the power-looms must be fed.[5]

In those days five miles was considered too far to travel back and forth each day to work. So the family left Brechin Road and moved themselves to Forfar. David Barrie's wages were now much better than those of a linen weaver, and the house he found for his family was correspondingly larger. For some reason Jamie was at home during this period, and a week or so after his tenth birthday he was caught up in the general excitement as the big cart was loaded up and the family set off for their new home. All except Margaret. The strain of leaving the place in which she had spent her entire life precipitated another emotional crisis, albeit less severe than the previous one that had felled her with such force. For three weeks she remained behind in Kirriemuir with her friend Bell Lunan.

Meanwhile, it was Jane Ann who oversaw the establishment of the family at the new house in Forfar. Jenann, as she was known, looked older than her twenty-two years. It was she who had for some time borne the brunt of the Barrie family's domestic responsibilities. Even before Margaret's illness three years earlier Jenann had taken charge of a large proportion of the many tasks incurred in the running of a Victorian household. Margaret Barrie oversaw the more delicate jobs, such as sewing, baking, taking care of the linen. But it was Jenann who was up early to clean out and light the fires and the range. It was she who fetched and carried and cleaned. If she ever resented this drudgery, we don't hear of it. It was Jenann's chosen work and it was done with the dedication of obsession.

She seems to have accepted self-effacement as her role, while one small outlet was the eminently acceptable Victorian craft of embroidery. Jenann was periodically subject to appalling migraines. Barrie wrote of her: 'My sister is down with one of the headaches against which even she cannot fight, and my mother . . . is most woebegone when her daughter is the sufferer.'[6] Just as Margaret had become that Victorian prototype 'the invalid', so Jenann was another, the sacrificial daughter. Remaining a spinster, she had no real life outside the home. The family, her mother in particular, was her life. In common with many other Victorian parents, Margaret received Jenann's intense devotion as her due. In turn Jenann's attachment to her mother made her possessive. Although the other children, one daughter in particular, were also devoted to her

> they scarce dared tend my mother – this one snatched the cup jealously from their hands. My mother liked it best from her. We all knew this. 'I like them fine, but I canna do without you.' My sister, so unselfish in all other things, had an unwearying passion for parading it before us. It was the rich reward of her life.[7]

A ritual regularly carried out by mother and daughter was later remembered by neighbours: Jenann would open the front door for her mother; Margaret then walked ahead down the garden path and waited until the gate was opened for her by Jenann.

Jamie returned to school in Glasgow with Alick, but within a year he was enrolled at Forfar Academy and was once again living with his parents. Major changes were about to take place in the Scottish school system and, like his father, Alick was preparing himself for the future. Scotland would soon appoint a body of school inspectors, part of a general centralisation process initiated from London. Having resigned his position at the Academy, he was effectively in training for the school inspector's post he hoped to be offered, and this left him unable to continue looking after Jamie.

In contrast to the cottage in Kirriemuir, the Barrie's new home in Forfar was virtually detached, with a high surrounding wall making the garden a secluded place compared with the almost communal living of the Kirriemuir tenements. Although the remnants of an old animosity sometimes surfaced between the people of Kirriemuir and Forfar, Jamie at least felt more at home in Forfar than in those lonely years in Glasgow.

A contemporary at school recalled the impression Jamie's storytelling had on him at this time:

> I remember one summer afternoon when I left school in his company . . . We turned into the Back Wynd, where we were greeted with the ring of hammer on anvil, and stopped for a minute, as all boys would, to watch Forsyth, the smith, sharpening chisels . . . plunging them when finished into a receptacle of water from which the steam rose as the heated iron sank.
>
> After leaving the smith's door Jim began to tell me a story, and was fairly under way with it when we turned into The Limepots . . . where presently we stopped before a high wall . . . There was a green door in the wall, and Jim invited me to enter so that he could finish his story, in which I was as interested as the teller. Inside the door was a flight of steps flanked by walls of stone. We ascended the steps and I saw Barrie's home for the first and last time . . . the cottage and garden were surrounded with stone walls, and when the green door was closed there was a strange silence as of a cloister. No one was about so we sat on the grass in front of the house while Jim continued his story. It was a 'strange eventful history' told with a sparkling eye, full of the minutest detail and entrancing to the listener. The story is long since lost to my memory, but I recollect that on my way home I pondered over the incident and thought to myself, 'He's a queer chap Jim. Where can he have got that story. It's not like any a boy ever told.'[8]

Unsurprisingly, David Barrie excelled at his new profession, and soon the new Gairie linen works in Kirriemuir had offered him promotion as their confidential clerk. Accordingly, barely two years after the family's establishment in Forfar, they were once again back in Kirriemuir. This time the Barries were able to improve still more on their standard of accommodation, and took on part of a new villa, called Strath View. Built of the local pink-red sandstone Strath View sits high above the Gairie at the junction of the Forfar and Glamis roads. Down below were the roofs of the two linen works; beyond these the houses of the town, at the edge of which were the familiar tenements on Brechin Road. The Barries' new home was a perfect vantage point from which to keep an eye on the town. In later years Margaret often sat watching from Strath View's lower windows.

Many others of Jamie's background, including his father, were required as children to work and help supplement the family income, but this was never asked of Jamie. Instead, by the age of twelve he had become a voracious reader. Unfortunately books were expensive to buy. And with the private library system in operation, the amount the Barries could afford to put aside each month didn't cover many. Nevertheless young Jamie and his mother managed to read numbers of books together. On these occasions he often reversed the customary parent–child roles, so that Margaret had the stories read to her. After *Robinson Crusoe*, her son became deeply attached to *The Pilgrim's Progress*, and enjoyed being a 'dark character' who could frighten his mother with his dramatisations from the story.

> Besides reading every book we could hire or borrow I also bought one now and again, and when buying (it was the occupation of weeks) I read, standing at the counter, most of the other books in the shop, which is perhaps the most exquisite way of reading.[9]

Jamie was an enthusiast of the highly coloured penny dreadfuls. Here he found absolute clarity as the brave and honourable heroes were pitted against the unmitigated wickedness of their enemies. There was also fairy tale and romance, and Jamie fell in love with a watercress seller whose story was serialised in *Sunshine*. He said of her, 'I lay in bed wondering what she would be up to in the next number: I have lost trout because when they nibbled my mind was wandering with her; my early life was embittered by her not arriving regularly on the first of the month.'[10] When Barrie wrote about his mother he was also investigating himself. He tells us: 'What she had been, what I should be, these were the two great subjects between us in my boyhood, and while we discussed the one we were deciding the other . . .'[11] Later he writes:

. . . on a day I conceived a glorious idea, or it was put into my head by my mother, then desirous of making progress with her new clouty hearth rug. The notion was nothing short of this, why should I not write the tales myself?[12]

He was soon galloping up and down the attic stairs with one chapter after another for his mother's approval.

They were all tales of adventure (happiest is he who writes of adventure), no characters were allowed within if I knew their like in the flesh, the scene lay in unknown parts, desert islands, enchanted gardens, with knights . . . on black chargers, and round the first corner a lady selling watercress . . . From the day on which I first tasted blood in the garret my mind was made up; there could be no hum-dreadful-drum profession for me; literature was my game.[13]

At twelve this may only have been a dim intimation of where his future lay, but Jamie's imagination had been fired.

In 1872 Alick achieved his ambition and was offered a post as one of Scotland's first schools inspectors. He was now in charge of the district of Dumfries on the west coast. Mary returned to live with Alick as his housekeeper, while also working as a part-time teacher. Alick's earlier theme was reiterated: Kirriemuir wasn't up to providing the education the family wanted for its sons. If Jamie returned to live with Alick and Mary Ann he could become a pupil at Dumfries Academy.

Unlike the move to Glasgow a few years earlier, Jamie tells us that he was fairly itching to experience life at this new school. He had acquired a fascination with tales of English school life by some of his favourite literary heroes, such as A. R. Hope, and had convinced himself it would be equally exciting at Dumfries. '[Hope] was the first author to whom I ever wrote a letter, and I remember carefully misspelling many of the words in it because the boys in his books spelt so badly.'

Books such as Robert Ballantyne's *The Coral Island*, Captain Marryat's *Masterman Ready*, and Fenimore Cooper's *The Last of the Mohicans* and *The Pathfinder*, helped inspire in Jamie the secret hope that at Dumfries the lodge keeper would have a peg leg; that he, Jamie, would be shinning up trees as lookout, and that his time would be crowded with plots to blow up teachers, pirates and other exotic villains.

I longed to go, with gunpowder in my box, to an English school. I had a friend of a like mind to whom, after I had gone to school in Dumfries, I sent a box of chalks, and he took for granted that they must be for blowing up masters and put them in the fire and awaited the explosion.[14]

At Dumfries Jamie threw himself into school life with an enthusiasm reaping its rewards to such a degree that many years later he was to say, 'I think the five years or so that I spent here were probably the happiest of my life.'

He soon found boys of like mind at the Academy, as eager as he to play out fantasies of shipwreck, desert islands and adventure on the high seas. One boy, Stewart Gordon, approached Jamie and demanded to know his name. It was rejected by Stewart who told the newcomer, 'I'll call you Sixteen String Jack.' He was then informed that Stewart's own name was in fact Dare Devil Dick, a name borrowed from one of the penny dreadfuls, and the new boy was invited to join the pirate crew. Their hero, Dare Devil Dick, 'wasn't much believed in by our relations . . . His school days had been rather trying. That was one of the reasons we sympathised with him.' After a disagreement with a master 'who would not give way', Dick had apparently deserted home for the high seas, whereupon he duly became a pirate.

Stewart Gordon was the son of the Sheriff Clerk and they lived in Moat Brae, a large and comfortable house set in rambling bosky gardens leading down to the river Nith. This garden and the river running beside it became a much-favoured spot, where for hours at a stretch Jamie, Stewart, his brother Hal and other school friends exultantly acted out their bellicose fantasies of capture, escape and vengeance.

Years later, in a preface to *The Coral Island*, Jamie would say that of all the writers of adventure stories 'Ballantyne was for long my man . . . I think I looked upon him as the writer of the Hundred Best Books, and wondered why that list ever needed to be a list of controversy.' In recalling how the boys took over the garden at Moat Brae, he describes its eventual place in his memory as 'an enchanted land for me. *Coral Island* . . . egged me on, not merely to be wrecked every Saturday afternoon for many months in a long-suffering garden, but to my first work of fiction, a record of our adventures.' Perhaps it wasn't actually his first work, but mere accuracy never held much attraction for Jamie. There was only one really important category, and that was Imaginative Literature. He continued:

We had a sufficiently mysterious cave, that had not been a cave until we named it, and here we grimly ate cocoanuts, stoned from the trees . . . Here too we had a fire, lit as Jack contrived to light his, by rubbing two sticks together. So we said (even in the Log Book); but of course, this fire came by more plebeian means, and never in our hearts did we believe in the efficacy of the sticks. No boy, so far as I knew, did believe in them. It seemed too beautiful a dream.[15]

Forty years later in 'a solemn London club', The Reform, James Barrie would gather with several young boys and watch as an American writer friend showed them that it *was* possible. And from the fire thus magically ignited the two men lit their celebratory cigars.

Games of make believe were not Jamie's only entertainments; any and every game was played with gusto. Football and cricket; skating on the frozen lochs; the dramatic and fierce 'prisoner's base'; marbles – at which Jamie was apparently such a fiend that he regularly wore through the sole of one of his boots scraping it along the ground. Then there was the fishing (for which he never lost his passion) and regular walks. With James Macmillan – a boy who died young, and whom Barrie later wistfully and significantly recalled as outshining them all at almost everything – he walked many times to a ruined castle four miles beyond Dumfries. Jamie was now old enough to comprehend and prize this other boy's particular rarity. As an old man he would ask,

What was it about James M'Millan [Barrie's abbreviation] that has stayed with me for so many years, and can still touch me to the quick? The other boys felt that there was something winged about him, just as I did. He couldn't play games and yet we all accepted him as our wonder . . . Where M'Millan was the others never had a look in. The others got his leavings. Literature was to be his game, and what play he might have made with it . . . He was a brilliant scholar, and had also a most original mind; and he would have done something if he had had half a chance . . . He was an influence for good in the school, which not all prize-takers are.[16]

At Dumfries Academy, although Jamie himself didn't take many prizes, he did work – enough anyway to avoid trouble, and sometimes even to take second place. But Alick was occasionally apprehensive about his chance of a place at university. Meanwhile their mother still hankered after a minister for a son. Something not to be achieved without a sound education.

Alick and Mary's household in Dumfries was not one of cheerless earnestness. Rather, it seems to have been a house full of books, easy cheerfulness and a degree of liberal-mindedness quite different from their parents' home. Alick's own learned tastes were rarely imposed upon his younger brother. Wellwood Anderson (Wedd) was a good schoolfriend of Jamie's, and his father owned the Dumfries lending library and bookshop. Jamie was allowed the run of the shop and its book-filled attics and here he read for hours at a time. His favourites were still adventure stories, but he now ranged more widely. Perhaps it was Alick who introduced him to another periodical, *Chatterbox*, in an attempt to wean him off the penny dreadfuls he continued to admire. He later recalled an article in *Chatterbox* describing the dire consequences for anyone so morally bankrupt as to read such stuff. As a result he went out at the dead of night, 'a shovel concealed up my little waistcoat – and deep in the bowels of the earth I buried the evidence of guilt'. Jamie's adolescent apprehension of impending adulthood and the ominous proximity of responsibility, revealed in this and similar stories, articulate something to be ceaselessly rehearsed: the problem of growing up. Burying the comics was one of his attempts – all of them doomed to failure – to put away childish things.

From an early notebook showing a temporary mania for lists, such as 'Fishing and Walking Statistics', we gain an idea of the intensity of Jamie's physical exertions. Having settled into a nervously preoccupied attendance upon his mother, outdoors he would often exercise himself until he collapsed into the sleep of healthy exhaustion.

Fished 12 times. Caught average of 2 doz + 6, in all 30 doz.
Walked 18 times. Average of 13 11/18ths, in all 245 miles.

Coupled with this physical energy was a robust youthful confidence, which drove Jamie and his friends to throw themselves into a series of literary experiments. In collaboration with James Macmillan, Jamie wrote one chapter of a book they called *Didymus*. He also finished four pieces for the school magazine, *The Clown*. Written out entirely in longhand, accompanied by the occasional illustration, the tone was typical of the facetiousness of adolescence.

Another passion was drama. In Jamie's parents' home, as in many other Presbyterian households, all drama after Shakespeare was suspect, and even he was often read in Thomas Bowdler's expurgated version. For centuries both Church and state had monitored and muzzled the theatre, wary of its capacity to rouse the populace to disturbing displays of anarchic behaviour. Beside its tendency to social disruption, in the more Puritanical sections of Scottish society the feeling that the theatre was ungodly was so pervasive that many homes expressly forbade any contact with it at all. As James Barrie would tersely say, 'To the Auld Licht of the past there were three degrees of damnation – auld kirk, play-acting, chapel' – their name for the Church of England.

Wedd's father, the bookseller, had no such inhibitions: his shelves had much of the post-Shakespearean drama it was difficult for the boys to find at school. They read, discussed and argued, and in addition to their feverish consumption of 'literature' they could now attend Dumfries's newly rebuilt theatre. This reinstatement put the Dumfries Theatre Royal on the provincial circuit of the stock companies, and the liberal head-master of the Academy encouraged his pupils to follow performances if their parents or guardians would permit. Between 1876 and 1878 Jamie rarely missed a show.

> I entered many times in my school days, and always tried to get the end seat in the front row of the pit, which was also the front of the house, as there were no stalls. I sat there to get rid of stage illusion and watch what the performers were doing in the wings.[17]

As a little boy in Kirriemuir Jamie had seen the unpolished itinerant acting troupes arriving in the town. Besides these there was Samm'l Mann's Tumbling Troupe, with its tumblers, jugglers, sword-swallowers and balancers, who visited twice a year. They came in summer for the Muckley Fair, and again at the end of the year for the Storm Stead. This was a time, as its name suggests, when the weather was harsh and the company might be trapped in the fields outside town by ice and snow. Nearly starving, they were sometimes unable to move on for weeks.

But when dusk fell the harshness of the lives of players and audience was temporarily dispelled as the lights were lit, and the drummer and fifer from the tumbling booth were sent out to call in the people. Here came the Fair Circassian, and the showman, who, besides playing '*The Mountain Maid and the Shepherd's Bride*, exhibited part of the tail of Baalam's ass, the helm of Noah's ark, and the tartan plaid in which Flora Macdonald had wrapped Prince Charlie'. Besides these there were *The Slave Driver and his Victims*, and *The Tragedy of Tiffano and the Haughty Princess*. Mere tableaux with vestigial plots, they were enough to hold the attention of an eager and uncritical audience.

On the Muckle Friday, the summer fair for which all Kirriemuir turned out, Jamie was breathless with anticipation as

> the square was crammed with gingerbread stalls, bagpipers, fiddlers, and monstrosities, who were gifted with second sight. There was a bearded man, who had neither legs nor arms, and was drawn through the streets in a small cart by four dogs. By looking at you he could see all the clockwork inside, as could a boy who was led about by his mother on a string . . . Some were literally spellbound by it all:

What a mockery the glare of the lamps and capers of the mounte-
banks were. It is a curious thing, but true, that our herd-boys and
others were sometimes struck with the stage fever. [The town] . . .
lost boys to the showmen even in winter . . .[18]

During the course of the nineteenth century, when the theatre went
through a revolutionary process of change, the impetus was to make play-
going more reputable. In 1800 fashionable society on the whole frequented
the opera, not the theatre. But the drive towards respectability was so
successful that by the century's end large audiences flocked to the theatres
from across the social spectrum. As a schoolboy in Dumfries Jamie had
witnessed a theatre in transition. He saw a mixture of the old traditions
played out in combination with the increasing vogue for historical drama
and the drive towards a new realism on stage.

At the Dumfries Theatre Royal the resident stock company of actors
churned out a stream of melodramas, burlesques and highlights selected
from Shakespeare, while the audience quickly grew familiar with the resident actors and their props, as each reappeared nightly in a number of
guises.

At our theatre there are no relays of actors: and the gentleman who
was Prince of Denmark from seven till eight, was the melancholy
Jacques and Macbeth a little later in the evening, was throwing kisses
from the foot of the balcony to Juliet about half-past ten, and had
an Irish Brogue as Handy Andy at eleven. Mercutio was killed only
to rush on to the next scene as someone else; and one man played
five different characters, including two of the witches in *Macbeth*.[19]

In 1877 the well-known actor-manager J. H. Clynes came to Dumfries,
and kept the theatre open for a whole winter. Clynes was Jamie's first
Hamlet, Othello and Macbeth, and even to the untutored eyes of the
Academy boys it was abundantly clear that this actor and his troupe were
superior to the performers they were accustomed to at the Theatre Royal.
Jamie was entranced. On the inaugural night Clynes led the company in
three different roles: contractions of plays by two leading playwrights,
Bulwer Lytton and Dion Boucicault, while the third drama included
excerpts from *Richard III*. It was at the Theatre Royal that Jamie first saw
As You Like It, a play which captured his imagination on that first night
and would later influence his own work. Occasionally Clynes brought
in 'star companies' for a few nights, and one of these was led by the great
comic actor J. L. Toole. At Dumfries Jamie saw Toole play two of his
most famous roles, while in the supporting cast was an actor named

George Shelton. By one of those quirks of fate, in years to come Toole would act in some of Barrie's earliest London plays, while George Shelton was to take the role of Smee in *Peter Pan* (a part he would make his own), and Boucicault's son – also Dion – would be its most famous director.

So affected were the boys from the Academy by Toole's acting that after the performer's second night half a dozen of them had fixed upon their profession. Fired up with dramatic enthusiasm they founded a drama club in which they first set down Toole's roles as well as they could from memory, then duly acted them out. Reminiscing many decades later Barrie said,

> I think I did greatest credit to our admired Wedd on one occa-
> sion when the curtain rose on my husband and me about to partake
> of breakfast, and in his stage-fright my husband pulled the table-
> cover and its contents to the floor . . . Adele was my name . . .
> but the unworthy youth who played my husband would call me
> Addle, to my annoyance . . . I went behind him, and, putting my
> arms around his neck . . . I said 'you clumsy darling', the house
> rose – I don't mean they went out – several of them cheered, led
> on by Wedd . . .[20]

In this fervent atmosphere Jamie also wrote his first play. He tells how, in order to escape from those feminine roles, he wrote *Bandelero the Bandit*, and 'took the part of all my favourite characters in fiction artfully rolled into one'.

The headmaster of the Academy continued in a liberal vein, allowing the boys to stage their plays for the public. When *Bandelero* was performed, however, it provoked an outraged letter from a clergyman. A member of the school governing body, he stormed, over several columns, that the play was grossly immoral – perhaps an overstatement. The controversy found its way into the local press and was taken up by several national newspapers. After Jamie and Wedd, with great audacity, had written to and been promised patronage by several notable actors and dignitaries of the day, including Henry Irving and the Duke of Buccleuch, they felt great satisfaction in seeing the clergyman climb down. Jamie Barrie's dramatic debut had achieved for him a most gratifying degree of noto-riety, especially for a boy who wanted more than anything to be *seen*.

Although we have no details, some time during 1877 Jamie and Alick's housekeeper sister, Mary Ann, died. This was also the year in which Alick married a young Edinburgh woman, Mary Cowan.

The following year was Jamie's last at school. At eighteen he was by now lagging behind the usual rate of academic progress. (In this period, many boys went up to university at sixteen or seventeen.) Alick had realised that Jamie was not scholarship material for university, and so the decision had been made to let him stay on at school until he was better prepared.

Although Jamie hadn't distinguished himself at the Academy, his time there remained of great value to him. The statement that his years at Dumfries were some of the happiest of his life was not made in jest. And in this frame of mind he made a momentous claim for the garden at Moat Brae, where he had played so fiercely those games of shipwreck, pirates and Indians. He said that there they had created 'a sort of Odyssey that was long afterwards to become the play of *Peter Pan*. For our escapades in a certain Dumfries garden, which is enchanted land to me, were certainly the genesis of that nefarious work.'[21] Whether this is strictly accurate, whether the genesis of *Peter Pan* lies further back in Jamie Barrie's childhood experiences and whether he would have been able to access the real genesis of his masterpiece, is open to debate. What is not in doubt is Barrie's estimation of Dumfries's importance in his life.

Within a few years his academic progress would cease to matter very much, but at this point his family saw it as crucial to his future. In that last year he distinguished himself by winning an essay prize, and also gaining the highest marks in the English Literature paper. Yet this wasn't enough for a bursary at Aberdeen, the chosen university for the sons of Kirriemuir bound for the professions.

3

'Literature was my game . . .'

At the end of the summer term of 1878 Jamie packed up and left Dumfries as a schoolboy for the last time. Leaving behind the final phase of childhood, he could no longer put off the first step into that dubious adult world. Returning to Kirriemuir, he was conscious that Alick, in whose house he had lived for most of the last ten years, was disappointed in him. Likewise his parents, David and Margaret. Jamie had announced that he was not going to university. He was determined upon another path. How he would go about following it was as yet unclear to him, but of one thing he was quite certain: he wanted to be an author.

Jamie's parents and brother were appalled. To be an author was not a respectable profession. Of course there was Mr Carlyle, that towering Victorian man of letters, whom Margaret Barrie held in such veneration, and whom Jamie had observed with awe at Dumfries on numerous occasions. Then there was Sir Walter Scott, whom many contemporary Scots regarded as a national hero. But the family were unanimous in believing that these two were honourable exceptions in a profession that was often disreputable, and, anyway, quite unreliable as a regular source of income. Besides, Jamie had done nothing to show that he had the slightest chance of becoming a second Scott or Carlyle.

Alick hurriedly returned to Kirriemuir from Dumfries and the discussions continued back and forth. No one was impressed when Jamie insisted that one day he would become a great writer. Nor, they insisted, was money a problem for his continuing education: Alick and his father would see to that. They refused to comprehend Jamie's indifference; he cared little that without a degree he would be barred from the Ministry, the Law, and anything other than the lower strata of medicine or teaching. The family's persistence was eventually repaid when Jamie reluctantly agreed: he would become a student at Edinburgh University.

Alexander Whyte, the minister at St George's Free Church in Edinburgh, had already begun to build the reputation that would make him one of

Scotland's most celebrated preachers. Here, thought Alick, was both a Kirriemuirian and one of his closest friends, who would be glad to keep an eye on the young Jamie. It also happened that Alick's wife, Mary Cowan, had a brother, an Edinburgh silk merchant, in whose house Jamie would be welcome. Last, and in Jamie's mind most importantly, at Edinburgh the Professor of Rhetoric and English Literature was David Masson. Masson, a disciple of Carlyle, was by 1878 renowned as teacher, biographer and major critic. Jamie thought briefly about the Law; he also thought about teaching, but in David Masson there lay the hope of inspiration.

Years later, when his own reputation as a writer was established, Jamie wrote of Masson, 'Though a man might, to my mind, be better employed than in going to college, it is his own fault if he does not strike on someone there who sends his life off at a new angle . . . I seem to remember everything Masson said, and the way he said it.' Masson's ex-student would call him a 'Gulliver in criticism', and wrote, 'There are men who are good to think of, and as a rule we only know them by their books. Something of our pride in life would go with their fall. To have one such professor at a time is the most a university can hope of human nature.'[1]

Most of Jamie's colleagues at the university were not well off; some lived in great poverty, frequently leading to ill health. The boy with whom Jamie shared his lodgings in his first year died in the following one. But poverty and hardship were regarded as the norm for undergraduates, and James Barrie recalled

> three undergraduates who lodged together in a dreary house . . . two of them used to study till two in the morning, while the third slept. When they shut up their books they woke number three, who arose, dressed, and studied till breakfast time. Among the many advantages of this arrangement the chief was that, as they were dreadfully poor, one bed did for three. Two of them occupied it at the one time, and the third at another.[2]

Nor was the desperate poverty of many students much alleviated by a sense of university community. Clubs, societies and meeting places were not common, and anyway membership usually required a portion of the funds that were always so scarce. Jamie was never well off as a student, but so long as he was careful neither was he ever desperate nor unable to afford the theatre, books, or membership of a debating society. In these societies the young men discussed such weighty subjects as 'Is Man the Creature of Circumstance?', 'Ought Extreme Measures be Taken for the

Suppression of Socialism?' and 'Is the Darwinian Theory of Evolution More Probable than that of Special Creation?'

The university lecture halls were for the most part the only places where students met their fellows. In a speech fifty years later, when his fame was such that James Barrie had been made chancellor of his old university, he spoke of the past.

> Unions and hostels, such as, alas, were not in my time, now give Edinburgh students that social atmosphere which seemed in the old days to be the one thing lacking: the absence of them maimed some of us for life.[3]

James Barrie could be melodramatic and emotional, yet it was not an overstatement to recall this period of his life as maiming. In comparison with the easy companionship and unselfconsciousness of his years at Dumfries, the four years he spent in Edinburgh were a period of suppression, strain and sometimes gnawing loneliness. This impression he left upon one of his fellow students would not have been untypical:

> I remember him distinctly – a sallow-faced, round-shouldered, slight, somewhat delicate-looking figure, who quietly went in and out amongst us, attracting but little attention . . . He was . . . then, as always, exceedingly shy and diffident, and I do not remember ever to have seen him enter or leave a classroom with any companion.[4]

From this period Jamie began to fall prey to the intense headaches and bouts of depression that would descend periodically, and without warning, for the remainder of his life. Between his studies, without the companionship found at Dumfries or home, there was too much time for brooding. Whatever his confusion and doubts, however, as a true son of Kirriemuir the young student drove himself to keep busy. Besides this there was, too, one real beacon of light. Through a combination of determination and doggedness, before the end of his second year Jamie had managed to persuade the editor of the *Edinburgh Courant* to take him on as a drama critic. Saving for his beloved theatre tickets was unnecessary when he had a complimentary seat in the best part of the house. Jamie was writing and, however paltry the sum, he was being *paid* for it.

Besides the nights at the theatre, and time spent writing up the performances, he was also roughing out ideas for articles. And, although his social life was limited, he was not a recluse. His sisters Isabella (Bella) and Margaret (Maggie) came to work as teachers in Edinburgh and Jamie saw them quite often. He was also made welcome in his brother's house

ies, and soon found that Alick's small children were genuine little ons when he visited. On these occasions his self-consciousness otten as he threw himself into games and stories, relishing the discovery that with the children he could temporarily put aside the pretence of adulthood. Meanwhile, a diary kept for a few months in 1880 gives a doleful impression of his routine and state of mind, epitomised by the concluding remarks for a week, which read 'Grind, grind, grind.'

Much later, in his play *The Wedding Guest*, he made a revealing observation: 'I lived too much in my art, and my solitary thoughts. I shrank from men's free talk of women, and yet when I left them it was to brood on the things they spoke of; theirs was a healthier life than mine.'[5] Meanwhile in Edinburgh Jamie complained to his notebook, 'Men can't get together without talking filth.' This precious attitude appears, as much as anything, to have been the result of his extreme shyness with women. It was also a natural defence against his sense of failure at making any impression on them at all. But if this young man couldn't attract attention by his appearance, he was to discover there were other ways by which he could hold centre stage.

While Jamie was in Edinburgh he was an assiduous churchgoer. On leaving Scotland, however, this practice ceased, except for those times when he returned to Kirriemuir; he had no intention of distressing his mother by confrontation. Apart from one or two bitter comments in his notebooks Jamie spoke little about religion. He never mocked it, undoubtedly upheld its moral precepts, and his working philosophy became a kind of stoicism. Interestingly, from his writing and notebooks it becomes clear that the older James Barrie was neither Christian nor anti-Christian. His mind was far from being a religious one, and yet there were times when he could capture real elements of religious sincerity.

In April 1882 the four years of 'grind' were finally at an end. Having taken his exams in the seven subjects – including History, Mathematics, Moral Philosophy, Natural Philosophy and Greek – that constituted an arts degree, James M. Barrie became an MA. Though he knew he had some of the most distinguished professors in the land, he was relieved to be leaving behind those years of boredom with some of the ideas only half understood and the resulting necessity for cramming. The impression is of a young man of delicate health, who was rather suspicious of himself and others; who was capable of hard work but only when he put his mind to it. It wasn't that he hadn't turned up for lectures or failed to turn in the essays, it was simply that he didn't engage with much of what he had been taught.

He returned home to Kirriemuir briefly and then travelled on to Dumfries and Alick's home for consultation and advice. His relatives were apprehensive. It was finally clear that Jamie would not make a teacher, doctor or lawyer. To his family's consternation he was still insisting on becoming a writer. Alick and their parents failed to understand how the young graduate could possibly wish to subject himself to a life so precarious and unpredictable. Neither could they understand how he would succeed. Yes, Jamie had been paid for his reviews by the *Courant*, but this was hardly a living. None of them knew anything about the details of writing as a profession, but neither, therefore, did they know effectively how to dissuade Jamie from following it.

Alick showed genuine sympathy and tolerance towards his younger brother, and it was he who first accepted that Jamie really did mean to become a writer. Despite the great differences in their characters, Alick had the imagination to understand that Jamie might lead a different life from the one he, and in particular their parents, had believed he might follow. Perhaps he had the wit to realise that he no longer quite understood his young brother.

None the less he still had a role to play; a sober and responsible elder, he could now see only one direction in which to guide his brother's pen. Confined by his own experience, Alick felt it his duty to steer Jamie in the direction of solemn labour, intellectual and scholarly, but here his imagination had utterly failed him. Neither, however, was Jamie himself any help, since he had little idea of how he might set about his chosen career. Once again Alick stepped in. Jamie would return to Edinburgh, and with board and lodging provided he was to set about becoming a writer. The model was of course Carlyle, the family's literary hero.

While Jamie went on with his reviewing for the *Courant*, the real job in hand was to produce something very serious indeed. Hour after hour he toiled in the library at research that now appears rather absurd in the light of his eventual *métier*. With Alick's encouragement the young scholar's projected work was *The Early Satirical Poetry of Great Britain (With Some Accounts of the Manner in which it Illustrates History)*. One remains astounded. In addition Jamie was to write a series of essays on equally recherché themes. If the *magnum opus* on satirical poetry ever got beyond a draft, or even notes, we do not know. What we do know is that he wrote a series of fairly derivative articles on current affairs, which he persisted in sending off to newspapers – they were all sent back – and made vague plans for grand historical romances and a farce.

Jamie continued in this fruitless labour before returning home for the Christmas and New Year celebrations. He was irritated and embarrassed at the queries he had to field from family and friends, who were curious and no doubt also sceptical about his progress. Jamie knew he had achieved little. With hindsight we can see that one of the important things he *had* been doing that autumn and winter was teaching himself the application necessary for hard work. Not intermittently as before, but with more consistent determination. Understating his talent, he was later to say, 'The most precious possession I ever had was my joy in hard work. I do not know when it came to me – not very early, because I was an idler at school, and read all the wrong books at college.'[6]

Like all the Barries Jamie was dogged, but his was not a particularly methodical doggedness. Trial and error was his method. He learnt what he had to learn by the long, slow process. And so all the notes, drafts and screwed-up pieces of paper in the overflowing wastepaper basket were the essential prelude to something happening. Nor, out of all this preparatory material, was Jamie quite able to envisage what the result would be after he had settled down at his desk. This would never really change. What did change was Jamie's realisation that this was the process he must endure in order to create. As yet, none of this was clear to him and he wrote on into the night.

His writing during this period was not in any important way creative. With his *Roget's Thesaurus* always beside him, and without quite realising it, Jamie was putting himself through a period of apprenticeship. In the process he already appears to have exhibited that combination of intense self-belief and the thick skin so necessary when receiving a returned manuscript or an editor's brush-off. Apart from the occasional lapse Jamie remained astonishingly undeterred. He was becoming ambitious. And although his aims were beyond his present capabilities, he wasn't going to allow a few failures to deflect him from his course.

It was Jenann, the elder sister always in the background, who was instrumental in Jamie taking his next crucial step. Jenann may have been hopelessly tethered to her mother – apparently oblivious to her own sacrificed life – but this didn't mean she was lacking in thought or initiative. Advertised in the *Scotsman* she saw that the *Nottingham Journal* was looking for a leader writer. With complete faith in her brother, and the practical sense to recognise his need for employment, she persuaded Jamie to apply for the post. In more than one publication he would later tell the story of how he had never read a leader. Desperate to find out how it was done, he said he pulled down the old newspapers that had been stuffed up the chimney to prevent draughts.

Jamie asked for a reference from his professor, David Masson, and another from the now distinguished Scottish minister Alexander Whyte. The *Nottingham Journal* were impressed by the eminence of these referees, and soon requested examples of his work. Although Jamie had at least glanced at many leaders, he had certainly never written one. Undeterred, rather than straining to write one or two of these specialised journalistic specimens, he sent off an old undergraduate essay on *King Lear*. Either an impressive demonstration of self-confidence or a risky show of fool-hardiness, this was a precedent for what would become Jamie's habitual way of behaving, and one that so often in the future was to meet with success.

The *Nottingham Journal* offered him the position at the sum of three pounds a week. To Jamie this seemed very reasonable, and was certainly enough. Above all it was regular payment, a salary. This was the opportunity that the feverishly hard-working and underpaid freelance journalists of the time dreamt of. It was also something that Jamie's family regarded as essential. 'If only you could be sure of as much as would keep body and soul together,' his mother had repeatedly sighed. With these thoughts in mind Jamie's new position looked remarkably good. An authority had given him its blessing and overnight his family was reassured. There was nothing romantic in their notions: if Jamie was being paid for it, this must mean that he was competent to write.

Jamie meanwhile, was torn between elation and fear. Elation because of hopes realised, and fear at the thought of his ignorance and inexperience. 'My mother was already sitting triumphant among my socks, and I durst not let her see me quaking.' Keeping his disquiet to himself, within a week her son had packed up, said his farewells and departed on the train for the Midlands.

Nottingham had only recently become a large town, so that in 1883 around its central streets and markets the old orchards and gardens still flourished alongside the factories and warehouses newly sprung up. Straddling an ancient agrarian past and a new industrial one, it was still famous for its Michaelmas Goose Fair, held in the great expanse of Market Square.

On his very first day in the offices of the town's *Journal*, the young Scot was immediately thrown into a maelstrom of activity. Although he rarely spoke about his time in Nottingham, the next eighteen months would prove to be a period so testing for Jamie that it amounted to a trial by fire. Fortunately he was ready for the challenge. With immense concentration and stamina he fulfilled the huge demands made upon him, and as the professional writer was forged Jamie would emerge a different young man. Not changed in essentials, but vastly more experienced, he was a little more hardbitten, with a new sense of worldly confidence to add to his innate conviction.

Not many would have had the resources to produce the great quantity of writing, week after week, month after month, that Jamie was required to turn out. From the beginning of his writing career, without any true comprehension of her son beyond a cunning ability to manipulate his emotions, his mother always feared he would 'dry up'. Contrary to her fears, the prodigious scale on which Jamie now showed himself able to write would continue unabated for years.

The *Nottingham Journal* had been established early in the eighteenth century. However, although the oldest of Nottingham's three daily papers, by the time Jamie arrived it had the smallest circulation. Two kindly and unbusinesslike brothers, of considerable wealth, had inherited the *Journal* from their father and appeared unaware of how much their newspaper had slipped behind the times. A few years later some thinly disguised commentary on his job in Nottingham appeared in *When a Man's Single*, Jamie's early romantic novel.

> The *Silchester Mirror's* offices are nearly crushed out of sight in a block of buildings left in the middle of the street for town councils to pull down gradually. This island of houses, against which a sea of humanity beats daily, is cut in two by a narrow passage off which several doors lead. One of these leads up a dirty stair to the editorial and compositing rooms of the *Mirror*, and down a dirty stair to its printing room.[7]

The *Journal* had an office, some printing machinery – in these days newspapers were still 'set up' by hand – and a staff who, by a communal spirit and effort of will, threw the paper together every day without any formal control. The owners took no part in its production, nor was there any editor. Each day a sub-editor, reporters and the foreman collected together enough columns so that the paper could go to press at about two or three in the morning. The sub-editor of the *Nottingham Journal*, H. G. Hibbert, later told how 'the key for the very large building, which housed thousands of pounds worth of machinery' was left for him under the doormat on Sundays so that he could gain admission and proceed with the preparation of copy, while the mechanical workers were free to attend evening service. Hibbert provided some details of 'Penny', the foreman compositor, who was left 'to get the paper out' as best he could. Penny divided copy into two classes: (1) 'noos', the importance of which he judged by the relative nearness of its place of origin; (2) 'tripe', which embraced all literary matter, such as leaders, reviews and special articles; indeed, everything the new arrival from Scotland had contracted to supply. Jamie continues his description:

The editor's room had a carpet, and was chiefly furnished with books sent in for review. It was more comfortable, but more gloomy than the reporters' room, which had a long desk running along one side of it, and a bunk for holding coal and old newspapers on the other side. The floor was so littered with papers, many of them still in their wrappers, that, on his way between his seat and the door, the reporter generally kicked one or more into the bunk. It was in this way, unless an apprentice happened to be otherwise disengaged, that the floor was swept. In this room were a reference library and an old coat. The library was within reach of the sub-editor's hand, and contained some fifty books, which the literary staff could consult, with the conviction that they would find the page they wanted missing.[8]

Penny is a figure then characteristic of the foreman–compositor in hundreds of newspapers across the land. And it was he who effectively ran the *Journal*.

Penny was a lank, loosely jointed man of forty, who shuffled about the office in slippers, ruled the compositors with a loud voice and a blustering manner . . . His politics were respect for the House of Lords, because it rose early, enabling him to have the paper set before supper-time.[9]

In an article called 'A Night in a Provincial Newspaper Office' Jamie described the frantic response to the late news of the death of a world-famous man of letters:

From the office boy to the editor, everyone takes the defunct sternly to task for dying at such a preposterous time of night. It is not creditable; the staff feels hurt; a literary man might have been more considerate. The editor disappears into his private room to look up Death, in the Familiar Quotation, preparatory to angrily dashing off an eloquent tribute to the memory of the deceased. The foreman bursts into the sub-editorial room to announce that he is 'flooded' with 'copy', to insist the racing must be 'slaughtered' if the two columns are coming from London, to state emphatically his low opinion of men of letters, and generally to have it out with somebody. Back comes the racing to be cut down to a couple of 'sticks'. The reporter who puts his head in at the door to ask whether a clear, bell-like voice is called a mezzo-soprano or a mezzotint, is told that his concert notice is doomed; and the great dramatic critic with his four French words and seven adjectives is 'held over until tomorrow in consequence of the unwonted pressure on our space'.[10]

In *When a Man's Single* Jamie gave an insight into the young jour-nalist's approach:

The reporter . . . was not quite the Rob of three months before. Now he knew how a third-rate newspaper is conducted, and the capacity for wonder had gone from him. He was in danger of thinking that the journalist's art is to write readably, authoritatively, and always in three paragraphs on a subject he knows nothing about. Rob had written many leaders, and followed readers through the streets wondering if they liked them.[11]

Rapidly becoming a practised hand at the daily leader, the chaotic way in which the newspaper was thrown together each night meant that Jamie was soon writing much more besides. Called upon to fill in gaps in the paper's columns, he realised that so long as he fulfilled its criterion – Is there space? – he was able to write on almost any subject he chose. This was hugely valuable and exhilarating practice. Even by the less corpo-rate, more individual standards of the day, Jamie's position was unusual. Most importantly its mix of eccentricity and autonomy was perfectly suited to his temperament; he was never any good at being led.

Within a week of starting at the *Journal* he was turning out at least two columns a day. The pressure must have been immense, yet he rose to the occasion, buoyed up by the heady knowledge that people were actually reading his work. Without fuss or obvious panic, armed with that sense of self-assurance that only a few had as yet discerned, Jamie sat down and wrote, and carried on writing. He turned out more than fifteen hundred words a day for six days a week. Besides this regular torrent he was tackling book reviews and several special articles each week.

As the months went by his style became more even and convincing. But from the beginning, Jamie's extraordinary facility, the vividness, and disrespectful, absurdist response to life and ideas with which he filled his columns made for a quirky freshness. He found that with time forever chafing at his heels he had become focused. It was clear that Jamie Barrie was a born journalist.

After a while, though, he grew concerned that the *Journal*'s readers might object to one person providing almost all the 'literary' material. Jamie quickly solved the problem with an original touch. He diversified his persona simply by becoming a number of people. Unconsciously permitting himself a level of experiment, this would become central not only to his writing, but also to his discernment of who he himself might be. As the leader writer he exemplified maturity, wisdom, even self-righteousness. As the book reviewer he was a younger, sharper, more witty and caustic man. On Mondays he was 'Hippomenes', while on Thursdays he became 'A Modern Peripatetic'. This constant mixture of pressure and variety helped to ignite his imagination. Each of his characters was thus enabled to develop their own personality, while each of them wrote, on the slightest whim, on absolutely anything that had struck the young journalist and lodged itself in his mind.

Jamie's consuming working routine at the *Journal* kept him in the office till long after midnight. Next morning he would get up late, make some preparatory notes for the day's writing, and then make his way back to the office. His aversion to the hard drinking and loose talking of his colleagues in the local pubs made it unlikely that he would form substantial friendships in Nottingham. He had only one day off a week, Saturday, and when not at the theatre would often fill this by making off into the country on one of his long walks. The sub-editor, Hibbert, besides being a fellow theatre-lover, was also a walking enthusiast, and they sometimes went out to the country together.

In addition to his enormous output for the *Journal*, within a few months Jamie ventured further and began to have articles taken by London publications. The first one appeared in August 1884 in the prestigious evening daily the *Pall Mall Gazette*, with the title, 'The Manufacture of Penny Numbers (by a Manufacturer)'. His next piece of London journalism appeared in *Home Chimes*. This curiously titled little magazine was begun by the immensely prolific, and long since forgotten, novelist F. W. Robinson. Robinson managed to attract a few established names, but more importantly he gathered together an impressive group of young writers, of whom several would go on to literary distinction. These included Swinburne, Brett Harte, Coventry Patmore and Jerome K. Jerome.

With these articles Jamie was making an attempt to launch himself on to a grander stage; his ultimate destination was London. But he was well aware that the odd London article wouldn't keep him alive. Meanwhile the *Journal* was making a loss and was forced to economise. Now that leaders could be syndicated from other newspapers the owners decided that they must let their leader writer go. And so it was, at the end of October 1884, after eighteen months of extraordinary exertion, the young journalist found himself back at home. The return may have appeared rather ignominious, but Jamie had had a taste of what he wanted, and mere dismissal was not going to unnerve him now.

In Kirriemuir he lived with his parents at Strath View, where he had lodging, a room which he filled with books and a window with a distant view of Glamis. The family attitude was ambivalent. About his father's thoughts we are never entirely sure, while his mother and his sister Jenann were at the same time convinced that their Jamie couldn't fail, and doubtful of him succeeding at such an insecure profession. Determined to make a living as a freelance journalist, Jamie wrote on, bombarding London editors with his work. Although much was rejected, a trickle of articles was published. He was forever on the lookout for new ideas, and in a later article for *Home Chimes* called 'A Journalist's Day' he wrote:

> There are few things that this journalist cannot turn to account. What would be a calamity to other men comes as a boon and a blessing to him. When his tailor misfitted him this spring he imme- diately made two guineas out of it; and thirteen shillings was his net gain last week for losing his luggage . . . His traps were put into the wrong van at a northern station, and instead of coming on with him to St Pancras, went to Euston. A few hours later they were delivered at his door, thus saving him a cab fare of three shillings. Having rested, he wrote a short article pointing out that it was an economical thing to let one's luggage go astray, and this he calcu- lates at another ten and sixpence. Deducting the small coin with which he tipped a porter to enquire into his missing things there remains a clear gain of thirteen shillings.

Another passage gives more clues as to how he developed his sources:

> This journalist had thought back upon every event of his life and utilised everything in it of practical value. He is now thinking back upon the lives of his friends with the most encouraging results. Naturally reserved, he was until lately a man of very few companions; but he has discovered that there are few persons so uninteresting as not to have, at the very least, a leaderette in them, and he now makes it his duty to extract it. He is the most genial of men when on the scent of a good thing . . . He only hates one kind of creature. That is the traveller who is full of miscellaneous matter and refuses to communi- cate it. He would rip that man to get at the articles.

The two guiding principles in Jamie's working life for the next few years were, that writing is a job which must pay, and that the creative imagination should be given free rein and be forever at work in search of new material. Given Jamie's background, his attitude was, not surpris- ingly, a practical one. He understood the romance of writing without being romantic about it, and as intuition came to be supplanted by reason, so a succession of articles quickly followed.

After a time, still under the guidance of Alick, Jamie was persuaded to apply once again for a regular salaried post, this time with the *Liverpool Post and Echo*. Fortunately he was turned down, and despite moments of grave self-doubt he ignored the rejection, mustered his self-belief and stubbornly ploughed on.

Not long after his return to Kirriemuir he had an article accepted by the *St James's Gazette*, a periodical in fierce competition with the prestigious *Pall Mall Gazette*. The *Pall Mall*'s first editor had been Frederick Greenwood, whose fifteen years of service came to an end when a political disagreement with the new proprietor led him to resign, along with all his staff. The indomitable Greenwood managed to find backing to establish a new periodical, the *St James's Gazette* – in direct rivalry with the *Pall Mall*.

At home Jamie had once again been listening to his mother telling those stories about the Auld Lichts from her youth. Margaret's reminiscences had always fascinated him, only now he listened with a purpose. Making dozens of carefully numbered notes in the minute books that were already a feature of his working life, Jamie was building up a small community of characters, old and young, drawn from past inhabitants of the town.

The initial article was written in the first person, by the elderly figure of a dominie (a schoolteacher) with a connection to Kirriemuir, now renamed Thrums. The old dominie sets down his memories of the townspeople back in the time of the Seceders, when Jamie's mother, Margaret, had been young. Jamie named the article 'Auld Licht Idylls', sent it off to Greenwood at the *St James's Gazette*, and waited. Greenwood liked it, changed the title and printed it as 'An Auld Licht Community' in November 1884. As Jamie would later write, 'In dispatching that article he thought he had exhausted the subject,' so he continued sending new articles to Greenwood and other editors on a variety of themes. The first of those he sent to Greenwood was returned and on it was scribbled the famous comment, 'But I liked that Scotch thing. Any more of those?'

At the time there weren't any more of those 'Scotch things', yet although surprised at Greenwood's interest Jamie knew better than to ignore such a request. Into the new year he continued writing and having work accepted by other publications, such as *Home Chimes*, while Greenwood's instinct, which had told him there was mileage in Jamie's 'Thrums' story, made him continue to press for more.

So I sent him a marriage, and he took it, and then I tried him with a funeral, and he took it, and it really did look as if we had him . . . My mother . . . was racking her brains, by request, for memories I might convert into articles.[12]

By March 1885, six of Jamie's Thrums articles, with titles such as 'An Auld Licht Funeral', 'An Auld Licht Courtship' and 'An Auld Licht Scandal', had been printed in the *St James's Gazette*. With ten of his articles accepted in London in two months, Jamie was becoming impatient. He was also becoming agitated; fearful lest his cowardice, or 'good sense', should stand in his way. Everything now depended upon the great metropolis, for conviction told him it was here his future lay.

Jamie's mother was afraid of what would happen to him if he went to London without any assurances, and tried to hold him back. Margaret loved her son, but her love was a constraining one, without boundless faith in his capacity to succeed. Jennan probably had faith; his father was out of his depth. Jamie once again travelled to Dumfries to talk it over with Alick, the brother whose kindness and sound judgement had always been available to him. Alick would have been aware of Greenwood's eminence as an editor, and perhaps it was he who suggested writing to the great man for his advice. The reply came quickly. Under no circumstances should Mr Barrie go to London. He must stay where he was until a more substantial body of his work had been published. But the advice came too late. However speedy Greenwood's reply, the young man could wait no longer. In his mind he had already left his homeland, and no one could now prevent him from setting out on his great journey south.

4

'To be forever known . . .'

Ignoring the advice of Greenwood, his brother and the rest of the family, Jamie set off for London on the Saturday overnight train. Writing about this momentous journey much later, he tells us that the date was 28th March 1885.

Strange that I cannot remember what the weather was like that night, I who have made so much of weather in the first pages of less moving tales . . . Our hero . . . sits awake in the corner of his railway compartment, well aware that the end of it must be to perch, or to let go, like a bat in the dark behind the shutter. He has a suspicious eye, poor gomeril, for any fellow-traveller who is civil to him. He is gauche and inarticulate, and as thin as a pencil . . . Expression, an uncomfortable blank. Wears thick boots (with nails in them), which he will polish specially for social functions. Carries on his person a silver watch bought for him by his father from a pedlar on fourteenth birthday . . . Manners full of nails like his boots. Ladies have decided that he is of no consequence, and he already knows this and has private anguish thereanent. Hates sentiment as a slave hates his master. Only asset, except a pecuniary one, is a certain grimness about not being beaten.[1]

His luggage consisted of a strong, square wooden box, a shared family possession taken to university by his brother and uncle before him. He continued his reminiscence:

Having reached London for the great adventure, he was hauling this box to the left-luggage shed at St Pancras when his eyes fell upon what was to him the most warming sight in literature. It was the placard of the *St James's Gazette* of the previous evening with printed on it in noble letters 'The Rooks Begin to Build'.[2]

This was none other than the title of an article Jamie had sent down from Dumfries a few days earlier, and after only a few minutes in the Great Metropolis here it was blazoned on the placard of one of London's most celebrated periodicals. As an old man he would write:

> I remember how he sat on his box and gazed at this glorious news about the rooks. He would have had singular pleasure in drawing the attention of all the other passengers to the placard, even though he had to drag them to it by force.[3]

His breakfast and a copy of the *St James's Gazette* bought, he read his article over and over, then set off in search of lodgings. These he found in Guildford Street, close by the British Museum, where he believed he would be spending much time in the great reading room. Tense with excitement at the thought that this huge clamouring city was where he meant to make his name, he was also well aware that 'the campaign was to be a hard one'.

The London of 1885 in which young Barrie had landed, although far smaller than today, was already a large city of immense energy and vitality. At well over four million the population had almost doubled in the previous fifty years. Overcrowded, overstretched, and rife with unplanned jerry-built dwellings, London's new inhabitants lived, many of them not far from Barrie's lodgings, in sometimes appalling conditions. On the other hand, the middle classes had grown and prospered, while the rich often lived in palatially grand houses teeming with servants. In London the gulf between rich and poor was as great as anywhere on earth.

The great old theatres, such as Drury Lane, showed extraordinary spectaculars and melodramas. Other theatres were hardly worthy of the name and stood alongside dubious clubs and erotic peep-shows, at the finale spewing out their noisy clientele on to the gas-lit streets every night of the week. Fifteen years later, in 1900, Karl Baedeker's travel guide noted that: 'London possesses about 50 theatres and about 500 music halls, which are visited by 325,000 people nightly.' The Russian novelist Dostoyevsky not long since had found the prostitutes so numerous and striking that he said, 'Here there are old women, here there are beauties at the sight of which you stop in amazement.' While these waited to dispense more tangible amusement than the theatres, the little match-girls, the flower girls, the tattered bootblacks and ragged crossing-sweepers all struggled in the chaos to maintain their desperate and meagre lives.

Above the rumble and clatter of horse-drawn carriages, cabs and drays, could be heard the cries of the costermongers. Flashily got up in their velvets, buttons and neckties – men and women alike – they roared out from behind gaudy barrows that theirs were the best, the very best fruit and vegetables in all of London town. Meanwhile, restaurants such as the Café Royal, Rules, Simpsons and Gatti's catered for the well to do, while the old taverns, chop houses, coffee houses and stalls were to be found on the corner of many streets. And, since it was often cheaper to buy ready-made food than to make it at home, traders of every kind noisily elbowed each other for the passing custom. The muffin man rang his familiar bell, while balanced permanently upon his head was the wooden tray with its 'fust-rate article, sir, werry much so'. The pie man called to the passers-by that his pastry coffins filled with meat or fruit could compare with none, and the oysterman claimed that no finer fish than his herrings, whelks and eels were to be had at Greenwich, or any other place.

In Barrie's neighbourhood – on the edge of Bloomsbury and bounded by Holborn and Clerkenwell – many of the winding, narrow streets had remained little changed since the seventeenth century. Perhaps even more than in the past, filth, deprivation and beggary were everywhere to be found. Often these desperate lives – thousands existed on the streets – were lived just one block or two away from the immense and overt wealth of fashionable areas such as Regent's Park, Belgravia or Mayfair. Most of those above the poverty line were still warmed by a steadfast belief in progress, and expansion overseas continued as vigorously as did industrialisation at home. Queen Victoria ruled Britain, which in turn ruled the waves, and the citizenry knew that theirs was the greatest, the richest, the most powerful nation on earth.

In the year Barrie arrived in London, Karl Marx's friend Engels described the East End of London as 'an ever-spreading pool of stagnant misery and desolation'. Marx's relatively obscure death, in 1883, hadn't heralded the march of the workers in the streets. None the less, although his philosophy of Socialism was neither known to the majority nor seen by the governing classes as a political option, there was a small and influ-ential audience (including the founder of the Arts and Crafts movement, William Morris) sympathetic to its theories. For the moment Socialism only had a small following because, for most of the British upper and working classes, it appeared synonymous with nihilism and anarchy.

In the mid 1880s three issues were constantly in the news: the Social Problem (i.e. the poor), Ireland, and the Empire. Barrie wrote an article on Home Rule, but whether he actually knew anything about the subject is unclear. He was intelligent, but an intuitive rather than a systematic thinker, with little real understanding of politics.

The issue of the Empire came to the fore with the death of General

Gordon in Khartoum early in 1885. Gordon had been given the job of withdrawing British troops from an exposed position in Sudan. With hindsight this was a fatal choice. Instead of a down-to-earth career soldier, good at logistics and careful long-term calculation, the delicate task of withdrawal was given to a dashing hero, a magnetic and inscrutable figure, famous for his evangelical piety and his dramatic achievements in China. Gordon was given to fantasies, at times he seemed quite mad, and this time he overreached himself. The whole affair was a disastrous failure; eventually Khartoum was stormed by the Sudanese and General Gordon was murdered.

W. T. Stead, the flamboyant editor of the *Pall Mall Gazette*, would soon popularise the myth of General Gordon as a Christian gladiator of the Empire, fighting to subdue anarchy and savagery. Even if there was an element of truth in the Gordon myth, much was omitted in order to make his image coherent. Although it was this same editor who had published Barrie's first London article in the *Pall Mall Gazette*, Barrie wasn't tempted to become one of the jingoist reporters putting forward the dubiously simplistic doctrines of figures such as Stead.

In the young Scot's cultural background echoed the voices of two quite different men: 'In our Scottish home the name that balked largest next Burns was Carlyle's.' And as these figures represent two of the most enduring strains in Scottish culture, so they are reflected in Barrie's belief system. On the one hand there was Burns, the robust democrat, 'a man's a man for a' that', and also a celebrator of an earthy sensuality. On the other hand there was Carlyle, the grandiose and dour moralist, the Jeremiah of the North. Forever taking the people to task for worldliness and sin in their daily lives, and railing against hypocrital pretence and the mad scramble for money.

Unlike his contemporary Arnold Bennett, Jamie had no great interest in success and money as ends in themselves. In 1885 in his modest room in a Bloomsbury lodging house, he was determined, however, to make more than survival money. And despite a huge and dominant capacity for fantasy he wasn't crippled by it, since it didn't interfere with his capacity for work. Writing was work, and work must pay. Also, it was by *work* he would be known – not by the gifts of appearance, or by eloquence. In spite of his overt veneration of his mother, Barrie makes it clear in *Margaret Ogilvy* that she clearly didn't think he was a Carlyle or a Walter Scott, so how could he possibly make a living at writing?

He tells us that, in his youth, the one person he thought believed in him was

an old tailor, one of the fullest men I have known, and quite the best talker. He was a bachelor . . . a lean man, pallid face, his legs drawn up when he walked as if he was ever carrying something in his lap; his walks were of the shortest, from the tea-pot on the hob to the board on which he stitched, from the board to the hob, and so to bed.[4]

The tailor asked to see the photographs the young boy Jamie had of 'the poets', and Jamie remembered how

> he spread them out on this board, and after looking long at them, turned his gaze on me and said solemnly,
>> 'What can I do to be forever known,
>> And make the age to come my own?'[5]

Jamie had marvelled at the old man's ability to penetrate his thoughts. But then the tailor surprised him by saying that it was actually of himself in his own youth he was thinking 'When that couplet sang in his head.' He told the boy that he too had longed to join Grub Street but that fear stopped him, and, Barrie goes on, completing the tale, 'while he hesitated old age came, and then Death, and found him grasping a box-iron'.

Second only to Barrie's desire to be known, was the obligation to keep the promise made to his mother after his brother David's death. He would look after Margaret Barrie so that she need never worry about anything again. It was irrelevant that his father now earned a salary sufficient that the Barries were no longer poor. While in Nottingham Barrie had already begun sending money home, and this he would continue to do until long after his mother's death.

Having come to the realisation that hard work was to be his main mistress, his life from now on accorded with Carlyle's dictum in *Past and Present* that 'Properly speaking, all true work is Religion.' Although it may appear that there are a great variety of ways of being a Calvinist, at heart they are all the same. Many years later in a speech Barrie declared, 'Doubtless He [God] could have provided us with better fun than hard work, but I don't know what it is.'[6] So he set about becoming a successful London journalist.

For week upon week he wrote, went for his habitual long walks, wrote more, had lonely meals and received rations from home. As an old man he wrote of himself, '. . . it must not be thought he ever went hungry to bed. There was jam and other delicacies from home, and abundance of bread and cheese and tea, and baked potatoes from the oven in the street.' He laboured at his writing, suffered from blinding headaches, and was frequently close to exhaustion. But somehow he kept going. On occasion, when he was short of ideas, he rifled through a pile of old newspapers kept expressly for this purpose in a corner of his room.

Whether stimulated by his afternoon walk, a newspaper story, the baker who sold him a bun or an incident in the street, the ideas poured out of Barrie by the score. He wrote to his friend Wedd that he went 'hounding about looking for subjects like a roaring lion'. The most trivial thing could set his thoughts in motion to generate the core of another fantasy, jotted down for a possible article. When he began, he frequently had no idea how an article was to end until, eventually, it would have formed itself into that tightly knit, always slightly subversive and entertaining prose.

The degree to which Barrie was conscious of his motives for anything he did (or wrote) remains unclear. The notebooks he kept throughout his life – to all intents and purposes material for his published writing – frequently appear to read as an extraordinarily revealing diary. Yet because they are almost always written in the third person, it is as if he is distancing himself from his own experience. Having put himself thus outside, it is as if he observes, without judgement, his innermost self. As we know, hard facts were of absolutely no concern to him. His way of approaching any situation, any person, was via some borderland between fact and fantasy, and the boundaries between the two were never clearly marked. He didn't invent in order to deceive – either others or himself – but the result of his inventions was that very few, if any, knew what this most unusual man ever really thought.

As the months passed the finished articles amounted to hundreds of pages, all written in a hand that in its impenetrability amounted to a kind of mask. Even after editor and printer had deciphered his script, Barrie had created another mask – the pseudonym – behind which he could shelter from view. In those days his name was 'Anon'.

Your philosophy, so far as I can see through the mists, was always to be at it with your pen and let the skies fall if they chose. Would you have looked up, Anon? You knew not what was going on around you, nor apparently cared to know . . . You were in the throng of National Events and International Convulsions, vast social Reforms, the rise and fall of parties, Women were getting Ready, the Religion of the Prosperous had passed from Golf to Lawn Tennis . . . there were Balls and Juncketings and Jubilees . . . and you only looked up to dip [his pen in the inkwell] . . . How long were you wound up to, Anon? Were you truly alive as you ticked away unheard? How long would your coat have been on fire before you noticed? O spare and diligent crumb, I know that in those two years some sort of ecstasy was drumming in your minute inside.[7]

Describing that early period in London like this, Barrie was never out of work. Writing about almost anything that came into his head, he had the supreme confidence to ignore a publication's house style, or indeed anything much that an editor might say to him. Despite this unwillingness, or perhaps inability, to conform, editors increasingly accepted his work. Distinguished periodicals, such as the *Fortnightly Review* and the *St James's Gazette*, could count on a high degree of literary sophistication from their readers. Yet, although the tone of these and other periodicals was rather grave and ponderous, 'lightness of touch' was not proscribed, and perfectly matched Barrie's present frame of mind. With that arresting mixture of dazzling talent, stubborn persistence and a wayward kind of charm, he somehow persuaded one grand London editor after another to publish his quirky pieces. With projected and fulfilled titles such as 'On Running After One's Hat', 'On Folding a Map', 'The Sparrow of the Housetop', 'Upstream in a Canoe', 'A Plea for Wild Flowers', 'The Joys of Wealth by a Bloated Aristocrat', 'On Living on Nothing a Year', and 'Vagabond Students', Barrie's articles were sometimes so light as to be inconsequential. On the edge of the absurd, without an agenda, they often had a mildly lunatic air; he was becoming an entertainer. He was luxuriating in the spectacle of life. As an old man he attempted an explanation:

I note one odd thing about his early articles, that they are mostly written, though anonymously, as the experiences of himself . . . By and by he nearly always assumed a character, writing as a doctor, a sandwich-board man, a member of Parliament, a mother, an explorer, a child . . . a professional beauty, a dog, a cat. He did not know his reason for this, but I can see that it was to escape identifying himself with any views. In the marrow of him was a shrinking from trying to influence anyone, and even from expressing an opinion.[8]

With hindsight one can see that Barrie was perfectly attuned to the belles lettristes traditions of the late Victorian and Edwardian period, in which he flourished and came to the height of his powers. He wrote for the modern equivalent of the arts and literary pages and instinctively understood that, as there were plenty of other writers good at being serious, there must be space for someone who was not only interesting but regularly amusing, too.

An increasing number of publications, including the *Edinburgh Evening Dispatch*, the *British Weekly*, *Chamber's Journal*, the *Era* and *Punch*, were now accepting his work. Even for a hard-working freelance journalist, over the next four years the young Scot turned out a huge amount of writing. It is almost impossible to trace all of it – even excluding the rejected pieces – but his printed journalism amounted to at least eight hundred articles. Meanwhile, his name, whether as Anon, Gavin Ogilvy or, finally, J. M. Barrie, was becoming known, and soon there would be little he chose to write that an editor would reject.

Though a compulsive entertainer Barrie's humour was often underscored by a strain of fatalism and darkness. Thus, in that early London article, 'The Rooks Begin to Build', the young writer sees man as 'that back bent clown'. Experiences were usually given a comic twist, but this was comedy that sparred, mocked and gibed; revering little, it refused to take much too seriously. Writing in a tone that was more often than not ironic, flippant or satirical, somehow Barrie got away with it. He also instinctively understood that the cool sophistication of most of his work must be leavened, so he gave it an acceptable degree of quaintness, or sentiment. He had his critics, but most people enthusiastically read his work. Finally, the whole was presented in prose of a fluency and grace that belied the hours of hard work devoted to its making.

Barrie's style, too, was developing, as much as anything from the sheer volume he turned out. His reading was broad but also selective, and if something didn't interest him he simply didn't read it. He was none the less perfectly aware of contemporary movements, and the potential complexities of style and the related battles raging among contemporary writers and critics. As a young man his own idiosyncratic style arose largely from an instinctive position. But as he grew to know where he stood there was much experiment, and frequent obscuring of his real opinions and intentions.

In those first London days, recalling the Barrie family's 'revered approach to Carlyle', he tells us that the great man was soon 'appearing in various guises in the *St James's*'. He continues: 'indeed he was the only writer I ever tried to imitate'. The young writer read Robert Louis Stevenson on style, 'but it depressed me also, and I had a childish notion . . . that style is . . . the way in which you paint your picture. The proper definition is of course far more difficult than that.'[9]

Barrie was highly intelligent and more than usually complex, but he shied away from lengthy analysis. Although he was a writer who would eventually stake out his own strange and unique artistic terrain, he was often unable to say quite what made him write as he did. At the same time he was much more self-aware than he later chose to reveal, and his use of apparent naïveté reflected the impatience he sometimes felt with his audience. He increasingly made use of irony and satire, and in 1890 wrote an article sending up the currently fashionable positions on literary style.

In *Brought Back From Elysium*, the setting is the library of 'a club in Piccadilly for high thinking and bad dinners'. Here, five novelists are gathered to question a 'select company of literary ghosts', who will be brought back from that resting place of the blessed, "the Elysian Fields", and questioned. The novelists represent five of the then most characteristic literary camps. They are a Realist, a Romanticist, an Elsmerian (*Robert Elsmere*, a novel), a Stylist and an American (a Modernist), who bears a marked resemblance to Henry James. Barrie chooses what were then some of the most highly regarded and popular literary figures from the past as his ghosts. We watch as Smollett, Scott, Fielding, Dickens and Thackeray are lorded over by their inquisitors.

> May I ask what was your first step towards becoming novelists? *the Elsmerian enquires.*
>
> *Smollett (with foolish promptitude)*: We wrote a novel.
>
> *Thackeray (humbly)*: I am afraid I began by wanting to write a good story, and then wrote it to the best of my ability. Is there any other way . . . ?
>
> *Stylist*: Pooh! Then there is no art in it.
>
> *Elsmerian*: And what was your aim?
>
> *Thackeray*: Well, I had reason to believe that I would get something for it.
>
> *Elsmerian*: Alas! To you the world was not a sea of drowning souls . . . you had no aims, no methods, no religious doubts, and you neither analysed your characters nor classified yourselves.
>
> *Stylist*: Style is everything. The true novelist does nothing but think, think, think about style, and then write, write, write about it. I daresay I am one of the most perfect stylists living. Oh, but the hours, the days, the years I have spent in acquiring my style!
>
> *Thackeray (sadly)*: If I had only thought more of style! May I ask how many books you have written?
>
> *Stylist*: Only one – and that I have withdrawn from circulation. Ah, sir, I am such a stylist that I dare not write anything. Yet I meditate a work.[10]

Although Barrie was a natural journalist, his ambition was to make himself known as a novelist, and in 1886 he decided it was time to begin. His first effort, *Better Dead*, was written at breakneck speed, with murder as a joke and the victims selected on the basis that they were appearing too often in the press. The plot was ridiculously flimsy and the book absurdly

Better Dead is little more than a succession of skits par-
nous. Even actresses, the professionals at whose feet Barrie
didn't escape his satirical pen. After months of publishers'
determination to see his book in print finally led him to
blisher to bring it out in November 1887. To the fledgling
novelist's huge delight Lord Randolph Churchill, one of the public figures
mercilessly lampooned in the book, sent a letter congratulating him on
his efforts.

Barrie's preoccupation with identity was revealed in another murder
story, *The Body in the Black Box*. Although a much better tale, this, too,
was refused by the publishers. An anonymous narrator stands looking at
his shadow in a shop window; he realises that his isolation is so great it
is only this, his shadow, that will acknowledge his existence. Mocked by
a clerk, the narrator stalks him for weeks, murders him and then takes
on his identity. Having assumed his place at work, the narrator finally
marries the clerk's fiancée. In this way he has succeeded in forcing society
to 'see' him; he has ensured that he does now exist.

This chilling story is more than a youthful Victorian writer's flirtation
with the still fashionable Gothic theme of the *doppelgänger*. Here, Barrie
is speaking about himself, about his own shadowy identity. Jamie, the
little boy, unlike his tall and handsome brothers, is searching for a reflection of himself in his mother's eyes. But his mother, the one who matters
most, doesn't see him – not even when David has died. And Jamie suffers
the horror of asking himself time and again: Do I really exist? This terrible
question is the source of ongoing pain. He will spend much of his time
in flight from it, his life turned into a kind of frenzy. Not surprisingly
his extraordinary and tragic creation, Peter Pan, leads a peculiar kind of
half-life in the Never Land, having little truck with memory, that dubious
human quality held in such high regard.

Barrie rarely boasted. Neither did he allow himself, or anyone else, to
say he was doing well. For all that, his growing assurance of manner was
noticeable; he said, and always half believed, that his finest coups were
down to luck. They were, but only in so far as huge effort and talent
can produce unpredictable rewards. During this period in which his name
became better known, Barrie initiated the management of his humility
as a kind of game. He wanted fame and financial success, and strove to
achieve them both. Yet as his gargantuan efforts began to show results,
he was acquiring a way of behaving that became a lifelong habit. First
courting success, he would then scorn its results, a frame of mind reflecting
his ambivalent relationship with money.

Several weeks after his arrival in London – when he was assured of work and wouldn't therefore lose face – Barrie sought out the fellow Scot whom he had met one day in the newspaper offices in Nottingham. T. H. Gilmour had already launched himself on London, combining part-time journalism with work as secretary to the politician Lord Rosebery. Soon after their reunion the two Scots were sharing rooms. A year or so older than Barrie, Gilmour was a man with a good clear head, a kind heart and apparently endless patience. Thus, for much of the next four years, until Gilmour's marriage at the end of 1888, the two young men shared a series of more or less smart rooms, depending on the state of their finances.

Despite the increasing sums Barrie was earning, and for which he was usually paid by cheque, he harboured a deep-seated Calvinist suspicion of banks and hadn't opened an account. If the cheques he received were open he cashed them, but if they were crossed he simply stuffed them into his pocket book or somewhere at the back of a drawer. After a time Gilmour persuaded Barrie that this was foolish and that if he wouldn't have a bank account then he, Gilmour, would cash the cheques via his own account. For the next five years then, until Gilmour was at last able to persuade him otherwise, numerous notes from Barrie reveal how his long-suffering friend was in the extraordinary position of acting as his banker. Barrie never appears to have seen these transactions as an imposition on Gilmour. Even in a profession well populated by neurotics, this was extreme. And of course being Barrie he made 'copy' out of the situation, soon writing a piece called 'From St Pancras to the Bank' in which he, his accommodating friend and the whole race of bankers are cheerfully lampooned. Gilmour had finally persuaded him to open a bank account.

We are told at the outset that in order to open an account 'the requisites are recklessness tempered with stratagem, a devoted but maddened friend . . . an ingratiating manner, and cheques'. Although Barrie says he had managed to outmanoeuvre his friend's attempts for a long time, 'I must open negotiations with a bank or starve. Of course he had me in his power, and I yielded . . . We sat . . . discussing which bank would be most easily duped, and other details.' Their choice of bank was directed towards those whose directors 'were not good business men. He [Gilmour] also consented to continue getting as much as possible for my cheques until we had outwitted the Banker.'[11]

After a series of tortuous manoeuvres they end in a public eating house where Barrie is ordered by Gilmour to produce all the cheques he has been able to discover littered about in his drawers, boxes, pockets and envelopes. His adviser then proceeded to the orderly arrangement of the cheques amid a breath-less silence, the people at the other tables laying down their knives and forks, and the waiters gathering around us open-mouthed, as the pile grew bigger . . . I wrote my name on the back of each cheque (this is compulsory), and then passed it to my Business Man, who made marks on a piece of paper. When all was over he said there were fifty-two cheques. As I had made it fifty . . . we counted again, and this time we both found there were fifty-two. [Barrie asks the reader] Have you ever been into a bank? . . . Bankers are of medium height, slightly but firmly built, forty or forty-one years of age, and stand in an easy attitude, with nothing about them to suggest their vocation save that they keep their hands in their trouser-pockets.[12]

Having thus implied the duplicity of all bankers he tells how you must

hand over your cheques and sign your name twice on different pieces of paper, so as to give them some sort of pull over you, and then after a last look at you, which is rather trying, they hand you your cheque-book. Cheque-books are in blue covers and are of a shape which makes them wobble in the hand like a trout . . . They probably saw from my face that I was not to be trifled with, and presently one asked with assumed lightness whether I would like anything now and if so how much. I said firmly that I should like ten pounds (in gold); and I got it too, without their knowing I would have closed with them if they had said that five would be more convenient. I soon wished that I had tried them with fifteen.[13]

Gilmour's amiability and his position had enabled him to make a good number of contacts and friends. He was happy to arrange introductions for Barrie, who in turn enjoyed this increased sociability, and was discovering that not everyone elicited in him the inhibiting social reserve of his student years in Edinburgh. The persona of the self-effacing writer would become one of his hallmarks, but increasingly it was a *persona*, which he defined and controlled for his own immediate ends. This *was* Barrie, but only a small part of him. Another, much larger part could be astonishingly self-assured, and confident that he was going to reach the top. Hand in hand with his reticence was a need to shine. His wit and humour began to flourish again as they hadn't since he was a schoolboy in Dumfries, and once his companions were willing to accept his central role Barrie could transform himself into an entertainer with unforgettable flair.

As a fellow lodger Gilmour was becoming familiar with his friend's moods, which were both erratic and extreme in their variability. In modern parlance Barrie would very likely be described as having manic-depressive tendencies. But he had come to accept his moods, with their swings from high to low, as unavoidable. He had learnt to live with them and, to some extent, to manage them. When, for example, every few weeks or so he went to visit his editor Frederick Greenwood, Barrie took care to do so only if he was feeling positive and buoyant. 'My moods are as changeable as the hoary ocean. There are times when I am the best of company, when my wit sparkles and cuts. At other times I walk in the shadows.'[14]

As Barrie grew in confidence so he projected more of his true nature, not only on the printed page, but also in real life. With his deep, measured voice and distinctive Scottish pronunciation, he was capable of entrancing an audience with a heady mix of enthusiasm, wit and humour. He was, however, just as capable of withdrawing into himself and brooding darkly for lengthy periods of time; it made little or no difference in whose company he found himself. For some this was too much, and incipient friendships could wither, leaving only those who were more patient, more confident and far-sighted to find out more.

At first it was mostly fellow journalists, colleagues and rivals with whom Barrie socialised, either in his rooms or at the little restaurants he could usually now afford. The theatre continued to exert its pull over him, and whenever he had time he was there; often making his pastime defray its costs by turning in theatrical criticism to one paper or another. And yet, long after he had become a world-famous playwright, Barrie said that it wasn't so much plays that held him in their thrall but the life of the theatre itself. At the centre of this life were the actors, but for Barrie most fascinating of all were the actresses, particularly if they were pretty.

A recurring theme, from his earliest writings to the end of his life, was his height. Small for his years as a child, it was clear that Jamie would never grow into a sturdy young man like his elder brother Alick. Barrie remained, like his mother, small, claiming 'bitterly' that his diminutive height – just over five feet – was the thing to blame for his authorship. In the oft-repeated claim there is at least a grain of truth.

Six feet three inches . . . If I had really grown to this it would have made a great difference in my life. I would not have bothered turning out great reels of printed matter. My one aim would have been to have become a favourite of the ladies, which between you and me has always been my sorrowful ambition. The things I would have said to them if my legs had been longer.[15]

Despite his lack of height, never the man to concede defeat Barrie began, as early as his student days in Edinburgh, his lifelong habit of falling in love with actresses. In 1883, while on the *Nottingham Journal*, he had fallen for Minnie Palmer, an actress in a touring company at the Playhouse there. Driven to write a one-act farce for her, *Caught Napping*, he was, however, struck dumb when faced with Miss Palmer in person. Both he and his literary offering made a poor impression and there was no choice but to admire from a distance.

Unburdening himself as Anon, 'that man of secret sorrows', he wrote: 'May I ask you lady novelists is this never to stop? Have you never tried a short hero? It has been established . . . that short men have souls, are subject to impression from the opposite sex . . . and marry as openly as their longer brethren. Why must they be inadmissible?' He wrote again of a train journey, during which he was installed in a carriage with five of the most exquisitely beautiful young women his imagination could conjure up. Settling themselves down, the girls' demeanour eloquently gave the 'verdict' on their fellow traveller: he was 'quite harmless', and the devastatingly lovely creatures then disregarded the young man for the rest of their journey. One, a 'tall poetical-looking girl . . . was the loveliest of my scorners'. She had 'eyes like lakes . . . while her voice . . . now deep and mellow, now soft and tender' was of the kind he thought 'to stir a man who was not harmless to his innermost core'. Each of the girls outdoes the last in loveliness until the young man finally withdraws broken-hearted, knowing he is unable to appear dangerous.

Did Anon ever hear ladies discussing him for the briefest moment . . . Alas, his trouble was that ladies did not discuss him at all . . . I remember (I should think I do) that it was his habit to get into corners. In time the jades put this down to a shrinking modesty, but that was a mistake; it was all owing to a profound dejection about his want of allure. They were right, those ladies in the train; 'quite harmless' summed him up . . . observe him in that compartment. Though insignificant he is not ugly. To be ugly, if you are sufficiently ugly, is said to attract the wayward creatures. The rubber that blotted Anon out is called . . . Individuality . . . You don't need to be handsome to be this sort of man . . . but the handsome ones can . . . do it on their heads . . . If you could dig deep enough into him you would find first his Rothschildean ambition, which is to earn a pound a day; beneath that is to reach some little niche in literature; but in the marrow you find him vainly weltering to be a favourite of the ladies . . . He is only striving hard for numbers one and two, because he knows with an everlasting sinking that number three can never be for him. If they would dislike him or fear him it would be something, but it is crushing to be just harm-less.[16]

As Barrie's professional reputation grew there was some amelioration. The capacity to prostrate himself before an actress never left him, and, with added opportunities offered by some of his new friends' sisters, he set about learning the art of courtship. During his second summer in London Barrie and Gilmour indulged in a grand expense by taking a houseboat on that luxurious green stretch of the Thames at Cookham in Berkshire. During the day he and Gilmour worked, but for two weeks of warm summer evenings there was also much cheerfulness and laughter as visitors came and went, including a pretty young actress, all providing scope for Barrie to improve his skill at playing the part of the exuberant, extravagant and romantic host.

Within two years of arriving in London, his talent, hard work and charm had gained Barrie the support of three powerful editors. They were Frederick Greenwood, who ran the *St James's Gazette*, Sandy Riach of the *Edinburgh Dispatch*, and the indomitable William Nicoll, who was the founder of *The Bookman* and the *British Weekly*. Barrie wrote regular articles for their respective publications and towards these three men he would always feel a deep gratitude, Nicoll becoming a lifelong friend.

Greenwood, while relishing his position of power, had a passionate devotion to literature. As an able journalist thirty years older than Barrie, he had been running high-quality British journals for years before they met. In the 1860s Greenwood edited first *Queen* magazine and then the *Cornhill*, one of the greatest literary periodicals of the day. With Thackeray as its first editor the *Cornhill* was responsible for publishing major writers such as Trollope, George Eliot, Hardy and, amongst the poets, Swinburne, Tennyson and Browning. Greenwood's extensive experience meant that his address book contained every literary contact a young writer could desire. Priding himself on his literary astuteness, he also enjoyed claiming the credit for a number of successful 'discoveries'. A self-made man, he believed his power was amply justified, but he also used his patronage generously. Happily for Barrie, Greenwood found him amusing and would introduce him to a man who was regarded as one of the most eminent literary figures of the day.

Novelist, poet – and journalist through financial necessity – in the last half of the twentieth century George Meredith's self-consciously intri-cate and epigrammatic prose has overwhelmed most readers and his work now receives little attention. However, at the time of his death, in 1909, although his writing had never made him rich, for a discerning public and many fellow writers, Meredith was a significant and revered literary figure. Virginia Woolf would describe him as 'possessed of an extraordinary power'. Long before this Meredith was sought out not only by his contemporaries, but also by younger novelists and poets, including Thomas Hardy, Robert Louis Stevenson and Henry James.

Meredith's most popular novel, *Diana of the Crossways*, was published the year before he and Barrie met, while his most celebrated work, *The Egoist*, was already well known. An article in the *St James's Gazette* had caught Meredith's eye, and enquiring after its authorship his friend Greenwood gave the young man a good press. Barrie may so far have read little or none of Meredith's work, but by the time he journeyed to meet him at Box Hill in Surrey he had ensured there would be real substance to his homage.

To Meredith's rather magnificent appearance, he added a powerful and enigmatic presence. While his pride was great and his sense of honour inflexibly high, his self-awareness was such that the greatest portraits in his novels were more often than not recognisable satires of Meredith himself. After the publication of *The Egoist* a young man remonstrated with Meredith, saying, 'It's too bad of you, Willoughby [the egoist] is me!' To which Meredith replied: 'My dear fellow, he is all of us.' As a writer determined to expose and scrutinise the excesses of the personality, his psychological writing had much to offer Barrie.

Meredith's proud and handsome face was further distinguished by the famous white hair and beard. His intense identification with nature meant that he needed the outdoors, until infirmity put a stop to it, and regularly walked long distances, alone or with friends. He was a controversial literary figure whose years of poor sales and consequent hardship made him at times impatient and bad tempered. Stern and uncompromising, he procured for himself some fervent enemies, while his brilliant and fluent conversation was renowned. The dramatic critic and literary editor Desmond MacCarthy wrote, after his pilgrimage to Meredith in old age, of the 'noble, ravaged handsomeness', the 'vitality that . . . still vibrated in his powerful voice'. Commenting on both Meredith's great love for and criticism of England and the English, McCarthy was moved to say that 'there was such a fund of invincible vitality in him' and marvelled at his 'determination to strike a spark from every topic, astounding in a paralysed old man'. With the years the number of Meredith's admirers had grown, while around him was a group of dedicated and loyal friends.

Until that time almost all of Barrie's new connections and friends were journalists of one sort or another, and George Meredith was the first major literary figure he came to know. Meredith not only looked the part, his reputation was that of a man who had laboured against great odds and yet continued to make few concessions in the name of success. And Barrie, with his yearning for heroes, would one day say of him, 'he was royalty at its most august to Anon'. For Meredith's own part, what old man could have resisted the young Scot's quicksilver wit and singular charm, when it so clearly sprang from such respect and admiration?

As the years passed and Barrie's own reputation grew, his respect for Meredith's work took the form of regularly promoting him in person and in print. Barrie's notebooks and essays are not, though, uncritical of Meredith's work; in the *Contemporary Review* his essay on Meredith is perceptive and far from mere adulation. He concluded that even if Meredith didn't always get it right, most modern novelists were by comparison 'mere petty twaddlers'. In common with most of their nineteenth-century readers, both Meredith and Barrie believed that one of the most important aspects of the novel was its need to present memorable characters. For Barrie, Meredith excelled in such characters. At the same time one of the themes in his work with which the younger man found himself strongly in sympathy was Meredith's perceptive and sympathetic treatment of women. After his death Barrie wrote approvingly of Meredith's female characters, 'the ladies of the future, they went their ways to tell the . . . earth of the new world for women which he had been the first to foresee'. The writers' friendship developed as they came together and talked over literature, and this continued until Meredith's death over twenty years later. In his own old age Barrie would write, 'I loved this man more every time I saw him.'

Thomas Hardy was an old friend of Meredith and it was natural that he should be introduced to Meredith's new young friend. Barrie met the quiet, unassuming and most unheroic-looking little man in the middle of Hardy's most prolific period of novel-writing: the period during which he had brought out *Under the Greenwood Tree* and the great novels, *Far from the Madding Crowd* and *The Mayor of Casterbridge*. Hardy wasn't averse to being fêted by the literary establishment and fashionable society, but he also suffered under the regular criticism made of him by reviewers. Although more obviously successful than Meredith, he remained an outsider whose work never sold in great numbers. While some of it was regarded as scandalous, he found the consistent condemnation of his 'pessimism' and 'immorality' wounding and difficult to withstand. Typical of this censure was the complaint that *Tess of the d'Urbervilles*, 'except during a few hours spent with cows, has not a gleam of sunshine anywhere'.

In Hardy, Barrie found the second of the great literary friends of his life, and in 1889 he wrote 'Thomas Hardy: the Historian of Wessex' for the *Contemporary Review*. Amongst living writers it was Hardy and Meredith

whom Barrie admired the most, and long after they were both dead he
would write, 'I am now undecided as to which was the greater of the
two.' Whichever it was, he would become one of their most insistent
advocates. Barrie's capacity for hero worship might at times have made
the diffident Hardy feel a little uneasy, but where Barrie worshipped he
also protected, supported, even nurtured. He was capable of immense
loyalty, and throughout his life was prepared to expend gargantuan efforts
on behalf of his friends.

Again, as with Meredith, Barrie's friendship with Hardy didn't colour
his estimation of the older man as a writer. Although he absorbed as little
of Hardy's style as he did Meredith's, Barrie championed Hardy's work.
He believed that Hardy was a writer under attack from the 'stylists', who
were increasingly as concerned with style and technique as they were
with content. Barrie thought that as a consequence they had lost sight
of the tradition of the *story* at the heart of the novel. For him, Hardy
was a writer whose modesty kept him in the background of the work
and made him, 'therefore, a storyteller'. He appreciated Hardy as a sharp
and unsentimental recorder of a passing age, the pre-industrial world that
in the last quarter of the nineteenth century was everywhere seen to be
dying. Of Hardy he wrote,

> Railways and machinery of various sorts create new trades and
> professions, and kill old ones . . . the shepherds and thatchers and
> farmers and villagers, who were, will be no more, and if their like-
> ness is not taken now, it will be forever lost.[17]

As a man who was realistic and unsentimental about the improvements
from which his times were benefiting, Barrie's comments here imply
much more than nostalgic regret. Indeed, his writings show a keen awareness that with the passing of this older world something greater than
trades was being lost. His respect for Hardy sprang also from sympathy
with a man whose life and work reflected that sense of unease at the
heart of so much late-nineteenth-century artistic endeavour: the loss of
faith. Many were precipitated into this, as much as anything, by the
profound influence of Charles Darwin's work *On the Origin of Species.*
Despite Hardy's lifelong struggle and failure to believe, and the impotent wretchedness of so many of his fictional characters' lives, tossed by
the randomness of fate, he remained a man whose quiet searching after
truth gave him a dignity that for Barrie endowed him with heroic stature.

Notwithstanding Barrie's gratification at the illustrious friendships he
was forging, and although avowedly ambitious, this never made of him
a mere collector of names. And, anyway, Meredith and Hardy were fêted

by far more distinguished figures than this young hopeful from Scotland. Retaining their friendship with him until their deaths, these two older writers undoubtedly saw in Barrie something more than the enterprising journalist of the moment. To them he was open about his hopes of becoming a novelist – literature 'was still my game'. They would have appreciated too that finance was the major impediment to his emancipation from journalism. (Meredith, for instance, could only achieve this when well beyond middle age.) For the moment Barrie would have to exhibit patience.

William Nicoll, the fiercely autocratic yet kindly and perceptive man of letters, must be given the credit for encouraging Barrie to broaden his range. Nicoll was impressed by an anonymous piece in Sandy Riach's *Edinburgh Dispatch*, and asked Riach for the name of its author. Not long afterwards Barrie was writing his first article for Nicoll's new periodical, the *British Weekly*. Under the aegis of Hodder & Stoughton, then a significant firm of evangelical publishers, the *British Weekly* had proved an almost immediate success since its launch six months earlier, giving Nicoll considerable leverage. Having practised as a Free Church minister until ill health made him move south and turn to full-time journalism, Nicoll intended that his new journal should act, amongst other things, as a goad to the Scottish Free Church. He wanted what he imagined were young men like Barrie to help him agitate.

Readers and editor alike greeted with enthusiasm Barrie's first article on his brother's old friend, the well-known minister Alexander Whyte. From then on, however, only occasionally, and in his own quirky way, did Barrie engage with the contemporary Scottish Church. Whether he knew from the start that he was entirely unable, or unwilling, to fulfil Nicoll's brief isn't clear. Whichever it was, despite Nicoll's well-known stubbornness and force of personality, somehow his young protégé managed to persuade him to print a succession of articles that had nothing whatsoever to do with the Church. In a periodical whose sub-title was *A Journal of Social and Christian Progress*, Barrie had the effrontery to write his second-only piece for the *British Weekly* on the new houseboat he and Gilmour had hired on the Thames. Incredibly, Nicoll published it, and Gavin Ogilvy, as Barrie styled himself, went on to become one of the journal's most popular contributors.

In May he had written to Gilmour from Scotland, 'Have been to kirk twice to-day . . . (an old fellow-student preaching, cunning, a donkey) and thought out a title, *When a Man's Single*. Nothing fixed.' While on the houseboat things did become more fixed. He had a plot, he had begun writing, and with the very slightest samples of the work he persuaded Nicoll to take it on. Like Dickens, Trollope, Hardy and most other nineteenth-century novelists, Barrie's new novel would be published as a serial. If it did well it might be taken up by a publisher and put into book form. From the autumn of 1887 to the spring of 1888, *When a Man's Single*, by Gavin Ogilvy, appeared in the *British Weekly*.

Better Dead was Barrie's horror 'shilling shocker', but *When a Man's Single* was his first attempt at a serious novel. Despite some interesting glimpses of embryonic Barrie themes, the book is a shapeless romp: a fiasco bursting with energy, humour and inexperience. Setting out as a 'problem' novel, it begins with a tragic episode. The young Scottish saw-miller Rob Angus is made 'single' when the little girl he has adopted has an accident and dies on her way to giving him a message. Rob then leaves his small home town and launches himself upon the world as an ambitious young journalist. But Barrie can't sustain the serious pace he has set himself, and *When a Man's Single* becomes a romance of unashamed entertainment. With a plot that lurches from the unlikely to the absurd, *When a Man's Single* soon acquires an upper-class cardboard heroine, whom Rob Angus eventually marries.

During the course of his ragged plot Barrie tosses in gossip, satire and almost anything else that will get him a laugh, but far more interesting are the colourful autobiographical passages on Angus's beginnings as a journalist in Silchester, i.e. Nottingham: ' "My God!" he groaned. "I would write an article, I think, on my mother's coffin." '

5

A Serious Purpose

Barrie's concerns with role-playing and the potentially shifting nature of a person's identity arose in large part because of his own struggle to discover who he himself might be. He was troubled, sometimes frightened, by his constant inclination to become someone else. In a few years he would say, of Tommy Sandys, his extraordinary central character in *Sentimental Tommy*: 'He is constantly playing some new part – playing is hardly the word though, for into each part he puts an earnestness that cheats even himself.' Barrie possessed a capacity for empathy to a quite pathological degree.

Emerging from this tendency was a theme that preoccupied him in his notebooks and articles throughout this period. Several of his friends had become engaged or were marrying – Thomas Gilmour married in 1888, Sandy Riach of the *Edinburgh Dispatch* in 1889. Barrie wanted, like his friends, to fall in love with a woman he could make a commitment to for the rest of his life. Meanwhile, his flirtations with actresses had continued and he often believed himself in love. But to his notebooks he repeatedly confided his intense fears about an inability to remain constant, and the frightening claustrophobia prompted in him by the thought of marriage. His predicament was very real, for if he was so regularly assailed with doubts about his ability to remain one kind of personality for any length of time, how could he remain constant and committed to any other person?

Detailing this recurring and lonely struggle with the idea of marriage, Barrie saw a yawning gap between its apparent significance and any ability to live up to it. Richard Abinger, the lawyer secretly working as a journalist in *When a Man's Single*, meditates,

> I wonder is it my fault that my passion burned itself out in one little crackle? . . . I am going to be married, though I would much rather remain single. My wife will be the only girl I ever loved, and I like her still more than any other girl I know. Though I shuddered

just now at the idea of matrimony, there can be little doubt that we shall get on very well . . . it is not the real Dick Abinger she cares for, and so I don't know if Nell's love is of the kind to make a man conceited. Is marriage a rash experiment when the woman loves the man for qualities he does not possess . . . ?[1]

Abinger goes on to ask himself, is a man a villain because 'love dies out of his heart'? and decides that 'Yes, after all Nell gets the worse side of the bargain. She will have for a husband a man who is evidently incapable of lasting affection for anybody.' And he concludes, 'That, I suppose, means that I find myself the only really interesting person I know.' There is no doubt that Barrie found J. M. Barrie the most fascinating person he knew.

Over the Christmas period of 1887, he was back in Kirriemuir on one of those lengthy visits home. In between fishing trips or long walks beyond the town into the glens, he sat in his little study above the porch at Strath View and wrote. Aside from the usual stream of articles, he was at work on another new project, secretly rewriting and collating his previously printed articles on the Auld Lichts, first written for the *St James's Gazette*. When William Nicoll had brokered the deal for Barrie with the publishers Hodder & Stoughton, they believed, mistakenly, that he would simply be collecting together his earlier articles. But the industrious young writer was putting together quite another kind of book. He would call it *The Auld Licht Idylls*.

Barrie could throw off an article with great speed and increasing finesse, but letting go of any longer piece of writing that wasn't journalism would always prove difficult. As his fiction-writing career progressed it became his custom to make numerous changes to his manuscripts, and, with this habitual reluctance to judge something finished, given the slightest opportunity he would always rewrite. Making numerous alterations, even on the final proofs – when all he was meant to be doing was correcting mistakes – Barrie must have been a trial for any editor. In years to come, as a playwright this habit would become entrenched to an almost obsessive degree.

Nevertheless, hard at work in Kirriemuir, despite debilitating headaches, he was thriving. A letter containing a series of instructions for Gilmour ends with the words 'Have a headache so won't write more.' Barrie seems by now to have accepted his headaches, and depressions, as exhausting but inevitable aspects of life that one simply had to endure.

These wretched episodes may sometimes have been brought on by the concern over his mother's health. After the death of her son David many years before, Margaret Barrie had effectively become an 'invalid'. This is not to say that she wasn't an ailing woman, simply that she declined into unstable health after David's death. Since someone had to pick up the pieces, a necessary counterpart to the role of invalid was the person whose life was sacrificed to care. This latter role had for many years fallen upon the shoulders of Jenann. As was the custom of the day, just as the Barrie family accepted Margaret's invalidism, so they accepted Jenann's self-sacrifice. Many Victorian families had their Jenann.

Whatever her position may have been over the last twenty years, in 1888 Margaret was nearly seventy and her status as an invalid was by now quite genuine. In addition to the headaches, to which, like Jamie and Jenann, she was always subject, her memory was now rapidly in decline. Her tendency to chest infections had always given the family concern, but in old age these were turning with greater regularity into potentially fatal bronchitis. Until she died seven years later, while jealously watched over by Jenann, there were many occasions when the family was urgently recalled. A letter to a fellow author during this time aptly describes one of these episodes and the degree to which it overwhelmed Barrie. He says he

had to come home suddenly owing to illness of my mother, and indeed we have had a fortnight of alarming days and nights, but she is much better again and so all's well with the world. Do you not feel after these anxieties how childish our hopes and fears about smaller things . . . have been? . . . this has interrupted everything and is the entire cause of the delay in answering your letter.[2]

The publishers at last managed to extract the final proofs from Barrie, and *Auld Licht Idylls* was published in April 1888. With this his reputation subtly altered, as reviewers wondered if this bright, witty young writer might contain within him the possibility of something more. And, indeed, *Auld Licht Idylls* was rapidly succeeded with another of its kind, called *A Window in Thrums*. An altogether more accomplished book, published in July 1890, *A Window in Thrums* began to sell immediately. By now the reviewers, or most of them, anyway, believed that Barrie's reputation as a writer was assured. His two books on Thrums, i.e. Kirriemuir, were examples of a popular new genre of writing.

Thomas Hardy and George Eliot had between them been producing their eloquent novels for over twenty-five years. Although quite different, it might be said that there were two subjects above all to which they applied their great art. Their writing distinguished, first, the loss to people's lives brought about by the industrialisation of Britain, and, second – and closely connected – the response to an increasing loss of faith. Hardy, Eliot and others, too, were observing a set of almost unimaginable changes and the effects of these upon individual lives. These were changes establishing Britain as the world's first modern society.

The population of Britain had grown at an astonishing rate. In the first year of the nineteenth century the country was largely made up of small traditional agricultural communities, but the following hundred years would see this transformed. During the course of this transformation a restructuring of British society would take place. When Victoria came to the throne, in 1837, there were seventeen million people living in Britain. At her death, in 1901, there were thirty-seven million. On Victoria's coronation only five towns in England could claim a population of over 100,000; by the end of the century there were at least twenty-three such towns.

By the latter part of the century Victorians of every persuasion were concerned about this huge growth and the radical changes accompanying it. People felt things so altered that they talked of life in the new industrial centres, such as Manchester, as being 'constructed on a wholly new principle'. There was constant concern about society disintegrating through a lack of 'order'. Ultimately, whether individuals actually 'believed' or not, the methods whereby people still held themselves, their families and their communities together, depended far more on Christian principles of care and charity than anything else. Individuals, and communities were frequently inadequate to the task and many suffered as a result. But until the development of an embryonic urban infrastructure, and a police force anything like that which we would recognise today, it was actually custom and morality – taught in the home and at Sunday school – that sustained society, rather than any existing laws.

The spirit of the times, however, was largely in favour of what some called the 'cult of material progress', and the majority saw its advantages as far outweighing any losses it might entail. While many undoubtedly benefited from these great changes, for many others it brought what Engels described as 'an increase in human misery'. There were dissidents, as there had been since the first days of the Industrial Revolution in the early 1700s, when loom-breaking Luddites and other kinds of noisy public pressure groups had risen up. But by the later nineteenth century there was a much larger number of people deeply concerned at 'the wilderness of our manufacturing world'. These were people quietly but seriously preoccupied by the great speed of change they were witnessing all around. No one could remember anything like it. Their memories served them well, for there had never been anything quite like it before.

People were preoccupied with time. Time changing, time passing and time speeding up. In one day a man was able to scythe a particular acreage of ripe grain. However skilful this man might be, he had an upper limit. A machine has no natural upper limit, and in theory might continue for ever. Men and women, their hand skills now frequently obsolete, became workers installed in factories to operate the new machines. Bound to their machines, the workers' lives were now bound by clock-time, rather than seasonal time, as they never had been in the past.

Everywhere it was clear that the old customs, crafts and skills, the great regional differences of British life, were inexorably in decline. And a small minority set out to document what they could before it disappeared. They recorded much, from the rituals and customs of farming and animal husbandry to the traditions and practices connected with the making of food, dairying, thatching, basket- and chair-making, and the hand-weaving of cloth. They took down the words and music, then later made some of the first ever recordings, of fishermen, of ploughmen, of tinkers, of carters and gypsies, singing to us across a century the haunting, sometimes ancient songs of all their different trades. It was clear that across the social strata not only traditions and practices, but entire ways of life would soon be irretrievably lost. Turmoil, then, was the dominating feature of nineteenth-century Britain, turmoil associated with the transformation of a small agrarian society into one that was industrial, urban and vast.

Barrie played his own part in recording the older, dying world. And that part of the pre-industrial world with which he was most familiar was the linen-loom weaving of Kirriemuir. Although the stories of *Auld Licht Idylls* and its sister publication, *A Window in Thrums*, are actually set around the beginning of the 1800s, some of Barrie's descriptions of the Kirriemuir poor, affectingly convincing passages observing their cramped and hard lives, are too authentic not to have been observed at first hand.

In a chapter in *Auld Licht Idylls* called 'Mysey Drolly', Mysey's son works desperately hard to keep his old mother with him at home and save her from relegation to the workhouse. Their poverty is such that 'The flooring was only lumpy earth, with sacks spread over it to protect Mysey's feet. The room contained two dilapidated old coffin beds . . . the two windows in the room faced each other on opposite walls, and were so small that even a child might have stuck in trying to crawl through them.'

In his youth Barrie saw mechanisation destroying the old hand-loom weavers' livelihoods, and in *Margaret Ogilvy* he tells how when he was a boy Kirriemuir was transformed into a different kind of town. He appreciated that the machines were responsible for reducing the weavers' often wretched poverty, and a crippling old age from the strains of their work. But he was also at pains to show how these improvements were accompanied by the loss of the weavers' famous independence. Now they were obliged to leave their workshops for factories that employed only the young and vigorous. With the older men unable to find work, the women must leave their children and homes to find factory work, and Barrie felt that the old certainties of home and family life were weakened. In _Auld Licht Idylls_ and then _A Window in Thrums_, while he is witty at his compatriots' expense, he also displays genuine sympathy for the hard lot of his own people. Showing them capable of dignity and independence, he describes the hardships of a community in decline.

To most of Barrie's largely urban readership, the claustrophobia of this small-town life, at times acidly drawn, was ignored, because what mattered more to them was believing that here was a way of life more rooted and constant than their own. Throughout the two Thrums books Barrie describes the stultifying religious principles and provincial mentality of the Auld Lichts with little mercy. And although this didn't worry most of his readers, his own family was torn between pride in their son's success and embarrassment at the portrayal of his fellow townspeople. They could not help but see it as a disclosure of intimacy, a problem for every writer. (His mother apparently kept the Thrums novels well hidden from view, as if she believed this would stop her fellow Kirriemuirians from reading them.) Although Barrie had set the books earlier in the century, it was clear to everyone that he was also writing about their own day.

When we remember that he was already noted for his reticence, the revelation of some of his most private sorrows in _A Window in Thrums_ is at first surprising. But as we come to know more of the man a pattern of behaviour emerges. This includes a mixture of extreme reserve, an unusual (for the period in which he lived) penchant for self-revelation and a singular ability to gain centre stage.

In _A Window in Thrums_, for the first time we see him edging his way towards greater coherence, writing without concern for the consequences – for himself, for his family, and even less for his countrymen. In conjunction with this artistic drive, Barrie's ability to persuade, or simply ignore the dictates of powerful editors was breathtaking in a writer so young. For example, when Hodder & Stoughton saw the concluding part of this book they were fearful the readers would be deterred, warning Barrie that the public didn't like sad books. When they begged him to alter the end the young man calmly replied, 'An author may not always interfere with his story ... It is a sadder book to me than it can ever be to anyone else ... but the thing had to be done.'[3]

The publisher's anxiety was shown to be ill-founded when the majority of the reviews were positive and the book sold well. Some reviewers nonetheless found parts of it 'tasteless and inaccurate'. A number of the Scots, a recurring theme, criticised Barrie's treatment of his countrymen, believing that he portrayed them as scheming, petty and insular. A good number of Barrie's Kirriemuirian neighbours may have been just that. With hindsight Barrie seems quite mild, especially compared, for example, with Caradog Evans in his pitilessly savage portrayal of the smallholders of West Wales. Looking further back, both Thackeray and Dickens were often harsh about the English. And Barrie never wrote anything as devastating as George Eliot's description of the brutal anti-intellectualism of some of the English rustics in *Silas Marner*.

It was said, too, that Barrie's treatment of the Scottish poor lacked realism, was sentimental, and in addition made them out to be a company of provincial buffoons. Because Barrie possessed that remarkable ability to craft well-written, easily read pieces of work, whose apparent intention was simply to 'entertain', most of his critics misunderstood that he was trying to achieve far more. They failed (and this failure would dog Barrie for the rest of his life, and beyond his death) to look further and see that he was *not* a simple writer and never a simple man. Indeed, perhaps his gift for humour was a fatal one. His use of it to soothe his audience into listening to some of the difficult things he wanted to say, lulled them into a frame of mind where hard thought was not always so acceptable. As Hugh Walpole perceptively observed in the year following Barrie's death,

> Although he meant all that he said, he also meant a great deal more than he said. It has been in part his misfortune that so many people have taken him at his surface-word. The majority of us have no time, as regards other people, for more than surfaces.[4]

Having said this, although Barrie's early journalism was largely ephemeral entertainment it was not dishonest, something his editors and his reading public knew full well. It *would* have been dishonest if he had joined the unscrupulous W. T. Stead, and turned out the dubious imperialist jingoism that Stead determinedly encouraged his journalists to provide.

Trollope, Hardy, and especially Conrad, were each profoundly knowledgeable about their subject matter. Just as Conrad knew both the practice and spirit of the British Merchant Navy – a reservoir of anecdotes as well as the code – so Barrie knew both the practice and the informing spirit (Scottish Calvinism) of the weavers, artisans and peasants of Kirriemuir. The figures in this book, as in all his works, are to a greater or lesser degree intentionally artificial and stylised. But their effect cannot have been so unrealistic, or Thomas Hardy would not have said of *A Window in Thrums* that it was 'a faithful representation of reality'.

Despite Barrie's early successes, he was still searching for a method of writing and a subject matter with which he could enduringly engage. It was not that the Thrums novels were insubstantial, but simply that he could not write so overtly about the rise of industrialism and its inherent depredations for the rest of his artistic life.

On one of the most potent artistic issues of the day, the drive towards Realism, Barrie takes a clear stand in these novels. He is against it. Contrary to the beliefs of his detractors, he was perfectly well aware that the Auld Lichts were not *literally* as he described them. Following the time-honoured route of countless other novelists before and since, he began with real people who were then transformed into something from which larger truths could be drawn. Barrie was clear that he had no wish to write as the Realists, such as Emile Zola in France, were trying to do, and believed that this vision of reality conveyed only a partial truth.

He illustrates this in one of his articles for the *Contemporary Review*, where he says,

> life is not a mechanical puzzle, nor are its black sheep made out of a suit of clothes and capacity for evil. The 'realist' may photograph a drunken peasant beating his wife, but that photograph is not the peasant, it is not the thousandth part of what goes to the making of a humble man . . . The spiritless drab whom you have photographed at his feet plighted her troth to him long ago in a country lane, or at a mean hearth . . . Beware lest even now, now that they have come to this, you should exhibit the thing in your camera as that man and woman. See them again many times and you will find that the soul is not dead.[5]

Barrie was trying to show that for him it was neither accurate nor illuminating to equate truth, that is reality, with bleakness, suffering and evil alone. Many of his contemporaries agreed.

Compared with, say, George Eliot's seamless artistry in her masterly depiction of the English peasantry in *Silas Marner*, *Auld Licht Idylls* and *A Window in Thrums* are flawed and uneven. Yet what Barrie set out to do had a serious purpose, capturing something difficult to define. He described the tenor, the mentality of his own people in an extended elegy for their passing way of life. Ironically, with the publication of *A Window in Thrums*, the young author's place of birth became a site of pilgrimage for earnest Victorian literary tourists. Whilst imagining the community's well-knit cohesive virtues, they sent home 'rustic' postcards of a 'Thrums' already in decline.

The Thrums novels were not, however, social observation alone. *Auld Licht Idylls* was a deeply personal reflection on Barrie's relationship with his fellow Kirriemuirians, his family and in particular his mother. At its conclusion, the chief character, Jamie, returns to Thrums for just twenty-four hours, only to discover that in his neglectful absence his entire family has died. A broken, despairing man, he revisits the familiar places one last time and is never again seen in Thrums. On this bleak note, Barrie ended his imaginative investigation into the possibility of separation from his mother. Without doubt this had become the underlying theme of his book.

Between 1887 and 1888 Barrie had published three books. Then, between 1889 and 1891, he brought out three more, while continuing with his huge journalistic output. At that stage more than one reviewer suggested he should stop for a while, and give himself more time.

6

'Genius in him . . .'

In the summer of 1887 Barrie was putting together a very different kind of project. A project that for years to come would be a source of comfort and great enjoyment. He formed a cricket club. Shere, a pretty Surrey village not far from Guildford, was one of the places he often passed through on long country walks with friends. In the little village one day with two of these, T. H. Gilmour and the New Zealand adventure novelist Marriott Watson, Barrie described how they 'talked so much cricket that it began to be felt among them that they were hidden adepts at the game, and an ambition came over them to unveil'. Having decided to challenge the Shere cricketers (the three young walkers felt assured of victory because the village team looked so old), Barrie, nominated as captain, was deputed to gather together a team.

His fascination with cricket had remained as intense as in those days when playing with the other little boys and their makeshift kit on the hill at Kirriemuir. Since his very first summer in London, Barrie had made regular pilgrimages to Lord's, sitting on the grass to follow the season's cricket. Determined now to collect together his own team – it had quickly become Barrie's team – he cajoled, wheedled and humoured until he had mustered an XI, of entirely unsuitable players. Unsuitable because, almost to a man, they were either completely inexperienced or else quite hopeless at the game. All Barrie's undeniable appeal and enthusiasm had been used to persuade a group of writers, with a few actors thrown in, that it was for the fun, the wonder of the game, not the winning, that they should leave their work and travel down to Shere.

Although possessing a minute knowledge of the game, Barrie was not a natural cricketer. His batting style was appalling, and his left-hand bowling action was very slow and off-putting. Added to this he was also utterly fearless in front of the ball – necessary with the calibre of players he had selected. Where other much larger men would duck and swerve away, no matter how fast or dangerous the ball Barrie faced it. His courage was tremendous, and it was his team-mates, not Barrie, who cried out or flinched at some of the blows he took. The intention was to play the game with as much high spirits and good humour as possible. Barrie believed that the cricket pitch was an arena for great sporting prowess, but just as importantly it was a stage on which to play out the human comedy. At the same time, no matter how much laughter the ludicrous quality of play engendered in competing teams and spectators alike, the rules, the customs, the spirit of the game were sacrosanct to the captain and those of his colleagues who actually understood how the game was played.

In the train down from London Barrie discovered that he had to 'coach more than one of his players in the finesse of the game: which was the side of the bat you hit with, for instance. In so far as was feasible they also practised in the train.' Two of the team were renowned African travellers, and when a name for this motley crew was discussed Barrie tells us that, having grown despondent about their chances, he asked the two explorers what was the expression for 'Heaven help us' in that part of the world they explored. It was 'Allahakbar', and thus his team acquired its name. Quite soon this was changed to the legendary 'Allahakbarries', in mock deference to the name of their captain.

Barrie loved all games, but cricket was his favourite. For him, in company with an inner circle of those who regularly played in the Allahakbarrie matches, there existed an implicit understanding of the ethos at the heart of cricket's arcane and meticulous regulations. No matter that the Allahakbarries were poor athletes, most of them understood that this game was the litmus test of one's honour, virtue and worth, both as an individual and as a member of society. The game of cricket was also the game of life in microcosm. Here, difference of background or position ceased to matter. It was the way in which you responded to the most difficult challenges, how good a sportsman you were, that mattered. And a good sportsman of course wasn't someone who always won. Much more importantly, he was someone who understood, with fortitude and coolness, how to lose well.

Before the first match Barrie encouraged his team to practise, with the result that 'one of the first balls that went down loosened two teeth in the head of the prospective wicket-keeper'. The strange-looking Frenchman, Belloni du Chaillu, one of the African explorer team members, kept stealing away every now and again and had to be dragged back. Chaillu was the first Westerner ever to see Pygmies and gorillas. An intense and volatile man, it was said of him that when he gave a lecture on his discoveries to the British Association their scepticism at his findings provoked such fury in him that he spat in their faces. Meanwhile, another team member 'hit the ball so hard that the Allahakbarries were at the beginning of a volley of cheers when they saw him coming out, caught at point by the curate . . . the top scorer was Gilmour, who swears he made five'.

At the end of the first match Barrie had scored all of two runs. After such total defeat most of the Allahakbarries decided that it had been a day of such ridiculous enjoyment they were prepared to take on anyone else who dared face them. And so it was that for a number of years, for a few days each summer Barrie rounded up this most eccentric of teams, for those brief interludes when grown men reverted to the simplicities of their youth. They behaved with innocent abandonment, and afterwards celebrated with more friends, food and drink.

Over the years the occasional participant was also a real athlete. Arthur Conan Doyle, subsequently a friend and collaborator of Barrie's, was one of them. Barrie later said Conan Doyle was the chief exception to the rule that 'the more successful as authors the men were the worse they played'. Indeed, one of the strongest ambitions of most players was to avoid any serious personal injury. One team against whom the Alahakbarries regularly competed styled themselves the Artists, and were probably even worse cricketers than the Allahakbarries. One of the Artists was heard to say, 'What? Spoil my painter's hands for a dirty leather ball?'

New recruits to the Allahakbarries came and went, but by the 1890s the list of those Barrie could muster gives an indication of his expanding circle. Amongst the players were Jerome K. Jerome, another novelist, A. E. W. Mason, the travel writer E. V. Lucas, George Meredith's sons Will and George, Tennyson's son Charles, the novelist Maurice Hewlett, E. W. Hornung (brother-in-law to Conan Doyle and future author of the immensely successful play *Raffles*), Owen Seaman, future editor of *Punch*, the illustrators Henry Ford (of Andrew Lang's fairy-tale books) and Bernard Partridge, H. G. Wells, the scholar Sir Walter Raleigh, the essayist and wit Augustine Birrell, P. G. Wodehouse and another writer, Charles Turley Smith.

Sometimes, no matter how persistent Barrie's efforts at collecting together his team, the Allahakbarries were a man or two short and had to scour around to make up their XI. About to play their second match, at the Worcestershire village of Broadway (then a favourite retreat for artists, actors and writers), a small group set off into the countryside in a horse cart in order to dragoon two more men into playing for them. Having 'captured' an artist discovered painting a cow in a field, they next found a soldier sitting outside a pub in conversation with two women. He was happy to play for the Allahakbarries, but only on condition that the women were allowed to accompany him as spectators. This was agreed, and to his team's immense satisfaction the soldier turned out to be a fine cricketer. On that day, unusually, the Allahakbarries won. When they last saw the soldier he was sitting triumphant outside another pub, with another two women beside him.

Among numerous other pieces, including a collection of previously printed essays called *An Edinburgh Eleven*, during the spring of 1889 Barrie published his critical essay on Thomas Hardy in the *Contemporary Review*. Then in May he was unanimously elected to membership of the Savage Club (one with strong literary and artistic connections). Writing to Gilmour Barrie cannot hide his satisfaction and crows, 'To think of it, and I was once obscure.' The following year he would be elected to the Garrick, this time saying to Gilmour, 'There will be a joy in the Garrick when I burst upon it like a sunbeam.'

Election to a London club was at that time a mark of social acceptance for any young man with aspirations. Despite his ill-fitting and untidy clothes, his country boots, his sometimes thick Scottish vowels, spoken in that incongruously deep voice, and one or more pockets failing properly to contain an assortment of manuscripts, letters, tobacco pouch and pipe, Barrie was now someone whose assurance was more than a façade. He was becoming 'known' and could count on a large number of friends and acquaintances with whom, between the writing, he somehow found time to socialise. For all his apparent loathing of the aesthete's *mot juste*, in both writing and conversation he had learnt how to use his natural wit, so that if he chose he was able to shine at any gathering.

In some sense always 'on stage', trying out one part or another, his increased confidence encouraged Barrie to project more freely those varied states he was capable of inhabiting. One mode of behaviour was a gloomy silence. From this, no matter where he was, it was virtually impossible to extract him.

Between occasional bouts of uncertainty, his belief in himself as a potentially successful writer was, however, unassailable. And yet en route to success, having been elected to a London club, he discovered that he was not really a very 'clubbable' man. Even with cricket, so aptly described as 'the only team game for rampant individuals', he had to take the lead. This rampant individualism meant that in those quintessentially English institutions the clubs of St James's, the Scottish artisan's son, Jamie Barrie, was incapable of either that particular admixture of bonhomie and confidence or the insouciance there required. As a Lowland Scot, he was a man only superficially reticent. His underlying passion lay close to the surface, and thus he was unable to school himself to the public school frame of mind. He simply did not possess the habit of suppressing his feelings, necessary to finding himself at home in an Englishman's club. Too intense, he was unable to make himself at ease.

Much later in life he would write to one of his oldest friends saying:
'As for the clubs, they are pleasant at intervals but it might fit in somewhere as an aphorism that nothing good ever came out of a club.' And
later he wrote,

> A few years ago I was elected to another club and went into it for
> the first time with a member who said he knew I didn't go much
> to my other clubs but hoped I would come oftener here, to which
> my reply, 'Dear Sir, I have now been oftener here than to my other
> clubs.' It was a very nice club but I have not been back.[1]

In July of 1889, after some time in Edinburgh, Barrie returned again
to Kirriemuir. Now established enough to feel confident about leaving
London, the image of his birthplace was becoming more attractive to
him. His growing circle of London friends and acquaintances was at the
same time encouraging him to better appreciate Kirriemuir's smallness,
even insularity, initially the principal source of his dissatisfaction.

While there, when he wasn't being cosseted by his mother and his
sister Jenann, or working in the little study, the young author was off
into the country to walk and fish. Like many of his contemporaries he
believed in vigorous exercise, after the hours and hours spent doubled
over his desk, the regular long walks must have done much to reduce
the frequency of his ferocious and debilitating headaches.

Barrie's growing appreciation of Kirriemuir is reflected in a letter to
Gilmour where he begins, 'Here I am in Arcady.' Meanwhile, in between
the outdoor pursuits he also wrote 'an article a day', began and completed
a long story for publication and for the best part of the next six months
worked steadily on his new book. This was to be the longest period he
spent in Kirriemuir since he had left to make his fortune in London
four years earlier. He hadn't yet quite made his fortune, that would come
to him, but meanwhile he was never short of money. Both as a successful
journalist and a promising novelist, Barrie's income continued to rise.

Another important event that year was a journey abroad with his friend
the distinguished African explorer Joseph Thomson. Thomson followed
what for many at the time was regarded as an inspired calling, and
throughout his life Barrie would always tend towards hero worship of
such men of action. This sprang not only from the appeal of their physical courage and initiative, but also their unselfconsciousness and simplicity.
Barrie was moved by the clarity emanating from those devoid of self-
absorption or introspection, who had found a purpose beyond themselves. So much otherwise himself he was fascinated by the difference.
As he said, 'I like well to be in the company of explorers.'

Not only explorers, but also soldiers appear to have been drawn in turn to Barrie. He was moved by what he called their 'light-hearted courage'. With them he seemed fully to extend his powers of imagination and empathy, and found himself 'stepping into other people's shoes and remaining there until he became someone else'. This led him to an imaginative empathy with lives so entirely different from his own. Many years later his secretary and confidante, Cynthia Asquith, would write that her husband, who had experienced the full horrors of the First World War, had commented, 'I would sooner talk about the war to Barrie than to any other non-combatant.'

In that summer of 1889 what for Joseph Thomson was the rather tame prospect of travelling within the confines of European shores, was for Barrie almost certainly the first, and hugely anticipated, trip abroad. After the years of hard grind this would be a real holiday. The two young men set off for a month of walking, with Barrie in high spirits. Sailing from Leith in Scotland they eventually made their way up the Rhine by steamer to Lake Constance, after which they walked in the Austrian Tyrol. Crossing an Alpine pass into Italy they stopped off at Lake Como, went over the Splugen Pass to Lucerne, and then wound their way north-east to Paris. From here, after five more days of sightseeing, they returned home.

Although parts of this journey were used as 'copy', one suspects that Barrie otherwise referred little to this historic four weeks because it wasn't a great success. There were two reasons. First, he couldn't properly enjoy any expedition that he wasn't leading. (His companion, who had already explored several regions of Africa as yet entirely unknown to the West, must have been irritated at being organised across some of the most well-trodden routes in Europe by Jamie Barrie, who had never before even left the shores of Britain.) Second, Barrie had little real need of travel as discovery. Although he could write beautifully evocative passages on landscape, he was not so different from his mother, for whom 'the descriptions of scenery were as ruts on the road that must be got over at a walking pace'.

He loved Scotland's landscape, but for him it was not a thing in itself. He was a practical and pragmatic man, but by far the greatest part of him lived deeply, and unpragmatically, in the mind. The grandest journeys of his life would take place in the vast regions of the imagination. Here he discovered or created – it is hard to know which – some strange landscapes indeed.

In the next and most important of his novels, Barrie proceeded to map out his own inner world. In doing so he would artistically extend himself more than ever before, establishing the particular terrain he was to inhabit for the rest of his life. This terrain was the interior, where he was to become an explorer of the mind. But before he could accomplish the difficult task of defining his province, it would be necessary to overcome a number of obstacles, some of his own making.

In the summer of 1890 Barrie did something with his growing income that he had been promising himself for some time. He rented a large house outside Kirriemuir and invited his family to stay. A summer holiday in a country house, for a whole month, was not something to which the Barries were accustomed. Jamie was encouraging them in behaviour which had no part in the austerely frugal Scottish tradition, and their instinct was to resist. Did they see the gesture as simple generosity, or was their gratitude at times tinged with resentment at his show of ostentation?

Whatever their thoughts, as usual Jamie's determination won out, and the family stayed at the head of the wild and beautiful Glen Cova in the little hamlet of that name. Remote even now, in 1890 the house and its dramatic surroundings must have left Barrie's family a little unsettled. Alick, Jamie and their father had always walked, sometimes great distances. For the rest of the family, despite appreciating the beauty of their native land, at times they felt at a loss and far from anything they knew.

No doubt Barrie's mother would have been concerned at the expense of the venture. Despite her son's increasing success, it would be some time before she really trusted his ability to succeed at his chosen profession. As Barrie said of her: 'She had a haunting fear that . . . something would one day go crack within me (as the mainspring of a watch breaks) and my pen refuse to write for evermore.' If there were any lengthy gaps between the pieces of writing (everything was sent up to Kirriemuir for her approval) 'Her face would say mournfully, "The blow has fallen – he can think of nothing more to write about."'[2]

Barrie himself was split between acute awareness of his mother's anxiety and his ceaseless craving for her approval. This was destined never properly to be satisfied because rooted in his earliest and most unreachable years. For herself, Margaret Barrie always retained the peasant's strong suspicion of anything unfamiliar. By comparison her son soared. In the meantime, the promise he had made after his brother David's death was ever present, and he recalled their mother's words: 'Do you mind how when you were but a bairn you used to say "Wait till I'm a man and you'll never have reason for greeting [crying] again?"' Until she died, indeed at every stage of his progress, Barrie never ceased to make offerings of propitiation to his mother to compensate her for not being his brother David and for his refusal to become a minister.

In what manner the Barrie family passed that long period of leisure at their country house that summer was in a sense immaterial. Jamie wanted to make a present of this holiday, above all to his mother. And, as would become routine, recipients had little choice but to accept when he chose to make a gift. In this instance it meant, too, that he insisted on the pleasure of playing host.

While spending time with his family at Glen Cova, Barrie was also hard at work on finishing his new book, a third attempt at the 'big' novel. *The Little Minister* first emerges in over four hundred meticulously numbered and detailed points, committed to his notebook two years earlier in the spring of 1888. His ideas continued to develop in the following two notebooks as he tried to come to grips with his novel. But, as he progressed, any real attempts at holding it all together in a conventional sense were finally thrown to the winds, as the book changed tack and became a love story on a most improbable scale.

The Little Minister tells of a young Auld Licht minister, Gavin Dishart, who arrives in Thrums to live at the manse with his pious mother, Margaret. Gavin falls for the beautiful, mysterious and anarchic gypsy girl, Babbie, who is already engaged to the slightly sinister Lord Rintoul. Outrageous odds are overcome and, in a race against time and her betrothed, Babbie throws her old life aside, and is married in a strange heathen ceremony by the gypsies' leader to the minister, Gavin Dishart. The improbability of the story is not only a result of Barrie's difficulty with extended narrative, which was something already observed in his Thrums books, really a series of episodes. In those first books Barrie had been edging towards more universal subjects, while also experimenting with ways in which to present them. He had rejected Realism and believed that it was a fallacy to think that all literature and drama can only work through naturalistic criteria.

His immediate cultural background, despite its Scottish Calvinism, was steeped in the more ancient local legends and fairy tales. And because he was already fascinated by ideas relating to illusion and transformation of all kinds Barrie was particularly receptive to these stories. Thus, one of the underlying and (deliberately) unsettling themes of *The Little Minister* is Babbie's connection to other worlds, which follow less apparently rational paths than this one. Babbie's different guises are used by Barrie not only to show her as woman the temptress, but also to suggest her possible origin in another world, which has invested her with powers to enchant and spirit away.

> Gavin had walked quickly, and he now stood silently . . . his hat in hand. In the moonlight the grass seemed tipped with hoar frost . . . Caddam [Wood] was very still. At long intervals came from far away the whack of an axe on wood . . .

For perhaps a minute Gavin stood stock still, like an intruder. Then he ran towards the singing, which seemed to come from Windyghoul, a straight road through Caddam that farmers use in summer, but leave in the back end of the year to leaves and pools . . .

She was still fifty yards away, sometimes singing gleefully, and again letting her body sway lightly as she came dancing up Windyghoul. Soon she was within a few feet of the little minister, to whom singing . . . was a suspicious thing, and dancing a device of the devil. His arm went out wrathfully and his intention was to pass sentence on this woman.

But she passed, unconscious of his presence, and he had not moved or spoken . . . Only while she passed did he see her as a gleam of colour, a gypsy elf poorly clad, her bare feet flashing beneath a short green skirt, a twig of rowan berries stuck carelessly into her black hair. Her face was pale. She had an angel's loveliness . . .

Still she danced onwards, but she was very human . . .

Gavin leaped into the avenue, and she heard him and looked behind. He tried to cry 'Woman!' sternly, but lost the word for now she saw him, and laughed with her shoulders and beckoned to him, so that he shook his fist at her . . . She reached the mouth of the avenue, and kissing her hand to Gavin, so that the ring gleamed again, was gone.[3]

For the smitten Gavin, after many adventures, to grasp the mystery of the gypsy girl became for him 'like chasing a spirit that changes to something else in your arms'. Meanwhile, when Babbie herself thought she must lose her lover, in misery

> she wandered westward over the bleak hill, and by-and-by came to a great slab called the Standing Stone, on which children often sit and muse until they see gay ladies riding by on palfreys . . . and knights in glittering armour, and goblins, and fiery dragons and other wonders . . . The Standing Stone is in the dyke that separates the hill from a fir wood, and it is the fairy book of Thrums. If you would be a knight yourself, you must sit on it and whisper to it your desires.[4]

The gypsy girl is not only beautiful but, as it turns out, a foundling, too. These qualities compound her aura of strangeness, making her for the young minister both exotic and forbidden. Simply by being a gypsy,

Babbie embodies the immemorial connection of her tribe with super-natural powers. These are reinforced by traditional fairy emblems, such as her regular appearance to Gavin in woods or near a well, the tradi-tional means of passing over into the fairy world. In addition, her unnerving mutability is reflected in her gift for replacing in an instant the Scottish dialect with a refined English tongue. She wears, too, the fairy rowan berries in her hair, and repeatedly dons or throws off her cloak as the prelude to her passage from this world into another. A lovable character, Babbie is also a deeply ambivalent force, sometimes seen as good, at others a figure implying much darker possibilities.

While the young minister represents reason, convention and respon-sibility, Babbie is a pagan thing, a creature of anarchy, humour and ungoverned instinct. At the same time, like the people from the 'other world', she remains a transforming presence for whom, and through whom, change may come about. It is with Babbie that her creator had moved a step closer to clarifying his direction. A direction leading towards the construction of other, artificial and unrepresentational, worlds, in order to reveal truths about the one that he found himself inhabiting. *The Little Minister* is, in however unresolved and mixed up a fashion, Barrie's first serious attempt at the development of fantasy and myth.

When the month of holiday at Glen Cova came to an end, the family dispersed and Barrie returned to Kirriemuir with his parents and Jenann. Back in his study at Strath View he kept up the astonishing output of daily articles, worked at finishing *The Little Minister* and enjoyed several social occasions brought about by his growing reputation. These included an invitation to a house party at Dalmeny, where Gladstone himself was to be present. This was recognition indeed, when one of the most distinguished statesmen of the day was interested to meet the Kirriemuir loom-weaver's son. This, however, was the public face of existence. By contrast his private world was still at times marked by social inadequacy, which later in life he recalled – exaggerated no doubt with an eye to its drama.

> He never knew whether he was most sorry for himself or for the lady whom he took in to dinner. She was usually kindly and cour-teous, striving in a way that went to his heart to put him at his ease, coming back to him refreshed by a talk with her other neigh-bour; but all in vain. On the rare occasions when he could say anything she was so nervously desirous to listen that she never knew what it was that he said.[5]

Barrie had by now developed greater self-assurance, but this was largely confined to his professional work, or his male friends and acquaintances. Although there were social occasions on which friends' sisters, or the young actress to whom Barrie was most recently paying court, might be present, these never amounted to anything more than fairly tame flirtations. In the notebooks for 1891 and 1892 (always in the third person) he writes:

> '. . . bashful with women but incident proving he felt they had only to know him to love him – he always wanted to kiss pretty girls tho' manner made him stiff with them – his reserve – the real man inside . . . How far his shyness is the real cause of all his weakness and badness . . . Got on with so few people that had to make much of the few. Thus missed flirting days of boyhood & they came later when he knew the world . . .'
>
> 'He never has contact with a woman – if he had this might have made him exult less in making women love him – & so he would have been a better man . . .'[6] A year or so later he notes
>
> 'Had he even a genuine deep feeling that wasn't merely sentiment? Was he capable of it? Perhaps not . . .
>
> His hatred of all kinds of loose talk – jarred on his delicacy – also his self-consciousness made him keep his vicious thoughts to himself. Perhaps the curse of his life that he had never had a woman. Did his upbringing or heredity account for his character to any extent?'[7]

In January of 1891 *The Little Minister* began its run as a serial in the periodical *Good Words*. Having done well for several months, it was then published as a novel in October of that year. The critics were not unanimous. Andrew Lang, the classicist-journalist and proto-anthropologist, wrote a generous critique, which nevertheless expressed some reservations.

> It is a novel full of happy traits of Scottish character . . . it contains some touching scenes . . . the landscapes are deftly touched, [the grandeur of Glen Cova on the recent family holiday had been much turned to account] but when it comes to the story, my power of credulity, which is huge, is staggered, and declines to do its office.[8]

George Bernard Shaw wrote a review reflecting the more 'highbrow' critics' attitude recently prevailing: if an artist was popular it was impossible that he could be any good. In part Shaw understood Barrie well, but he was one of those critics who could never encompass the darker, more profound aspects of his work.

Mr Barrie is a born story teller; and he sees no further than his stories – conceives any discrepancy between them and the world as a shortcoming on the world's part, and is only too happy to be able to re-arrange matters in a pleasanter way. The popular stage, which was a prison to Shakespeare's genius, is a playground to Mr Barrie's. At all events he does the thing as if he liked it, and does it very well. He has apparently no eye for human character; but he has a keen sense of human qualities, and he produces highly popular assortments of them.[9]

Meanwhile, Robert Louis Stevenson, exiled to the island of Samoa in the belief that the climate would help him regain his health, wrote to his friend Henry James with some extraordinarily astute comments about Barrie:

Hurry up with another book of stories. I am reduced to two of my contemporaries, you and Barrie – O, and Kipling – you and Barrie and Kipling are now my muses Three. And with Kipling, as you know, there are reservations to be made . . . But Barrie is a beauty, *The Little Minister* and *The Window in Thrums [sic]* eh? Stuff in that young man; but he must see and not be too funny. Genius in him, but there's a journalist at his elbow – there's the risk.[10]

This was high praise indeed. Yet Stevenson identified the problem a number of the critics were having with the book, when he wrote to congratulate Barrie on his work.

The Little Minister ought to have ended badly; we all know it did; and we are infinitely grateful to you for the grace and good feeling with which you lied about it. If you had told the truth, I for one could never have forgiven you. As you had conceived and written the earlier parts, the truth about the end, though indisputably true to fact, would have been a lie, or what is worse, a discord in art. If you are going to make a book end badly, it must end badly from the beginning. Now your book began to end well. You let yourself fall in love with . . . and smile at your puppets. Once you had done that your honour was committed – at the cost of truth to life you were bound to save them . . . Write to me again in my infinite distance.[11]

Stevenson's astuteness lies in noticing how Barrie lets his narrator convince his audience of the story 'at the cost of truth to life', and he sees exactly why Barrie's novel is mixed up and unresolved. Barrie himself understood the problem. He knew that, as he was using the accepted devices and logic of novel writing, he had written a novel that *should* end badly, and that the ending would finally place the whole fantasy of Babbie and Gavin Dishart in perspective. Thus he had written in his notebook, 'Tragic love affair ending unhappily and the minister being preached out of his church by the old minister.'

The Little Minister fails, then, because Barrie played havoc with the 'rules'. On the one hand he had written a fairly conventional love story, while on the other hand he interspersed it with the illogicality of the supernatural, of fairy tale, legend and myth. As yet there was nothing Barrie could have done about his problem, because in writing *The Little Minister* he was trying – as in an important sense he had done since boyhood – to have it both ways. He was continuing to play with the idea that it was possible to inject fantasy into the real, without suffering any consequences.

Whatever the critics thought of it, *The Little Minister* was a success with the reading public. The majority would have agreed with the prophetic comments of one of Barrie's most prestigious editors, Robertson Nicoll, of the *British Weekly*. In April of that year Nicoll wrote to Marcus Dods saying,

> Barrie will succeed and that soon. He is one of the men – more numerous, I fancy, than we think – who are in every way improved by success – softened, humbled, and redeemed from cynicism, and I do not know any man of letters with such a future. My admiration for him constantly rises.[12]

In 1890 his name had already been sufficiently prominent for *Punch* to feature him in a series of *Prize Novels* – short parodies of the most popular writers of the time. Amongst the select few with whom he was included were Jerome K. Jerome, Robert Louis Stevenson, George Meredith, Jules Verne, Emile Zola, Olive Schreiner and Rudyard Kipling. By the summer of 1891 this accolade was magnified when the *British Weekly* brought out a sixteen-page supplement devoted entirely to Barrie and his writing. This was the first time he was portrayed as a personality to his reading public, and – along with a photograph of him subsequently displayed in half the bookshops of Britain – the supplement enhanced his reputation still further. If there were any previous doubts as to his sticking power outside journalism, by the end of 1891 Barrie the novelist was being discussed across the Empire. Meanwhile, on the other side of the Atlantic, his popularity meant that American (pirate) editions of his work were appearing almost as quickly as it was possible to run them off the presses.

After the publication of *The Little Minister* Barrie's readers would have to wait a full five years before he produced another novel. During this period he was subject to a series of events whose consequences were set to affect him for the rest of his life. With the publication of his next novel, *Sentimental Tommy*, in 1896, Barrie would emerge as a writer who had made the decision to investigate and write about fantasy rather than simply being a fantasist. This was to be the most testing and significant decision of his artistic life, and would colour all his subsequent work.

During that immensely busy year of 1891 his growing success did not make him immune to failure. Three years earlier he and his friend Marriott Watson had decided to write a play together. This was probably at the suggestion of Barrie's friend, the defiant and stoic poet-playwright W. E. Henley. (Henley is best remembered for his poetry collection *In Hospital*, which includes 'Invictus' and the lines

Out of the night that covers me,
Black as the Pit from pole to pole,
I thank whatever gods may be
For my unconquerable soul.

It was written during a year's hospitalisation to save his foot, the other having already been amputated through tubercular arthritis. Henley's personality shines through.)

Because of Barrie's and Watson's busy working schedules it took over a year to complete their play, *Richard Savage*. Then, to the young playwrights' dismay, no one wanted to take it on. Undeterred, their resolve was such they made up their minds to pay for it out of their own pockets. *Richard Savage* appeared as a matinée on 16th April 1891, and the *Times* reviewer summed up the critics' feelings when he wrote: 'The spectator is enabled to witness the poet's suicide, not only without a pang, but even with some sense of relief.' *Richard Savage* was not performed again.

Barrie of course immediately made currency out of his failure by converting it into a stubbornly cheery article, which began:

Yesterday Mr Anon produced his first play, and being interested in the fellow I bought the newssheets this morning to see what they thought of it and him. They agreed that it was among the most hopeless things ever offered to our kind friends in front.[13]

The failure of *Richard Savage* left Barrie more downcast than beaten, for he had more than this one play at stake. A series of slowly organised thoughts for another work had been developing in those little notebooks for the last four years. This second play was Barrie's alone.

Much later, as a world-famous playwright, he would describe drama as: 'a walk of literature I at first trod rather contemptuously'.[14] He even said that he 'preferred writing books and still think they were more my game'. (Here Barrie was mistaken, for the discipline and economy of the theatre, which forced him to get the plot and structure right, was exactly what he needed to counter his runaway fantasy. In addition, the theatre permitted a projection of himself into the 'separate roles of his characters without having to establish a realist context'.[15]) He would say: 'In my first years . . . I never contemplated becoming a dramatist, and would have thought you harsh had you said it was the thing for me. No one would have been so astonished as Anon.'[16]

As much as anything Barrie's astonishment must have arisen because, since his youth – when he already knew that he wanted to write – he had known that the status of the drama was nothing in comparison with that of the novel. And here one remembers that from the outset he was pragmatic about success and the best way to achieve it. Every seriously aspiring young writer of the period wanted first and foremost to become a novelist.

In spite of this attitude we know that Barrie's fascination with the theatre was established early on. One of the reasons he survived the loneliness and boredom of his years at university was undoubtedly because he visited the theatre as often as he could. Later, in London, he continued making theatrical criticism pay for his fixation. When other kinds of journalism became more lucrative he may have dropped the criticism, but during the five years Barrie had so far spent in London he never ceased to be one of its theatre's most passionate devotees.

Here he wasn't so unusual, for the Victorian dramatic theatre was attended every night of the week by huge numbers of people. Paradoxically – unlike opera and ballet – in spite of the theatre's popularity the cultural bias of the time was against it. Indeed, drama was regarded as so secondary that when commentators were contemplating what they saw as a hierarchy of the arts, drama was not included at all. During the nineteenth century British theatre had fallen into disarray; the middle and upper classes had largely deserted it as a form of entertainment. Other writers, painters and musicians were honoured by the educated and by fashionable society. The poet laureate Tennyson was made a peer in 1884, the composer Sullivan was knighted in 1883, but even in the later years of Victoria's reign few playwrights or players were fêted in the same way.

Two notable exceptions were the revered Shakespearean actor Henry Irving, and Oscar Wilde, until he fell from grace.

Prior to the 1870s great actors such as William Charles Macready had struggled to reform theatrical culture. During the 1870s actor-managers, such as Samuel Phelps, the Bancrofts and Charles Kean, were consolidating these efforts. In 1878 Henry Irving became leading actor and manager at the Lyceum, while the 1880s saw John Hare and the Kendals managing the St James's. In spite of all the efforts of these large personalities, the theatres rarely ventured away from the path of adapting or reviving older plays. The repertoire was dominated by flash, rowdy spectaculars, melodramas and highlights from the classics. Indeed, Barrie himself had written criticising Henry Irving, for a similar lack of originality.

Having worked hard at domesticating itself, by the 1890s a large section of London theatre was leaving behind its louche image and becoming almost respectable. During the last decades of the century a number of theatres were given major overhauls, acquiring subdued colours and the architectural features of classical refinement. At the same time, in this growing atmosphere of respectability, a more critical and ambitious drama was also becoming acceptable to the middle-class audiences who were now returning to the theatre. This new discrimination on the part of audiences was soon appreciated by some writers, too, as they recognised creative opportunities where previously there had been almost none.

Barrie was as conscious as any critic of these changes in the air and, recognising that the stage would not necessarily ruin a reputation, he permitted himself the luxury of some experiment and fun. How he saw his relationship to the theatre in the long term is not entirely clear. But, whatever he might have said or believed, his engagement with it ran deep. On the one hand he revealed an extraordinary ability, a need, to dwell in the realm of fantasy and illusion, while on the other he demonstrated the characteristic hard-headed practicality of any actor-director or playwright, consumed by a desire to understand the structure of make-believe. He might later protest that he never really intended to become a playwright, but the theatre remained for him something infnitely mysterious and magical. Its quirks, eccentricities and character were as fascinating as the constant interplay between its earthy practicalities and the shimmering fabric of illusion. As he later wrote, 'the theatre and the oddities of its life drew me to them'. At the very heart of it all was the same implicit enquiry that drove on Barrie himself: who or what was a person, and what was actually real?

Richard Savage was a failure but, as Barrie said, he was 'not one who tossed unfavourable criticisms aside, I took my revenge instead in considering them carefully and trying to draw sustenance from them; an ordeal at first'.[17] Having considered, he launched himself into a new play, for the moment called *The Houseboat*, and the decision to make another sally into the theatre would be discharged with his usual tenacity. As to the play's staging, for the moment its author would have to wait.

Meanwhile, at the Garrick Club, then a haunt of any actor of distinction, Barrie met Henry Irving. They talked, and, although nothing immediate was forthcoming, Barrie worked some of his magic, even upon this luminary of the stage. But another member of the Garrick, Irving's old friend the comic actor J. L. Toole (who, as a schoolboy, Barrie had venerated at the Theatre Royal in Dumfries), gave Barrie an idea. At this point Toole was also at the height of his fame, and in common with his friend Irving also ran his own theatre.

In April of 1891 the great Norwegian dramatist Ibsen was the talk of London. A single matinée performance of *Ghosts* two months earlier, and *Hedda Gabler*, which had recently opened at the Vaudeville, were causing outrage, while *A Doll's House* was about to be revived. Despite the scandalised response of a number of critics and sections of the audience, with the help of advocates such as Bernard Shaw, Ibsen's work was becoming popular enough for antagonistic critics to refer to it scathingly as 'this Ibsen craze'.

In October of the previous year, 1890, Barrie had written an anonymous piece in W. E. Henley's *National Observer*, a dialogue satirising the dramatic features of Ibsen's then much discussed work. Barrie's article, *The Ghost of Ghosts*, was precursor to the next move. A month after the failure of *Richard Savage* he made up his mind, sat down to work, and in a matter of days had written a one-act Ibsen parody and sent it off to Toole. *Ibsen's Ghost* is an irreverently witty dialogue between several Ibsenesque figures, in which the playwright's most characteristic features are coolly satirised. With encouragement from Irving, Toole agreed to put on the play as a single performance pre-matinée curtain-raiser. After brief rehearsals *Ibsen's Ghost* was performed on 29th May 1891, with Toole wittily luxuriating in the lead role of Barrie's 'Ibsen'.

Five days later the critic William Archer (Ibsen's great British advocate and his first translator into English) was writing in *The World* that Barrie 'was the pioneer of Ibsen parodists (so far as the stage is concerned) . . . the burlesque is irresistibly amusing . . . a piece of genuinely witty fooling, which ought not to be missed'. *The Times* called it 'a clever little parody', while the *Manchester Guardian* said: 'It lacks coherence, but contains so much invention in humorous details that the audience laughed and applauded from beginning to end.' A later critic wrote, 'it is a genial though serious attempt to pour contempt on the vogue of Ibsenism then at its high noon'.[18]

Audiences were soon clamouring to see the little preamble – this was the status of the curtain-raiser – in preference to the main play that followed. At first *Ibsen's Ghost* was anonymous, but its immediate popularity encouraged Barrie to admit authorship, in turn encouraging even larger audiencess. Normally one of these short burlesques would only run for about fifteen performances. Instead, Toole played *Ibsen's Ghost* to twenty-seven increasingly packed houses. This successful little parody, which ends with Hedda Gabler seeking release from her troubles with the aid of a child's popgun, didn't make a dramatist of Barrie, but his triumphant send-up of the new naturalism had whetted his appetite for the theatre still further.

By the end of June and the month's run of *Ibsen's Ghost*, Barrie was once again organising his friends to play for the Allahakbarries at Shere. These matches had acquired more cachet as Barrie's reputation and the number of his friends and acquaintances had grown. It was in this summer of 1891 that he first persuaded Arthur Conan Doyle to become a member of the team, discovering to his delight what an asset this genial bear of a man was to prove. The same summer Barrie had also acquired sufficient status to join both the Author's Club (as an original member) and the Society of Authors. Then, in July, the sixteen-page supplement devoted to him appeared in the *British Weekly*. His star was in the ascendant.

It was a shorter holiday than usual in Scotland that summer. Following *The Little Minister*'s serialisation, Barrie wanted to be back in London for its launch as a novel that October. His mother and sisters, Maggie and Jenann, marked his rise minutely. Jenann's faith in her brother was less circumscribed than their mother's, but even Margaret was beginning to appreciate the degree of her son's success. Meanwhile, Alick's pride in this oddest member of their family would for a while yet be informed by a greater understanding of Jamie than their father's outlook qualified him to master. To David Barrie, his youngest son must always have remained largely unknown.

Another cause for family celebration that autumn was the announcement of Barrie's younger sister Maggie's engagement. Since childhood Barrie had been particularly close to her, and as her chief protector his thoughtfulness towards her was unfailing. Maggie was a more malleable character than her brother, and acquiesced in the colourful image of herself which since childhood he had provided. She enjoyed being fussed over, having a champion, luxuriating in his solicitousness, and made no objection to Barrie's regular management of her life. Perhaps her beloved Jamie had even taken a hand in his sister's engagement to the young Free Church minister James Winter. How much Maggie might have differed from Barrie's 'creation' of her isn't clear, but certainly she remained devoted to him throughout her life. As time passed and she basked increasingly in his reflected glory, many found Maggie less sympathetic than her brother did, but Barrie's tendency to project on to others thoughts and feelings he wished them to have was an urge that would always remain irresistible to him.

By all accounts Maggie's fiancé was a sympathetic young man, while Margaret Barrie was most gratified at the prospect of such an addition to the family. Her beloved David had died before he reached her goal: the Church. Her son Jamie had eschewed it, but here at least one daughter would be *marrying* into it.

7

Mary

It was more than the forthcoming publication of his book that prompted Barrie's early return to London that summer. Instinct told him that following the success of *Ibsen's Ghost*, it would be unwise to remain for too long out of London. The revisions to the new play, *The Houseboat*, were now completed and Barrie anticipated that Toole's success with the Ibsen parody would encourage him to cast a more sympathetic eye over anything else he might be offered. Barrie's intuition was correct, and by the middle of October, with Irving's encouragement, Toole had purchased all the rights to Barrie's new play. Having effectively bought a permanent option he wasn't, however, under any obligation actually to stage it, but with Toole's *Ibsen's Ghost* coup in mind its fledgling playwright hoped that sooner or later Toole would consider it. Despite the failure of *Richard Savage*, in a year of serial successes for Barrie, with the purchase of his first real play by Toole and the launch of *The Little Minister*, he could reflect on October 1891 as a particularly satisfying month.

In January of the new year Toole did indeed announce that he would be staging *The Houseboat*. At the last minute it was discovered the title had previously been used and so it became *Walker London*; walker then being a vogue word for a trickster. Toole reassembled the actors from *Ibsen's Ghost* and rehearsals began almost at once. While Barrie was gratified at Toole's confidence in his play, and exhilarated at the prospect of its staging, characteristically this had little effect on his behaviour. The patterns were already too well established. He worked immensely hard, believed that he would succeed, and without cynicism happily paid court to those whom he admired. At thirty-one he could already claim as his friends two of the most distinguished living English writers. Yet, while always treating anyone he admired with grave respect, he did not ingratiate himself. Whatever private fears he might have been subject to, Barrie wasn't really capable of behaving with subservience.

In addition, his force of personality was such that to change his mind once it was made up, to curb or coerce him, was a truly formidable task.

Thus, unperturbed by either Toole's standing in the theatre or his furious protestations, Barrie insisted that he wasn't satisfied with the choice of second-lead actress. With just one dramatic success behind him the young playwright refused to budge. He was after all famous for his journalism and novels, and he now quietly reiterated that without *his* choice of actress there would be no play. The actress he had in mind was quite unknown, and pretty. Her name was Mary Ansell.

Jerome K. Jerome's reputation had been assured in 1889 with publication of *Three Men in a Boat*. He was touring one of his plays in the provinces with a travelling company, for which Mary Ansell was playing the ingénue. In his autobiography, *My Life and Times*, Jerome tells how Barrie asked him if he could recommend an actress for the new play. 'He didn't want much,' recalled Jerome.

> She was to be young, beautiful, quite charming, a genius for preference, and able to flirt. The combination was not so common in those days. I could think of no one except Miss Ansell. It seemed unkind not to give her the chance. I cancelled the contract and sent for her . . .[1]

Mary Ansell was neither a genius nor especially sophisticated, but she was intelligent, quick-witted, pretty and tantalisingly flirtatious. She was also ambitious. Although her father, a publican, was dead, and her mother was not left well off, Mary Ansell wasn't going to allow modest circumstances to limit her prospects. Mrs Ansell and her daughter were not close, and so there was no objection to her leaving home. The stage – as yet one of the few options for a girl who wanted a career and some independence – was Mary Ansell's goal. In order to further this ambition she took a gamble; a bold move reflecting her determination and resolve. Rather than wait, perhaps for ever, until a manager noticed her in a production and sought her out, Mary saved, or borrowed, enough money to put into a touring company of her own. In this way she had been playing, albeit mostly in the provinces, for some time. Her looks were of course an asset, but they didn't make an actress of her, and she wasn't yet in great demand. When the call came to meet Barrie, any young actress thirsting for parts on the London stage would have congratulated herself on her good fortune.

Toole himself may have been angry and frustrated at the young Barrie's challenge to his authority, but Irene Vanbrugh, to whom Toole had given the lead, was privately outraged. Not only was Barrie insisting on putting forward an actress in place of someone already chosen, but the new second lead, Miss Ansell, was to have a *higher* fee than Miss Vanbrugh. In addition, Irene Vanbrugh had now realised that although her part as the bluestocking Bell Golightly was the lead, it was much less characterful than the exuberant Irish girl, Nanny O'Brien, played by Mary Ansell. Vanbrugh later recorded how she

> approached the shy little author, confident at seventeen that my position as Toole's leading lady would intimidate him into giving me a choice of either part. How young but how foolish I was and how quiet but firm he was.[2]

The actress also wrote candidly about her feelings. 'Mary Ansell . . . was delightful and extremely pretty. I acknowledge this now more freely than I did at the time because I was jealous of her success; especially as the author was in love with her.' And it certainly did appear that Barrie had been swept off his feet. By the time *Walker London* was staged, at the end of February, the playwright and Mary Ansell were regularly seen together in public. Barrie's notebooks for this spring and on into the summer of 1892 are filled with ideas for a new play, clearly reflecting his preoccupation with the young actress. Beginning as *The Bookworm*, this play would slowly develop until it eventually became *The Professor's Love Story*.

This tells the absurd story of Professor Goodwillie, so absent-minded and emotionally undeveloped that he fails to recognise first, that he has fallen in love and second, with whom, believing instead that he is ill. His doctor diagnoses the 'malady'. The professor is horrified and flees to Scotland in an attempt to escape, taking with him his secretary, Lucy White, the very source of his unease. Lucy White is already quite aware not only that the professor loves her, but that she is in love with him.

Meanwhile *Walker London* had its premiere on 25th February 1892, and what would become the typical response to Barrie's writing was here prefigured. Most critics came to regard him as a dramatist of great technical skill, who turned out conservative plays with just enough edge to give them popular appeal. His drama would quickly be categorised by these critics as a drama of the surface. Consequently, a more reflective reviewer would later write that Barrie's masterly skill in dramatic construction and his famous whimsicality had obscured his other virtues, which included 'his deep psychological meaning'.

This came about in part because his family background, and his training as a journalist, gave Barrie the understanding that without some kind of private funding a working writer cannot be aggressively unpopular and survive. Over and again he makes this point, with regard to both his drama and his humour; while his prose heroes are made to reinforce the point: 'When I say a humorous thing myself I'm dependent on other fowk to tak note o' the humour o't, bein myself tae'n up with the makkin o't.'[3]

Underneath the apparent conventionality there was already a high degree of the unorthodox in Barrie's early works, whether journalism, novels or plays. Resisting classification, he was enigmatic and difficult to pin down, and with time less and less likely to follow any artistic mainstream. He was also aware that in order to say some of the uncomfortable things he wanted to communicate, they had to be presented with an appealing surface. With these thoughts in mind his work would become increasingly layered. As he enticed his audience by the brilliance of the surface – famously referred to as his 'lightness of touch' – below there were further, more challenging meanings for those who were prepared to look. That many critics, and no doubt many in his audience, failed to do so was in part because his work was so disarmingly approachable. This quality would eventually lead one critic to write, 'No dramatist has ever been more perilous to criticism than Barrie within a week of his death.'[4]

Walker London was a success. It ran right through the rest of 1892 and on into the middle of the following year, before going on tour for several more months. It played in New Zealand, South Africa, India, the US and several British provinces. Meanwhile, five days before the launch of Barrie's play, Wilde's *Lady Windermere's Fan* had also received its London premiere. Wilde had irritated critics and actors alike when, at the curtain call,

> a fat man in evening dress, wearing a fur-lined overcoat, had strolled into view smoking a cigarette and, the applause subsiding, had continued to smoke while he assured the audience that he was so glad the acting had not quite spoilt his little play.[5]

This studied condescension was repeatedly criticised in the play's reviews, which complained that it was nothing more than a series of dialogues, and a vehicle for Wilde's own epigrammatic wit. This was something out of which J. L. Toole cleverly made currency when taking his own curtain call on *Walker London's* first night. By implied contrast with Wilde, he recounted how Barrie's nerves had been so extreme he had left the theatre, and neither did he smoke. That Barrie didn't smoke was of course arrant nonsense, but in contrasting him with Wilde, Toole's comments enhanced the popularity of Barrie and his creation by adding to the already complex myth of his modesty.

In *Walker London* Barrie had disclosed an experimental mind with an instinctive feeling for the theatre. Here, both actors and designers were in agreement that he had created a play of extraordinary visual inventiveness. As well as this, while Barrie revelled in his play's light-heartedness, he had also given *Walker London* real themes. Themes which anticipated what were to remain some of his chief concerns: the self-delusion of lovers; the mistaken belief that life must be judged on rational grounds alone; and the impossibility of different social classes really communicating with one another until certain prejudices had been dislodged.

Old Toole made a hefty profit with his young protégé's farce, while the young protégé himself, having sold it outright to the savvy Toole, made nothing further than the initial sum of three hundred pounds. What he did make was something much more valuable to him than money at this point in his career; a leap forward in his understanding, and his apprenticeship as a writer for the stage.

Despite a few subsequent flops, such as the one-act satire, based on Thackeray's great heroine Becky Sharp, performed in 1893, Barrie learnt quickly from his early efforts for the stage. The critics noticed how his plays became less laboured, and saw that what was to become his legendary understanding of dramatic structure and stagecraft was developing fast. In *Walker London*, for example, he confined the entire three-act play to one strikingly creative set. The designer, Joseph Harker, would later say that this set was the most rewarding he had made in the whole of his career. The dramatist and critic Harley Granville Barker – to become an outstanding figure in progressive theatre at the beginning of the twentieth century, and in turn a campaigner on Barrie's behalf – would later write that *Walker London* was 'evidence enough of the extraordinary scenic inventiveness to be cultivated later'.

Barrie was not only achieving more *dramatic* lightness of touch. His intense personal involvement in the making of *Walker London* was also to set a precedent for the rest of his working life. 'When he was rehearsing *Ibsen's Ghost*, he had no idea what he wanted; dress and business he left despairingly to the company. But when he rehearsed *Walker London* he had precise views about everything.'[6]

He was capable of an exhausting intensity, and would usually dictate the course of any communication. At the same time he was renowned for his reticence. Inadequate though it is, the justification he himself gave for it was his Scottishness.

You only know the shell of a Scot until you have entered his home circle at social gatherings where you and he seem to be getting on so well, he is really a house with all the shutters closed and the

door locked. He is not opaque of set purpose, often it is against his
will – it is certainly against mine, I try to keep my shutters open
and my foot in the door but they will bang to . . . Now, it seems
to be a law of nature that we must show our true selves at some
time, and as the Scot must do it at home, and squeeze a day into
an hour, what follows is that there he is self-revealing in the superlative degree, the feelings so long dammed up overflow, and thus a
Scotch family are probably better acquainted with each other, and
more ignorant of life outside their circle than any other family in
the world. And as knowledge is sympathy, the affection existing
between them is almost painful in its intensity . . .[7]

Barrie's force of personality, at times overpowering, was juxtaposed
with an endearing willingness to put his own needs to one side if he
perceived that someone else's were greater. Often a surprise to those who
were irritated by his urge to control, once his sympathy was stirred Barrie's
readiness to listen patiently, to console and sustain were qualities cherished by his friends. He possessed, too, that rare and welcome quality: he
found no difficulty in giving praise. In old age he complimented a close
friend on that very quality which he himself possessed in abundance:
'Your first instinct is always to telegraph Jones the nice thing Brown said
about him to Robinson; you have sown a lot of happiness that way.'

These sensibilities often meant that, although he had good men friends,
as time passed Barrie was often easier in the company of women. His
empathy with them didn't, however, arise from the wisdom of experience. In many ways he didn't understand women. And yet, an intuitive,
female part of him responded to some of their deepest feelings and
concerns. In this respect Barrie was quite different from his contemporary Bernard Shaw, who sometimes appears to have had difficulty in
understanding that there might be others, besides the activist New Woman,
who possessed any sensitivity or strength of character at all.

Meanwhile, Barrie's courtship of Mary Ansell continued. The actress
must have been flattered by the attentions of someone so clearly a man
of the moment, but her liking for him didn't spring from his growing
reputation alone. Her lively intelligence was combined with an astuteness which enabled her to appreciate that his Scottish humour was an
essential part of Barrie's character. When the spirit moved him that remote
sadness in his beautiful blue eyes would temporarily ease, and the diffi-
dence was replaced by a jubilant gaiety. Counter to this, his by now notorious unpredictability was something Mary Ansell appeared capable of
handling. Revealing little of his moods Barrie rarely smiled, and with a
perverseness that never ceased to unsettle all but his closest associates, he

often sent up those very things dearest to him with a completely impassive countenance. Where even his good friends sometimes found him impossible to gauge and grew impatient, many acquaintances refused to persevere.

Barrie's notebooks for this period are full of references to a novel with the working title *The Sentimentalist*. Much of it is straightforwardly autobiographical, revealing equivocal feelings. So, while the gossip columns were reporting a blossoming romance between Mr J. M. Barrie and Miss Mary Ansell, Barrie was writing:

> This sentimentalist wants to make girl love him, bullies and orders her . . . yet doesn't want to marry.
> – Such a man if an author, wd be studying his love affair for book. Even while proposing, the thought of how it wd read wd go thro' him . . .
> – She pretends she doesn't want to marry him – really this cause of her doubts – she can't be sure he loves her.
> Her way of peering over her fur collar.
> – Her ordering clothes for him, &c. – Motherly feelings. If she an actress, shd he not be a dramatist? Tho he and she had married wd she have been happy not acting? Probably not.[8]

Driven to hold centre stage, Barrie would also write of a deep sense of isolation, exemplified by the comment, 'He is really a house with all the shutters closed and the door locked.' With time, refining his wit and refusing to contain his quirkiness, he would become a public figure of depth and pathos. And yet he always remained at his most relaxed when smoking and talking with no more than one or two. Writing to a friend after a hectically social time away he said, 'I wish I could drop in on you about nine p.m., put another log on the study fire and tell you all about it.'[9] Barrie's inclusion in an ever-expanding social scene, spilling over into the intense bustle and energy of literary London, meant that his new life in England was utterly different from the quiet solitude also necessary to him and learnt during his boyhood in Scotland.

For the ambitious young journalist, however, finding a larger place than Kirriemuir in which to hammer his career into shape had been imperative. At another level the artist in him had felt compelled to leave behind the arid constraint of his parents' vision, his birthplace, even his country, in order to expand and find his own. Fortunate in being equipped with that immense self-belief, Barrie rarely experienced the provincial's customary sense of vulnerability when faced with the rigours of city life:

> Big as the place is, I don't think it has the effect of making you
> feel your own littleness, else could you not slave so hard in it. For
> they do slave in London, do they not? The gospel of work, work
> till you drop often means that you are to live a life bounded on
> north-south-east-and-west by the mighty trifles of your own pen.[10]

Despite this disclaimer, for a long time yet it was to be the 'mighty trifles'
of his own pen that more than anything else were to fire Barrie's spirit.
In the process he became an honorary Londoner. He might refer to a
temporary absence, saying, 'I was not sorry to leave London', but he had
also quickly grown to love this great city. Indeed, by the time he died,
London was the place in which Barrie had spent by far the major part
of his life, and he would write, 'It eternally thrills me and has been to
me all the bright hopes of my youth conceived.'

Even so, in those first London years the distance from his origins never
entailed Barrie's rejection of them, and his frequent journeys home to
Scotland were as much as anything essential psychic refuelling. He was
also making the best of necessity. With the decline in Margaret Barrie's
health throughout the 1890s, again and again, at a moment's notice, her
son would leap on to the northbound train. With each emergency, as his
journey brought him closer to home, he dreaded that this time it would
be the end. During repeated episodes awaiting his mother's recovery, he
discovered that Kirriemuir had become for him a good place in which
to work. He also described 'those many night alarms, when lights flick-
ered in the house and white faces were round my mother's bedside'. And
in *Margaret Ogilvy* he relived

> Those long vigils when, night about, we sat watching . . . the awful
> nights when we stood together, teeth clenched – waiting – it must
> be now. And it was not then; her hand became cooler, her breathing
> more easy; she smiled to us. Once again I could work by snatches,
> and was glad . . .[11]

Barrie's mother persistently searched for herself in his female characters.
As a result, in her single-minded and self-absorbed fashion she would
regularly interrupt to comment on the authenticity, or not, of her son's
fiction. For the rest, what he had so far printed was pored over by Margaret
and Jenann, provoking Margaret's observation, 'It is a queer thing that
near everything you write is about this bit place. You little expected that
when you began.'

8

'You must decide . . .'

At Strath View, preparations for Barrie's sister's much anticipated wedding to the minister James Winter were going ahead. Then suddenly, on the day of Barrie's thirty-second birthday, his friend Gilmour received a bleak piece of news:

Dear Gilmour
    A telegram announces that Winter has been thrown from his horse and killed.
    Yrs
    J. M. Barrie

Not only had poor Winter, the immaculate friend and perfect lover, been killed by a fall from his horse, but the animal had been a gift from Barrie. In one of those characteristic gestures of largesse that would become common as he grew in prosperity, Barrie had given his friend James Winter the horse so that he might visit his new parishioners more easily.

The Barrie household was silenced and the curtains were pulled shut. Barrie's parents and Jenann were in deep mourning, while Barrie himself, the inadvertently guilty brother, was overcome with remorse. The bride-to-be lay uncomprehending, refusing to communicate, in the terrible darkness of her room. Searching himself for the words that might give her the smallest hope, Barrie cautiously made his way to Maggie's bedside.

He felt that the responsibility for James Winter's tragic death was his own. Having arrived at this conclusion, the only recompense he could offer was to devote himself unstintingly to his sister's care. Despite Maggie's lack of dynamism, her brother would later say of her, 'No one could understand me much who did not know what she has been to me all her life.' He would therefore strive to protect and console her, remaining always at her side. In her present state of collapse Maggie was incapable of decision and willingly handed herself over to her brother, accepting entirely his tendency to arrange and shape her life. Reflecting on it all in his notebook he wrote: 'Novel. After death, a character talks beautiful resignation, &c. Yet what is the feeling at heart? A kicking at the awfulness? A bitterness? no-one in these cases gets at others' real feelings. Each conceals from other.'[1] Next Barrie composes an embarrassing letter of tribute, to be read out at the funeral in Caithness and forwarded by him for publication in the *British Weekly* and the *Pall Mall Gazette*, where Marriott Watson was now literary editor. Of his sister Maggie he says,

> She has not physical strength to be with you just now in body, but she is with you in spirit, and God is near her, and she is not afraid . . . God chose his own way, and took her dear Jim, her dear young minister, and she says, God's will be done.[2]

Hardly an accurate description of Maggie's state. Moreover, one feels that God, in his wisdom, might here have preferred that the siblings exercise just a touch of restraint. Contrary to this public testament of faith, Barrie's private feelings at the minister's death were not those of resignation. His notebook reads:

> Here was killed so & so
> Brave gallant man.
>
> Knocked out of the world
> by God
> While doing his duty.
> Left by his God to die
> in a ditch.
> God is love.[3]

Earlier Barrie had written in his customary numbered notes

250) Man (disbelieving) telling girl God's will &c. because knew this only way of saving her life . . .
256) How long ago it may be since yesterday.
257) Walking on tiptoes for invalids till always walk on tiptoes.
259) No reward from God in this world (except own conscience).
260) Bones creak in night when you stealthily move about room of invalid not to wake her.
261) Strange after loved one's death to see papers again and see all

the world crying out against pinpricks – as we ourselves did but the other day and will do again.[4]

After six weeks of giving themselves up to unrelieved suffering, Barrie decided that the best regimen for Maggie's health would be to take her away. While alone, the siblings' misery could run its unhindered course. Maggie's total surrender to her grief, and her inability (or unwillingness) to overcome it with a measure of stoicism, reminds one of her mother's response at the time of her son David's death many years before. Perhaps here even the earnest Barrie family were a little overwhelmed by the intensity of Jamie's and Maggie's mourning.

The sorrowing brother and sister travelled south to seclude themselves in a Surrey cottage at Shere, lent to Barrie for as long as he might wish to stay. Friends had offered other retreats, while letters of sympathy and proposals of help had flooded in. Despite all this Barrie chose to keep both his own and Maggie's friends at a distance. His sister needed absolute quiet and rest, and in the months of their incarceration he remained her attentive companion. Maggie herself meanwhile endured the lengthy bout of suffering, perhaps encouraged to do little else.

Even this punishing routine failed for long to keep Barrie from his writing. The curious situation in which he had placed himself may temporarily have stopped him working, but this never led to any slackening in the pace of his mind. Bit by bit Maggie's morning walk, supported by the ever-solicitous brother, was put a little later, as once again his thoughts began to clarify beyond his notebooks. The play he was developing and the experiments with his novel moved forward, as page after page was covered with that small illegible hand. July and August passed, by which time Barrie was travelling up to London once a week. The world, and the need to keep up with its movement, could not be put aside for ever.

That summer Barrie didn't assemble the Allahakbarries to play cricket. He was unable to muster that robust state of mind necessary to superintend the camaraderie, the cheerful rivalry and witty dinner repartee of an Allahakbarrie weekend in the country. Gradually, though, he did begin to re-emerge, sometimes making the short journey to the elderly Meredith – about eight miles from Shere. Although the younger author was subdued, he was slowly warming to the need of his friends. Did he see Mary Ansell during this period? No mention of her exists for this period. Thoughts preoccupying Barrie not long before the Reverend Winter's death, however, led him to jot down a series of notes for his play *The Professor's Love Story*.

68)   B[ookworm] realises he has been leading a selfish life engrossed in own work & not playing citizen's part in world . . .

65) Discuss the question whether men of genius shd marry.
72) – Doctor maintains to sister . . . that B's marrying wd be the remaking of him – he has got so sunk in books he'll drown, he'll become a parchment, a mummy . . .
73) – Doctor says a sister can never be like a wife – nor a brother a husband . . .
77) 'If it wasn't for women men wd never learn anything.'
80) Many a woman's a widow at my age.
82) Heroine poured cold at first . . .
85) Doctor . . . says love must come to all at some age.[5]

For the moment Barrie appears to have been incapable of acting on the prescription that 'love must come to all of us at some age'. He was unable to do anything more than retreat into the emotionally less challenging role he had defined for himself as his sister's chief prop.

In August *The Professor's Love Story* was at last finished, and Barrie sent it to the stately Henry Irving by whom it had been commissioned. Although as an old professional Irving would pay Barrie the compliment of saying, 'You have a remarkable way of getting your characters off – always a difficulty with playwrights and players,'[6] none the less he found he didn't like the play, and neither would he perform in it. Nor, when he was sent it, would Irving's friend Toole. Barrie was most disappointed, but, as was his custom when faced with setback, he collected himself, and carried on. There was, however, a certain cooling towards Irving. Meanwhile, the persistent little playwright continued sending *The Professor's Love Story* out. And each time it came back. No one seemed to want it. Once again Irving took a hand in Barrie's fortunes, and once again he would be the catalyst for the young man's success.

Possibly feeling a little guilty at having refused the play he had commissioned, Irving recommended it to the actor-manager E. S. Willard, back in England after an annual stint with his touring company in the United States. Willard was looking for a new piece to take back with him across the Atlantic and bought the American rights to the play. Barrie later said he had fifty pounds for it. Despite funds put by, caring for his sister over these last months had seriously curtailed his output. Although at the time he was pleased to receive anything for *The Professor's Love Story*, he would live to regret this impatience.

In December 1892, when Willard put on the play in America, Barrie had no rights to any royalties and watched as the actor-manager reaped all the rewards. But when Willard brought the play to England two years later the playwright had acquired an agent, who negotiated a well-framed contract giving him not only a royalty, but a favourable one at that. Despite

Clova, the closest of the glens to Kirriemuir

Kirriemuir in the earlier part of the 20th century, with the Gairie works chimney, and Cemetery Hill in the background

The Tenements. Barrie was born in the
right-hand end terrace.

A grave-faced Jamie Barrie, at about six years old

Jamie (front left) aged about twelve, at school

Burnbank Terrace in Glasgow, where Jamie
lived with his brother Alick as a boy

Margaret Barrie in old age with James

Barrie's older brother Alick, and his wife Mary

Strath View, the family home in
Kirriemuir from 1872, where Barrie
did much of his early writing

Barrie's father, David, as an older man

Barrie's mother, Margaret, and sister, Jenann,
a few years before their deaths

The prospering author in confident pose in the late 1890s

Mary Barrie,
two years after her marriage

A favourite photograph

Mary Barrie looks over
her collar as Grizel does

Sylvia and Arthur Llewelyn Davies. Barrie thought Sylvia the most beautiful creature he had ever met.

Mary Hodgson, nursemaid to the five Llewelyn Davies boys

Charles Frohman, without whom *Peter Pan* would probably never have been staged

Sylvia Llewelyn Davies
and her son George

Leinster Corner, the house in which
Peter Pan was written

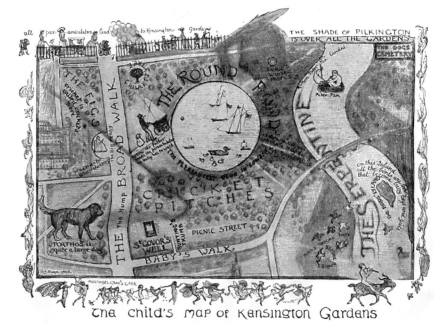

The child's map of Kensington Gardens

The Child's Map of Kensington Gardens, from *The Little White Bird*, 1902,
in which Peter Pan's character is first developed

The Llewelyn Davies boys as
The Boy Castaways of Black Lake Island:
an element in the creation of *Peter Pan*

Bevil, the son of Sir Arthur
Quiller-Couch, and Porthos,
the Barries' St Bernard

the reviewers' edgy, sometimes critical note – they found *The Professor's Love Story* improbable – they correctly predicted another Barrie success.

Its plot is unlikely and the play has dated, but at the heart of Barrie's most Shakespearean comedy are two themes that would become central in his work. The first, and perhaps most significant, is his preoccupation with the passage of time. The second is his great interest in different types of strong women, his belief in their superiority, and by contrast the weakness, even silliness, usually characteristic of men.

In a later play, of 1908, *What Every Woman Knows*, the central character, Maggie, is a case in point. An intelligent and knowing woman, she understands certain aspects of life instinctively, while the man who becomes her husband, John Shand, can only arrive at this knowledge through a series of educative experiences. As the one who 'knows', Maggie is the guiding figure, whose schemes provide both the play's movement and it's comedy. Referring to John Shand in an early draft, Barrie wrote, 'Woman cd do the work better (any woman knows that)', and on numerous future occasions his women will demonstrate different manifestations of this same idea. Pre-eminent among his knowing and powerful women – though still only a girl – is the heroine of *Peter Pan*, the young Wendy Darling.

While *The Professor's Love Story* plays out the themes of love and courtship in high and low life, a lesser but still important theme that Barrie's subtly mocking pen will delineate over time is what he perceives as the inane and wasteful lives of the English upper classes. After the disciplined high seriousness of Lowland Scotland, and the ferociously industrious environment of Kirriemuir, he must have found the indolence of the late-Victorian upper classes particularly shocking. In *The Professor's Love Story* this is exemplified by Lady Gilding's stepson, Sir George, who makes the decision to investigate the life of the poor by nothing less than sending his family out to labour in the *fields*, 'wearing dresses such as those worn by the common things while harvesting'. This is Barrie's trial run for the brilliant comedy pervading what was to be one of his most famous plays, *The Admirable Crichton*.

As *Walker London* continued its successful run, he was sometimes seen in the wings – on more than one occasion with his friend Thomas Hardy. (A lifelong habit, and perhaps the greatest compliment Barrie could pay, was to invite someone to a rehearsal of one of his plays.) Now cautiously trying out the possibility of leaving his sister for periods, he was even beginning to encourage the occasional visit from friends. Whether he admitted it or not, Barrie needed to free himself from this rigorous twinning with his sister, and he finally began edging towards a more realistic life. In September, brother and sister left the cottage at Shere and took up lodgings in London at Gloucester Walk, just off Kensington Church Street.

Mary Ansell was still playing the second lead in *Walker London* and, even if only on his visits to the theatre, Barrie must have seen her. We do not know what the actress thought about his retreat from the world. He, however, would have explained, with aching sincerity, that the tragedy of Winter's death must be put before everything else; this included themselves. Of course, neither he nor Maggie could now ever marry. Did he confide this last thought to Mary Ansell or only to Maggie? Whatever was said regarding long-term arrangements, from this period Barrie began to be seen about with the delightful Miss Ansell once again.

James Winter's death and its aftermath was a deeply affecting period for Maggie and her brother, and their grieving was unfeigned. Yet, from this distance, there is something about the whole episode that appears to verge on the melodramatic. Barrie's intensity sometimes led him to behave in a manner that can be described in no other way.

The one surviving letter from Margaret Barrie to her son is from this period and thanks him for his devoted support of Maggie.

My dear beloved Jamie my heart keeps blessing and thanking you but my love no words can say, and especially your present, my heart fails words for my first birthday gift. My dear beloved son God bless you and prosper you [you] are a precious God given son to me, the light of my eyes. And my darling Maggie is safe with God and you till we meet.
    Your loving mother[7]

In that summer spent cloistered with his sister, Barrie also received the first of a number of letters from Robert Louis Stevenson, exiled far away on his remote South Sea island in search of health. With Stevenson's letter, which had taken months to arrive, Barrie apparently put behind him some of the doubts he had harboured about his fellow Scot's writing. He was flattered and responded immediately to Stevenson, accompanying his letter with a copy of *Auld Licht Idylls*. The two writers quickly became friends via a regular correspondence, enduring until poor Stevenson's early death four years later. From that summer onward Barrie consistently defended the older man. Although Stevenson's romantic life and dramatic personality made him an intriguing character, he was an embattled figure. The critical reputation of the author of *The Strange Case of Dr Jekyll and Mr Hyde*, *Treasure Island* and *The Master of Ballantrae* was by no means assured. After Stevenson's death Barrie was one of those involved in trying to erect a memorial to his memory. Writing to a friend at the time he said: 'The "people" of course are as they always were, indifferent to RLS and think this confounded "art" an absurdity

. . . there is fierce enough local opposition to the thing [the memorial] in influential circles.'[8]

Stevenson had repeatedly asked Barrie to travel out to visit him and his family on their plantation in Samoa, and declared, 'We would have some grand cracks! Come, it will broaden your mind and be the making of me.' The projected adventure sadly never took place; and then Stevenson was dead. But what went on in Barrie's imagination was often of greater importance than any particular action, and in his head the discovery of a new hero was significant enough.

Friends occasionally succeeded in drawing Barrie away from his sister. He wrote to Arthur Quiller-Couch, 'I am writing plays to stop myself from thinking', and was persuaded to travel to Cornwall in the autumn to stay with Quiller-Couch and his wife. Styling himself 'Q' for the duration of his prolific and distinguished literary career as critic, novelist and poet, Quiller-Couch made his name in 1887 with a novel, *Dead Man's Rock*. In 1900 he edited the first, and tremendously influential, *Oxford Book of English Verse*. He would remain a close friend of Barrie, not only appreciating the man, but also considering his work more perceptively than many other critics. Quiller-Couch had left London for his beloved Cornwall, from where in 1912 he moved to Cambridge to take up the Chair of English. In 1906 Barrie would write to him: 'I think it's true that you are what I miss mostly in London. It would have made a big difference to me if you had been here all these years.' And in 1909, he wrote: 'I miss you much and always. On the whole I've cared for you more than any other of our calling.'[9]

Away from his sister with the Quiller-Couches for a few days, Barrie was freed from the shackles of responsibility. Quiller-Couch's wife was sympathetic and welcoming, and here Barrie felt able to smoke and talk for hours at a time. Meanwhile, in playing with their small son, Bevil, to whom he was devoted, he was temporarily permitted to slough off the strains of adulthood in fantastic and happy games of make-believe.

In the autumn of 1892 Barrie became caught up with an idea put to him by the renowned theatrical manager Richard D'Oyly Carte. D'Oyly Carte had made a fortune with Gilbert and Sullivan's operas; their collaboration had appeared charmed until they quarrelled and D'Oyly Carte convinced himself he could succeed on his own. For a time he had been trying out other collaborations, when the popularity of *Walker London* suggested Barrie as a possibility. Barrie was of course immensely flattered that such a celebrated man of the theatre wanted his help.

With a mixture of bravado and genuine confidence he charmed D'Oyly Carte and his wife, enthusing them with his plot, until all three persuaded themselves that Barrie was capable of writing the libretto for a new comic opera. His excitement at the idea of this new challenge convinced him it was possible, and he was commissioned to begin immediately. Barrie, however, was not another Gilbert, and such an undertaking was to prove beyond him; his genius lay elsewhere.

In between toiling over his notes for a new novel, *Sentimental Tommy*, he launched himself on this massive, entirely misguided, and ultimately debilitating task. Christmas came and he took Maggie away to the coast, where they stayed on into January. Then, in London once again, the librethist struggled against more headaches and, as always, a tendency to colds and coughs. In early February he went north, intending a short visit, but the tensions he had been labouring under for months finally proved too much even for this obdurate worker. In Edinburgh physical and mental exhaustion caught up with him and Barrie became seriously ill. He was in a breakdown state, exacerbated by a serious bout of bronchitis. Maggie immediately travelled up to Scotland to nurse him, and soon Mary Ansell gave up her role in the cast of *Walker London* and left London to join them.

Mary Ansell and Barrie had spent much time together recently: suppers *à deux*, the theatre, walking in Richmond Park at weekends. In spite of his consistent unpredictability, Mary enjoyed his company very much: she liked the humour, the quicksilver mind, the attentiveness. She was intrigued by his elusiveness and would later write, 'I only loved clever men. And clever men, it seems to me, are made up of reserves. It is out of their reserves they bring their clever things.'[10] Barrie, meanwhile, took care to reveal few doubts or inadequacies, and when he was on good form Mary was exhilarated by the challenge of his company.

With her desire to succeed as an actress, Mary Ansell wasn't a conventional Victorian girl. This didn't, though, make her a Bohemian, and she remained conscious that Barrie's attentions hadn't so far included any professions of commitment. By now she couldn't help wondering if he really knew his own mind. Perhaps, therefore, her offer of assistance to Maggie was a calculated one. Whatever the motive, Maggie found it difficult to refuse help from this pretty, stylish young woman, who so clearly fascinated her brother.

Barrie was almost unfailingly sensitive to others' feelings. He must have noticed the antipathy between his sister and the actress, indeed he added to his notebook the comment 'two women fighting for man and his life/ill'. One is unsure how much he actually articulated difficult thoughts to himself. Instead, his sensitivity would very often take a subterranean course, and sooner or later appear in his writing. Divided soul that he was, Barrie appears to have been only dimly aware of this habit. The parallels are clear between aspects of his relationship with Mary Ansell and his possessive sister, and the similarly triangular tension he was simultaneously creating in his novel, *Sentimental Tommy*, between Tommy Sandys, his sister Elspeth and the heroine of the story, poor Grizel.

However much Mary Ansell and Maggie Barrie may have had to grit their teeth over personal differences, their ministerings were successful, and the patient improved. Soon Barrie went on with Maggie to stay at Kirriemuir, while Mary returned to London alone. Recuperating in Kirriemuir, Barrie was forced to admit that he just couldn't finish the libretto for D'Oyly Carte's opera in time, so he asked his friend Conan Doyle if he would step in to help. Reportedly Barrie's telegram read, 'Come at once if convenient – if not convenient, come all the same.'[11]

Although Doyle's hands were tied as far as the plot was concerned, always a good-natured man, he agreed and did his best. Afterwards he would say, 'The only literary gift which Barrie has not got is the sense of poetic rhythm, and the instinct for what is permissible in verse.'[12] The opera, called *Jane Annie* with music by Ernest Ford, was finished and performed in May 1893, and, although it ran for a few weeks, between them Barrie and Conan Doyle had written a complete flop. At the end of the first night a young friend came into their box and Barrie later said, 'Doyle expressed my feelings by saying to him reprovingly, "Why did you not cheer?" But I also sympathised with our visitor when he answered plaintively, "I didn't like to, when no one else was doing it." '[13] When George Bernard Shaw reviewed the opera in the *World* he described it as 'the most unblushing piece of tomfoolery that two respectable citizens could conceivably indulge in publicly', while the *Academy* called it 'one of the weakest librettos ever written; and the number of weak librettos has been large'.

Barrie – of whom Conan Doyle would say 'there is nothing small except his body' – habitually rose above failure, and in no time had sent Conan Doyle a parody of *Sherlock Holmes* written on the flyleaves of a copy of *A Window in Thrums*. In these flyleaf *Adventures of Two Collaborators*, Barrie and Conan Doyle are mercilessly satirised. Luckily, the forgiving Doyle didn't let this unfortunate episode of theatrical failure mar a good friendship.

That summer, having endured responsibility for his sister for more than a year, Barrie must have felt relieved when Maggie announced her second engagement. Her brother's life, his friendships, had become circumscribed by her presence and he was in need of his old freedoms once more.

Maggie's new fiancé was none other than William Winter, brother to James, the man she was to have married. William's visits to Maggie were initially to console and pay his respects. But if Tommy Sandys' behaviour

in *Sentimental Tommy* bears any resemblance to Barrie's, then this particular pairing may have come about in some measure as a result of subtle
manoeuvring on the part of Maggie's brother. Indeed, Maggie and
William's attachment and eventual match would never have gone ahead
without Barrie's blessing, for Maggie would do nothing without his
approval. A notebook entry for a story at this time reads:

> Girl's lover to whom about to be married dies. Mother instrumental
> in getting her to marry another man. Yet in end it is seen secretly
> mother thinks daughter shd have remained virgin to old love &
> herself feels has shamed herself before old love's memory.[14]

By all accounts as honourable and decent as his brother, in the autumn of
that year William Winter married Maggie Barrie in a quiet, one might
almost say apologetic, ceremony. When the Barrie family occasionally
wondered if William just might have been profiting from his brother's
death, perhaps it slipped their minds that William, too, was in mourning.
Whatever the thoughts that went through this good-natured and long-
suffering man's head, during a marriage lasting forty-two years Maggie
never quite permitted her husband to forget that he was really her second
choice.

The newlyweds moved to Medstead in Hampshire, where William
carried on his work as an academic coach to school pupils. Barrie was
with them for much of that autumn. No doubt his accommodating
brother-in-law wouldn't have objected, while his sister may still have
needed his company. His thoughts regarding his own future, and Mary
Ansell's possible part in it, were confused. By remaining out of town so
much that autumn, Barrie was hedging, but he easily convinced himself
it was because work on *Sentimental Tommy* was proving so difficult. The
notes went back and forth with him from London to Hampshire, as he
struggled to decide what he was doing. This is surely reflected in Tommy's
response to Grizel's cry:

> 'But you must decide!' . . .
> 'I needna,' he stammered, 'till we're at Tilliedrum. Let's speak
> about some other thing.'
> She rocked her arms, crying, 'It is so easy to make up one's mind.'
> 'It's easy to you that has just one mind . . . but not if you had
> as many minds as I have!' was Tommy's tormented reply.[15]

That autumn Barrie's brother Alick met Mary Ansell, and apparently
she confided in him. Although Mary was a member of a profession

Margaret Barrie thought was close to the devil, Alick found her sympathetic. He also quietly advised her to be patient. But Mary Ansell had already been patient. She had known Barrie for almost three years, and in 1893 a woman of thirty-three was obliged to act with prudence if she wasn't yet married. (Whether Barrie knew its falsehood is unclear, but Mary professed to be only twenty-six.[16]) Barrie meanwhile was torn over offering her his hand, when all his instincts were telling him that it was a dangerous thing to do. He would write:

> Into the life of every man, and no woman, there comes a moment when he learns suddenly that he is held eligible for marriage. A girl gives him the jag, and it brings out the perspiration . . . soon thereafter, or, at worst, sooner or later (for by holding out he only puts the women's dander up), he is led captive to the Cuttle Well.[17] [This is the place in Thrums where betrothals were made.]

Barrie's preoccupation was publicly recorded as long before as 1887, when he had written an article for the *Edinburgh Evening Post* entitled 'My Ghastly Dream'.

> When this horrid nightmare got hold of me, and how, I cannot say, but it has made me the most unfortunate of men. In my early boyhood it was a sheet that tried to choke me in the night. At school it was my awful bed-fellow with whom I wrestled nightly while the other boys in the dormitory slept with their consciences at rest. It assumed shape at that time: leering, but fatally fascinating; it was never the same, yet always recognisable. One of the horrors of my dream was that I knew how it would come each time, and from where. My weird dream never varies now. Always I see myself being married, and then I wake up with the scream of a lost soul . . . My ghastly nightmare always begins in the same way. I seem to know that I have gone to bed, and then I see myself slowly wakening up in a misty world.

On the morning of 1st December, after an evening hosting a banquet for the Allahakbarries, Barrie rushed for the Edinburgh train; his mother was once again dangerously ill. As he sat beside her in Kirriemuir she passed in and out of consciousness and sometimes mistook him for her long-dead father. He wrote in his notebook, 'An old woman's thoughts on death – secret feelings, wistful, afraid, wandering mind . . . her love for her father – as aged she thinks she is young again, & he is alive. She thinks her son is him.'

Slowly, to his immense relief, she recovered, and he decided to stay on, working at his novel over Christmas and into the New Year. A fortnight after presiding at a Burns Night dinner he wrote an article for the *Observer* entitled 'Wrecked on an Island'. This was Barrie's last piece of miscellaneous journalism, and also the first time he put into print his fascination with islands. Concluding the article on a melancholy note he said, 'but, alackaday, these joys are only for the imagination'.

Something finally put an end to Barrie's vacillation over marriage and he came to a decision. On 1st March he was elected to one of London's most distinguished clubs, The Reform, and immediately afterwards he made the journey home to Kirriemuir. With much apprehension he was travelling north to tell his mother that he and Miss Ansell had become engaged. No one must know yet, not even friends, for Barrie was unable to proceed any further until he had been given his mother's blessing. Or was it permission? If he couldn't persuade Margaret Barrie out of her doubts then, just as his disapproval would have brought a halt to his sister's marriage plans, there could be no marriage between the actress and Margaret Barrie's son. But circumstances were swiftly to take a hand.

No one now knows exactly what passed between Barrie and his mother, except that he went out on one of his long walks. Apparently he lay down – to think? – on the damp ground. He caught a cold, and as usual this became bronchitis, only this time it was worse than normal and he rapidly developed both pleurisy and pneumonia. It was the longest and most serious illness he had ever experienced. The tension caused by his attempt to sever himself from his mother may well have precipitated this episode of dangerous illness. For weeks his life hung by a thread. At first his sister Jenann tended not only her ailing mother but also her critically ill brother. The doctor was unsure as to the prognosis, while the national newspapers kept up a running commentary – accurate or not – on the progress of the young author's affliction.

Leaving his practice in Bristol, Dr Murray (husband to Barrie's sister Isabella) travelled up to Kirriemuir to assist the local doctor. Soon afterwards, while the newspapers speculated, Mary Ansell left London and also made the journey to Scotland. Between them they helped the exhausted Jenann and battled for Jamie's life. Slowly the patient's health began to improve. It appeared he was not going to die.

By the end of June, although as yet still weak and prone to infection, Barrie was well enough to appreciate the telegrams, letters and articles heralding the success of the first English performance of his play, *The Professor's Love Story*, being staged by Willard at the Comedy Theatre in London. Hardly had the reviews begun to come out when someone got wind of Barrie's engagement and word was rapidly spread throughout the press. This was the first any of his friends had heard of the forthcoming marriage between Mr J. M. Barrie and his pretty fiancée, the actress Miss Mary Ansell. To his friend Quiller-Couch on 1st July Barrie wrote,

> I could make a long letter of it but am shaky with a pen . . . My lungs are quite right again, and I have only to pick up strength now. Miss Ansell, who has an extraordinary stock of untrustworthy information on diseases of the human frame, knows all about quinsey and says she sympathises in full. Yes, it is all true though it was in the papers, and I am just recovering from the pleasure of a letter on the subject – yours – which is not comic. Even so long ago as when I was going to you in Bedford Gardens I was beginning to hope that this would come about, and I am not in a position to deny, as the Speaker would say, that the obvious happiness of you two seemed to me a most enviable thing. We have worked hard to get married unbeknown to the lady journalists but vainly. In about a week it will be, – up here, so that we can go off together straight away, she to take charge.[18]

Barrie did indeed want the companionship and stability he saw that a good marriage could bring. But he omitted to tell Quiller-Couch that his apprehension about such commitment and the consequent loss of freedom consumed him with fear. What proved the final spur to his decision we do not know; he appears never to have spoken about it to anyone. Both the engagement and then the marriage ceremony itself were successfully kept a secret from the newlyweds' friends. Neither is there reference to it in their letters, or the books they subsequently wrote. Meanwhile, in keeping with Barrie's long-standing custom of committing his major preoccupations to his notebooks, a few days before his marriage to Mary Ansell he jotted down – as always as if for a projected story – some ominous lines:

> – Our love has brought me nothing but misery . . .
> – Boy all nerves . . . 'You are very ignorant.'
> . . . How? Must we instruct you in the mysteries of love-making?[19]

The wedding was a very quiet affair. Under Scottish law the ceremony was permitted to take place in Barrie's parents' home, at which only immediate family were present. It was said that the bridegroom was still weak, and unable to deal with any large gathering of people. Shortly after the ceremony the young couple left Scotland for a month-long honeymoon in Switzerland, where Barrie would continue his recuperation.

Although his income was now sizeable and promised to become larger, several months later the newlyweds had still not found somewhere permanent to live. Meanwhile, on the advice of friends, who appreciated Barrie's lack of skill at striking a bargain, he had put his work into the hands of one of the best contemporary agents, Arthur Addison Bright. It was Bright who had recently negotiated a good contract with Willard for the British staging of *The Professor's Love Story*, which, as its success grew, was providing a good steady income for its author.

After brief spells in a number of London lodgings, the Barries spent part of the autumn with Maggie and William in Hampshire. Then, in November, they travelled down to Cornwall to spend several cheerful weeks near the Quiller-Couches. Barrie had written saying:

> The sort of thing we want would be two sitting rooms, one of them such as I could work in and smoke in, and a good bedroom. An extra bedroom would be an advantage in case anyone came to see us. Also we have a dog which needs a bit of garden ground to grow in, which he does a foot or so a night.[20]

The couple were now acompanied by a St Bernard puppy, Porthos, discovered by Mary in Switzerland and sent on after their honeymoon. Porthos grew at an alarming rate and appeared even larger beside his master and mistress, each as small and delicate as the other. Although nominally Mary's dog, Porthos's chief affections were quickly appropriated by his master, who daily threw himself into a series of ingenious and lengthy games with the ever eager puppy.

In later, sadder times, Mary Barrie would write in a volume of autobiography:

> Perhaps my love for dogs, in the beginning, was a sort of mother-love. Porthos was a baby when I first saw him: a fat little round young thing. The dearest of all in a litter of St Bernards ... [Porthos] passionately loved his master. He really loved him more than he did me. It was a case of Mary and Martha. I gave him medicine, and kept him clean, and generally looked after him, but his master played with him. And he was a genius at games. They had fearful wrestling matches. These went on until both were exhausted. And they ran races, in and out of the rooms, up and down the stairs, out of the

front door, in by the back, over and over again . . . When it was all
over I went round collecting the debris.[21]

In spite of being spoilt, Porthos was an animal of great character, whose
size meant that he was unfailingly conspicuous. The Quiller-Couches' boy,
Bevil, now almost five years old, was captivated, as was Barrie by the boy. It
wasn't so much childrens' innocence Barrie cherished, it was consistent unpredictability he celebrated. He loved – and encouraged – the child's bouts of
anarchy and awkwardness. He wasn't troubled by the ingratitude, selfishness,
conceit or primitive savageries, and delighted in the way these states could
change so rapidly to warmth, kindness or a touching generosity. Joyfulness
and love one moment, fury and hatred the next; and then all is forgotten in
a competition to see who can be first to reach the top of a tree.

These traits, disconcerting to most adults, were the very qualities that
Barrie found so fascinating. In celebrating what it was to be a child he
was also perfecting his appreciation of the problem of growing up, the
theme that was the undercurrent to all his thoughts. On the one hand
he was a responsible married man, while on the other he had built his
life around a complex set of schemes devised to keep the adult world at
bay. His passion for cricket, draughts, the games with his dog – a dog
remains for ever a kind of child – were part of the fabric he constructed.
He understood far better than most what was lost, and what was gained
by growing up, by maturity and civilisation.

Barrie none the less wanted the best of both the worlds – fantasy and
reality – he always straddled. Accordingly, he treated children as if they
were his equals, and used his genius for transforming himself into one
of them, playing with absolute dedication games of make-believe like no
grown-up they had ever known. Indeed, it was a rare child who could
resist the magic of Barrie's presence; a rare child who wasn't entranced
by the stories of pirates, fairies and islands strange and far away; by performances of such astonishing anarchy and imagination that they found
themselves drawn into some of the most unforgettable games they would
ever remember playing.

Pamela Maude, whose father was to act in many of Barrie's plays,
recalled the spell he cast over children:

He was unlike anyone we had ever met or would meet in the future
. . . Mr Barrie talked a great deal about cricket and wanted Margery
[her sister] to like it and be boyish, but the next moment he was
telling us about fairies as though he knew all about them. He was
made of silences but we didn't find these silences strange; they were
so much part of him . . .

Mrs Barrie was lovely . . . but we could not feel at ease with her. She did not talk to us and she never smiled when we were with her. Mr Barrie did not talk and he did not smile, and yet he was our companion. When we were away from him he seemed to be with us; he was more present than our parents or Mrs Barrie, who were beside us.

Mr Barrie held out a hand to each of us in silence, and we slipped our own hand into his and walked, still silently, into the beech wood. We shuffled our feet through leaves and listened . . . for sudden sounds, made by birds and rabbits. One evening we saw a pea-pod lying in the hollow of a great tree trunk and we brought it to Mr Barrie. There inside was a tiny letter, folded inside the pod, that a fairy had written. Mr Barrie said he could read fairy writing and read it to us. We received several more, in pea-pods, before the end of our visit.[22]

Barrie's Scottish heritage, the heritage of fairy stories and spirits, gave him these creatures as an enduring part of his inner landscape. And as the man who would create Tinker Bell, the most famous fairy in modern literature, he could see perfectly the fairies' similarity to children. He understood that like them small children are creatures as yet without real character. Indeed, as creatures of temperament and mood, both fairies and children abjure it. Children are like the weather, not the structure of the soul. To be an adult is to have intentions, and by implication to understand that time is a real and pressing thing. For small children (and fairies), however, as incarnations of self-indulgence, time is rejected, it has no meaning; there is no past or future, because there is only now, now, *now*.

It is clear that in playing with children Barrie was not only put in touch with his own childhood, but that play also acted as a catalyst for his work. This was not all, for he took a double stance. Play, or crucially the fantasy element of it, not only liberated his imagination, it was also an integral part of what he wrote. His writing was not only infused with fantasy, but, as the central subject of his most important work, it was also something he stood outside to observe and discuss. As a writer Barrie didn't separate the notions of entertainer, maker or explorer. He presented his explorations to his audience as light-hearted entertainments, in a manner which was acceptable to the popular taste of the day. Centred in the borderland between fantasy and reality, these explorations were sometimes grim and dark. And Barrie instinctively understood that his messages would not be palatable without a certain amount of sweetening and diversionary amusement. In the past the role of Chief Messenger had been a dangerous one; in bringing bad news to the King he might well lose his head.

But what was the position of Barrie's companions, the children, in his explorations of make-believe? In story after story, folklore warns of the dangers of venturing unprotected into the land of the fairies, or of remaining there for any length of time. Either the adventurer runs the risk of being lost there, never to return, or, if they do, their bewitchment will often make the everyday world of real men and women appear so drab and grey as to be almost unendurable. Barrie was an adept, who had been toughening himself for decades in the techniques of survival in those strange regions. But even he was not impervious to their effects and the disappointment and dullness of 'return', and would write, 'I fancy I try to create an artificial world to myself because the one I really inhabit . . . becomes too sombre.'[23]

Although 1894 was a momentous year for Barrie, it ended with the premature death of Robert Louis Stevenson, a friend from halfway across the globe. While the Barries were in Cornwall, far away on his Pacific island Stevenson was losing his long battle with tuberculosis. He and Barrie had never succeeded in meeting, but this was not for lack of Stevenson's trying. Although Barrie referred to their exchange of 'thoughts that run to columns of the *Times* in length', his letters to Stevenson appear to have been lost. Barrie commented on this in his notebook in 1922: 'Odd that with so much of R. L. S. none of the letters *to* him published. Perhaps not kept.' We are thus left to guess at their content through Stevenson's replies:

They tell me your health is not strong. Man, come out here and try the Prophet's chamber. There's only one bad point to us – we do rise early. The Amanuensis states that you are a lover of silence – and that ours is a noisy house – and she is a chatterbox . . . We would have some grand cracks! . . . come, it will broaden your mind, and be the making of me . . . [5th Dec 1892]; We all join in the cry, 'Come to Vailima!' My dear Sir, your soul's health is in it – you will never do the great book, you will never cease to work in L., etc till you come to Vailima. [7th Dec 1893]; This is the last effort of an ulcerated conscience. I have been so long owing you a letter, I have heard so much of you from the Press, from my mother and Graham Balfour, that I have to write a letter no later than today or perish in my shame, but the deuce of it is, my dear fellow, that you write such a good letter that I am ashamed to exhibit myself before my junior (which you are after all) in the light of the dreary idiot I feel [14th July 1894][24]

Stevenson picks up again later:

> No, Barrie, 'tis in vain they try to alarm me with their bulletins.
> No doubt you're ill, and unco ill, I believe, but I have been so often
> in the same case that I know pleurisy and pneumonia are in vain
> against Scotsmen who can write (I once could). You cannot imagine
> how near me this calamity brings you . . . Keep your heart up and
> you'll do . . . Mount, sir, into a little frigot of 5,000 tons or so and
> steer peremptorily for the tropics . . . [29th July 1894][25]

Then in August, lonely, homesick, aching for a fellow spirit, and understanding that his health was worsening, Stevenson had written, 'I tell you
frankly you had better come soon. I'm sair failed a'ready; and what I may
be, if you continue to dally, I dread to conceive.' Many years later Barrie
recalled to his friend Quiller-Couch their sad walk around the harbour
at Fowey on hearing news of Stevenson's death, and how they had
mourned his loss to the world.

In March the following year another scare over Margaret Barrie's health
sent her son, her new daughter-in-law and their dog rushing for the
Dundee train. Once again she pulled through, but now her memory was
failing and she spent as much time in her youthful past as she did in the
present. Barrie saw his mother's decline, yet he was unable to discover a
route by which its inevitability might become any easier for him to bear.

House-hunting continued and he wrote to a friend, 'We have not fixed
on a house yet, but unless something else turns up it will be the Chiltern
Hills (in Buckinghamshire). I wasn't happy in London, chiefly perhaps
because I wasn't working, but it impressed me as a werry hollow place.'[26]
By June he appears to have recovered his old enthusiasm for the city and
with Mary had finally settled on a house in Gloucester Road. Just a short
walk across Kensington Gore and then Porthos was free for his daily run
in Kensington Gardens, part of that large green breathing space adjoining
Hyde Park. In those days much of Kensington Gardens had still an
unmanicured pastoral feel to it, as sheep grazed the long grass, and the
Serpentine island and its inlets were, as now, alive with wildfowl. As long
as the Broad Walk and the Round Pond were avoided, it was possible to
walk through large stretches of woodland and almost believe one was in
the country.

Externally number 133 Gloucester Road looked ponderous and undis-
tinguished, but inside, Mary Barrie, who was noted for the stylishness of
her own appearance, could for the first time exercise her artistry on a
house. She was luxuriating in the knowledge that she and Jim – she

could never bring herself to call Barrie by his Scottish diminutive –
would at last be living in a house of their own. With a team of workmen
to help her, Mary made 133 into an elegant yet welcoming place. She
spent considerably on the house, but as a practical woman she also oversaw
its organisation, financial and otherwise. In addition she did her best to
curb her husband's slapdash habits with cheques, and they no longer lay
fallow in drawers or his jacket pockets. If Mary may on occasion have
tried to moderate her husband's feelings for his homeland, his dedication to his family, and in particular his mother, it goes unrecorded. Certainly
the roots of his attachment were most complex and any attempts at
weaning him from his mother would have been met with a most stubborn resistance.

On the first floor of Gloucester Road, above the front door, was Barrie's
study. Here, hour after hour, the dog Porthos lay, keeping a vigilant watch
over his master, while he in turn wrote or indulged his now unfailing
habit of pacing up and down and smoking interminably. Barrie's illness
the previous summer had meant there was no cricket, but this year in
collecting together his team of Allahakbarries he enjoyed asking several
of them to stay as guests at Gloucester Road. When he and Mary married
she had given up the stage, and for the moment devoted herself to domesticity and learning to be a wife. In their new house there were many
cheerful evenings for friends, while Mary, who was probably at her most
confident in her own home, flourished and showed herself a congenial
hostess. George Meredith, now ailing, came to stay while visiting his
doctors in London. Undeterred by his fame and reputation, whenever
they met Mary's lively and intelligent company was a fillip to Meredith's
sometimes sombre mood.

9

Dreams and Reality

In the summer of 1895, the Barries celebrated a year of marriage by returning to Switzerland for another holiday in the clear mountain air. Unable to leave without monitoring his mother's health, Barrie first took his wife to Scotland. By now Mary must have passed some of her mother-in-law's rigorous tests of seemliness and propriety – and devotion to her son – for the days in Kirriemuir passed uneventfully enough. No doubt it helped that, although presently in good health, Margaret was increasingly frail in body and mind, often unaware of any difference between past and present time.

All seemed well with Margaret, and Jamie and Mary duly left for their holiday in the Engadine, while each day Jenann sent to their luxurious mountainside hotel a letter assuring them of her mother's continuing health. Barrie could now well afford the elegant luxury the Hotel Maloja had to offer. Whether this was adequate as compensation for a wife whose husband was often silent or unable to leave his work is another matter. On 1st September, only hours after Barrie had received that day's reassurance from Jenann in Kirriemuir, another communication arrived. Barrie later wrote:

> The telegram said in five words that she [Jenann] had died suddenly the previous night. There was no mention of my mother, and I was three days' journey from home. The news I got on reaching London was this: my mother did not understand that her daughter was dead, and they were waiting for me to tell her.[1]

Jenann had died of cancer. Whether she or her mother had known she was suffering from a mortal illness is unclear, but Barrie would write, 'though we did not know it my sister was dying on her feet'. If Jenann did understand her fate there was, typically, no word of complaint. That night, after her tirelessly thoughtful ministerings to her failing mother were completed, she had gone quietly to bed. Next morning, when she didn't appear, the household was appalled to discover that during the night she had died. The family gathered, and unable to make Margaret Barrie comprehend the terrible news, for fear of what it might do to her if they persisted, it was decided to wait for Jamie. In the following days, as he made his way back across Europe to Scotland with Mary, despite the family's silence Margaret Barrie probably understood that the faithful daughter, whose life she had used up, was now gone.

Exhausted and deeply apprehensive, when Barrie at last reached Kirriemuir his brother Alick and their other sisters were waiting at Strath View to give him the final chapter of the story. The thing he had for so long dreaded had come to pass: his mother had died before he reached her. Margaret Barrie had slipped away just twelve hours before her youngest son could make his farewells. And so he arrived to find not one but two dead women laid out in the rooms at Strath View.

On 6th September 1895, the day of her seventy-sixth birthday, Margaret Barrie was buried in the cemetery on Kirriemuir's hill, beside her beloved son, David, and the daughter, Jenann, whose life had been sacrificed to such passionate devotion. The devotion of which Barrie would write, 'the fierce joy of loving too much, it is a terrible thing'.

Although Margaret's husband was still in reasonable health, at almost eighty-one he was unable to live alone. Strath View actually belonged to Margaret Barrie's brother, David Ogilvy, but at that moment no one in the family wanted to live there. David Barrie's relationship with Margaret's brother had always remained on a good footing, so he moved to Motherwell where his daughter, Sarah, would care for both elderly men. (Sarah had long ago been adopted by her uncle David Ogilvy the minister.) Thus, not long after the double burial service on Cemetery Hill, Strath View was closed up, and for the time being the Barrie family left the town of their birth behind.

Back in London, the Barries' friends noticed how Jamie remained particularly quiet. Overcome by his loss, for long periods his mind was far removed from his life in the south. And at these times it was quite impossible to penetrate the black cloud which had engulfed him. Mary meanwhile carried on, mustering her energy to offer her husband sympathy and support. With that tendency to submerge himself in a welter of emotion, although Barrie's gloom was understandable it must at times have been very difficult to live with. But was there something more? Notwithstanding all her efforts, Mary must that autumn have realised that, although wife and partner in name, no love or kindness she could offer seemed enough to fill the space left in her husband's life by the departure of his mother. Without having set out to take her mother-in-law's place, Mary had come to realise that Barrie's attachment to his mother was impregnable. She must by now also have begun to wonder how much of his real emotional space could be reserved for anyone else. Her husband's consuming worship of his mother would not diminish with her death.

Apparently resigned, however, Barrie obscured the depth of his loss when he wrote to his friend, W. E. Henley:

> My dear Henley
>   It is all as you say. My mother died full of years and honours . . . She was always the glory of my life, and now I sit thinking and thinking, but I cannot think of one little thing I cd have done for her that was left undone. That leaves me with a kind of gladness even now. What saddens me most is the loss of my sister, who had given a whole life's devotion to her.

As the autumn passed his thoughts turned to his notebooks. Blackness never stopped Barrie's pen for long. His need to write, to create, was compulsive. He also knew, both through instinct and force of habit, it was work that kept him sane. Learning more than most since earliest childhood how to draw strength from escape into his imagination, as the years transformed this therapeutic measure into writing, this was not without its drawbacks. A means to managing his life, writing also encouraged Barrie to avoid what was uncomfortable. In this way, the problems he would one day be forced to confront were accumulating. Meanwhile, his mind was experiencing a storm of activity and the notebooks were once again filling up. Life in Gloucester Road was slowly recovering its positive pattern; friends and new guests once again came to cheerful, amusing dinner parties, and the great sad-looking dog continued acting as a benign and uniting force in his master and mistress's house. Privately friends asked each other why there were as yet no children.

With *Sentimental Tommy* at last finished and due to appear by instalment in *Scribner's Magazine* in the new year, Barrie turned his attention to the introduction Charles Scribner had asked him to write. The novel was above all about childhood, and with much of his own thrown in it seemed quite natural to Barrie that the introduction should become an appreciation of his mother

Late in life he would say to a friend that 'the taking of myriad notes first has always been my way, and occupied me longer than the actual writing'. The writing of *Sentimental Tommy* was the product of a series of apparently unrelated ideas turned over in Barrie's mind for years. As early as 1888 we can see the first stirrings noted down. Odd words and phrases, such as 'Double Dykes', 'Thrums in London', led gradually to thoughts about someone called 'a Sentimentalist', in turn connected with an illegitimate young girl who is cursed. As yet it is unclear whether a father or a lover is the villain, but their association with the alcoholic 'Painted Lady' is not a good one, and by 1892 Barrie knows that the story's ending will be tragic.

In January of 1896 *Sentimental Tommy* finally began its serialisation in *Scribner's* with a long first instalment designed to whet the readers' appetites. (It was published as a novel in the autumn of that year.) The serial quickly attracted attention on both sides of the Atlantic, with a large following soon waiting in anticipation of what the outrageous Tommy Sandys would dare to think up next.

Sentimental Tommy, and the second part of the novel, *Tommy and Grizel*, contain passages of such breathtaking self-revelation that it has always been tempting for biographers to read them simply as Barrie's own thinly disguised story. These extraordinary books are, however, more complex than that. *Sentimental Tommy*, in particular, is a profound meditation on the nature of fantasy, reality, childhood, the passage of time and, by implication, one's end. In the introduction to the American edition Barrie wrote that the book wasn't what he'd meant it to be.

> Tommy ran away with its author. When we meet a man who interests us, and is perhaps something of an enigma, we may fall a-wondering what sort of boyhood he had; and so it is with writers who become inquisitive about their creations. It was Sentimental Tommy the man that I intended to write here; I had thought him out as carefully as was possible to me; but when I sat down to make a start I felt that I could not really know him at one and twenty unless I could picture him at fifteen, and one's character is so fixed at fifteen that I saw I must go farther back for him, and so I journeyed to his childhood. Even then I meant merely to summarise his early days, but I was loath to leave him, or perhaps it was he who was loath to grow up.

With this book Barrie had come to maturity. He was now completely himself and a master of his craft. In the simple sense *Sentimental Tommy* is a work of genius; it is an original making, a breaking of new ground. With his creation of the audacious Tommy Sandys, more than in any other novel of its period, Barrie had captured the high ground, making the literary territory of childhood his own.

Sentimental Tommy is not a novel of development; rather it is a series of episodes, a picaresque novel of the mind in which Tommy hardly changes at all. Almost fully formed when the novel opens, he has temperament, but it is doubtful whether he ever develops any character. Although the book is structurally flawed, its power emerges not from any formal elements, but from the astonishing vividness and virtuosity of the writing. It was said at the time that no one in the future could write about children without first reading *Sentimental Tommy*. Indeed, nothing like it had ever been written before.

Barrie set down what he had intuitively understood, and exemplified each time he played with children. With greater perceptiveness and clarity than any other writer before him, he understood that children's play arises from a realm of inner activity – the realm of our inner lives, which we refer to as fantasy or the imagination. Barrie showed that it is this inner world that crucially connects the adult to his child self. He described how it is the imagination that we take with us from childhood into adulthood, which nourishes our inner world – indeed, without it there can be no psychic health – for the remainder of our lives.

With the incorrigible Tommy Sandys, Barrie is saying that if we lose our life of fantasy we lose it at our peril. Therefore, in growing up we must not 'put away childish things' entirely, because not only is the imaginative-play aspect of childhood something we carry with us into adulthood, but, crucially, without it we cannot become fully adult. With his observations on Tommy's outrageous nature Barrie makes a series of momentous steps. Standing back, he reflects, and, sometimes with moving exactitude, addresses the central and ongoing problem of his own troubled life: this was the struggle to confront the relationship between fantasy and reality. As a novelist he presents Tommy Sandys as a symbol of both the question and the answer. In creating Tommy, he understands that the answer to this question doesn't lie in a series of statements set in stone. Through Tommy the answer must, like a child's nature, be forever alive, shifting and full of texture.

During the course of the book we watch then, as Tommy manufactures a plethora of ways in which to exert his imagination, to indulge his fantasy. But ultimately these all become means by which he avoids facing the truth. Hence, '"I believe it was," said Tommy. He had not thought of this before, but it was easy to him to believe anything.' And later: 'But his tendency to be anyone he was interested in implied enormous sympathy (for the time being) . . .'[2]

Young Tommy is a fantasist so remarkable he has difficulty in telling the difference between what is real and what is not, and this in turn leads him to a nagging uncertainty about who he actually is. As the beleaguered schoolmaster, Cathro, says of him:

He is constantly playing some new part – playing is hardly the word though, for into each part he puts an earnestness that cheats even himself, until he takes another . . . A single puff of wind blows him from one character to another, and he may be noble and vicious, and a tyrant and a slave, and hard as granite and melting butter all in a forenoon. All you can be sure of is that whatever he is he will be it in excess . . . Sometimes his emotions master him completely, at other times he can step aside . . . He baffles me.[3]

For Tommy the distinctions between fantasy and reality are so tenuously drawn that when Barrie says of him: 'He passes between dreams and reality as through tissue paper', the image is most apt. Images such as this are combined with Barrie's remarkable feel for dialogue to generate an atmosphere more powerful than any he has so far devised.

As the novel opens, little Tommy Sandys is living with his mother, Jean, in the East End of London.

Tommy first comes into view on a dirty London stair, and he was in sexless garments, which were all he had, and he was five . . .

This stair was nursery to all the children whose homes opened on it, not so safe as nurseries in the part of London that is chiefly inhabited by boys in sailor suits, but preferable as a centre of adventure, and here on an afternoon sat two. They were very busy boasting, but only the smaller had imagination, and . . . he used it recklessly . . .

Shovel, a man of seven, had said, 'None on your lip. You weren't never at Thrums yourself.'

Tommy's reply was, 'Ain't my mother a Thrums woman?'

Shovel, who had but one eye, and that bloodshot, fixed it on him threateningly.

'The Thames is in London,' he said.

''Cos they wouldn't not have it in Thrums,' replied Tommy.

''Ampstead 'Eath's in London, I tell yer,' Shovel said.

'The cemetery is in Thrums,' said Tommy.

'There ain't no queens in Thrums, anyhow.'

'There's the auld licht minister.'

'Well, then, if you jest see'd Trafalgar Square!'

'If you jest see'd the Thrums townhouse!'

'St Paul's ain't in Thrums.'

'It would like to be.'

After reflecting, Shovel said in desperation, 'Well, then, my father were once at a hanging.'

Tommy replied instantly, 'It were my father what was hanged.' . . .

[A gentleman – an unusual sight – passes them on the stairs.] Shovel had experience, and 'It's a kid or a coffin,' he said sharply, knowing that only birth or death brought a doctor here . . .

'Hello, it's your old woman!' cried Shovel. 'Is she a deader?' he asked, for funerals made a pleasant stir on the stair.

The question had no meaning for bewildered Tommy; but he saw that if his mother was a deader, whatever that might be, he had grown great in his companion's eye. So he hoped she was a deader.

'If it's only a kid,' Shovel began with such scorn that Tommy at once screamed, 'It ain't!'[4]

Tommy was wrong. It was Elspeth, his sister, announcing her arrival into the world. At first Tommy resents his displacement, and meditates chucking her out of the window, but his parent is a good enough mother, and he becomes reconciled. In fact, the two children became inseparable. Elspeth sticks like a leech, which is not surprising, since their mother works long hours and is often exhausted. Tommy's father, Tom Sandys, is a brute: a hard and wicked man, who uses his wife contemptuously. He comes back occasionally, and then finally to die.

Of this man who was his father he could get no hold. He could feel his presence, but never see him. Yet he had a face. It sometimes pressed Tommy's face against it in order to hurt him, which it could do, being all short needles at the chin . . .

There came a time when the man was always in bed, but still Tommy could not see his face . . .

An old man with a white beard and gentle ways, who often came to give the invalid physic, was standing at the bedside, and Tommy and his mother were sitting on the fender. The old man came to her and said, 'It is all over,' and put her softly into the big chair. She covered her face with her hands, and he must have thought she was crying, for he tried to comfort her. But as soon as he was gone she rose, with such a queer face, and went on tiptoe to the bed, and looked intently at her husband, and then she clapped her hands joyously three times.[5]

A few years pass, and the mother becomes ill, is dying. Knowing this, she determines to send her children back to Thrums. As a girl of seventeen she was betrothed to Aaron Latta, a weaver of Thrums, and was soon to be married. But at a dance she met Magerful Tam (Masterful Tom), the man who proved her undoing. Later on she resisted, and would have held him off, if Aaron had not let her down. Aaron was a coward, and did not defend her, so lost her to Magerful Tam.

The writing has both economy and a terrible power. D. H. Lawrence treats the same elemental theme, and illuminates it, but his version has not the chilling force of Barrie's writing. This has particular relevance when one remembers that Lawrence had read Barrie's work and greatly admired *Sentimental Tommy*, and its sequel, *Tommy and Grizel*. Indeed, Lawrence identified strongly with Barrie's anti-hero, Tommy, who finds the difference between reality and fiction so difficult to locate. Lawrence told his lover Jessie Chambers, whom he repeatedly broke with, that if she wanted to understand his predicament she should read *Sentimental Tommy*, who says, 'I want to love you, you are the only woman I ever wanted to love. But apparently can't.'

Lawrence was frightened of being like Barrie's Tommy, and repeatedly wrote about the man who was so much the detached, observing, self-conscious self that this imprisoned him in himself and prevented him from engaging directly and unconsciously with anyone. Like Barrie, Lawrence was deeply attached to his mother, calling her 'my love of loves'.[6]

In *Sentimental Tommy* Jean writes a letter back to Thrums to prevent her two children being left to starve in London. She asks someone to go to Aaron Latta and plead with him to come and collect them. After her death Latta does go down to London, and brings back Tommy and Elspeth, who then spend the rest of their childhood in Thrums. Tommy quickly becomes the leader of his age group, and all follow him willingly, except Grizel, the pretty, illegitimate daughter of the alcoholic Painted Lady, who lives at Double Dykes.

> The double dykes were built by a farmer fond of his dram, to stop the tongue of a water-kelpie which lived in a pool below and gave him a turn every night he staggered home by shouting, 'Drunk again, Peewitbrae!' and announcing, with a smack of the lips, that it had a bed ready for him in the burn. So Peewitbrae built two parallel dykes two feet apart and two feet high, between which he could walk home like a straight man. His cunning took the heart out of the brute, and water-kelpies have not been seen near Thrums since about that time.[7]

As the story evolves we see that the tension and calamity at its heart is the relationship between Tommy and the dignified young Grizel. Tommy is the world's most outrageous and compulsive fantasist. Forever inventing new aspects of his life, he finds it unsatisfying if his friends are too easily convinced.

To trick people so simply, however, is not agreeable to an artist, and he told them his name was Tommy Shovel, and that his old girl walloped him, and that his father found dogs, all which inventions [were] accepted as true. What is more noteworthy is that, as he gave them birth Tommy half believed them also, being already the best kind of actor.[8]

Poor Grizel, meanwhile, is a sunny and persistent realist: 'She wanted to ask Tommy now, and the next time she saw him she began at once. Grizel always began at once, often in the middle, she saw what she was making for so clearly.' Her sadness lies in being unable to fathom Tommy's many selves, his inability to understand the difference between what is real and what is not. She asks him if it's true that her mother, clearly suffering from consumption, will die, and Tommy replies,

'I – I oh, no, they soon get better.'
He said this because he was sorry for Grizel. There never was a more sympathetic nature than Tommy's. At every time of his life his pity was easily aroused for persons in distress, and he sought to comfort them by shutting their eyes to the truth as long as possible. This sometimes brought relief to them, but it was useless to Grizel, who must face her troubles.
'Why don't you answer truthfully?' she cried with vehemence. 'It is easy to be truthful!'[9]

One day Tommy is questioning Grizel about her mother.

'She walks up and down the Den, talking to the man.'
'And him no there?' cried Tommy, scared.
'No, there is no one there.' . . .
Tommy reflected, and then he said, 'She's daft.'
'She is not always daft,' cried Grizel. 'There are whole weeks when she is just sweet.' . . .
'Her name is Mary, I've heard?'
'Mary Gray is her name, but – but I don't think it is her real name.'
'How, does she no use her real name?'
'Because she wants her own mamma to think she is dead.'
'What makes her want that?'
'I am not sure, but I think it is because there is me. I think it was naughty of me to be born. Can you help being born?' . . .
'Where does the Painted Lady get her money?'

'Oh,' said Grizel, 'that is easy. She just goes into that house called the bank, and asks for some, and they give her as much as she likes.'[10]

As a literary artist Barrie doesn't of course solve the problem put forward in the book by sequential argument. He does it by dramatisation. Tommy is dominated by fantasy, while Grizel lives by an equally intense attachment to reality and truth. They are drawn to each other by their common vitality and sympathy, but the profound opposing forces are always there to see.

Each has a hard childhood. Tommy grows up with a mother who is broken in spirit, with an occasional, wicked father. Using his unfailing imaginative powers, he continually evades the burdens of a harsh and dreary reality. Grizel also lives with a broken, abandoned mother; someone who has retreated into sentimental delusion, interspersed with fits of outright madness. Grizel's response is the polar opposite to Tommy's: she holds rigidly and obsessively to accuracy and truthfulness. For her there is no leeway. She makes no distinction between imagination and lies, finding both methods equally reprehensible.

'Hod ahint a tree!' cried Tommy, hastily, and he got behind one himself; but he was too late; Elspeth was upon them; she had caught them together at last.

Tommy showed great cunning. 'Pretend you have eggs in your hand,' he whispered to Grizel, and then, in a loud voice, he said: 'Think shame of yoursel', lassie, for harrying birds' nests. It's a good thing I saw you, and brought you here to force you to put them back. Is that you, Elspeth? I catched this limmer wi' eggs in her hands (and the poor birds sic bonny singers too!) and so I was forcing her to—'

But it would not do. Grizel was ablaze with indignation. 'You are a horrid story-teller,' she said, 'and if I had known you were ashamed of being seen with me, I should never have spoken to you. Take him,' she cried, giving Tommy a push towards Elspeth. 'I don't want the mean little story-teller.'

'He's not mean!' retorted Elspeth.

'Nor yet little!' roared Tommy.

'Yes, he is,' insisted Grizel, 'and I was not harrying nests. He came with me here because he wanted to.'

'Just for the once,' he said, hastily.

'This is the sixth time,' said Grizel, and then she marched out of the Den.[11]

Tommy's inability to commit is epitomised in the following:

> [He] swithered wretchedly on one foot: 'I didn't put them on to come with you,' he explained, 'I just put them on in case I should come wi' you.'
>   'Are you not coming?'
>   'How can I ken?'[12]

Writing shortly after *Sentimental Tommy*'s publication the *Academy* said in 1896:

> We have laughed, we have wept, we have on occasion hardly known whether to laugh or weep; we have been captured at the beginning and held to the end . . . and it suddenly flashes upon us that there is no plot . . . [it is] a series of short stories – always connected with Tommy, but not always connected with each other. The boy lives in the present, rarely recalling the past, rarely regarding the future. Life goes by him in episodes. He has not the sustained passion or the permanent ambition that makes connecting links.

Despite the hastiness and prudery of some of *Sentimental Tommy*'s reviewers, there were others, like the critic above, who had taken trouble with this strange book and its author. On both sides of the Atlantic a number of reviewers understood what a remarkable thing it was Barrie had achieved. One talked of 'being reduced to a crude and unmitigated joy. Perhaps Tommy's innumerableness, his frequent embarrassment in determining which he really was, his impersonal pride in his respective selves, is the most striking feature of this profound . . . study of a child's soul wondering at itself.'[13] The *Bookman* said Tommy would 'take a permanent place in the affections of the English reader'. He was 'in many respects a creation unique in litera-ture'. In 1899 it was correctly recognised that it was the author's master-piece 'and that after reading *Sentimental Tommy* one is prepared to maintain that the advantage in some of the highest points, lies by no means with Dickens'.[14]

The narrator in *The Little Minister* had tried to convince his audience of his fantasies 'at the cost of truth to life'. But in *Sentimental Tommy* a subtle change had taken place. Here the narrator makes it clear that he is crit-ical of the fabulous Tommy Sandys, and the damaging effect his fantasies have upon the lives of those around him. Through Tommy, Barrie made the choice not to be dominated by fantasy but to both *investigate* what fantasy might be and to explore its effects on other people. The choice was not an easy one, and he wrote to his friend Quiller-Couch about his review of the book, 'You have found out some things about me and about the book that I thought were only known to myself.'[15] He may have been referring to Quiller-Couch's comment that Barrie 'had written this book in a mood of indignant revulsion from the picture of a soul, which . . . might have been his own'.

However much this might have been true, Barrie's ability to portray the struggle each of us has to accept reality in place of the easier and more seductive realms of fantasy was to become the most powerful and far-reaching aspect of his future work.

Barrie's American publisher, Charles Scribner, now reminded him that with the growth of his worldwide reputation, pirated editions of his work were increasing. Copyright had for centuries been the bane of every published author's life. Traditionally there was little means of redress when either whole sections of a work were used by someone else or, as in Barrie's case, entire books were brought out by a publisher who gave no royalties to the author. Just as writers such as Charles Dickens had impotently railed against the problems of copyright, from the beginning of Barrie's book-publishing career much of his work had been pirated in the States, with correspondingly fat profits for those prepared to do it.

In 1891 the Copyright Bill had finally made this practice illegal. However, as several of Barrie's most popular books were published before that date, none of these was covered and so the rogue publishers continued collecting the profits, rather than the British publishers or the author himself. Scribner suggested a plan benefiting both the author and his new publisher, which would avoid this continual leaching of the rewards of Barrie's labours. Scribner's would print a uniform edition of Barrie's works. In this edition the texts would be slightly revised by Barrie, he would write an introduction for each book and they would also have some illustrations, all of which would be protected under the new copyright laws. Thus all other publishers would be prevented from using Barrie's work, because unless the reader now bought one of these new editions he was neither getting the authorised version of his works nor the new introductions. Appreciating the extent to which his books were selling in foreign markets, Barrie was in favour of the plan; the series would be called the Thistle Edition.

Having launched himself into writing *Sentimental Tommy*'s preface for Scribner, it soon became apparent that it was outgrowing the scope of a normal introduction. Barrie carried on regardless, and eventually it became clear that the length of the piece meant it would have to be a book in its own right.

As *Sentimental Tommy* was based in Thrums and used the stories of the Auld Lichts Barrie had heard as a boy, inevitably he was thinking about his own past; a past linked more inextricably with his mother's than that of any normal child. As the words flowed from him, Barrie discovered that, instead of finding it painful to write about his mother, Margaret had become the subject of his book. He had found a way to assuage his grief.

His friend William Nicoll was so impressed with what he called 'the beauty and pathos' of the manuscript, he insisted that his firm, Hodder & Stoughton, must publish it. But how should the book be described? Was it a memoir? A tribute? Barrie refused to describe it, or categorise it. He simply called it *Margaret Ogilvy, by her son J. M. Barrie*, and to a casual reader, or misguided critic, the book did appear to be just that, a biography of the artist's mother.

How little the critic of the *Athenaeum*, for instance, understood Barrie when he wrote, 'This book has . . . the added virtue of being entirely and obviously a sincere study from life.'[16] The *British Weekly* misguidedly wrote that to criticise *Margaret Ogilvy* would be almost sacrilegious, because

> it stands unmatched in literature as an idyll of the divinest of human feelings – a mother's love . . . this is Mr Barrie's finest and noblest book . . . It has been so written that no book of the generation is so likely to outlive us all as this.

Another periodical, the *Critic*, was closer to the truth when its reviewer wrote, 'It is not precisely a biography on the one hand, nor a work of fiction on the other. It lives in the borderland between imagination and fact . . .'[17]

Barrie's imagination was indeed at work, and as he wove the story of his mother's life, he himself became a central part of it. *Margaret Ogilvy* became Barrie's vision of their joint past, something he was driven to shape in this way because this was the only way he could bear it to be. *Margaret Ogilvy* was the final offering to his mother, the final act of propitiation for not being his brother David. Just as the book was the vision of his mother Barrie found it necessary to create, so *Margaret Ogilvy* was in equal measure the fabrication of a version of autobiography that Barrie found endurable.

We read that harrowing interpretation of his brother David's death. We see its devastating effect upon their mother as she withdraws, broken, to her darkened room, and we note the complex methods her youngest son devised to survive the pain of his mother's retreat. Finally, we witness the little boy's pitiful efforts at self-elimination, concluding with Barrie's sorrowful admission, 'I had not made her forget the bit of her that was dead; in those twenty-nine years he [David] was not removed one day farther from her . . . When I became a man . . . he was still a boy of thirteen.'

The story moves on and Barrie constructs a vision of his early life; his first yearnings for literary fame. We are given the tale of the old tailor who impressed the young Barrie so much with Cowley's lines, making believe they were written for him.

> What can I do to be forever known,
> And make the age to come my own?

We read how those innumerable talks with his mother 'made her youth as vivid as my own . . . she told me everything . . . and so my memories of our little red town are coloured by her memories'. Memories filled his life until he imagined he felt all her feelings, including the frustrations at premature responsibility, so that 'when she told me her own experience we discovered that we [were] very like each other inside'. He says, 'What she had been, what I should be, these were the two great subjects between us in my boyhood, and while we discussed the one we were deciding the other, though neither of us knew that.'

Despite the sometimes cloyingly sentimental portrait of his mother presented in *Margaret Ogilvy*, there coexists Barrie's self-belief and heady ambition, his romanticising and exaggeration, his painful search for approval, and in conjunction these become oddly compulsive reading. His craving for maternal approval produces references such as 'my 1000 letters that she so carefully preserved, always sleeping with the last beneath the sheet, where one was found when she died'. But Barrie's need for approval, extending beyond the grave, combined with the creation of a personal history more bearable than the truth, is all so brilliantly constructed, so skilfully presented, that in the end we no longer quite know where either the real Barrie or his mother might lie.

When it was published, despite the overwhelmingly good reviews and the large sales, there were also those who found *Margaret Ogilvy* unsettling and 'in bad taste'. In his inimitable way Barrie had, more than ever before, succeeded in creating an unprecedented sense of intimacy with the reader by giving free rein to that confessional style so in advance of his time. It was this level of indiscretion that brought *Margaret Ogilvy* its detractors. They believed the book 'suffered from indelicacy', that 'the subject was too sacred and the details too intimate to be given to the public'. One of the most significant of its critics was Barrie's older brother, Alick.

Whatever some of his doubts may have been about Barrie's work, Alick had always been supportive. Indeed, without his years of thoughtful and generous sponsorship Barrie may never have advanced beyond those first uncoordinated attempts at authorship. But with *Margaret Ogilvy* it was just too close: the subject was after all Alick's mother, too. Indeed, the whole family were critical, but it was Alick who withdrew some of his support. He believed that what Jamie had written was inaccurate and an exposé of the family's privacy, seeing its publication as offensive and unacceptable. But Alick was unaware – how could he be otherwise – that Jamie's creativity was something over which the young author had only limited control. (He was after all an artist, in every one of whose hearts there lies a shard of ice.) So, how could Jamie apologise for this piece of writing, integral to his quest for his own identity? Besides, in his mind the book was a tribute to their mother. What was said, what was written between the two brothers is not known. But family legend has it that after this episode they were not on such close terms again.

It was understandable that poor Alick should find his brother's apparent misconstructions and motivation difficult to understand. It was understandable that he should object to Jamie's false picture of the humbleness of their origins, to some of the 'facts' which were simply wrong, and to the portrayal of their mother as a simple-minded peasant. Even the title of the book, *Margaret Ogilvy*, was an irritant. A 'foreigner' would be unlikely to know this, but in giving his mother her maiden name, Ogilvy, Barrie was imposing a more rural, less sophisticated set of habits upon her than she actually practised. Countrywomen in Scotland often continued to use their maiden name after marriage. The family, fellow Kirriemuirians, knew that this was something Margaret Barrie, a woman very much concerned with the social mobility of her family, would *never* have done.

The Barrie family may be forgiven their grievances against their famous brother, but what is not so forgivable is the naïveté and literal-mindedness with which some critics then, and in the future, launched their attacks on this extraordinary little book.

One may very well wonder why *Margaret Ogilvy* was ever written, except for private circulation, but Barrie threw the portrait of his mother into the whirlpool of commerce: in cold fact, cashing in on his own popularity. Not many men would deliberately expose their own domestic affairs in this fashion, but Barrie was one of the few; and we can only conclude that commercial success after a chilly boyhood, had turned his head. On the other hand, it is difficult to determine whether or not Margaret Barrie is true to the facts of the woman's life.[18]

On the one hand Barrie was very astute, and on the other only half conscious of what he did. *Margaret Ogilvy* was a complex and heartfelt book, but it certainly wasn't Barrie throwing his mother 'into the whirlpool of commerce'. He was *driven* to express himself, and *Margaret Ogilvy* was the result.

It doesn't take a particularly painstaking reading of his work to see that Barrie's truth is never so simple, so literal, as to be 'true to the facts'. Neither, though, did he intend to hoodwink his reader. He was searching after something essential; *Margaret Ogilvy* was, after all, a *portrait* of his mother, and Realism for him was uninteresting. What he wrote here, indeed what he was forever searching after, was something much broader than that. In *Margaret Ogilvy* he was trying to mediate a vision; a vision of his mother and himself.

Unable to draw any succour from her religious belief, Margaret Barrie had turned her son David's death into a cult of his memory. Her leading characteristic was pride, and this was attended by vanity, its more plebeian cousin.

When it was known that I had begun another story my mother might ask what it was to be about this time.

'Fine we can guess who it is about,' my sister would say pointedly.

'Maybe you can guess, but it is beyond me,' says my mother, with the meekness of one who knows that she is a dull person.

My sister scorned her at such times.

'What woman is in all his books?' she would demand.

'I'm sure I canna say,' replies my mother determinedly. 'I thought the women were different every time.'

'Mother, I wonder you can be so audacious! Fine you know what woman I mean.'

'How can I know? What woman is it? You should bear in mind that I hinna your cleverness . . .'

'I won't give you the satisfaction of saying her name. But this I will say, it is high time he was keeping her out of his books.'

And then as usual my mother would give herself away unconsciously. 'That is what I tell him,' she says chuckling, 'and he tried to keep me out, but he canna; it's more than he can do!'[19]

This illuminates the heart of Alick's discomfort and may account for the unease we ourselves feel when reading the book. At an unconscious level Alick was surely aware of a streak of ill-disciplined worldliness, a spiritual vulgarity in his mother which he, his father and his sister Jenann did not share. It was also a quality in Margaret that no one in the family had combated. Jamie, however, in this respect more like his mother, had revealed this to the public at large, and *this* was his unforgivable act.

In *Margaret Ogilvy* one cannot fail to notice two glaring omissions. Throughout the story of Barrie's life, his father is mentioned in only one or two anodyne phrases, such as: '. . . one who proved a most loving as he was always a well-loved husband'. In addition, nowhere in the entire book is there a mention of Mary, Barrie's wife.

10

America and Fame

With publication of *Sentimental Tommy* and *Margaret Ogilvy* imminent, in the autumn of 1896 the Barries boarded ship for the
United States with their friend William Nicoll. Barrie had
been persuaded to visit the United States as much as anything by the
thought of meeting one of his American literary heroes, George Cable.
Cable did for the southern American states what Barrie was supposed
to have done for Kirriemuir with his Thrums books. In addition, Barrie's
agent, Arthur Addison Bright, was keen to engineer a meeting between
Barrie and the New York impresario Charles Frohman. Despite Barrie's
misgivings, Bright had been trying to persuade him to turn *The Little
Minister* into a play. Eventually Bright had begun work on it himself and,
through the influential New York agent Elizabeth Marbury, he had
managed to negotiate a provisional contract with Charles Frohman, in
his own way as outstanding as Barrie himself.

On arrival in New York, to the visitors' consternation, accompanying
the reception party was a large deputation of reporters. As publicity of
this kind was something Barrie prided himself on avoiding, he was
dismayed. As early as 1894, when he was being approached regularly for
interviews, he said to a friend, 'McClure's Magazine dogs me as if it wanted
my hand in marriage.' And later: 'Never shall man or maid interview me.'
Despite this he was complicated in his attitude to a public image, and
learnt to manage the name of J. M. Barrie with considerable sophistication.
Many years later a well-known reviewer would say, 'No other dramatist
has given so much delight to so many people and at the same time lived
so apart from public life. The newspaper "interviewer" has long regarded
him as morbidly elusive . . .'[1] Barrie was genuinely a private man, but at
the same time he understood with a shrewd instinct the notion of
remaining mysterious. He gave out just enough information to keep his
public beguiled.

During those weeks spent in America reporters continued to besiege
the visitors. On one or two occasions Barrie did speak to them, only to

regret it afterwards. Regardless of whether he spoke to the journalists or not, there were regular banner headlines about the celebrated Scottish author now staying in the United States. Having dodged the journalists, first in New York and then in cities as far away as New Orleans, from morning till night the visitors were fêted and entertained.

For seven weeks America was clamouring to meet them; even their kinsmen were attentive, with an invitation to visit Lord and Lady Aberdeen in Canada, where Lord Aberdeen was then Governor-General. Barrie felt Canada was too far, turned them down and instead, while squeezing in short bursts of sightseeing, his party spent days and nights in trains travelling to Washington, Boston, Harvard, Concord, Northampton and Salem, and everywhere parties were thrown and receptions held in their honour. In Washington the Barries enthusiastically tried out the new craze – bicycle riding – and bought one each on returning home.

During his tour Barrie was flattered at the distinguished literary company interested to make his acquaintance. This included luminaries such as William James, the philosopher brother of Henry; novelist and man of letters William Howells; Charles Eliot Norton, influential Harvard professor and critic; and Charles Scribner, Barrie's American publisher, soon to become one of the foremost in the country. A couple of years later Barrie recorded: 'I had the distinction of supping with Colonel Roosevelt . . . We began at eleven and I left at two.'[2]

The last few days back in New York were a frenzy of lunches and supper parties. One was given by the Aldine Club, where a piper marched up and down, thistles and heather decorated the dining hall, the company ate haggis, and more than a hundred publishers and writers thumped on the tables and cheered, as William Nicoll waxed emotional and Barrie amused in their valedictory speeches. After such overwhelming hospitality the exhausted travellers were relieved to be returning home. Nicoll wrote to his future wife, 'We have done very well, have got on splendidly together, have met with unbounded kindness, but I am so homesick.'

Finally, it was time to board ship. Following a rough passage back across the Atlantic, Barrie would write enthusiastically, 'We had a roaring time in America.' In addition to the immense stimulation and good publicity for his books, the visit to the United States set in motion the first steps in a relationship that would eventually develop into one of the most important of Barrie's life.

Charles Frohman was a theatrical producer of genius. He was so prolific that at the turn of the century a list of his productions amounts to a record – including both actors and playwrights – for the English-speaking stage. From German-Jewish immigrant parentage, Frohman had grown up in New York. Like Barrie he was a small man with boundless energy, and since boyhood this had been directed unswervingly towards the stage. By 1896 his success was tremendous, and although prepared to take enormous risks on plays and actors, money for its own sake held little interest for him. He never quite knew how rich he was, and was vague about exactly how many times he had made and lost fortunes. He ran a huge organisation of his own making, but what mattered above all was the continuing crusade of his work. Frohman brought fame and fortune to many actors and a number of playwrights. A man almost completely without education, he had an immensely quick mind. He was not only hard-headed and obstinate, but also idealistic, broad-minded and kind. Much later, after his death, Barrie wrote of him,

> His energy . . . was like a force of nature, so that if he ever retired from the work he loved (a thing incredible) companies might have been formed . . . for exploiting the vitality of this Niagara of a man. They could have lit a city with it.
>
> He loved his schemes. They were a succession of many-coloured romances to him, and were issued to the world not without the accompaniment of the drum, but you would never find him saying anything of himself. He pushed them in front of him, always taking care that they were big enough to hide him . . . I have never known anyone more modest and no one quite so shy . . . A sense of humour sat with him through every vicissitude like a faithful consort.[3]

The initial stages of Frohman's relationship with Barrie have become confused in the retellings. At best we can say that Frohman read the play version of *The Little Minister* while Barrie was in New York; we cannot be sure that they met on this occasion. Frohman returned the manuscript, saying that it just wasn't quite right. What he wanted was a vehicle in which to launch a young actress he believed he could make into a star. The story has it that watching this actress, Maude Adams, one night in her current production, Barrie turned to his wife and said that he had found his Babbie, the heroine of *The Little Minister*. The only way this could happen, however, would be if he completely rewrote the play in order to make Maude Adams's part more prominent.

Soon after the Barries' return from America, the publication of first *Sentimental Tommy* – dedicated to 'my wife' – and then *Margaret Ogilvy* brought immediate success. Some reviewers may have been unsure about *Sentimental Tommy*, but the public had no doubts, and British and American sales amounted to over twenty-five thousand copies in the first year. Meanwhile, *Margaret Ogilvy*; a book unlike anything its Victorian audience had come across before, sold 40,000 copies in a matter of weeks, and went on to do just as well in the States. With limited editions in the first year the books together sold over 120,000; figures which even by today's standards are large. In 1896 few writers were doing better. A dozen or so were doing as well, but in the days before the introduction of book clubs or societies this was a remarkable achievement and made Barrie one of the most talked-about writers of the day. Knowing little of the financial details, but content to allow Mary and Gilmour to organise them, at the age of thirty-six Barrie was becoming an affluent man.

Shortly afterwards he travelled with Mary up to Edinburgh, where he was to give a speech to a mixed company of students and worthies. As a prominent Scottish writer he had been deputed to help drum up support for Robert Louis Stevenson's memorial; two years after his death nothing had yet been arranged. The issue had become a sticking point and Edinburgh was divided, with the students and the older intelligentsia on one side and the mass of the establishment on the other. Stevenson's reputation had always been poor with the respectable Godfearing Scottish establishment; they were suspicious of his moral and religious outlook, and at the time didn't anyway think too much of most fiction.

This was Barrie's first public appearance in Edinburgh since his rather lacklustre graduation fourteen years earlier. Now he was a famous writer returning to his academic roots. Championing his hero Stevenson, he gave a rousing and (what was to become a hallmark) eccentric speech. As a natural performer his speech-making would grow increasingly polished over time. None the less, although it was always done with an assumed spontaneity and nonchalance, in reality he spent hours, sometimes days, preparing these talks, by which time he had driven himself to a state of intense anxiety.

Years later, as a very famous man, he would write of trying to urge himself 'to face the ordeal of public speech'. Yet at the same time he loved it, especially the actor's recognition that when it was going well the audience was indeed in the palm of his hand. On this occasion he asked the permission of the chairman, Lord Rosebery, to put his hands in his pockets to 'keep them at rest', because he said he was unsure what to do. At the end of his address a thousand students roared their appreciation and Rosebery and Sidney Colvin – Stevenson's literary executor and future editor of his letters – gave Barrie their enthusiastic votes of thanks.

In the early summer of 1897 the country was preparing to celebrate Queen Victoria's Diamond Jubilee, and the Barries were once again staying in the village of Broadway. As the names of the players and guests had grown more celebrated with each passing year, the Barries were in

Broadway to commemorate the first Allahakbarries match fought there, and won by just a run. This time they were staying with the de Navarros; Mary de Navarro, née Anderson, was much celebrated at the time for her beauty and her acting. At the Jubilee match the artists included Frank Millet, Alfred Parsons, Herman Herkomer and the illustrator Bernard Partridge. Conan Doyle played for the writers again, as did Gilmour, the influential journalist-editor H. W. Massingham and the poet-playwright John Davidson. At Broadway this year one of the new players, Charles Turley Smith, was destined to become one of Barrie's closest friends.

'Turley', as his friends called him, made his living as a reviewer, publisher's reader and occasional novelist. An unassuming man of rare sympathy, he possessed a kindly common sense, unfailing humour and an indefinable aura of stillness. Turley's stillness, his gentleness and courtesy, meant that his many friends, soothed by this benign presence, felt their lives more manageable and improved by having spent time in his company. Sharing, as Turley and Barrie did, an equal obsession with cricket, each also kindled the other's charm and wit. With time their friendship would progress to one of undemanding and unpossessive intimacy; in later years they would write to one another almost every week.

That spring Charles Frohman made his annual visit to England, where he habitually took up residence in a suite at the Savoy Hotel. His custom was to read through a large number of scripts, then interview a stream of authors and actors. Out of this quantity of reading and meetings he would plan a new clutch of plays. Barrie's agent, Bright, went to see Frohman with the rewritten script of *The Little Minister*, and this time Frohman said he would take it for his protégée Miss Adams. He wasn't, however, prepared to take a risk on it in England as well, so Bright must find a London producer.

Shortly after Bright and Frohman's meeting, Barrie happened to be playing billiards with the actor-manager Cyril Maude at the Garrick Club. (Maude had acted in Barrie's earlier dramatic mistake, *Richard Savage*.) It seems Barrie told him something of the *Little Minister* story, after which Maude moved fast. He and Frederick Harrison, with whom he was presently running the Haymarket Theatre, asked to read the play, were enthusiastic, and rapidly negotiated a deal through Arthur Bright. *The Little Minister* would go into rehearsal and open at the Haymarket in the autumn of that year.

In July the Barries were holidaying in Switzerland and France. Barrie was in thrall to the glamour of France, Paris above all, and could now easily afford to visit several times a year. Most often he and Mary went with a small party of friends, and, in common with many other travellers, away from his own milieu Barrie threw off some of his inhibitions and relished playing up the more urbane, flamboyant side of his character.

At the end of that summer, although the New York rehearsals for *The Little Minister* were under way, Charles Frohman continued asking Barrie for more alterations to Maude Adams's role. After several weeks this arduous process was complete, the rehearsals were at an end, and the play got off to an uncertain first night in Washington on 13th September. (Frohman always gave his plays a short preview outside New York.) On its arrival in New York any doubts were swiftly dispelled as *The Little Minister* and its star took the city by storm. For more than six months it played to capacity audiences, outdistancing all other Broadway records. Finally, it went on tour and repeated this success in theatre after theatre across the United States. In those days immediately before the advent of the cinema, the theatre was still very much at the heart of entertainment, and Barrie's play struck a popular chord. American playgoers flocked to see Maude Adams's performance and she, like Barrie, became a major star.

That autumn, when rehearsals began in London, Barrie sat in every day. Stimulated by the process, he was always open to suggestions. A production was a collaboration with his players, and as the rehearsals progressed, if convinced by an actor Barrie was ready to cut, revise or even produce new material. The final production was unmatched by the challenge of what had gone before. It wasn't the first night Barrie loved, it was his part in the slow process of a play's genesis unravelling before his eyes. Thus, at the Haymarket he watched, walked up and down, smoked, encouraged, altered, and flirted outrageously with his heroine 'Babbie'. Winifred Emery seemed made for the part of the wild and fearless gypsy girl, who is wooed by the little minister, and Barrie fell hopelessly under her spell.

The presence of his own wife at a number of rehearsals, together with Winifred Emery's husband, Cyril Maude, both as producer and in the title role of the little minister, Gavin Ogilvy, appeared to make little difference to Barrie's extravagant compliments. With unerring predictability he fell for a pretty leading lady. If in this instance Winifred Emery and Cyril Maude were embarrassed, they took the playwright's behaviour in good part, while Mary Barrie appeared unruffled by her husband's overtures to the beautiful Mrs Maude. In public at least, Mary never showed irritation at Barrie's serial attentions to beautiful women, managing these episodes with consistent dignity. Barrie himself appeared oblivious to the effect his behaviour might have on any of those around him.

Whatever her feelings, Mary Barrie knew from experience that her husband's very public captivation would in private be a much more limited affair. She understood that Barrie's relationships were unlikely to progress any further than flirtation. And, yet, although the flirtations were in themselves unimportant, they were increasingly a reflection of more serious flaws in the Barries' marriage. After three years they were still without children. And while Mary survived what was for her the pain of this deficiency by mothering Porthos and excelling as a homemaker and hostess, her husband mastered the situation by hard work, socialising and becoming attached to the children of his friends.

The Little Minister opened at the Haymarket on 6th November. Surpassing expectations, it repeated its American triumph and ran for over eleven months. Frohman was jubilant. Indeed, the play was such a success that much later Barrie confided to Lord Esher that it had made him over eighty thousand pounds – in 1897 an enormous sum, today worth about fifty times that amount. In spite of this, in years to come, when his great plays were behind him, he knew that *The Little Minister* was a crude thing. Bright had begun reworking it, Frohman had demanded more, and against all his instincts Barrie had permitted his hands to be tied. Knowing that he had gained commercial success at the price of artistic integrity, he was determined not to let it happen again. In 1928, when he put together the collected edition of his plays, Barrie made clear his final judgement on *The Little Minister*: he left it out.

If his personal estimation of his play was low, its success had turned him into a hugely celebrated international name. Before this latest triumph his writing had made him comfortably off, yet, with his Calvinist upbringing acting as a check against an extravagant lifestyle, in a sense Barrie had no use for the great wealth he now possessed. Of limited comfort to him at the time, *The Little Minster's* success was, none the less, a means to greater artistic autonomy. Its author was now financially free to write whatever he liked for the rest of his life. At the same time Frohman was interested in anything else the playwright might have to offer. It didn't matter that at that moment Barrie had nothing, there would be much more to come. For the time being he was preoccupied with the second part of *Sentimental Tommy*, to be called *Tommy and Grizel*. The book inched its way forward, with a chapter here and a scene there, periodically Barrie allowed himself to be distracted, or taken up by a flurry of new ideas.

11

Sylvia

Barrie's friend and fellow cricketer Henry Ford claimed it was in his studio in Kensington that the playwright first met Sylvia Llewelyn Davies. Ford said, 'she was wearing a corduroy jacket made by herself. He [Barrie] saw, fell victim, and was instantly conquered.' A more appealing version of what could be described as the fateful meeting between Barrie and Sylvia Llewelyn Davies is enshrined in family legend.

'Copyright performances', as they were called, were sociable occasions on which a playwright would bring together a group of friends, allocate parts and then ask them to read through the play. Yet more friends acted as the audience, in other words 'witnesses', thus making the performance one duly termed 'copyright'. In 1897 this was the only method open to a playwright to protect the dramatic rights to his or her play. Mary Barrie had become friendly with Kate Lewis, one of the lawyer George Lewis's daughters. (This was the same Kate Lewis admired by Oscar Wilde, and a close friend of the young Max Beerbohm.) Soon Kate Lewis and her sister were asked to read at a copyright performance of *The Little Minister*. According to the American writer Richard Harding Davis, who was present, this was a 'truly remarkable performance' in which Mary Barrie played Babbie the gypsy and insisted – against her husband's wishes – on dancing on and off while playing for most of her part. Harding Davis played her father and 'had a great scene in which I cursed her, which got rounds of applause'.

George Lewis was one of the most distinguished trial lawyers of the day. He had, amongst numerous successes, averted a public scandal for the future King Edward, embroiled in an adulterous affair, when the aggrieved husband threatened to cite him as co-respondent in the divorce. Lewis, an intelligent, urbane man, was now Barrie's solicitor, and, while the two men would become good friends, Lewis's wife Elizabeth was to prove one of Barrie's staunchest female supporters. This blossoming friendship led to an invitation to the Lewises' annual New Year's Eve party at Portland Place.

Lady Lewis was one of London's noted hostesses. Her guest list was a stimulating mix of interest and distinction, and regular habitués of Portland Place included Max Beerbohm, George Meredith, Henry James and the painters Burne-Jones and Sargent. Portland Place parties were significant occasions on the London calendar, and seventy-two artists, musicians, writers, lawyers and politicians customarily sat down to the New Year's Eve dinner. Later, when the theatres had closed, the actors and actresses would arrive. Later still, after a home-made entertainment presented by some of the assembled company, the new year was toasted in. The composer Sir Hubert Parry and his wife were old friends of the Lewises. The Parry's daughter, Dorothy (Dolly), was to marry the British attaché in Copenhagen, Arthur Ponsonby – a noted socialist and son of Queen Victoria's Principal Private Secretary, Sir Henry Ponsonby. Dolly, who became an able diarist, would write of another occasion, 'It was a very good party indeed – the Lewises make things go so – [Lady] Lewis is so kind . . .'

Usually eschewing large public gatherings, that night Barrie had relented, and on this, the eve of 1898, he found himself sitting beside a young woman whom he later described as the most beautiful creature he had ever seen. Numerous accounts of the period struggle to interpret Sylvia Llewelyn Davies, her vitality of expression, her compelling femininity and her unconventional beauty. Seven years earlier, in 1891, the fourteen-year-old Dolly Parry captured with adult discernment something of the elusiveness of Sylvia Llewelyn Davies's appeal after a stay at the Parrys' seaside home in Sussex. She wrote:

Arthur and Sylvia left. Very sorry indeed. Discussed Sylvia freely of course, after she had left. Without being strictly pretty, she has got one of the most delightful, brilliant, sparkling faces I have ever seen. Her nose turns round the corner – also turns right up. Her mouth is quite crooked. She is much too fat. Now for her virtues. Her eyes are very pretty, hazel and very mischievous. She has pretty black fluffy hair, but her expression is what gives her that wonderful charm, and her low voice.[1]

Despite a ten-year age-gap between Dolly and Sylvia, a deep affection sprang up between them, growing with the years until it became the closest of friendships.

Meanwhile, in the following description of his fictional character Grizel, clearly based on Sylvia, Barrie's comment that there was sadness in her face signalled an almost prophetic capacity regarding his own life that sometimes appeared in his writing. Sylvia (Grizel) was

tall and graceful, and very dark and pale. When the winds of the day
flushed her cheeks she was beautiful, but it was a beauty that hid the
mystery of her face; the sun made her merry, but she looked more
noble when it had set, then her pallor shone with a soft radiant light,
as though the mystery and sadness and serenity of the moon were in
it . . . Her eyes . . . were unusually far apart, and let you look straight
into them and never quivered, they were such clear, grey, searching
eyes, and they seemed always to be asking for the truth.[2]

Sylvia Jocelyn Llewelyn Davies was a member of the du Maurier clan;
sister to the actor Gerald, and daughter to the artist and writer George,
who acquired such fame and fortune in 1894 with the publication of *Trilby*,
the autobiographical novel about his early life. The du Mauriers were
renowned for their good looks, their quick-witted sophistication and
penchant for mockery and humour. Their refusal to take life too seriously
typified an aspect of the gaiety and intellectual disdain of the 1890s.

The du Maurier tone was set by Sylvia's father, George. Having led
the life of an impoverished Bohemian art student in Paris, although
possessing nothing like the artistic distinction of his friend James McNeil
Whistler, in his ambition to become an artist George du Maurier found
a good measure of success. More conventional than Whistler, du Maurier
had married a pretty and respectable girl and, while fathering five children, had gone on to acquire a reputation as a dextrous illustrator for
writers such as Thackeray. Du Maurier eventually became a popular satirist,
making the larger part of his living as a mainstay of the magazine *Punch*.
In this role he became, *par excellence*, the not too unsettling, gracefully
prodding satirist of fashionable middle and upper-class English life. When
he later took to writing he was more astonished than anyone at the huge
success of his second novel, *Trilby*, which made him a household name.

Based on his early and cheerfully abandoned student life in Paris with
three friends, *Trilby* rent asunder any relationship du Maurier might have
retained with one of them, James Whistler. In *Trilby* he concealed Whistler's
identity as poorly as his satirical portrait hid the envy he had nursed over
Whistler's recognition as a great artist. On publication the notoriously
litigious Whistler was, with some justification, incensed, and soon launched
a series of public counter-blasts against du Maurier, who adamantly
refused to retract. The situation grew worse, until finally Whistler tried
to engage the services of their long-standing mutual friend Sir George
Lewis in suing du Maurier for libel. Ever tactful, Lewis wrote, '. . . naturally it is impossible for me to act against him. I hope, however, that no
proceedings will be taken.' Both sides were eventually persuaded and with
some reluctance beat a retreat.

Sitting beside du Maurier's daughter that evening, and realising who she was, Barrie told her that he had named his dog Porthos after the St Bernard of the same name in *Peter Ibbetson*, her father's first novel. Sylvia Llewelyn Davies in turn described how she had named the latest of her three sons after the same novel's chief protagonist, in honour of her father, who had died the previous year. While Barrie thought her the most beautiful creature he had ever met, neither of them could possibly have foreseen how this New Year's Eve meeting would set in motion a relationship that was to colour the remainder of their lives.

Five years earlier Sylvia du Maurier had married Arthur Llewelyn Davies, a brilliant scholar and promising young barrister. Describing their first meeting at a dinner party, Barrie's friend Henry Ford observed that Arthur Llewelyn Davies was sitting beside an unusually graceful and charming young woman who 'displayed liberally the most beautiful neck, shoulders and bosom to an admiring world . . . and I dimly perceived that his fate was sealed. A few weeks later the engagement of Arthur L.D. was announced to Sylvia du M.'[3]

Arthur was as handsome as Sylvia was beautiful and together they made an extraordinarily fine-looking couple. This at least was a mark in Arthur's favour for, knowing that their families had little in common, the du Mauriers (Sylvia's mother in particular) had been ill disposed to the match and insisted on a lengthy engagement in order to assess Arthur's prospects in his chosen profession.

Over the years George du Maurier had cultivated a persona that flaunted a certain philistine disdain. This was projected on the one hand at the self-consciously refined *fin de siècle* aestheticism of the likes of Jimmy Whistler and Oscar Wilde, whom du Maurier caricatured in *Punch* as Jellaby Postlethwaite the aesthetic poet, and on the other hand at the solemn intellectualism of such people as the Llewelyn Davieses. Sylvia's brother-in-law, Charles Millar, characterised the du Mauriers' attitude when he described the importance the whole family gave

to the appearance of their friends and new people they met . . . People in general were divided into good-looking, amusing, and bores . . . One must never be *au serieux* about anything . . . The family in general had a rooted dislike of serious topics of any kind, at all events in the presence of each other.[4]

The young man Sylvia du Maurier had married was from a radically different milieu. Arthur Llewelyn Davies was the son of a family as noted in its way as the du Mauriers; though in the Llewelyn Davieses' case it was for their courtesy, their intellect and their learning. Arthur's clergyman father, John, had previously been Honorary Chaplain to the Queen. A radical, and a determined supporter of workers' rights, the Reverend Llewelyn Davies's honesty (one might say naïveté) had led him to destroy his chance of ecclesiastical promotion when he delivered a sermon at Windsor – in Queen Victoria's presence – in which he passionately denounced Imperialism. Naturally, the Queen was furious, and her prime minister saw to it that the outspoken vicar was soon transferred to the far north. Until then, Llewelyn Davies's early brilliance at Cambridge, advancing to a position as a distinguished scholar and theologian, had led to the general opinion that he would eventually be offered a bishopric.

A bishopric was now out of the question, but as rector of Kirkby Lonsdale in Westmorland John Llewelyn Davies continued in his scholarly pursuits, practised mountain climbing and cultivated his radical views on the rights of workers and women's suffrage. These views were largely shared by both his siblings and his children: his sister had founded Girton College, Cambridge, his only daughter, Arthur's sister, Margaret, was an early suffragette with many friendships in the early Socialist Movement, and his son Crompton drafted the peace treaty that established Irish self-government. The philosopher Bertrand Russell said of Crompton, 'He combined wit, passion, wisdom, scorn, gentleness, and integrity in a degree that I have never known equalled.'

The Reverend Llewelyn Davies's wife, Mary, apparently failed to attend a single one of her husband's sermons in thirty-six years of marriage. Strong enough to weather such differences, their marriage was remarkable for the mutual devotion of husband and wife, while at the same time Mary's seven children adored her.

It was she who welcomed their future daughter-in-law, Sylvia du Maurier, with warmth to the Westmorland rectory. A milieu which was high-minded, a little self-righteous and yet immensely gracious; so different from the easy-going artistic London household in which Sylvia had grown up. She was immediately drawn to her future mother-in-law and afterwards was moved to write,

Dearest Mrs Davies
I feel I must just write a few lines to you, to thank you *with all my heart* for being so very kind and sweet to me . . . The recollection of my first visit to Kirkby will be very dear to me, and I shall never be able to thank you enough. I am very, very fond of you. I was, I think, the moment I saw you.
Always affectionately yours
Sylvia du Maurier[5]

Dolly Parry captured the atmosphere at the rectory when she later wrote,

How romantic it is to think of Sylvia coming to Kirkby, to the outwardly severe-looking Georgian Rectory adjoining the grave-yard on one side, and looking over the lovely Fells, where Mr Davies walked nearly every day. I like to think of Sylvia feeling the warmth within, and the love and sympathy she found in Arthur's mother. And Arthur's brothers, austere outwardly, felt, I feel sure, very soon the charm of this lovely sweet feminine creature.[6]

Having in turn been struck by Sylvia's charm, Mary Llewelyn Davies replied in kind, thus initiating what was to become a deep bond of friend-ship and affection.

My dearest Sylvia

Thank you very much for your dear note and for all your loving words. It is delightful to think that your visit to us has established an intimacy and affection which will, I hope, go on always increasing. It quite surprised me how you got into my heart in so short a time ... Write as often as you feel inclined. Kindest regards to your father and mother.

Your loving Mary Ll.D.[7]

Although Mary's son Arthur showed promise as a barrister (George Lewis was responsible for many of his early briefs), progress up the profes-sional ladder was to be slow, and there was little in the way of family resources to supplement Arthur's income. Meanwhile, Sylvia worked for the noted theatrical costumier Ada Nettleship, Augustus John's formidable mother-in-law, making clothes for noted players such as Ellen Terry. In 1892, after a two-year engagement, during which Emma du Maurier seems to have persisted in her reluctance to find her future son-in-law agreeable, the young couple were at last permitted to marry. Whatever the du Mauriers' concerns may have been, and despite the couple's sharply contrasting backgrounds, Sylvia and Arthur's marriage proved above all to be one of singular devotion and happiness.

Two years later, with one little son, George, and another on the way, Sylvia and Arthur took a holiday house near the du Mauriers' and Davieses's mutual family friends the Parrys. The young Dolly Parry had written in her diary three years earlier that

We have never seen such a pair of undemonstrative lovers, as Sylvia and Arthur. They hardly ever speak to each other even when in a room by themselves. Sylvia is a delightful thing. I can't imagine her with Margaret D. [Arthur's sister] at all – with her love for pretty dresses, and the stage. She is always dancing about the room.[8]

A year later, when Sylvia and Arthur had become familiar visitors to the Parrys at Rustington, an entry in Dolly's diary reads, 'Talked a good deal with sweet Sylvia, who told me a good deal about all her family, etc. They all love one another so much, which is so rare now in families'.[9] In 1894 Dolly, now sixteen, wrote: 'Arthur and Sylvia to tea. They seem very flourishing and contented on £400 a year – but it is a miracle.'

They returned to London after their holiday, and on 11th September their happiness was increased with the birth of a second son, called John after his maternal grandfather, but always known as Jack.

A year later, fate struck the young Llewelyn Davieses a harsh blow when in quick succession they suffered two painful losses. In February Mary Llewelyn Davies died suddenly of a heart attack, leaving both her son and daughter-in-law feeling bereft. Dolly Parry later wrote that only when Mary Llewelyn Davies died did she quite realise 'the depth of Sylvia's feeling for her – in fact I don't think I ever came across a mother and a daughter-in-law so deeply attached. Sylvia could not talk about it.'[10] Then, only eight months later, the du Mauriers lost their beloved father, George, who died aged only sixty. Thanks to the great success of *Trilby* he was able to bequeath a small legacy to Sylvia, which put the young couple in a more comfortable position. In addition, Arthur had inherited the last part of a leasehold on a larger house in Notting Hill, and here Sylvia gave birth to their third son, Peter, just five months after his grandfather du Maurier's death.

Not only was Sylvia Llewelyn Davies blessed with that mysteriously irresistible beauty, but both men and women also warmed to a disposition found almost universally appealing. She was quick, interested and intelligent, and had the du Maurier sense of mischief. As early as 1891 Dolly had commented in her diary: 'Went to Phil's [Phillip Burne-Jones] party at the New Gallery. We invited Arthur and Sylvia. The latter looked so pretty and was delightful. She was very wicked and coughed and winked her eyes when Kenneth [Muir] got hold of us.'[11]

Sylvia also possessed the du Maurier sense of taste; indeed she possessed an artistry that enabled her to present herself, her boys and wherever they were living with unusual flair and originality. A natural talent with the needle, developed while working for Ada Nettleship, led Sylvia to make many of her own and her boys' clothes. For them she devised beautiful and slightly unconventional clothing 'out of nothing and other people's mistakes'.[12] Eventually these would be copied for the children's costumes in *Peter Pan*. Thus, in combination with their winsome looks, from babyhood the Llewelyn Davies boys appeared subtly different from the other children out with their nurses in nearby Kensington Gardens.

On their afternoon walks with Porthos in the gardens the Barries may already have noticed these good-looking boys, distinctive in their red velvet berets made from their great-grandfather's old judicial robes. And the boys may in turn have observed this small man and his wife out walking and playing with the brown and white St Bernard dog, whose great size made some of the children in the gardens run back to their nurses in fear. Whether or not they had yet spoken, following Barrie's chance meeting with their mother over dinner, the trio of little boys soon met the small man, Mr Barrie, and his wife. After the Lewises' New Year's Eve supper the Barries and the Llewelyn Davieses began to socialise, and into the spring of 1898 the friendship between the families swiftly developed. Although their backgrounds were essentially different, with their artistic sensibilities in common Mary Barrie and Sylvia Llewelyn Davies appeared to have reason enough for becoming friends.

Barrie himself was of course already smitten. In his mind the Llewelyn Davieses quickly became the perfect family. Worshipping motherhood as he did, Sylvia was soon personified as the ideal mother, surrounded by her perfect clutch of small, strong-minded boys. In the spring of 1898 the eldest, George, was a confident and independent five-year-old, his younger brother Jack was three, and the youngest, Peter, had just passed his first birthday. Out with their nurse, Mary Hodgson they were often pleased to see Mr Barrie walking his dog in the gardens. He and Porthos entertained the little boys, who were intrigued by the brilliant games he was so adept at inventing. George in particular delighted in Barrie's stories, and was encouraged to join in with their making; stories in which he and his brothers were always the heroes, and vanquished every foe in sight.

Barrie was soon inviting himself to the Llewelyn Davies home, and become a favourite with the older boys, George in particular. Arthur and Sylvia Llewelyn Davies's social manner was more measured, more *comme il faut* than Barrie's. Consequently, as his visits to 31 Kensington Park Gardens increased in frequency over the following months, the young couple were left relatively powerless in the face of his determined friendship.

What the attitude of the immensely correct and austere Arthur Llewelyn Davies was, regarding this earnest little Scotsman's attentions to his wife and children, goes unrecorded. If he found Barrie's uninvited presence disconcerting, he appears to have been too courteous to comment, publicly anyway, on his lack of social grace. Besides, demurral would as likely as not have made no difference. Barrie's persistence was terrier-like; he had referred in *Margaret Ogilvy* to doggedness as one of his foremost qualities. Once he had decided that one was to be his friend there was little to be done in the face of the onslaught. He was by turns entertaining, charming, funny, selfless and immensely generous. By contrast he could also be selfish, demanding, moody, possessive and proprietorial. One of the ways in which these last two qualities were made evident was in his habit of planting postage stamps on new friends' ceilings by flicking them up on a coin. There, as badges of ownership, Barrie intended them to remain.

At the same time as this drive to dominate and possess, he had an equal craving to *be* dominated and owned. Gradually, he was to find that these profound and opposing needs would be fulfilled in almost equal measure by the Llewelyn Davies family, whose lives he saw as charmed. Sylvia was quickly put on a pedestal – something she accepted with bemusement – and Barrie was enchanted by her children, who were in turn enthralled by his gift for creating magical games such as they had never experienced before.

Thus was initiated the complex association between James Barrie, his wife and the Llewelyn Davieses. It was an association out of which grew bonds that would, in different ways, mark each one of them until the end of their days. For Barrie's part, in addition to his consuming preoccupation with his mother, the charismatic Davies family were, in spite of themselves, to provide him with a set of relationships to absorb him for the rest of his life.

From the beginning it was Barrie who drove the friendship, and in May 1898 he was writing to Arthur,

My dear Davies

Mrs de Navarro has issued her challenge for the match [cricket] at Broadway for Saturday June 11, and wants us to go down on the previous day, for which she is arranging sports of an undignified character. She also invites us to supper and a ball. I hope you will contrive to make this suit you and that Mrs Davies will come too, as she is particularly wanted and is said to be good at managing boys.

Let me know, as rooms have to be booked.

Return on Saturday.

Yours ever

J. M. Barrie[13]

Arthur's son Peter later said that he didn't know if his parents went to Broadway but he did know that 'the occasion would not have been A's cup of tea'. It is interesting to note the same slightly proprietorial air with which Barrie wrote inviting his friend H. G. Wells to the Broadway match.

> Are you coming to my cricket match . . . against a team of artists, etc. and got up by Mrs de Navarro? . . . We had a great team last year, and none of us can play. We are going down the previous day, for which she has arranged sports, etc. of a wild nature, a supper also at which there are great doings . . . Our train leaves Paddington Friday morning at 9.50. Book second class to Evesham and bring evening dress.[14]

A bewilderingly eccentric yet clear indication of Barrie's urge to bind himself to the Llewelyn Davieses is revealed in a letter of dubious taste he wrote to Sylvia some time during that year. It was dated the day before her marriage to Arthur, which had actually taken place six years earlier, in 1892.

> Dear Miss du Maurier
>   And so you are to be married tomorrow! And I shall not be present. You know why. Please allow me to wish you great happiness in your married life. And at the same time I hope you will kindly accept the little wedding gift I am sending you . . . It reaches you somewhat late, but that is owing to circumstances too painful to go into.
>   With warmest wishes to you and Mr Davis [sic]
>   Believe me dear Miss du Maurier
>   Yours sincerely
>   J. M. Barrie[15]

By constructing this complex fantasy he implies not only that he knew Sylvia before her wedding, but also perhaps that he knew her better than Arthur did. And that there existed between them a greater intimacy, both then and at the time of the Llewelyn Davieses' marriage, one of the most important events in their lives.

Whatever hesitation their parents might have felt about Barrie and his wife, to George and Jack, the older Llewelyn Davies boys, Barrie was without question a friend. The actor Cyril Maude's daughter, Pamela, later characterised the child's accepting response to Barrie when she wrote:

He was a tiny man, he had a pale face and large eyes and shadows around them . . . He had always been in our lives, like Mr Gilbert [of Gilbert and Sullivan]. Our parents called him Jimmy. He was unlike anyone we had ever met. He looked fragile, but he was strong when he wrestled with Porthos, his St Bernard dog . . .[16]

Pamela Maude didn't find Barrie's silences odd or oppressive and was puzzled to hear her mother say to her father, 'Jimmy didn't say one word during the whole of lunch . . . it is difficult for poor Mary.' To the children indeed: 'He was made of silences, but we didn't find these silences strange; they were so much part of him his silences spoke loudly.'

Barrie's notebooks were soon charting the development of his relationship with the Llewelyn Davies boys, especially George, for whom he was to develop a singular devotion:

  – George admires me as a writer [because] thinks I bind & Print.
  – George burying face not to show crying.
  – Little White Bird book described to me by George
  – Telling George what love is . . . in answer to George's inquiries abt how to write a story.
  – What George said while walking me round the Round Pond [in Kensington Gardens] (abt what to have for his birthday – ship – Greek armour – book &c. . .
  – The queer pleasure it gives when George tells me to lace his shoes, &c
  – The boys disgrace one in shops by asking shopkeeper abt his most private affairs. Shopkeeper &c takes me for their father (I affect rage).[17]

And the rage was indeed affected, for Barrie was moved by the recurring thought that these boys could indeed be his own children. As he struggled on with *Tommy and Grizel*, this other set of notes would evolve over the next four years into another book: *The Little White Bird*. Through chronicling the development of his relationship with young George Llewelyn Davies, in *The Little White Bird* Barrie is once again digging deep into personal and artistic preoccupations. Embedded in this most odd book is a crucial stage in the evolving story of the boy Peter, who had already made an appearance in just one paragraph at the end of *Tommy and Grizel*:

The new book . . . was *The Wandering Child* . . . It would make little stir in an age in which the authors are trying who can say damn loudest. It is but a reverie about a little boy who was lost. His parents find him singing joyfully to himself because he thinks he can now be a boy forever, and he fears that if they catch him they will compel him to grow into a man, so he runs farther from them into the wood and is running still, singing to himself because he is always to be a boy . . . The moment he conceived the idea . . . he knew that it was the idea for him . . . He forgot at once that he did not really care for children.

'It is myself who is writing at last, Grizel,' he said as he read it to her.

She thought (and you can guess whether she was right) that it was the book he loved rather than the child. She thought (and you can guess again) that in a subtle way this book was his autobiography.[18]

Subsequent to Barrie's meeting with Sylvia, the description of Grizel, originally based largely on Mary, turned more on a description of Sylvia, until the two women became inextricably intertwined. And when (at the end of 1899) Barrie's friend Bernard Partridge came to illustrate *Tommy and Grizel* for its serial publication in the American *Scribner's Magazine*, Barrie said he didn't know what most of the characters looked like, but that Grizel resembled Mrs Llewelyn Davies, and that she had consented to sit for Partridge if he liked the idea. He must have liked the idea because it is clearly she who is the model in the illustrations for *Tommy and Grizel*.

Barrie's almost feminine capacity for emotional sensitivity was at times matched by an equal degree of emotional blindness, even callousness. Although not a cynic, his divided soul made it possible for him to oscillate between complete consciousness and complete unconsciousness of what it was he did. Thus he begged for Tommy, '. . . you must not think him calculating and cold-blooded, for nothing could be less true to the fact'.

Driven to want Sylvia's image in his book, was it sensitivity of a kind on Barrie's part that made her appear as the model for Grizel in the American edition alone? Was this an acknowledgement of the embarrassment such public relegation to second place would cause his wife, or had she forced his hand?

Mary understood that she had little or no control over her husband's infatuations. For several years she appears to have done her best to accommodate him, and we know that she managed his ubiquitous fascination for his leading ladies with a greater measure of dignity than he himself did. To a large degree Mary evolved a civilised *modus vivendi* with her husband that left her, for example, able to socialise with people like the Llewelyn Davieses, for it was not only her husband who sought their friendship.

It was now seven years since Barrie had begun writing the first volume of *Sentimental Tommy*, and his attitudes, both as man and artist, had developed. He was also now a married man. Less brimful of humour than in *Sentimental Tommy*, the outrageous hero's exuberance is more muted in *Tommy and Grizel*. With a plot founded upon the fraught and finally disastrous relationship of the ill-fated young couple, the central problem is still Tommy's capacity for fantasy. When Tommy has constructed a particularly outrageous fabrication, involving nothing less than breaking his friend Corp's leg, Grizel rebukes him until in his defence Tommy mournfully declares,

> 'I wish I were different but that is how ideas come to me, at least all those that are of any value.'
> 'Surely you could fight against them and drive them away?'
> This to Tommy who held out sugar to them to lure them to him![19]

With her profound inability to imagine why he can't change, Grizel tells him she doesn't like his book if it is written at such a cost, and in desperation for him she finally cries, 'If writing makes you live in such an unreal world it must do you harm.' Meanwhile the narrator informs the reader that

> To expose Tommy for what he was, to appear to be scrupulously fair to him so that I might really damage him the more, that is what I set out to do in this book, and always when he seemed to be finding a way of getting round me (as I had a secret dread he might do) I was to remember Grizel and be obdurate . . .[20]

Tommy constantly refers to his inability to progress beyond boyhood, and, while knowing he is no longer a child, over and again he expresses his urge to return to that ideal state.

> Poor Tommy! He was still a boy, he was ever a boy trying sometimes, as now, to be a man, and always when he looked round he ran back to his boyhood as if he saw it holding out its arms to him and inviting him to come back and play. He was so fond of being a boy that he could not grow up. In a younger world, where there were only boys and girls, he might have been a gallant figure.[21]

Almost falling in love with the idea of love, Tommy then

> pressed her wet eyes reverently because thus was it written in his delicious part, his heart throbbed with hers that they might beat in time, he did not love, but he was the perfect lover, he was the artist trying in a mad moment to be as well as to do.[22]

Although clearly feeling great sympathy for him, Barrie eventually lets Tommy choke to death in an accident arising out of his unfaithfulness to Grizel. Caught on some railings in an overcoat given him by her, Barrie has Tommy die, because ultimately he has failed to relinquish his life of fantasy. And this may in part be Barrie's judgement upon himself, for a failure successfully to do just that.

In writing this book, he reveals aspects of himself that are at times excruciating to witness. In Tommy Sandys the fantasist, his creator is undoubtedly describing a version – albeit often magnified – of himself. Indeed, *Tommy and Grizel* mercilessly quarries both Barrie's own personality, and the effects of his personality on his marriage, for material to further his investigation into the fantasist's life. Intertwining the progress of Tommy Sandys and Grizel's relationship with his own and his wife's, Barrie gradually reveals the full and tragically destructive force of Tommy's fantasy on Grizel's life. In the period (through the second half of 1898 and into 1899) when Barrie was completing *Tommy and Grizel,* although Mary remained discreet, one of the heartrending underlying themes of *Tommy and Grizel* must be the slow but inevitable disintegration of the Barries' marriage.

> But he could not love her. He gave her all his affection, but his passion, like an outlaw, had ever to hunt alone ... did there remain in him enough of humanity to give him the right to ask a little sympathy of those who can love?[23]

> Ah if only Tommy could have loved [the way Grizel did]. He would have done it if he could. If we could love by trying, no one would ever have been more loved than Grizel[24] ...

And he wanted to confess to her

> ... Grizel, I seem to be different from all other men; there seems to be a curse upon me. I want to love you, dear one, you are the only woman I ever wanted to love, but apparently I can't.[25]

When Tommy makes an attempt to explain himself to the young doctor Gemmel, who despises him for what he has done to Grizel, Tommy again gives the self-consciousness of the artist as the reason for his inability to be a 'proper' man. And surely it is Barrie talking when Tommy says, 'If I have greetin [crying] eyes it was real grief that gave them to me, but when I heard what I was called it made me self-conscious.'

Using *Tommy and Grizel* and the notebooks as sources (because these are all we have to go on), in the painful confrontations one guesses at between Mary and Jamie Barrie, the following words of Grizel's must be the essence of what Mary said to Barrie himself: 'It was not that I did not love your books . . . but that I loved you more.' In 1899, after five years of marriage, had Mary come to the realisation that she could only sustain so much pretence? After a passage in which Barrie has declared with feeling, 'Oh men, men, will you never understand how absolutely all of her a woman's love can be?' he says, 'If she gives you everything, how can she give you more? She is not another person, she is part of you'.[26]

Is it Mary speaking when Grizel eventually asks, 'How much self-respect do you think is left for me?' And after everything Tommy realised that he 'could not make himself anew'. Ultimately the problem was that Tommy had tried

> to become a lover by taking thought and Grizel, not letting on that it could not be done in that way . . . He was a boy only. She knew that despite all he had gone through, he was still a boy. And boys cannot love. Oh is it not cruel to ask a boy to love?[27]

Barrie repeats versions of this phrase so often and at times with such rawness that it must have been a cry from the heart. *Tommy and Grizel* is a sad book. If one reads Barrie and his wife's predicament into it, and his powerlessness to do anything about it, the book becomes immensely more so.

The success of *The Little Minister* had made Barrie's name as prominent in the United States as it already was in Britain. On both sides of the Atlantic any item of news about him was enthusiastically reported, and usually exaggerated. And while Barrie's elusive public persona added to the mystique, many thousands of readers waited, curious as to what he would give them next. Throughout the spring of 1898 and on into 1899, while working on *Tommy and Grizel,* as usual there was much more than the one work being created in that fertile brain.

The growth of Barrie's relationship with the Llewelyn Davies boys acted as a vital catalyst for the ideas in his notes for *The Little White Bird.*

At the same time he wrote two introductions for fellow writers' work: one for his friend the American George Cable, and another for the late Mrs Oliphant, the prolific and successful Scottish novelist with whom Barrie had corresponded for a number of years. He also wrote a 'duologue' for the actors Cyril Maude and Winifred Emery, and by 1899 was at work on another new play, for the moment called *The Two Kinds of Women*, but eventually to be *The Wedding Guest*.

While Barrie's inner life was progressing in its habitually febrile manner – incorporating and transforming all available experience into his art – sociability appears to have been carried on at an equally feverish pace. He was leading life at a run.

In the summer of 1898 he once again threw himself into organising the Allahakbarries' cricket match. Making the most of any opportunity to talk about the game, Barrie gave several speeches in which cricket was a core theme. Years later, in 1926, he was asked, alongside the then Prime Minister, Stanley Baldwin, to give a speech in honour of the visiting Australian cricket team, and remembering his own experience as a boy, described where he thought the heart of cricket could still be found.

> And let us not forget . . . that the great glory of cricket does not lie in Test Matches, nor county championships . . . but rather on village greens, the cradle of cricket. The Tests are but the fever of the game. As the years roll on they become of small account, something else soon takes their place, the very word may be forgotten; but long, long afterwards, I think, your far-off progeny will still of summer afternoons hear the crack of the bat and the local champion calling for his ale on the same old bumpy wickets.[28]

At the end of June the Barries set off for their annual holiday in Scotland, this time taking a house for two months near Grandtully on the Tay. Despite a constant stream of visitors, Barrie continued hard at work on *Tommy and Grizel*. This included the further incorporation of Sylvia Llewelyn Davies into the book, which occasioned lengthy revisions. It was during this summer in Scotland that Cyril Maude and Winifred Emery were invited to stay with their two little daughters. Maude did much serious fishing, provoking the caustic remark in Barrie's notebook, 'Actor fishing all day & never catching anything – surprising till you realise he is playing the part of the fisherman.'

Barrie may have misread Maude here. Maude's fishing might have been without affectation, but as Barrie himself was a master of such an endless variety of roles, he was hypersensitive to this tendency in others. His note also reveals a prejudice he never really overcame. With one or two notable exceptions, he had little time for actors. Actresses, on the other hand, were on the whole held in the highest regard; they were muses to whom one paid court with outrageous flirting. His notebooks show he was none the less quite aware of the affectation involved. A note reads, 'Of all the moods in which my leading lady indulges the worst is the agreeable mood. When she is agreeable she is unbearable.'[29] Another note observes, that 'to kiss an actress is merely to sign you bear her no ill will'.

The actress was, however, fundamental to the mystery of the theatre, an idea now ingrained in Barrie's consciousness: the stimulating puzzle of the theatre with its constant shifting back and forth between illusion and reality. One senses that his difficulty with male actors – competitors, perhaps, in emotional sensitivity – derives from the fact that men in general were more problematic for him than women. Indeed, with his chameleon temperament, Barrie must have created a similar level of discomfort in many men, whose approach to life was a clearer and more straightforward one than his.

While in Scotland, he cheerfully took Maude – on their bicycles, still a novelty in 1898 – to Kirriemuir. Having taken the part of Gavin Dishart in *The Little Minister*, Maude was curious to see the town and Barrie's family home. For several reasons this was a significant visit for Barrie. It was the first time he had returned to Kirriemuir since his mother's death almost three years before, and the family home, Strath View, remained uninhabited. The occasion must have been made more peculiar by the fact that the cyclists were invited to stay the night with the Lyells at Kinnordy House, a mile outside the town. Lord Lyell was the town's squire, living in his recently rebuilt Scottish Baronial house on the large estate effectively surrounding the town. Within the Kinnordy estate was Caddam Wood, a significant feature of Barrie's childhood and his writing; the place made more mysterious for him by the gypsies' annual arrival there to set up camp.

No doubt the man who had begun as the boy from the Kirriemuir tenements, now welcomed into 'the big house', had a strange mixture of thoughts that night. Although Barrie would always be of Kirriemuir, in a sense he no longer belonged. Separated from his old life not only by time, but also by the other life he had forged, and by his increasing wealth, it was only in his memories and imaginings that he could ever really return.

When the two months' lease of the house by the Tay was up, the Barries stayed on and travelled around Scotland together until October. Back in London their social life was once again busy. Entertaining and being entertained despite, as his future secretary and friend Cynthia Asquith

so aptly put it, being 'too genuine, too true to his immediate self to coun-
terfeit an unvarying cordiality', Barrie was much lionised. In the new
year of 1899 another friendship began and would flourish. Maurice
Hewlett, civil servant, poet and novelist, had recently come to promi-
nence with his novel *The Forest Lovers.* The Hewletts, together with the
Llewlyn Daviesis, George Meredith's son Will and his wife, and another
friend, A. E. W. Mason (failed actor turned successful novelist and future
MP, best known for his novel *The Four Feathers*), were for the moment
the inner circle.

In February 1899, after wringing the end of *Tommy and Grizel* out of
himself, Barrie wrote to Quiller-Couch,

> I am glad I have finished your story, it reminds me that after all one
> does at last get to the end. Oh that 'final canter up the avenue'.
> They should see the author belabouring the brute.
>
> I see the finish not so far off of my own, but it cracked some-
> where about the middle and needs a deal of sticking plaster.[30]

Henceforth, although there would always be significant references, he
was to leave behind his birthplace, 'the dearest place in the world', and
its characters, as the major source for his writing.

In May, with William Nicoll, Barrie organised a celebratory dinner at
the Savoy in honour of his old professor Masson's seventy-eighth birthday,
attended by a distinguished literary company. In the middle of the month
the Allahakbarries were out in force. Playing first a group of artists at
Denmark Hill, they played again on 1st June, once more on the 17th
and a week later pitted themselves against the Savile Club. Then in July
they were down in Broadway for another long Worcestershire weekend
of cricket and festivities. It was in this year, 1899, that Barrie produced
a more extended commentary – he had made the first in 1893 – called
The Allahakbarries' Book of Broadway Cricket. The company of writers and
artists played, made fools of themselves and were consistently sent up by
Barrie in his little booklet of thirty-three pages, decorated with drawings and photographs.

But this was to be the last of the Allahakbarries at Broadway. Many
of his friends, and especially Barrie himself, had become too well known
for the press to ignore. And that July they descended on Broadway in
search of copy. Barrie was furious. Though by now it shouldn't have
surprised him that his fame could generate this kind of response, having
forged the role of the mysterious celebrity he was jealous of his privacy.
Ahead of his time here, Barrie's appreciation of how to manage his public

'persona' was part of the mystique, and he wanted control over when and how his privacy was to be breached. The anger and frustration he felt at failure to keep control has a familiar twenty-first-century ring to it.

While Barrie's fame grew, so also the new popular press – under the auspices of magnates such as Alfred Harmsworth, founder of the *Daily Mail* – was at the same time hugely increasing its circulation. In 1881 George Newnes had established *Tit Bits*, and almost overnight readership reached 800,000. The press was in the first stages of becoming more recognisably like our own.

Accompanied by a pretty and fashionable wife, Barrie would soon be able to count among his friends and acquaintances a good number of the richest and most prominent figures of the day, and, shocking to a number of contemporaries though it was, the press would happily fabricate a story if that was the only way to have a piece on Barrie in their columns.

After the cricket the Barries left for the Schwalbach, in Germany, where Mary was to take a course of the waters. It appears she had been ill, and not for the first time, because in February Barrie had written to a friend, 'Mary is quite well, but unfortunately it seems that she must have another of those operations again, which depresses me though she makes light of it.'[31]

The couple returned from Germany and took a small house at Rustington. George Meredith, now sixty-one, was staying with his daughter nearby, and the Llewelyn Davieses were once again at the Mill House, about half a mile away. Barrie had at last sent *Tommy and Grizel* off to the typist (with typewriters now in fairly common use, manuscripts were expected at the publisher's typed up), and this August was something like a real holiday for him. Friends either visited the Barrie's cottage by the sea or, like the Gilmours, came to stay. Barrie and the Llewelyn Davies boys also spent much time playing together – cricket, of course, but Barrie also taught the boys many of the Scottish games of his childhood, some of his own invention: spyo, kick-bonnety, peeries, egg-cap, capey-dykey and smuggle bools.

That summer of 1899, the Barries and the Llewelyn Davieses had been friends for a year and a half, and Barrie had come to know the boys well. Crucially, almost all his time with them was spent playing. This was playing that involved great ingenuity and expenditure of energy, and was frequently bound up with the creation of stories, of heroes, pirates, wrecked islands and strange fairies. All the while, in collaboration with the boys, a more significant story was developing. This concerned the little figure previously referred to as the 'Wandering Child', whom we first glimpsed in that single paragraph towards the end of *Tommy and Grizel*.

The 'Wandering Child' had by now acquired a name, Peter, to which would soon be added a second one, Pan. And as the story continued to develop, its setting was confirmed as Kensington Gardens, the place where the Davieses most often played. It was here they had first discovered that in Barrie's company the world was filled with magical possibilities. To them he was an infinite source of mystery, amusement and entertainment, and they delighted in his friendship. Their parents' attitude is more difficult to decipher.

Arthur Davies was essentially a private person. Gentle, and at times stern, he was a man of simple tastes, whose beliefs, like those of the rest of his serious and intelligent family, were held with a quiet passion. One of his greatest pleasures was to spend time with his wife and sons. The taxing and time-consuming work required to rise to the top of the legal profession meant that he saw less of them than he would have liked, making the summer break a period to savour.

With the Barries only half a mile away, what might Arthur's thoughts have been on the matter that August? We have no record of any objections he may have voiced about the time Barrie spent playing with his sons. Time when, in some critical sense, they were spirited away from their father. With this in mind Arthur must surely have objected to Barrie's insinuation into his family life, but what could he do? He was too well mannered to take the author to task over his behaviour, especially when it was carried out with such determination and charm. Besides, what exactly would he have said? Crucially, Sylvia doesn't appear to have objected to Barrie's regular presence.

With that unusual beauty her contemporaries struggled to define, Sylvia's appeal was made more engaging by her possession of that rare quality, sympathy. Almost everyone loved her, and therefore perhaps Sylvia was unsurprised by the knowledge that she held any number of men, and some women, quite captive – indeed a part of her must by now have grown quite accustomed to it, in the most gracious and unassuming way.

The almost inevitable element of ruthlessness attaching to great beauty is accepted as quite natural in an artistic milieu. Added to this, in her father's house Sylvia had grown up accustomed to the charisma of glamour given by literary and artistic power. Perhaps, in combination with his wealth, Sylvia was nourished by Barrie's aura of artistic power, and thus she may well have thrived on the open adulation of this little man whose life lay at the centre of an artistic world. Sylvia's childhood and youth had been spent in a very different milieu from the earnest intellectualism of her husband's family, which was neither a glamorous nor a worldly one. She may have discovered a great sympathy for her mother-in-law, but this didn't mean that Sylvia had taken on the Davies mantle.

At the same time, there was never any doubt about Sylvia's deep attachment to her husband. Indeed, although tongues might eventually wag, the mutual attachment of husband and wife was always absolutely clear to those who knew the Davieses at all well. Barrie's money and prestige, however, offered Sylvia something more than Arthur could provide, and this must have irritated her husband. Both the Davieses cannot but have found Barrie's presence invasive, but Sylvia minded much less, and it appears that nothing was ever said in public on the matter.

As an adult their son Peter would say, 'It is clear enough that father didn't like him, at any rate in the early stages. Did J. M. B.'s entry into the scheme of things occasionally cause ill-feeling or quarrellings between mother and father?' The boy's nurse, Mary Hodgson, would later write,

> What was of value to the One had no value to the Other. Your father's attitude at all times was as 'One gentleman (in the *true* sense) to Another'. Any difference of opinion was *never* made 'Public Property' in the house . . . The Barries were overwhelming (and found your mother's help, grace & beauty a great asset in meeting the right people, etc.) – aided by Mrs du Maurier – always ambitious for her favourite daughter . . . The du Mauriers in a way stood in awe of your Father. There were times when he defied the lot – & stood alone – and his Wife stood by him![32]

True though this may have been, Mary Hodgson was by no means a neutral witness. Her interpretation of events was coloured by considerable animosity towards Barrie, and sustained over many years to come.

With the holiday season at an end, everyone returned to London. In September the Barries travelled up to Kirriemuir, stayed with various relations at Strath View – once again opened up – and then went on to Edinburgh to visit Barrie's father, uncle and sister. Here their return was delayed as they waited for David Barrie's health to improve.

On quite another scale, national affairs loomed as the problems between Great Britain and Germany grew. The Dutch Boers wanted freedom from the British, and the President of the South African Republic, Kruger, led them into war. This war was to shake much of the complacency of late-Victorian politics and, sowing seeds of doubt about Britain's Imperialist role, would raise problems for the Liberals. Two and a half years later, when mismanagement had unfolded a confusing saga of muddle and defeat, the Boers were finally driven to accept British sovereignty, and hostilities were called to a halt.

A month after the war had begun, in November of 1899, Barrie was writing to a friend, 'We are well, except in the morning when we tremble so over the newspapers and what they may contain.' In February he wrote, 'We are both as well as people can be who know that Buller has crossed the Tugela. I went to the House the opening night, a poor show. Balfour bewildered, neat, Bannerman lumpy, with his little joke – no rising to the occasion anywhere . . .'[33]

At the end of the year, although Barrie had been hard at work filling his notebooks, he had given his public nothing, having published no more than the privately printed booklet on the Allahakbarries. Even so, with Gilmour's investments combined with royalties – which included translations of his novels, so that *The Little Minister* was soon to be seen as *Maly Farar* on the bookstalls in Prague – and the play of *The Little Minister* still on tour, that year Barrie made over twelve thousand pounds. This was a sum, even considering his generosity to charities, to his father, his uncle and other family members who appeared needy, that far exceeded his needs. Barrie would be forty with the new century, and there is little doubt that his wealth would sometimes prove a barrier to communication. Yet he was sincere when he wrote, 'I loathe snobbishness so much that I hate to write of it . . .'[34]

His success was beginning subtly to isolate him from some of his friends. It also meant that unless people were very strong-minded – or gave up and went away – the sheer force of Barrie's personality, the tendency to dominate and have his own way, was becoming more difficult to foil. He was discreet and didn't vaunt his wealth, but there were occasions when, together with his self-belief the combination was unappealing.

12

The Boy Castaways

With the New Year came a new century whose tone was already anticipated. As long ago as the 1870s the contemporary atmosphere had been described as 'full of missiles', and 'one where all is in doubt, hesitation and shivering expectancy'. The journalist T. H. Escott felt everywhere 'old lines of demarcation being obliterated, revered idols being destroyed', while another writer, Elizabeth Chapman, had written of 'a general revolt against authority in all departments of life, which is the note of an unsettled, transitional, above all democratic age'.

Oscar Wilde and his aesthetic followers were only one of the many groups in revolt against established values. In Wilde's case, any earnestness was abhorred (his last play, with its punning and ironic title, *The Importance of Being Earnest*, was performed in 1895). Wilde's attitude led Yeats to say of him that he 'tricked and clowned to draw attention to himself'. Wilde and his followers believed that convention should be dispensed with and life always lived in search of new and expanding experiences. As in Ernest Dowson's poem *Cynara*, they cried for 'madder music and for stronger wine'.

Another important strand of rebelliousness took the form of a sophisticated primitivism, a 'simple' return to nature, practised by those, like Edward Carpenter, in retreat not only from what they saw as bourgeois traditions, such as the family, but from the proliferation of the machine. Carpenter wanted a world 'not of riches, nor of mechanical facilities, nor of intellectual facilities'. Instead he sought 'freedom and joy'. Both Wilde and Carpenter were socialists of a sort. But most devoted to the cause were Sydney and Beatrice Webb, leading figures in the newly formed Fabian Society.

Meanwhile, the playwright and critic William Archer made his contribution to the attack on prevailing mores with his translations and productions of Ibsen. Rightly called the founder of modern prose drama, Ibsen was the first to look with any real persistence at the forces of the unconscious. At the same time he not only dealt with women's rights but, as he said, 'with human rights', too. In 1900 there was no doubt that although a great many were still very poor, a greater number were better off than seventy years earlier. With this increasing wealth came more leisure, and as the cities continued to expand, Britain became an urbanised and, slowly, a more democratised society.

Preoccupied as they were with time, and space, to the Victorians it appeared that everything was speeding up. And in the process Nature as a whole (even before Darwin) was often seen not as the Romantics had perceived it, as something from which one took succour, but more as an impersonal, alienating element, subject to harsh and immutable laws. From this emerged Tennyson's vision suffused with doubt:

> Though Nature, red in tooth and claw
> With ravine, shrieked against his [God's] creed.

This sentiment evoked what Barrie's friend Meredith had described as 'the army of unalterable law'. In 1948 the historian Humphrey House offered the opinion that the Victorians knew they were peculiar. 'Heirs of time' they might have been but they were also deeply conscious of belonging to an upstart generation, leading House to say of them:

> One minute they are busy congratulating themselves on their brilliant achievements, and the next they are moaning about their sterility, their lack of spontaneity. In either mood they are all agog at being modern, more modern than anybody has ever been before. And in this they were right. They took the brunt of an utterly unique development of human history; the industrialisation and mechanisation of life meant a greater change in human capabilities in the practical sphere than ever before had been possible.[1]

In the first month of the new century *Tommy and Grizel* finally went into publication with its launch in *Scribner's Magazine*. It was to run until the autumn, when Cassell in Britain and Scribner's in the United States would simultaneously publish it as a book. As usual Barrie's difficulty in finishing a project meant that with the arrival of the proofs he felt compelled both to correct and to rewrite.

Meanwhile, Mary Barrie's long search for a cottage in the country finally produced results; she found a place in Surrey. It was Mary who set the visual tone in the household at Gloucester Road, and to this she added her skills as a capable hostess. But now, with more space and grounds, she was to have scope for her abilities as a designer of houses

and their gardens, too; the house she had found needed completely refur-
bishing, and was set in a large expanse of overgrown garden.

The Barries now spent less time alone in each other's company, and
more with other people. When Mary wasn't playing hostess to their
widening circle, her husband spent much of his time either at work in
his study, in attendance at one of his clubs, or shining at one of the social
occasions at which he was now in constant demand.

In her book *Dogs and Men*, when describing the devoted St Bernard,
Porthos, Mary wrote,

> For a dog makes a most admirable accompaniment to a husband.
> He supplies those . . . ways . . . so dear to a woman's heart, and so
> necessary to her well-being, that come tripping along so gracefully
> before marriage, but at the end of the first year have tripped away
> – less gracefully – into oblivion . . . To quote an instance. Those
> silent meals. Haven't most of us experienced them [probably rarely
> as much as Mary] . . . When the mind of your man is elsewhere,
> lord knows where, but nowhere in your direction. Just when the
> silence is becoming unbearable, your dog steps in and attracts your
> attention. He lays his head on your knee, or he presses your hand,
> as it is in the act of conveying a succulent morsel to your mouth.
> '. . . asking for food? You interrupt.' Quite true. But to be asked for
> anything is a relief. And with . . . what an adoring glance he rewards
> you for the titbits you pop into his mouth. Your heart begins at
> once to warm up again. The whole balance of life is restored.[2]

We do not know what Mary's thoughts were about the completion of
a novel in which her husband painfully and transparently dismantled their
marriage. Was it Mary who insisted that certain passages be cut between
the manuscript and publication of *Tommy and Grizel*? And was one of
the deleted sentences on the last page of the manuscript a prime example
of Barrie's unnerving capacity to make accurate observations about his
life, without the accompanying ability to do anything about them? 'What
God will find hardest to forgive in him, I think, is that Grizel never had
a child.'

When later Mary said of herself and the cottage in the country that
she had 'been wanting something to occupy my days', one feels a measure
of relief on her behalf. Relief that with no children or her acting career
to occupy her days, she had found something beyond the hope of attention a distant husband was failing to provide. Perhaps Barrie had been
humouring Mary in encouraging her to find them somewhere else
outside London. Apparently, though, when she announced that she had

found a house her husband's interest in the venture cooled. This provoked Mary into using some of the funds she had invested with Gilmour to take on the lease herself. For the moment she had a new project, and her energy and aptitude were enthusiastically employed in the remaking of the cottage and its gardens.

The house was not far from Farnham and Tilford, and its name, Black Lake Cottage, came from the expanse of water nearby. This was a shallow lake, home to a number of herons, and surrounded by woods of tall Scots pine. With higher ground behind, a vantage point from which to look out beyond the trees, the house stood, like one in Barrie's tales, along a dusty road in a clearing in the wood with no other house nearby. Although only thirty-eight miles from London, in 1900 this part of Surrey felt far away, and after leaving the Waterloo train one finished the journey by bicycle or horse-drawn vehicle, arriving at the peace and quiet of the woods, the garden and lake.

Mary organised and supervised builders, decorators and gardeners to help her transform the house into a pleasant and welcoming retreat. We don't know when Barrie became more enthusiastic – perhaps when his wife incorporated a study for him into her re-planning of the house – but by July, when the last of the workmen were leaving, the couple began to settle themselves in. Barrie was definitely taking the house seriously now, and after the previous year's influx of journalists at Broadway he decided that the venue for this year's Allahakbarrie cricket weekend would be his own little country retreat.

As many as possible were squeezed into Black Lake Cottage, while other friends were fitted with lodgings nearby. The extended weekend of cricket and golf-croquet, the walks, the round of convivial meals skilfully arranged by Mary were, with the house, voted a great success. And this despite the advent of a new game for the Allahakbarries, over which Barrie managed to rule – but then he seemed to rule all the games he played, with the exception of draughts. His fascination with games was nothing less than a mania. His competitiveness as a boy on the football pitch, the cricket pitch, at marbles in the dust, and any other game requiring a good eye and a sense of strategy, was prodigious. More than that, with games such as the newly developed golf-croquet he effectively made his own rules, and to these everyone must bow. Faced with Barrie's sorcery and force of personality, his friends appear to have accepted that there was no point appealing once he had decided upon a new rule. Thus, whenever his circle came together they played by Barrie's rules.

One of the more unusual guests at Black Lake that summer was the American Charles Frohman. Having once again been introduced, by the actor Seymour Hicks, at the Savoy the previous year, Frohman and Barrie had discovered an empathy for one another not found before. Perhaps it was Barrie's indefinable brand of charm that won Frohman over, or the realisation that central to both their lives was a passion for the stage. They were both small men with compensating abilities to make people laugh. Although, like a number of people who amuse others, Barrie preferred being at the centre of the laughter, something in Frohman's gentle and sympathetic demeanour meant that Barrie was always delighted at his quick spontaneous humour.

On a professional level Frohman's great success with *The Little Minister* in America had helped him to recognise Barrie's potential as a playwright. And though Barrie had as yet given the American nothing more, Frohman made it clear that he was very interested in anything he might have to offer. (Meanwhile, Barrie still believed he was a novelist.) By now, too, each was rather fascinated by that distinct aura of power issuing from the other's success. During the past year, emerging from their professional relationship and mutual respect, a real and lasting friendship had grown up between these strange and driven men.

In the middle of June, Sylvia Davies gave birth to her fourth son, Michael, and the family were consequently unable to visit the Barries' new house. Barrie left little time before travelling over – often taking Frohman with him – to visit the Davieses where they were staying not far away. After August at Black Lake, the Barries were back in London for September. More than a year after its completion, a new play, *The Wedding Guest*, was finally going into rehearsal under Dion Boucicault (junior) at the Garrick Theatre, where it was to be performed at the end of the month.

Boucicault was an immensely knowledgeable and painstaking producer, who insisted on choreographing his actors' behaviour on stage down to the last inflection and movement. Unlike many of his contemporaries his style was neither lofty nor amateurish. Instead, Boucicault was one of the first of the modern producers whose expertise extended to all aspects of the theatre. The actress Lillah McCarthy once said that his production methods were like a game of chess, in which every piece (actor) had its proper value and purpose. Boucicault would eventually work with Barrie on most of his finest plays, but their first encounter was not entirely auspicious.

A gifted autocrat who believed he knew best, in the theatre Boucicault almost always got his way. As Barrie's conduct was much the same, inevitably there were clashes. But, unusually, Barrie didn't always come off best. His subtle observations and suggestions were largely ignored as Boucicault's convictions simply overrode them, leaving Barrie to wail to his friend Gilmour about his 'bleeding and broken play'. In the same vein, when writing to invite Sylvia and Arthur Davies to the play, he said, 'I fully expect the men of the world to stamp on the thing, but never mind.'

Barrie's apprehension proved well founded, for his audience was left perplexed. His name by now had such status that, as the drama critic H. M. Walbrook would write,

> A Barrie first night had become a social event, and the audience was what is called 'brilliant' with well-known faces everywhere in the reserved seats. All had gathered in the expectation of a dramatic surprise, nor were they disappointed. Indeed, of the many Barrie First-Night audiences the one of that autumn . . . was certainly one of the most astonished. For here was their gentle ironist, their optimist, their sentimentalist ladling out scenes as harrowing and remorseless as those of Ibsen himself![3]

Barrie's name had sufficient pull that throughout his life as a dramatist his plays attracted most of the greatest actors of the day – in the case of *The Wedding Guest*, however, they were almost all unknowns, and Walbrook believed that the play was not well served by its cast

Ibsen's great advocate William Archer was one of the lone exceptions when he wrote saying that previously Barrie had only 'trifled with the stage', but now the critic wanted 'to offer a sincere welcome to our new dramatist'. Despite Archer's support – and though it played for fifteen weeks – Barrie's problem play was not considered a success. The audiences were puzzled and the critics didn't like it

The *Times* called it 'curiously naïve and curiously mannered', and ended by saying that Barrie would be best sticking to novels and leaving the stage alone. This proved to be a remarkable mistake, but it did help Barrie to clarify his aims.

He was deeply disappointed by the critics' response, but, as we have seen, he was not one 'to toss unfavourable criticism aside'. Ever responsive to his audience, he concluded that his expression must develop through a different form. While his purpose became an increasingly focused and serious one, he was also pragmatic enough to endorse Henry Irving's dictum that 'the drama must succeed as a business if it is not to fail as an art'.

Unlike other art forms, the theatre cannot progress significantly with the aid of private patronage. Rents for the building and payments to actors and playwright meant that in the days before state patronage of the arts, the theatre had to find mass support from its public in order to keep the doors open. And here Barrie's training as a journalist, combined with his instinct for communication, helped him to understand what his audience wanted. Appreciating well enough that an empty theatre meant he would neither make a living nor make himself heard, he saw that his message would have to be mediated in an acceptable way. He was discovering that, within a context of structure, with an apparently happy ending, he could still project a subtle message. In 1902 the *Times* critic tried to spell out this intangible quality at the heart of Barrie's work – why did a Barrie play with a happy ending often leave the audience unaccountably sad? He wrote:

> For the charm of a genuine Barrie, while it is undeniable, is at the same time not very easily explicable. In the ultimate analysis we believe that the pleasure of a genuine Barrie will be found not so much in what the work – whether novel or play – says as in what it implies.[4]

The Wedding Guest's premiere was followed by publication of *Tommy and Grizel*:

> No book in recent years has been awaited with such great expectation, and no book is likely to prove a greater disappointment. And yet . . . it is a great, and in the main, a successful work . . . Barrie has made a success as great in its way as Thackeray . . . Tommy . . . is a type, and one new in fiction. He is the artistic nature carried to its farthest development, a portrayal of what a man is in whom the imagination makes the ideal more real than the actual.[5]

Blackwood's Edinburgh Magazine said, 'He has bided his time; he has spared no pains . . . And the result – the appalling, the damning result – is *Tommy and Grizel*! For . . . let it be said at once [it] is a dire and dismal failure . . . a lamentable and grievous disappointment . . .'[6]

The public meanwhile, bought many thousands of copies.

Even by Barrie's notable rate of production, 1901 was to be an unusually prolific year. It began, though, with endings. On 22 January a national event signalling a momentous change took place. After sixty-three and a half years on the throne, Queen Victoria died. (Barrie's friend von Herkomer would paint her on her deathbed.) Hers had been the longest reign in British history. At eighty-two Victoria's death was not entirely unexpected, yet millions had lived their whole lives knowing no other monarch, and many could not imagine their country, or the Empire, without her. As if to mark the transformation of daily life that would take place in this new century, in the summer of 1901 the Barries purchased their first car. Their steam automobile, for which they hired a chauffeur, Alfred, was a great topic of conversation, for few of their friends had even travelled in a car let alone owned one.

This first car was more of a toy than anything practical. Steam-propelled, and set high up off the ground, it moved along with a bell warning of its approach. With no gears or clutch it was steered by a tiller rather than a wheel, and was more likely to break down than to carry passengers reliably from one place to another. Although it was probably Mary's idea, Barrie enjoyed the game of driving around in this slightly ridiculous contraption, which regularly caused a minor sensation as it passed along the as yet largely unmetalled roads. A year or so later, as much more sophisticated vehicles took to the roads, the steam car was dispensed with. Mary bought a Lanchester, the first of a series of much grander vehicles the Barries were to own, and hired a new chauffeur. Yet Barrie grew increasingly to dislike what he saw as these symbols of ostentation and extravagance. His needs were simpler, and by the latter part of his life he had grown to dislike all cars, their noise, speed and destructiveness. Viewing them as examples of modernity and the kind of machines that had destroyed the older, pre-industrial world of his youth, Barrie would take a cab or hire a car rather than own one himself.

When he wasn't maintaining a busy social life he shut himself in his study, and was simultaneously hard at work on at least three different pieces of writing. One of these, *The Little White Bird*, was progressing steadily, spurred on by Barrie's association with the Davies boys. He saw them often, both at home and out in Kensington Gardens with Mary Hodgson. The two eldest, George and Jack, were now eight and almost seven respectively, while Peter was four, and Michael still in a pram. Barrie's rapt child audience was encouraged to take part in the making of his stories in a creative cycle of repetition, reduction and enlargement. And like all good child audiences this one was quick to pounce on any inconsistencies, misrememberings or exaggeration, throwing these out with the authority of the most imperious editor.

In July the Barries were once again settled at Black Lake for the summer, and for the third year in succession the Davieses were holidaying at Tilford close by. All domestic details at Black Lake were organised with Mary's customary flair, and a steady stream of guests enjoyed croquet, cricket and good talk, seasoned with a series of pleasant meals.

George, Jack and sometimes little Peter joined Barrie in transposing their Kensington Gardens games and stories to the woods and shores of Black Lake. These more expansive surroundings gave them greater scope than the gardens in London, and day after summer's day they were fired by the adventure and romance of island shipwreck, hazardous combat with wild animals, lurking Redskins, and always the pirates, waiting in their ship on the deep lagoon to capture the shipwrecked heroes. Tirelessly obliging, Porthos joined in to act out a variety of parts, from pirate's dog to 'terrifying tiger'. Sometimes the master of ceremonies, Barrie became so caught up in the potency of the drama that his enthusiasm was indistinguishable from the children's.

Years later, he was asked to write a preface to *The Coral Island*, in which he would memorably say, 'to be born is to be wrecked on an island'. Following loosely the story of *Coral Island*, the adventures at Black Lake grew and developed. A punt was commandeered, variously to become a longboat, a pirate ship or 'the ill-fated brig *Anna Pink*'. Fortunately, the 'South-Sea Lagoon' was really quite shallow, because more than one prisoner was made to 'walk the plank' into its 'dark depths'. Garden tools and a number of real weapons, such as bows and arrows and long-bladed knives, were used – by the end of the summer Jack's lip would be split by an arrow from George's bow. This hardware was necessary to keep, for example, the dreadful and cowardly pirate Captain Swarthy, Barrie's present incarnation, at bay. At times Sylvia and Arthur grew alarmed at the realism of their sons' and Barrie's exploits, and felt obliged to step in and modify the ferocity of the game.

When Barrie was able to drag himself back to his incarnation as an adult, he recorded the perils and feats of that summer in a series of photographs of the boys and Porthos. August came to an end and with it this most idyllic of holidays. More than a quarter of a century later Barrie would recall it in his strange Dedication to *Peter Pan*. Asking the 'boys' if they remembered how they had cried out to the gods, saying, 'Do I just kill one pirate all the time?' he went on to say:

> Do you remember Marooner's Hut in the haunted groves . . . and the St Bernard dog in the tiger's mask who so frequently attacked you, and the literary record of that summer . . . which is much the best and the rarest of this author's works.

When the Davieses returned to London, the Barries remained at Black Lake for several more weeks. Poring over his photographs Barrie decided he would put together a selection of them, and construct a book out of the summer's adventures. Before long, at considerable expense, he would have just two copies printed and bound by his friend Walter Blaikie at the publishers Constable. One copy was for Barrie himself, while the second he presented to Arthur, the boys' father. 'Rarest of this author's works', Barrie called his book *The Boy Castaways of Black Lake Island*,

and made it a kind of tongue-in-cheek homage to all the adventure and shipwreck stories inspiring so many of the games he played with children. In the preface to *The Boy Castaways*, which was ostensibly written by the four-year-old Peter, Barrie wrote:

> The strange happenings here set forth ... are expansions of a note-book kept by me while we were on the island ...
>
> The date on which we were wrecked was this year, in August, 1901, and I have still therefore a vivid recollection of that strange and terrible summer, when we suffered experiences such as have probably never before been experienced by three brothers.

On opening the jolly red and black cover of *The Boy Castaways*, one discovers that, following the pastiche preface, sixteen chapter headings are written in the same idiom. Beginning with a dedication: 'To Our Mother, in Cordial Recognition of her Efforts to elevate us above the Brutes', the book's chapters have the titles:

I. Early Days – Our amusing Mother – her indiscretions.

II. Schools and Schoolmasters – Mary's bullying ways [this undoubtedly refers to the boys' nurse] – George teaches Wilkinson a stern Lesson – We run away to Sea.

III. Fearful Hurricane – Wreck of the *Anna Pink* – We go crazy for want of food – Proposal to eat Peter – Land ahoy!

IV. First Night on Black Lake Island – A Horrible Discovery ...

V. Gallant Behaviour of Jack – We make Bows and Arrows – We set about making a Hut.

VI. Tree-cutting – Madame Bruin and her Cubs – George to the Rescue – Pig-sticking and its Dangers.

VII. We Finish the Hut – George and Jack set off on a Voyage of Exploration round the island ... Night in the Woods – Startling Discovery that the island is the Haunt of Captain Swarthy and his Pirate Crew.

VIII. Dead Men's Point – Corpsy Glen – The Valley of Rolling Stones.

IX. Exploration Continued – We find Captain Swarthy's Dog – Suspended Animation – We are attacked by Wolves – Jack saves George's Life.

X. The Hut meanwhile – The Pirates set upon Peter ...

XI. We board the Pirate Sloop at Dawn – a Rakish Craft – George Hew-them-down and Jack of The Red Hatchet – a Holocaust of Pirates – Rescue of Peter.

XII.   Trial of Captain Swarthy – He begs for Mercy – We string him up.

XIII.   The Rainy Season – Malarial Fever . . .

XIV.   We build a Boat – Narrow Escape from a tiger – Skinning the Tiger.

XV.   The Pleasures of Tobacco – Peter's Dream of Home – Last Night on the Island – We sail for England, Home and Wilkinson's.

XVI.   Advice to Parents about Bringing up their Children.[7]

And that is all. One searches in vain for a text, because the book consists of nothing but the lengthy chapter titles, thirty-five photograph illustrations and their captions. Why did Barrie leave the chapters empty?

If we see *The Boy Castaways* as one of his elaborate jokes, it was also a flattering record and a homage to his relationship with the little Davies boys and their make-believe life together. But, as always, one must be wary of accepting Barrie's deceptively simple descriptions or estimation of events. Read carefully enough his words were essentially the truth. 'The strange happenings here set forth . . . are expansions of a notebook kept by me while we were on the island.'

By putting into pseudo-book form his and the boys' private world of fantasy and adventure, Barrie was once again blurring the distinction between illusion and reality. He was, as was his custom, challenging the idea of what was truly real. The shared adventures were real, but they were also something made up and existing only in the imagination of those who had taken part in them. Thus the empty chapters of *The Boy Castaways* insist that the imagination is not only powerfully real, but also something intangible. Their shared imaginative world was Barrie and the boys' secret society.

The boys, and no doubt their mother, must have been greatly flattered by the book, but one is left in some doubt as to how impressed the boy's father would have been. It is worth noting that almost as soon as Barrie had presented him with the precious second copy, Arthur left it on a train. Many years later, in the Dedication to *Peter Pan*, Barrie wrote: 'The literary record of that summer . . . which is so much the best and the rarest of this author's works . . . was limited to two copies, of which one (there was always some devilry in any matter connected with Peter) instantly lost itself on a train.' Arthur's copy was never discovered, and his son Peter would later remark of this apparent carelessness, 'doubtless his own way of commenting on the whole fantastic affair'.[8]

The Boy Castaways was a significant part of Barrie's experimental process,

and although Peter Pan and any fairies are not explicit, they are prefigured in a number of elements. As Barrie would later write to 'the boys':

> They do seem to be emerging out of our island, don't they, the
> little people of the play, all except that sly one, the chief figure, who
> draws farther and farther into the wood as we advance on him? He
> so dislikes being tracked, as if there were something odd about him,
> that when he dies he means to get up and blow away the particles
> that will be his ashes.[9]

13

A Second Chance

dventures aside, throughout 1901 Barrie worked on what were to become two of his most famous plays; plays that would mark his arrival as a mature dramatist. The first, *Quality Street*, had been completed before the historic summer holiday, and was to receive its premiere under Charles Frohman that autumn in the United States. Frohman was excited at presenting Maude Adams as the star of another Barrie play, and had backed the production with considerable emotional and financial resources. It opened in Toledo in the middle of October and Barrie was soon writing to Frohman 'to thank you most heartily for all the thought and care you have given to *Quality Street*. I see it has been immense – and Miss Adams for the wonderful things she seems to be doing with Phoebe [the heroine, Phoebe Throssel]. She is a marvel.'

From the start the play was received well, and on arrival in New York in November its success was assured for Frohman, Adams and Barrie. The response from the public was rapturous. This was repeated when in the following year *Quality Street* came to London. As always the critics took a more complex view, but many were appreciative.

> The play is an invention, a creation, a thing nobody but Mr Barrie could have done. It was produced by a totally different order of mental effort from that which goes to the making of the everyday comedy of commerce, however witty and agreeable.[1]

A number of reviewers were relieved that Barrie had apparently returned to the kind of thing they thought he did so well – light comedies of manners. This inspired the *Illustrated London News* to write,

> Quite the most exquisite thing the London stage has known for some time is [J.M.B.'s] new comedy . . . an idyll of Georgian days, in which the prim manners and precise speech of old-world gentility

are cleverly revived, and the unpretentious history of two spinsters is told with all a Jane Austen's sympathy and humour.

Set in the time of the Napoleonic Wars, a genteel street in a little town is home to a group of maiden ladies, who read romances and remain oblivious to much of the outside world and its bellicose dramas. The outside world, however, is set to impinge on their lives when the younger of the Throssel sisters, Phoebe, loses her admirer, Valentine Brown, to the war. We see them again ten years later when, through lack of funds, the pretty drawing room in which romances were read has become a schoolroom. Here the sisters humorously and pathetically survive, with equal fortitude, both the brazen youthful insensitivities of their pupils and the impenetrability of algebra.

With the return of one of their ex-pupils and Phoebe's admirer, we are shown how the sisters have taken on the mantle of middle age before their time. Now regretful, given the chance to throw off her premature ageing and responsibilities, Phoebe dresses up as her own 'niece' and is thus asked to a ball by Valentine Brown. In her newly acquired role Phoebe is able to 'act' the part of a pretty, frivolous, witty and romantic young heroine. In this 'role' she chastises Brown for his insensitivity – years ago he could have asked her to marry him and didn't – whereupon he confesses that it is not the 'niece' he loves but her aunt.

In the last act the Throssel sisters farcically strive to rid themselves of their mythical niece. The neighbours have noted her appearance and await her dramatic exit, while the sisters grow more and more agitated at the thought of a lifetime spent with a niece who is an illusion. After a devoted maid tells all to Brown, he enters into the charade, takes away the 'niece' wrapped in a bundle, and returns to propose to her 'aunt', Miss Phoebe.

As usual, most of the critics took the easiest route with Barrie's new play and responded to it at its simplest level, or misunderstood it altogether. *Quality Street* is not a pretty, romantic comedy but rather a satire on the contemporary romance, while presenting in its place something Barrie believed to be much more lasting and important. As always using his sly humour, his immense care with language and his great theatricality, he turns on its head the very notion of the passionate nineteenth-century romance – usually a fairly unsubtle projection of male fantasies – his audiences were expecting.

In *Quality Street* Barrie gives them a heroine who is not passionate, beautiful and vacuous, with a head full of fantasy, but instead is a new kind of woman: intelligent, realistic, modest and witty. In the stage directions

Barrie is at pains to instruct the actress not to act the romantic heroine but to understate in everything.

In the London debut, however, Barrie's leading actress did not serve him well. Ellaline Terriss, who was very pretty, well known for her head-strong temperament and accustomed to a great deal of adulation, played the part of Phoebe Throssel. (A good proportion of the male population was in love with her, and her image graced many a boy's wall.) Clearly she was unable to subsume her own personality within the modest and intelligent middle-aged woman she was portraying, and led the ever-perceptive Max Beerbohm to say of her: 'Miss Terriss ... walks and talks very prettily, and is very pretty altogether. But never for a moment does she forget herself, still less merge herself for us in the part she is playing.'

However, when Fay Compton played Phoebe in the 1921 revival of the play she followed Barrie's directions with great care and sensitivity. As a result it was said of her:

> Those who saw Miss Compton in this scene will not soon forget her acting. Every tone, glance, and movement was significant, and the character in all its complexity lived ... All through the play Miss Compton acted very quietly ... No actress who has not a sense of the comicality as well as the tears of life will ever be able to play the part of Phoebe Throssel correctly ... from many spectators she has, when rightly acted, drawn more tears than laughter, though a good many of those tears have been shed over the last act and have been tears of happiness.[2]

Just as Barrie needed a subtle and intelligent audience to appreciate the full import of his plays, so he had need of actors of subtlety and under-standing to fully represent their *dramatis personae*.

The idea for the second play of 1901 came to Barrie in the Easter of 1900 and, untypically for him, he had 'seen' the entire plot almost at a sitting. Instead of his customary disjointed series of notes, the major scheme of this new play was put down consecutively in one long draft. Once Barrie had begun, his mind must have been so utterly focused that the ideas were unstoppable. Unusually, the notebook runs on for page after page until he has finished. It is rough, but the four acts of the play are quite recognisably there. After many changes of title, this was the play that would become famous as *The Admirable Crichton*.

Barrie's intense preoccupation with the significance and nuance of words meant that he would search doggedly for a title until he felt he had precisely captured the essence of each new work. There is purpose, then, in choosing as this play's namesake a Scottish linguist, poet and adventurer of the sixteenth century, named James 'the Admirable' Crichton. Crichton's career included episodes in which he 'travelled to Paris in 1577, where he is said to have disputed on scientific questions in twelve languages . . . disputed doctrines of Thomists and Scotists . . . [and was] a good swordsman; killed in a brawl in Mantua'.[3] Although Barrie had trawled through many possible titles for the new play, clearly Crichton had interested him for some time, became he had written down 'The Admirable Crichton' in a notebook in the early 1880s.

'Movement' was of central importance both to the form and the content of Barrie's mature plays. In his earlier drama there is a great interest in disguise and role-playing – Barrie's perennial fascination with identity and illusion – but beginning with *Quality Street* a new kind of movement was introduced and is evident in all the major plays. In the first act Barrie sets the scene and establishes the context. In the second, usually taking place some years later, the circumstances have radically altered. This is what happens in *Quality Street, What Every Woman Knows, Mary Rose* and *Little Mary*. If the change in circumstances doesn't take place over a fairly long passage of time, then it is brought about by a radical change of geography. *The Admirable Crichton, Peter Pan* and *Dear Brutus* all have shorter time-spans, but their change of location is the most radical.

In *Peter Pan* the characters move from Bloomsbury to Never Land, while in *Dear Brutus* they are transported into a magic wood. Finally, as in *Dear Brutus* and *Peter Pan*, Barrie has his characters move through time and space with some kind of return to their starting point. And it is through this device that we see how much the characters have learnt, or not, through their experience. Just occasionally, as in *Quality Street*, the return, when Phoebe Throssel throws off her disguise and returns to her present self, brings about a change for the better: Phoebe receives a proposal.

But more often, as in *Dear Brutus, The Admirable Crichton* and *Peter Pan*, the return to the 'starting point' brings darker and more ambiguous messages. Barrie asks whether, given a change or a second chance, we can undo the past. Certainly we know that Barrie himself believed we are rarely given that second chance.

We can point to various 'sources' of inspiration for *Crichton*, as it became known in the trade. More than anything, one senses that these were useful triggers for something that had been bubbling away in Barrie's imagination for years. For example, a notebook entry some time before reads: 'Play. Scene. Servants entertained in drawing room by mistress + master à la Carlisle family.' This referred to Rosamund, Countess of Carlisle, who apparently 'combined advanced radical principles with a manner which terrified members of every class'.[4]

After the play's staging, another Scottish aristocrat, Lord Aberdeen, felt compelled to write to Barrie objecting to the satirical treatment of his family; the 'liberal' and rather driven Aberdeens were also in the habit of reversing roles with their servants. Typically, Barrie didn't respond one way or another to Aberdeen's accusation. He was far too slippery for that.

The Admirable Crichton begins in Lord Loam's household, which is presented to us as dominated entirely by class. Lord Loam thinks himself very radical when, once a month, he has his household reverse its roles and the noble lord and his three haughty daughters wait on their reluctant servants. This situation gives Barrie ample opportunity for much humour (and satire at the expense of the indolent and ineffectual leisured classes). The butler, Bill Crichton, a staunch conservative, strongly disapproves of the whole affair.

Act II finds Lord Loam, his daughters, their cousin the Hon. Ernest Wooley, the kind vicar, Traherne, the butler, Crichton, and the maid, Tweeny, all wrecked on a desert island while sailing on Lord Loam's yacht 'on a voyage to distant parts of the earth'. In the end their voyage is as much a matter of personal discovery as of navigation.

When it comes to leadership, the ineffectuality of Lord Loam and Ernest is quickly apparent, and to everyone's agitation Crichton feels it increasingly necessary to take charge. To him it is 'natural' that 'there must always . . . be one to command and others to obey'.

Two years after their shipwreck on the island we see that Crichton's position as leader is not only accepted but rejoiced in for the energy and initiative he demonstrates, his 'superiors' now following him with conviction. Lord Loam's daughters are also much changed. From young women so indolent that dressing in the morning without help was an exhausting experience, they now dress themselves, in trousers made of animal skins, and luxuriate in the knowledge that they are not only free from social pressures, but are also adept at hunting and fishing.

> This splendid boy clad in skins, is what Nature has done for Lady Mary. She carries bow and arrows and a blow pipe, and over her shoulder is a fat buck, which she drops in triumph. Forgetting to enter demurely she leaps through the window.[5]

In this 'natural' society, with practical and organising abilities now paramount, the priorities of birth and class have become obsolete. And while Crichton has shown clearly that it is he who possesses the qualities of outstanding leadership – ruling his island regime with a benevolent but iron hand – his old 'superior' Lord Loam cheerfully fulfils his role as the simple handyman, 'whose flabbiness has dropped from him; gone too is his pomposity; his eye is clear, brown his skin; he could leap a gate', and exuberantly entertains his fellow islanders with his home-made concertina. He has become the minstrel-fool, while Crichton is, disturbingly, on the way to becoming a king. He has the girls make a robe for him, provoking Ernest's outburst, 'I think he looks too regal in it.' To which Traherne retorts, 'Regal! I sometimes fancy that is why he is so fond of wearing it.'

In the fourth and final act the rescued party have returned to the conventions of their previous life. But unlike *As You Like It*, perhaps Barrie's favourite Shakespearean play, with the reversion to the court, in this case Lord Loam's Mayfair house, the characters do not remain their regenerate selves, but revert to lives of indolence, condescension and hypocrisy. Once more in England, Lord Loam, from an unassailable position of absolute power within his household and his society, passion-ately lectures: 'Can't you see, Crichton, that our divisions into classes are artificial, that if we were to return to Nature, which is the aspiration of my life, all would be equal.' But Crichton sees further and says: 'The divisions into classes, my lord, are not artificial. They are the natural outcome of a civilised society.' (To Lady Mary) 'There must always be a master and servants in all civilised communities, and whatever is natural is right.'

As to Crichton, his position is left ambiguous, and the embryonic rela-tionship implied between him and Lady Mary on the island is put aside once they return to their old lives.

Whereas in most of Barrie's plays a pleasant surface plot carries under-tones and messages more subtle, and often far darker than are immedi-ately obvious, in *The Admirable Crichton* it was apparently clear to everyone what Barrie had achieved. He had written a biting and sometimes hilar-ious political satire which held up a mirror to the present social order, headed by a parasitical aristocracy. And, like all the best humour, those at whom it is most directed often find it the funniest. Barrie set against those who dominate, those without power, who none the less have more clarity, dynamism and enterprise. When dealing with questions of class and its hierarchy, Barrie makes clear his belief that the Natural Order works quite differently.

Shipwrecked on the island, the more enterprising and dynamic Crichton rules over his aristocratic employers. But once back in 'civil-isation', although all the characters revert to the vapidity of their previous lives, and Crichton is once again subservient, it is still he, the enigmatic butler, who we sense is the ruling intelligence of the play. In Crichton's ambiguous final position Barrie may well be cautioning against making the simple judgement that civilisation is a dubious improvement on the primitive. From the evidence of his early notebooks we know that Barrie had read Darwin, and more than one reviewer pointed out the connections in this play. But Barrie was a highly intelligent, if intuitive, thinker who took from both Darwin and Carlyle only that which he could make into something quite his own. The end of *Crichton* was much debated, and without a clear final statement it has been criticised for a fatal ambiguity. Typically, Barrie changed the ending several times over the years, but it would be quite consistent with his art to say that in *Crichton* his aim was to reflect a fractured world without clear answers or paths. As Bill Crichton says: 'circumstances alter cases'.

Over the Christmas period of 1901 Barrie took the older Davies boys to see a new play, a pantomime, with the author, Seymour Hicks, and his wife, Ellaline Terriss, taking the leading roles. Hicks had called his pantomime *Bluebell in Fairyland*. Set around the lives of struggling young workers in Covent Garden, the plot follows the various encounters here and in the fairy world of a flower-girl, Bluebell, and her young man, a crossing-sweeper, Dicky. Bluebell finally rejects Fairyland and the possibility of material wealth to marry Dicky. Both the children and Barrie were fascinated by the play, and he retold and acted out its roles for any child who would listen.

At the end of December Barrie faced another family loss when his older sister Isabella unexpectedly died. They had not met often in the last few years, and while Isabella had been occupied raising her five children Barrie was engrossed in making his life as a writer. This life had progressed and developed in such a way that the milieu in which he now moved, plus the handicap of his wealth, meant that he was one of those who had outgrown his roots.

Whether he had much in common with them or not, Barrie's feeling for his family, including what they represented to him as symbols of his rooted past, always remained strong. He nurtured the *idea* of his family, and financially assisted a number of them at various times. The reality of engagement was more problematic, but his sadness at his sister's early death – she was forty-three – was genuine. And so was his offer of financial assistance to his brother-in-law left with five children, none of whom had yet reached the age of independence. Dr Murray felt able to manage without his brother-in-law's support, though six years later, when he, too, became ill and died, Barrie would, in his own way, be generous to his nieces and nephews.

Early in 1902 his friend the writer Anthony Hope (pseudonym of

Anthony Hope Hawkins, who gave up the law to write after the great success of his novel *The Prisoner of Zenda* in 1894) had successfully proposed Barrie, seconded by Lord Rosebery, as a 'person of distinguished eminence' for membership of the Athenaeum Club. This new mark of approbation was characteristic of Barrie's increasing status, and for which it was his established custom to affect little regard. Having discovered that he was, to use Dr Johnson's description of *his* friend Hawkins, 'not a clubbable man', Barrie would rarely present himself at the Athenaeum. However, although in one sense he was too confident to need much approval for his work, at some level his self-belief required such sustenance. Superficially this was because it made him progressively socially acceptable, a part of the establishment, and Barrie was always fascinated by power, especially when that power was an *éminence grise*. More importantly, it was because honours, popularity and applause were indicators, as they were for Tommy Sandys, that he existed.

And one of the happiest proofs of existence for Barrie was friendship. He already knew many people, and his fame would lead him to know many more, but there were only a few with whom he felt truly at ease. That spring, at the Hewletts', he was to meet a couple, Edward and Elizabeth Lucas, who were to become two of those intimate few. E.V., as friends called Lucas, was a prolific writer of journalism, essays, biography and travel, who had acquired much of his broad education while employed in a Brighton bookshop. He worked for a time for *Punch*, edited Charles Lamb and became chairman of the publishers Methuen. A brilliant professional amateur, E.V. Lucas's ambition to succeed at writing novels and plays was frustrated by his *just* not being good enough. He had a dry sense of wit, and was hospitable and generous to others struggling to survive as writers. A. A. Milne wrote of him after his death: 'One would save for him the little gleanings of the week; ridiculous things, odd things, damnable things; heard, read, discovered: thinking, "I must tell E.V. that," knowing that his comment would give just that extra flavour to one's emotion.'[6] Meanwhile, according to a mutual friend of hers and Barrie's, Elizabeth Lucas was

> Subtle, sympathetic, quick-minded; she could be, as occasion needed, delightfully ribald or delicately ironic. I remember Charles Whibley saying she was one of the only three women he knew who was equipped with a sense of irony [a mark in her favour for Barrie]. Charles Whibley, and several other men, remarked on her possession of another faculty then also rare in women. Beside her quick sure taste in furniture and decoration . . . and her skill in gardening

. . . she had, they acknowledged with surprise, a palate, and a very well-trained palate, for wine.[7]

That year Mary's search for a house to improve on 133 Gloucester Road at last brought results. After seven years they were to leave behind the words Barrie had had inscribed above the drawing-room fireplace, and which he described as 'the wisest of Greek sayings': 'If we would love our fellow men we must not expect too much of them.'[8]

Leinster Terrace was part of a pleasant row, probably built for comfortable merchants in the early nineteenth century. Although backing on to the haughty grandeur of Lancaster Gate, Leinster Terrace itself was on a more intimate scale. At the bottom of the garden was an old stable, which Mary would convert into a garage, with a new study for Barrie in the stable boy's hayloft above. She had the house painted white and made the garden pretty, achieving an effect of rural simplicity. No larger than Gloucester Road, Leinster Corner, as Mary called it, was altogether more appealing. Adjoining Bayswater Road, directly across the road from the house were the great trees and the green northern reaches of Kensington Gardens. The proximity of Barrie's new home to the gardens was not a coincidence, for Mary loved this green haven as much as did her husband.

Not long after their move to Leinster Corner Mary bought another dog. As a short-lived breed, the St Bernard, Porthos, had died the previous year at the age of eight. In her memoir, *Of Dogs and Men*, Mary wrote:

> I missed everything that Porthos had been to me. What was the use of going out, when there was no dog to dance happily by my side? What pleasure in coming back, when no wild greeting awaited me?
>
> It is very easy to see why women love their dogs so devotedly. From nobody else do we get such flattering attentions. A man takes you as a matter of course. You are there, just as his dinner is there. Unless you do something extremely odd, you cease to surprise him. But every time your dog looks at you, it is as though it were for the first time. 'What an amazing person you are,' he cries, 'and how exquisite!'
>
> 'You're a funny old darling,' you reply, but nevertheless believe it . . .[9]

Barrie named the puppy Luath after Robert Burns's poem *Twa Dogs*, in which Luath is the poor man's dog and represents the peasantry. Mary continued:

Porthos very early had said farewell to wild puppydom. But it clung to Luath for many years . . . He took life so eagerly . . . He lived in the present. Porthos might be interested in his past . . . but the present was always good enough for Luath . . .

Domesticity is what he was cut out for. He would have been a nurse; he should have been the father of a large family, above all he should have been a mother. An adverse fate denied him these delights; but he managed to manoeuvre something of them all into fourteen years of life that never failed to bring him unreasoning happiness.[10]

Mary walked in the gardens with her dog and her husband almost every day. Unlike Porthos, whose greatest loyalty lay with Barrie, Mary believed that as a new arrival in the house, because she had nursed Luath through a mortal illness, he remained more devoted to her.

What races we ran in the Gardens! Hiding behind trees, 'Catch me, catch me if you can.'

I am quite aware that my games, even at their wildest, were not a patch on those he had with his master, for he was an adept at games. But I didn't worry myself about it. I knew I was the favourite . . . he was never really comfortable, to tell the truth, unless we were together. He hated those walks when friends joined us and we got separated.

Dear Luath. He was always that kind of dog. He never probed into the complexities of life. Life to him was a very simple affair. Home, food, games, and a walk out every afternoon, all together, what more could you want?[11]

It was June when the Barries moved in to Leinster Corner. The Allahakbarries had already begun the cricket season, so from his new address their captain was soon making preparations for that year's cricket and festivities at Black Lake. With the last guests gone he intended staying on in the country until rehearsals began for the London staging of *Quality Street* in the early autumn. These plans were soon to be cut short, and there would be no more cricket that year. With little warning, Barrie's father died.

Although at eighty-seven David Barrie was becoming senile, he was also quite well and active. So when he was knocked down by a horse and cart in Kirriemuir High Street, and appeared no more than bruised, the family thought that a good rest would soon help him over any shock. The old man was put to bed. Lying peacefully to recover, he appeared so tranquil and untroubled that his son was not recalled from London.

The invalid's calmness, however, was misleading and no one realised that he wasn't actually improving. His family then, were quite unprepared for his death, which came on 26th June 1902. Jamie and Mary were immediately summoned, once again making the long train journey north. Barrie had been devastated at his mother's death, seven years earlier. Now forty-two, what were his thoughts as he followed his father's coffin in the funeral procession up on to Cemetery Hill?

Those of Barrie's friends who had known him at the time of his mother's death were concerned lest his reaction to his father's death should overwhelm him in the same way. But they misjudged the profound difference in Barrie's relationship with each of his parents. His notebooks are empty of comment, and there was no memoir, no *Margaret Ogilvy*, for his father. Apart from remarking that David Ogilvy was 'the kind of Scotchman that I admire the most', Barrie appears to have had very little else to say about him. Although he had inherited his father's great industry and doggedness, and that determination to further himself, there the similarity ended. He respected his father for his achievement, but the earnest, narrow literalness of David Barrie's religion, for example, was anathema to his son. Indeed, these two had so little in common that the image of Jamie Barrie as a changeling comes to mind. Rather than shutting himself away, surrounded by an impenetrable gloom, this time Barrie withdrew only to his study, where he put the finishing touches to *The Admirable Crichton*.

His star was so far in the ascendant that immediately the rehearsals for *Quality Street* were over and the play opened, rehearsals for *Crichton* were to begin. Hardly had the notices for *Quality Street* ceased when, by the first week of November, Barrie was in the position of having not one but two really major successes on the London stage at once.

Throughout rehearsals for *Quality Street*, when Barrie wasn't practising his habitual silence or watchfulness, he flirted outrageously with the lead actress. With equal predictability, Mary Barrie looked on without comment. Instead, in the theatre for many of the later rehearsals, her presence may well have kept things in check. She was quite able to appreciate the element of humour in rehearsals, and to tolerate her husband's idolisation of his leading ladies. But Mary also knew when the joking and foolishness was beginning to hold up progress, and in her own way she let this be known. Although her manner could sometimes be abrupt, and her particular intelligence meant that she grew impatient with too much silliness, as an ex-actress her sharp eye for detail and nuance would make a valuable contribution to the staging of more than one of Barrie's plays.

At these rehearsals his demeanour was one of studied indifference. A line he jotted down in his notebook reveals the consciousness with which this was done: 'Hare watching my face for laughs'. And one knows that Hare would almost certainly have got none. The many selves that constituted J. M. Barrie meant that while, on the one hand, he could make the production of a play an extraordinarily collaborative venture between himself and his actors, on the other hand, his determination to control was rarely in abeyance.

The stance of indifference, which was part of Barrie's highly crafted public presentation of himself, included the premise that as long as those around you found it difficult to gauge your thoughts or feelings, they would remain at a distinct disadvantage. A few years later, having attended one of Barrie's rehearsals, this studious impenetrability was touched on by Thomas Hardy:

> If any day a promised play
> Should be in preparation
> You never see friend JMB
> Depressed or in elation.
> But with a stick, rough, crooked and thick,
> You may sometimes discern him,
> Standing as though a mummery show
> Did not at all concern him.[12]

After *Quality Street* Frohman became the most important of Barrie's sponsors. Frohman's belief in his friend was now unqualified, and he instructed that all Barrie's set directions were to be meticulously followed. From now on, once he had agreed to stage a Barrie play Frohman never insisted on a contract. No matter what the cost, the play would go ahead; and the sets for *Crichton* were costly.

Barrie's interest in the use of theatrical effects of all kinds arose out of his fascination with the theatre as illusion. This was evident in his stage instructions as far back as that early play *Walker London*. In *Crichton* his stage effects were the most dramatic and the most powerfully integrated of any he had yet employed. They anticipated, too, the use of effects on an even grander scale, in a play where they would soon be used more dramatically than in anything yet staged. Meanwhile, the props, the visual effects, the lighting, and even many of the actors' movements in *Crichton*, were all calculated to reinforce the play's meaning. Irene Vanbrugh, who played Lady Mary, recalled:

It was a production full of mechanical difficulties. In one scene there was the clearing of a patch on a desert island. The lighting of a log fire, a pot to be brought to the boil at a given moment, all needed very careful timing. The properties were extremely original and had to be made with the greatest care in every detail to give the true impression of hand-made effort.[13]

This was epitomised by the famous scene in which, having indicated that he should be the shipwrecked party's leader, Crichton provokes a mass exodus in reaction. Darkness is falling and he stands absolutely still, caught in the motion of leaning forward to stir a pot on the fire. His absolute stillness emphasises his action, until eventually the implied smell of the food, representing the power of Nature, draws the aristocrats back to squat subserviently around the fire, waiting to be given their meal.

Dion Boucicault and Charles Frohman were at one in their determination to see Barrie's complicated props and effects realised. From Lord Loam's grand Mayfair residence to the desert island with its mixture of realism and illusion, to the vast quantities of scenery, the special electrical effects (electricity was still a novelty), the newly built props, to the specially designed dresses by Barrie's friend, the illustrator Bernard Partridge, in all these things Frohman and Boucicault were convinced that every last detail was crucial. This stretched the capacities and patience of the skilled stage staff and, ironically for a play in part about the problems of class and hierarchy (in 1902, for instance, it was regarded as quite shocking to have a butler in the lead role, and women in trousers), they came out on strike in protest at the difficulties of their work.

Stagehands from other London theatres were hurriedly brought in, but on the first night there was chaos behind the scenes. Nevertheless, though the play ran over time and finished after midnight, the audience remained fascinated and amused. Responding to the final curtain with resounding applause, they called for the author as the cast returned again and again to take their bows. The author, however, was no longer in the house. After an interminable delay at the end of the second act he could bear the strain no longer and, leaving behind Mary and the Davieses, had gone out into the streets to walk off his nerves.

The response of that first-night audience was justified when the reviews appeared. For the first time the critical acclaim for a Barrie play was as pronounced as its popular appeal. The eminent critic William Archer would write: 'Rarest of virtues on the English stage – it gives one something to think about.' And later he added, 'Say what you will about the piece . . . it is, above all, the product of a unique mind, of an original humourist doubled with an inexhaustibly inventive man of the theatre.'[14] The critic Max Beerbohm considered *Crichton* 'quite the best thing that has happened, in my time, to the British stage'. While *The Bookman* would say:

It is at once one of the most amusing and one of the bitterest in all the range of English drama. Barrie has often been accused of sentimentality. Yet here . . . there is a fatalism, a bitterness, a denial of an exit from the coils of life, which that self-confessed foe of sentimentality, GBS [George Bernard Shaw] himself, never has achieved.

And in this remarkable year, when there were packed houses for *Quality Street* and *The Admirable Crichton*, and the reviewers were almost unanimous in saying that *Crichton* was the best thing Barrie had done so far, his commercial success was set to continue still further. Only a few days after *Crichton's* launch, Hodder & Stoughton published *The Little White Bird*, the book that had taken its author four long years to write. Since August it had been appearing as a serial in the United States, and Scribner's now followed Hodder in bringing it out as a book.

The story is narrated by a retired army captain, 'W', a barely disguised Barrie, a 'gentle, whimsical, lonely old bachelor'. A writer, who goes for long walks with his St Bernard dog, Porthos, in Kensington Gardens. He tells the little boy, David – based on George Davies – that over a period of time he had observed from his window a nursery maid, David's mother, Mary, whose marriage he has engineered. The captain describes how a letter he had written was responsible for bringing David's parents together, and is impatient at the thought that his power might not be appreciated. He says, 'You don't seem to understand, my boy . . . that had I not dropped that letter, there would never have been a little boy called David.' As Barrie's stories for the Davies boys had developed, so, according to Captain W, the creation of children did not come about through childbirth.

David knows that all children in our part of London were once birds in the Kensington Gardens: and that the reason there are bars on nursery windows and a tall fender by the fire is because very little people sometimes forget that they no longer have wings, and try to fly away through the window or up the chimney.

Children in the bird stage are difficult to catch. David knows that many people have none, and his delight . . . is to go with me to some spot in the Gardens where these unfortunates may be seen trying to catch one with small pieces of cake . . . The first time I ever saw David he was on the sward behind the Baby's Walk. He was a mistle thrush, attracted thither that hot day by a hose, which lay on the ground . . . [He] was on his back in the water, kicking up his legs.[15]

Caught by the leg with a string, the little mistle thrush eventually became the boy David, who is often wistful for his bird past.

> 'Think of your mother,' I [the captain] said severely.
>   He said he would often fly in to see her. The first thing he would do would be to hug her. No, he would alight on the water jug first, and have a drink.[16]

With his ability as narrator to control time – past, present and future – the captain gives David the chance not to have become a boy. On reflection David decides that it would hurt his mother too much and he accepts his human fate. At first, in competition with David's mother in all things 'creative', the captain 'creates' his own fictional son, Timothy. Later, when he and David have become friends, the captain finds he must now compete with the boy's nurse, Irene, for the little boy's attentions – another woman to be kept away. While many of David's mother's personal traits were clearly based on Sylvia Llewelyn Davies, so, too, the nurse, Irene, was undoubtedly modelled on the Davieses' nursemaid, Mary Hodgson.

In a chapter called 'A Grand Tour of the Gardens' Barrie describes Kensington Gardens: 'a tremendous big place, with millions and hundreds of trees where there are many different Walks, and where many different games are played'. He describes the famous round pond, to which

> paths from everywhere crowd like children . . . [and] there are men who sail boats . . . such big boats that they bring them in barrows, and sometimes in perambulators, and then the baby has to walk . . .
>   The Serpentine begins near here. It is a lovely lake, and there is a drowned forest at the bottom of it. If you peer over the edge you can see the trees all growing upside down, and they say that at night there are also drowned stars in it. If so Peter Pan sees them when he is sailing across the lake in the Thrushes Nest. A small part only of the Serpentine is in the Gardens, for soon it passes beneath a bridge to far away where the island is on which all the birds are born that become baby boys and girls. No one who is human, except Peter Pan (and he is only half human), can land on the island . . .[17]

From the fantastic imaginings through which Barrie has guided the children, a boy called Peter has suddenly emerged. On the published frontispiece of *The Little White Bird* is a 'map' of Kensington Gardens, and here, included with the gardens' imaginary places and inhabitants, he appears for the first time.

First glimpsed in that paragraph at the end of *Tommy and Grizel*, Peter was introduced as 'the little boy who was lost', and who was 'singing to himself because he is always to be a boy'. Barrie had concluded this paragraph by saying, 'That is really all, but T. Sandys knew how to tell it.' And now Peter acquired his second name – and became Peter Pan. Living in a state of eternal childhood, Peter's other name, Pan, reflects his affinity with the pipe-playing god, symbolising a state of nature, who luxuriates in immediate gratification and lives unhindered by social constraint.

In *The Little White Bird* Barrie describes one of the ways in which his writing is inspired by interaction with a child:

I ought to mention here that the following is our way with a story: First I tell it to him, and then he tells it to me, the understanding being that it is quite a different story; and then I retell it with his additions, and so we go on until no one could say whether it is more his story or mine.[18]

Earlier Barrie had said:

If you ask your mother whether she knew about Peter Pan when she was a little girl, she will say, 'Why of course I did, child'; and if you ask whether he rode on a goat in those days she will say, 'What a foolish question to ask; certainly he did.' . . . Of course Peter is ever so old, but he is really always the same age, so that does not matter in the least. His age is one week and though he was born so long ago he has never had a birthday, nor is there the slightest chance of his ever having one. The reason is that he escaped from being human when he was seven days old; he escaped by the window and flew back to Kensington Gardens.

If you think he was the only baby who ever wanted to escape, it shows how completely you have forgotten your own young days. When David heard this story first he was certain that he had never tried to escape, but I told him to think back hard . . .

And the boy David gradually remembers that indeed he had lain in bed planning to run away the moment his mother was asleep, but she had caught him halfway up the chimney.[19]

When he eventually makes his escape from the nursery, Peter Pan causes pandemonium in Kensington Gardens. Believing him to be human, the fairies flee from him in terror. After repeated rejection he returns to the island on the Serpentine – adjoining Kensington Gardens – to search out the old leader of the birds, Solomon Caw, and 'put his strange case to him', to discover what is wrong. Peter is distressed when Solomon tells him the problem: he is no longer a bird but has become a baby human. 'I suppose,' said Peter huskily, 'I suppose I can still fly?' But he has lost faith, and the narrator tells us:

> The moment you doubt whether you can fly, you cease forever to be able to do it. The reason birds can fly and we can't is simply that they have perfect faith, for to have faith is to have wings. And the old crow Solomon tells Peter that he is now a . . .
>
> 'Poor little half-and-half! . . . you will never be able to fly again, not even on windy days. You must live here on the island always.'
>
> 'And never even go to the Kensington Gardens?' Peter asked tragically.
>
> 'How could you get across?' said Solomon. He promised, very kindly, to teach Peter as many of the bird ways as could be learned by one of such an awkward shape.
>
> 'Then I shan't be exactly human?' Peter asked.
>
> 'No.'
>
> 'Nor exactly a bird?'
>
> 'No.'
>
> 'What shall I be?'
>
> 'You will be a Betwixt-and Between,' Solomon said, and certainly he was a wise fellow, for that is exactly as it turned out.[20]

For this 'Betwixt-and-Between' the capacity for sadness and regret is severely limited. With his panpipes Peter becomes the fairies' favoured musician and is taught once again how to fly. He is also given two wishes by the fairy queen, Mab. His first wish is to go home to his mother, but with the right to return to the gardens if he finds her disappointing. Queen Mab tells him that although she can give him the power to fly so that he can return home,

> '. . . I can't open the door for you.'
>
> 'The window I flew out at will be open,' Peter said confidently. 'Mother always keeps it open in the hope that I may fly back.'
>
> 'How do you know . . .'
>
> 'I just do know,' he said.[21]

And so Peter returns more than once and looks lovingly at his sleeping mother, often crying in her sleep for her lost son, but each time he is reluctant to give up his play in the gardens and flies back once more. At the same time, we are told

> You must not think that he meditated flying away and never coming back. He had quite decided to be his mother's boy, but hesitated about beginning tonight . . . after all there was no hurry, for his mother would never weary of waiting for him.[22]

After months of procrastination, eventually Peter decides, 'I wish now to go back to mother for ever and always,' and reluctantly the fairies have to let him go.

> He went in a hurry in the end, because he had dreamt that his mother was crying, and he knew what was the great thing she cried for, and that a hug from her splendid Peter would quickly make her smile. Oh! He felt sure of it . . . and this time he flew straight to the window, which would always be open for him.

But Peter's cheerfully ruthless self-absorption and neglect of time mean that when at last he flies to his mother's window he is faced with an appalling truth:

> The window was closed, and there were iron bars on it, and peering inside he saw his mother sleeping peacefully with her arm round another little boy.
> Peter called, 'Mother! Mother!' But she heard him not; in vain he beat his little limbs against the iron bars. He had to fly back, sobbing, to the Gardens, and he never saw his dear again. What a glorious boy he had meant to be to her! Ah, Peter! We who have made the great mistake, how differently we should all act at the second chance. But Solomon was right – there is no second chance, not for most of us. When we reach the window it is Lock Out Time. The iron bars are up for life.[23]

At the end of November Arthur Davies wrote to his father, in Westmorland:

Dearest Father
    I don't know what your arrangements are for Christmas, nor if you are likely to have the Vicarage very full. I should like to come,

if possible, bringing one boy or perhaps two. It is just possible that Sylvia may be induced to come too, but that is not likely . . .

Sylvia is at present on a trip with her friends the Barries, by way of celebration of the huge success of Barrie's new plays and new book. The party is completed by another novelist, [A.E.W.] Mason, and they seem to be living in great splendour and enjoying themselves very much . . . Barrie's new book is largely taken up with Kensington Gardens and our and similar children. There is a whole chapter devoted to Peter.

My work is moderately prosperous but no more . . .

Your Affect. son

A. Ll. D.[24]

Arthur can have done no more than glance at *The Little White Bird*, for the 'chapter' devoted to his son Peter is instead the five chapters devoted to Peter Pan. The book was clearly not to Arthur's taste, and here we catch a rare glimpse of what his feelings might have been towards Barrie. The Davieses had known the Barries for more than five years, and spent a good deal of time in each other's company. But Arthur had no inclination to do anything more than glance at Barrie's book. In addition he pointedly refers to Barrie and his wife as Sylvia's friends. Meanwhile, his comment on the unlikelihood of Sylvia joining in any family celebrations in Westmorland has a note of weariness to it. Arthur must have minded. He must have minded, too, though having no need of it himself, that he couldn't offer Sylvia the luxury Barrie was able to indulge in if he chose.

And Barrie's trips to Paris were luxurious. Despite virtually refusing to speak French, he felt a special preference for the glamour of Paris, and on these occasions was the perfect host. He was conspicuously devoted to Sylvia, and in company with the handsome, charismatic Mason, who was a great admirer of women, Sylvia must have found this a most satisfying holiday. It is difficult to imagine Mary's feelings. Perhaps she just didn't allow herself too many. Later in the summer, whatever Arthur's thoughts may have been, he, Sylvia and the boys were once again staying at Tilford near the Barries at Black Lake.

When the visitors left, Dolly Ponsonby – who had written so perceptively about Sylvia when she was younger – wrote an entry in her diary about a visit to her marital home at Shulbrede Priory, in Sussex. Her comments are arresting.

Friday Aug 22nd 1903

Sylvia, the Barrys [*sic*], Peter & Michael came in a motor from Farnham to tea. Jim Barry with a child clinging to each hand at once went and sat in the dining room chimney corner looked so characteristic . . . Sylvia beautiful and satisfying, loving the house & appealing to 'Jimmy' about it, while I tried to make myself pleasant to Mrs Barry – commonplace, 2nd rate & admirable – It is a strange ménage – It was very charming to see Girly [Dolly's daughter, Elizabeth] give her hand to Jimmy and with Michael on one side and her on the other they walked down the garden path & into the field – His devotion and genius-like understanding of children is beautiful & touching beyond words – as he has none himself.[25]

And here we catch a fleeting glimpse of prevailing attitudes in the disso-nance between Dolly Ponsonby's comments, on the one hand regarding the beautiful Sylvia and Barrie's genius-like understanding of children, and on the other hand in the description of Mary. Through his gifts and success Barrie had transcended his humble origins. Without such demon-strable gifts as her husband's, many contemporaries judged Mary with more haughtiness. At the same time Dolly could perceptively add to her comments that Mary was 'admirable'.

At the end of October, as a result of a meeting with the theatre enthu-siast Viscount Esher – then secretary to His Majesty's Office of Works – Barrie was given a strange honour; he was presented with a key to the Kensington Gardens. To visit the gardens when they were locked up and everyone else gone home seemed an odd wish, and not something he particularly wanted. None the less, it was clearly a mark of esteem, and Barrie officially swore that he wouldn't misuse the key. Viscount Esher wrote to his son, having had to clear the whole business with the Duke of Cambridge, that, 'It would have been far easier to get the little man a baronetcy.'

A few days later, on 1st November, the Barrie family were deeply shocked to discover that at only forty-nine Sarah had died overnight in her bed at Strath View. Beside his younger sister, Maggie, Sarah was Barrie's favourite sibling. Although their lives had developed quite differ-ently and communication was therefore limited, Barrie had felt great sympathy for this sister, and her death inevitably kindled memories of their past. It was Sarah, for instance, who had met him for walks in Edinburgh in his lonely student days; she was always a sympathetic listener.

Once again the youngest brother took the northbound train from London, and followed another funeral procession up on to Kirriemuir's Hill. Both his parents, his brother and six of his sisters now lay here in the cemetery, and Barrie felt keenly the loss of that nourishment he had always drawn from a firm rootedness in his family. Back in his study in London after the ceremony, although his grieving was modest compared with the utter morbidness following his mother's death, he did retreat into a period of silence, and friends and engagements were put off.

14

Origins

Barrie was much absorbed by Sylvia Davies's condition; she was expecting her fifth child, and this imminent birth may have been the trigger for a momentous literary nativity. On 23rd November 1903 Barrie sat down at his desk and wrote:

ANON

Play

He then drew a detailed stage set, entitled 'The Darlings' Night Nursery, Scene I', and began at last to write *Peter Pan*.

Having noted down the various elements of the story disparately for months, Barrie only gradually realised that they belonged together in one place: the pirates and shipwrecks of *The Boy Castaways*, the menacing and cowardly pirate, Captain Swarthy, the faithful and steadfast dog, and the strange little boy who had run away from his parents to Kensington Gardens in order to avoid growing up.

If the impending birth in the Davies family was the final trigger, certainly one more added to their number reminded Barrie that the Davies boys were growing up. George would be eleven in a few months, Jack was nine, Peter was almost seven, and little Michael three-and-a-half. And twenty-eight years later, with the final publication of the play of *Peter Pan*, Barrie would say in his baffling Dedication to the Davies 'boys' that he always knew he 'made Peter by rubbing the five of you violently together, as savages with two sticks produce a flame'. What Barrie meant was not that Peter Pan was an amalgam of the five boys, but rather that through their intense contact with him he was inspired to create the marvellous boy. He goes on:

> What was it that made us give to the public in the thin form of a
> play that which had been woven for ourselves alone? Alas, I know

what it was, I was losing my grip. One by one as you swung from branch to branch in the wood of make-believe you reached the tree of knowledge. Sometimes you swung back into the wood, as the unthinking may at a cross-road take a familiar path that no longer leads home; or you perched ostentatiously on its boughs to please me, pretending that you still belonged; soon you knew it only as the vanished wood, for it vanishes if one needs to look for it. A time came when I saw that no. 1 [George], the most gallant of you all, ceased to believe that he was ploughing woods incarnadine, and with an apologetic eye for me derided the lingering faith of no. 2 [Jack]; when even no. 3 [Peter] questioned gloomily whether he did not really spend his nights in bed.[1]

Struggling with the mystery of growing up, Barrie had written of Tommy Sandys' failure to do so in *Sentimental Tommy* and *Tommy and Grizel*. Although he suggested that Tommy's was an honourable failure, none the less he was unable to relinquish his childhood. Terrified by the prospect of adult life, he had attempted to return to the imaginary land of his fantasies.

He came night after night trying different ways, but he could not find the golden ladder, though all the time he knew that the lair lay somewhere over there. When he stood still and listened he could hear the friends of his youth at play, and they seemed to be calling . . . but when he pressed forward their voices died away.

Robbed of many of the carefree elements of his own childhood, Barrie had learnt early that children were able to strike a vital, joyful spark in him, could help him to participate in the abandonment of adult thought and responsibility. But as an artist he remained always just on the outside, as much observer as participant. For years the child in Barrie had been driven to take part in exuberant games with children, while simultaneously the adult artist in him made descriptions of these games; descriptions which grew to be his anatomy of childhood.

In 1903, plays that included child characters were primarily for adults, and above all about 'real life'. Those performances put on specifically *for* children were based on books and were not plays, but simple pantomime-type entertainments. *Alice in Wonderland* had been dramatised in this way in 1886, while Thackeray's *The Rose and the Ring* was given similar treatment in 1890. The first real play written specifically for children appears to have been Seymour Hicks's *Bluebell in Fairyland*, which had fascinated Barrie so much in 1901. Although *Bluebell* belonged to the genre of pantomime, it had broken with convention by mixing real, believable children and adults with fantasy. And while *Peter Pan* is an expansion and development of Barrie's own abiding themes, there is no doubt that *Bluebell in Fairyland* also spurred on his creative development of them. In early 1902, not long after seeing *Bluebell*, he had noted down an implicit criticism of the pantomime element in Hicks's play: '. . . what children like best is imitation of real boys and girls (not so much *comic* incidents) . . .'

Later in the year, Barrie jotted another note, which immediately brings to mind the paragraph near the end of *Tommy and Grizel* about the 'Wandering Child', who escapes from his parents because he is fearful that they will compel him to grow up. It reads:

The mother treated from the child's point of view –
Peter: Mother, how did we get to know you?
– Play: The happy Boy: boy who couldn't grow up – runs away
from pain and death – is caught *wild* – (and escapes)[2]

Here for the first time a more evolved version of Peter Pan has emerged.

The elements making up *Peter Pan* inescapably reflect certain ideas and preoccupations of the time. Barrie's originality lies in how he treats them.

Peter Pan appeared at what is now recognised as the high point of a golden age of children's literature in Britain: the last quarter of the nineteenth and the early years of the twentieth century. In this period virtually all the books we now think of as the classics of children's literature were written. Before this flowering, children's literature consisted largely of edifying tracts lecturing on the perilous results of disobedience and non-conformity. With the advent of children's fiction in the eighteenth century these themes were sometimes modified by humour or illustrations of daring deeds, but the intention was still the same. Translations of the brothers Grimm and Hans Andersen's fairy tales in the 1820s and 30s were very popular and helped make fantasy acceptable. And in the 1880s and 90s Barrie's friend Andrew Lang would make his contribution to the genre with his fairy novels and the famous collections named after colours, *The Blue Fairy Book* being the first.

The publication of Edward Lear's *Nonsense Poems* in 1845 is one of the major precursors of this new wave of writing, which began seriously to flourish with Lewis Carroll's *Alice in Wonderland* in 1865. The strain of popular literature from which Lear's and Carroll's writing sprang drew upon the traditional violence and anarchy of the long-established nursery rhymes, and thus set a cheerful precedent for anarchy and irreverence in the growing number of stories for children.

Of the hugely popular boys' adventure stories, Ballantyne's *The Coral Island* and Robert Louis Stevenson's *Treasure Island* are only the most famous; a later example is Arthur Ransome's *Swallows and Amazons*. Beatrix Potter wrote *The Tale of Peter Rabbit* in 1902 and Rudyard Kipling's *Jungle Book*, *Just So Stories* and *Puck of Pook's Hill* had all appeared by 1906. Kenneth Grahame's seminal descriptions of the egocentricity and ruthlessness of children had appeared in *The Golden Age* (1895) and *Dream Days* (1898), while his great animal fantasy, *The Wind in the Willows*, was published in 1908. A. A. Milne's *Winnie the Pooh* was a continuation of the late-Victorian and Edwardian love affair with childhood and the 'other world' children were believed to inhabit. No doubt some of this great outpouring of children's literature was a response to growing leisure and literacy and the expansion of the married middle class. But we could also speculate that it came about when it did partly as a widespread retreat into fantasy, a form of escape, from those difficult and confusing times.

In the last years of the nineteenth century, no matter how much people avoided facing up to it, the absolute power of Britain and her Empire was in decline. No longer unquestionably the supreme world power, her society was less secure. Justification for the Empire, upon which so much of the country's wealth was founded, was becoming more difficult for some to formulate. Justification, contemplated for long enough, will always lead to thoughts of foundations and origins. And thinking about our origins leads naturally to childhood, a state founded above all upon fantasy and play.

It is probably no accident that around the turn of the twentieth century Barrie was in the midst of his major period of writing, because what he was doing chimed with a series of contemporary intellectual developments. Put simply, during the nineteenth century a small group of progressive and profoundly influential men had been part of a movement that would change irreversibly the attitudes of the Western mind. Beginning in 1859 with *On the Origin of Species by Means of Natural Selection*, Charles Darwin had explained *living forms*: how they adapt, diversify and change. In 1867 the first volume of Karl Marx's *Das Kapital* had appeared; in this he set out to explain human *society*. Then in 1900 Sigmund Freud published *The Interpretation of Dreams*; this looked at the human *individual*.

By any account an extraordinary piece of work, Freud's book was a masterpiece entirely relevant to the times. Grossly simplified, it espoused two major ideas: first, that beneath the wildly irrational surface of the dream world there lies a hidden rationality. As Polonius said of Hamlet, 'Though this be madness, yet there is method in't.' Second, that the irrational elements revealed in dreams are always related to sex. Freud drew his evidence for this from the inner worlds of emotionally disturbed people. The conclusion was that compulsive neuroses, hysteria, delusions, etc. have as their root cause some serious disturbance of sexual development.

At virtually the same time Barrie was writing about the nature of fantasy and reality, and the overlap and interconnection between the two. This is the leitmotif of *Sentimental Tommy*, *Tommy and Grizel*, and most of *Peter Pan*. These works are above all about inner worlds. In *The Interpretation of Dreams* Freud is preoccupied by exactly the same things.

It was inevitable that at some point the methods of natural science – developed so successfully during the course of the nineteenth century for the investigation of things – would be applied to the internal world of human beings. Thus, using the methodology of natural science Freud attempted to formalise vast amounts of accumulated insight into the human psyche. Writers had already collected large amounts of similar material over several centuries, and remaining within the fold of literary art Barrie was doing his version of the same thing. It was the impetus of the two men that differed. Freud's original impetus was therapy, while Barrie's was understanding.

In the late-Victorian years attitudes towards children subtly altered and softened. Adults gradually came to see childhood not simply as a stage on the path to adulthood, but rather as one with its own inherent value. A child was no longer simply an embryonic, and therefore implicitly deficient and incomplete adult, but rather a creature in its own right. One, moreover, who symbolised hope and optimism. The child, especially when associated with nature (i.e. not the looming confusion of the Victorian city, but usually some kind of rural idyll), came to represent innocence and goodness, and was thought to have greater access than the adult to the worlds of the spirit and the imagination. Barrie has Tommy Sandys weave a story in which his hero says sadly to his boy, 'I shall never be able to show you to the lair, for I cannot find the way to it,' and the boy is touched, and he says, 'Take my hand, Father, and I will lead you to the lair; I found the way long ago for myself.'[3]

Springing from this growing respect and sympathy for the state of childhood, for the first time in the Western tradition, instead of dressing children as small adults, a style of dress was developed for them different from that of their elders. As time passed this changing attitude included a tendency towards sentimentality, epitomised in that Victorian icon of childhood, the painting *Bubbles* by Millais. Another of Millais' paintings, *Cherry Ripe*, depicting the child milkmaid with cherries in her lap, was published in the 1897 Christmas edition of *The Graphic*, and sold 600,000 copies almost at once.

Perhaps partly in reaction to an age where change and uncertainty were beginning to undermine or compromise a sense of permanence, the Victorian middle classes also created an image of the home and the family as places of safety and retreat: as ideals after which they strove. Increasing numbers of better-off parents with more leisure time were more sympathetic not only to their children's physical needs, but also to the development of their emotions and their imagination. The worship of the ideal, secure family – at whose heart was the child – became for some a secular attempt to compensate for the prevailing and unsettling doubts about religious faith.

Within the social groups who could afford to put these notions into practice, the sacred innocence of childhood and the corrupting effect of adulthood led to a belief, frequently represented in painting and literature, that life arrested in childhood or youth was noble and beautiful. In an age of high infant mortality, death might at least ensure that innocence and youthful perfection remained forever preserved.

Towards the end of the century the cult of childhood developed further, so that in some quarters it was even held that only youth had any real significance. This in turn led to an obsession with the preservation of eternal youth. Oscar Wilde's *The Picture of Dorian Gray* is the archetypal 'decadent' expression of the glory of youth and reluctance to progress beyond it. And in early death, therefore, the most fortunate of these sacred and innocent creatures – the lucky few of A. E. Housman's hugely popular *Shropshire Lad* – would never be exposed to the inevitable corruptions of adulthood; 'The lads who will die in their glory and never be old' was only one example of many. Not surprisingly this was one of Barrie's favourite lines. Crucially, in his writing, and in his life as an artist, Barrie struggled with and travelled beyond these themes. At the same time, as a divided personality, many of his personal preoccupations led him instinctively to subscribe to them. Hence he was driven to say, 'Nothing that happens after we are twelve matters very much.'

In the post-Freudian late twentieth-century it became commonplace to suggest that a juxtaposition of sexual inhibition and the idolisation of childhood led towards an uncomfortable and barely suppressed sexual ambivalence towards children. The most famous example is probably Lewis Carroll's relationships with little girls, and his need to photograph them, often scantily clad. That it was quite public and done with decorum (he always wrote to their mothers asking permission to meet and photograph them) makes little difference to us.

Carroll's interests were not then on the whole seen as socially unacceptable. His contemporaries, more generous-minded than we are, appear to have interpreted his behaviour as eccentricity rather than perversion. It is notable that, of the most famous late-nineteenth and early-twentieth-century children's writers, Edward Lear, Lewis Carroll, J. M. Barrie, Kenneth Grahame and A.A. Milne all struggled with their attitudes to childhood and growing up. The inference usually now drawn from this is that the problem lay with their sexuality.

Under the influence of popular Freudianism − how many of us have ever read even one of the texts, whose collected extent stretches to twenty-three recondite and learned volumes? − we are all-knowing and convinced that we understand far more about the sexuality of previous periods than those living at the time ever did themselves. Since Freud, contemporary wisdom has it that sex is at the root of all motivation, and consequently we believe that our insights into the sexual behaviour of the past are authentic, and have authority. But how much do we really understand about Victorian or Edwardian attitudes to sex, or how they interpreted such texts as this passage from Barrie's *The Little White Bird*?

> David and I had a tremendous adventure. It was this − he passed the night with me. We had often talked of it as a possible thing, and at last [his mother] consented to our having it.
>
> The adventure began with David's coming to me at the unwonted hour of six p.m., carrying what looked like a packet of sandwiches, but proved to be his requisites for the night done up in a neat paper parcel . . .
>
> We were to do all the important things precisely as they are done every evening at his home, and so I am in a puzzle to know how it was such an adventure to David. But I have now said enough to show you what an adventure it was to me . . .
>
> At twenty-five past six I turned on the hot water in the bath, and covertly swallowed a small glass of brandy. I then said, 'Half-past six; time for little boys to be in bed.' I said it in the matter-of-fact voice of one made free of the company of parents, as if I had said it often before, and would have to say it often again, and as if there was nothing particularly delicious to me hearing myself say it. I tried to say it in that way.
>
> And David was deceived. To my exceeding joy he stamped his little foot, and was so naughty that, in gratitude, I gave him five minutes with a matchbox. Matches, which he drops on the floor

when lighted, are the greatest treat you can give David; indeed I think his private heaven is a place with a roaring bonfire.

Then I placed my hand carelessly on his shoulder, like one a trifle bored by the dull routine of putting my little boys to bed, and conducted him to the night nursery, which had lately been my private chamber. There was an extra bed in it tonight, very near my own, but differently shaped, and scarcely less conspicuous was the new mantelshelf ornament: a tumbler of milk, with a biscuit on top of it, and a chocolate riding on the biscuit . . .

David watched my preparations with distasteful levity, but anon made a noble amend by abruptly offering me his foot as if he had no longer use for it, and I knew by intuition that he expected me to take off his boots. I took them off with all the coolness of an old hand, and then I placed him on my knee and removed his blouse. This was a delightful experience, but I think I remained wonderfully calm until I came somewhat too suddenly to his little braces, which agitated me profoundly.

I cannot proceed in public with the disrobing of David.

Soon the night nursery was in darkness but for the glimmer from the night-light, and very still save when the door creaked as a man peered in at the little figure on the bed. However softly I opened the door, an inch at a time, his bright eyes turned to me at once.

'Are you never to fall asleep, David?' I always said.

'When are you coming to bed,' he always replied, very brave but in a whisper, as if he feared bears and wolves might have him. When little boys are in bed there is nothing between them and bears and wolves but the night-light.

I returned to my chair to think and at last he fell asleep . . . Long after I had gone to bed a sudden silence filled the chamber, and I knew that David had awaked . . . and a little far-away voice said in a cautious whisper, 'Irene!'

'You are sleeping with me tonight, you know, David,' I said.

'I didn't know,' he replied, a little troubled, but trying not to be a nuisance . . .

I think he had nigh fallen asleep again when he stirred and said, 'Is it going on now?'

'What?'

'The adventure?'

'Yes, David.'

Perhaps this disturbed him, for by and by I had to inquire, 'You are not frightened are you?'

'I am not,' he answered politely, and I knew his hand was groping in the darkness, so I put out mine and he held on tightly to one finger.

'I am not frightened now,' he whispered.

'And there is nothing else you want?'

'Is there not?' he again asked politely. 'Are you sure there's not?' he added.

'What can it be, David?'

'I don't take up very much room,' the far-away voice said.

'Why, David,' I said, sitting up; 'do you want to come into my bed?'

'Mother said I wasn't to want it unless you wanted it first,' he squeaked.

'It is what I have been wanting all the time,' said I, and then without more ado the little figure rose and flung itself at me. For the rest of the night he lay across me, and sometimes his feet were at the bottom of the bed and sometimes on the pillow, but he always retained possession of my finger, and occasionally he woke me to say that he was sleeping with me. I had not a good night. I lay thinking . . .

Of David's dripping little form in the bath, and how when I essayed to catch him he had slipped from my arms like a trout. Of how I stood by the open door listening to his sweet breathing, had stood so long that I forgot his name and called him Timothy.[4]

When the little boy David comes to stay for the night, for a brief moment the captain, who longs for a son of his own, can pretend he has one. On reading this passage, it is virtually impossible not to imagine a series of barely repressed desires, which leave us deeply unsettled. The passage, however, was *not* written in a secret journal, kept under lock and key. It was published in a popular book that sold many thousands of copies across the English-speaking world. *The Little White Bird* wasn't banned or criticised for its perversion. Instead, the objections contemporaries made to its content were not that it was sexually dubious, but that at times Barrie was exhibiting too much whimsy and sentiment. Although on reading about Captain W and David we may conclude that a large fraction of the Edwardian reading public must have been proto-paedophile, contemporaries received this piece of writing effectively *without* comment.

A great shift in understanding, in human intentions and consciousness, in assumptions of all kinds, has taken place since 1902, and interpreting the past by imposing our own attitudes and beliefs upon it is a dubious practice.

If one agrees that every age has its characteristic obsessions, two of the most prominent nowadays must be environmental degradation and sexual abuse. As the task of illuminating the obsessions of one's own period is an almost impossible one, perhaps all we can do here is to set down a few notes and quotations relating to paedophilia, homosexuality and love. This is a vast and hazard-strewn field, beyond the scope of this book, so what follows can offer no more than a few hints.

As late as the edition of 1956 the *Shorter Oxford Dictionary* thought it unnecessary to have *any* entry on paedophilia, whereas by 1990 even the much smaller *Concise Oxford* gives a definition: 'Paedophilia . . . Sexual desire directed towards children'.

In the West paedophilia has customarily been disapproved of, and never more so than now. In many Western legal codes paedophile activities, of various specified kinds, are designated as crimes. This derives from the contention – for which we have plenty of supportive evidence – that whatever the attitude and feelings of the older of the two involved, too early exposure of a very young person to active sexual experience is damaging to that person's later emotional and sexual life.

The extract above from *The Little White Bird* is equivocal in its implications, and is one of the reasons why in recent decades it has been suggested that Barrie was a paedophile. Against this we can set two comments made late in life by the youngest of the Llewelyn Davies boys, Nico.

> Of all the men I have ever known, Barrie was the wittiest, and the best company. He was also the least interested in sex. He was a darling man. He was an innocent; which is why he could write *Peter Pan.*[5]

Nico also said:

> I don't believe that Uncle Jim ever experienced what one might call a stirring in the undergrowth for anyone – man, woman, or child . . .[6]

Behind contemporary Western thinking about sex and love looms the hugely influential figure of Freud, a visionary and proselytiser, an indefatigable theoriser and a formidable writer. His mature reflections on these themes include the following:

> [Some people] avoid the uncertainties and disappointments of genital love by turning away from its sexual aims and transforming the instinct into an impulse with an inhibited aim . . . Perhaps St Francis

of Assisi went furthest in thus exploiting love for the benefit of an inner feeling of happiness . . .

People give the name 'love' to the relation between a man and a woman whose genital needs have led them to found a family; but they also give the name 'love' to the positive feelings between parents and children, although we are obliged to describe this as 'aim-inhibited love' or 'affection' . . .

Genital love leads to the formation of new families, and aim-inhibited love to 'friendships' which become valuable from a cultural standpoint because they escape some of the limitations of genital love, such as, for instance, its exclusiveness.[7]

It would appear that variants of Christian love, *agape* – the love of a man and a woman, a parent's love for a child, the friendship of two men – all arise from 'genital needs', either in original or 'aim-inhibited' form. This is a very large claim. Its justification seems to rest upon a kind of evolutionary premise: that specialised love, friendship, for example, has *evolved* out of 'genital needs' love. Therefore friendship is really no more than 'aim-inhibited' love arising out of genital needs.

World views, such as Christianity, Leninism or Freudianism, cannot be directly or empirically tested. And no single event, situation or experiment will throw much light on or greatly affect our attitude to these momentous ideas. If most of us, however, have our own methods of gaining a foothold here, we use a mixture of two overlapping criteria. One is intellectual and explanatory, while the other is emotional and pragmatic: we ask ourselves, 'Does this accord with how I see the world? Does this articulate more clearly and help me to make sense of life?' Then we ask, 'Does this lead to a fuller, richer life for me?'

Across the spectrum of human history, psychological science is a novice in the field of love. Two and a half thousand years ago the lyric poets of Ancient Greece were already trying to express its joys and despairs. Good imaginative writers of every generation have so far left the psychologists far behind in the exactitude and range, in the precision, accuracy and breadth of their observations and thoughts. The imaginative writer is a natural historian of love, and tends to be sceptical of attempts at large-scale theorising.

Sonnet number 20 is one of Shakespeare's one hundred and fifty-four autobiographical sonnets, some of the most illuminating and sustained reveries on love written in any language. In sonnet 20 the poet is passionately in love with a youth, and is telling him that his feelings, however intense, are not in this instance homoerotic. The young man has vanquished Shakespeare with his beauty, yet, since nature has additionally furnished

him with a penis, he is more obviously capable of satisfying the sexual
needs of women, than of this male admirer.

> A woman's face with Nature's own hand painted,
> Hast thou the Master Mistress of my passion;
> A woman's gentle heart but not acquainted
> With shifting change as is false women's fashion;
> An eye more bright than theirs, less false in rolling,
> Gilding the object whereupon it gazeth;
> A man in hue all hues in his controlling,
> Which steals men's eyes and women's souls amazeth.
> And for a woman wert thou first created;
> Till nature as she wrought thee fell adoting,
> And by addition me of thee defeated
> By adding one thing to my purpose nothing.
> But since she prick'd thee out for women's pleasure,
> Mine be thy love, and thy love's use their treasure.

Hartmann, in Anita Brookner's *Latecomers*, is a man in love with his
baby granddaughter.

From his first sight of Flora, with her damp dark hair and tiny
purposeful mouth, Hartmann was lost to reason. He worshipped her,
cunningly contrived to ingratiate himself, to integrate his presence into
her sensibility, her receptivity, removed her from her mother's arms
and sat down happily with her, talking to her even when she was fast
asleep. When no one was looking, when his wife and daughter were
in the kitchen or were engaged in talk, he would give Flora a gentle
nudge and wake her up. She might cry a little, but after a few minutes
was always pleased to see him, opening her blue eyes at him as he
lovingly wiped away her tears . . . When Hartmann saw the contrast
between the bloom of the infant's face and the wrinkling flesh on the
back of Yvette's well-kept but ageing hand, he felt overwhelmed with
love for them both, felt an overflowing of such loving-kindness that
he would have to go out for a walk. In any event, once Flora was
removed his home seemed to him momentarily intolerable. Yvette,
although she looked at him with a sceptical eye, understood. He was
in love, she knew, and there was no point in trying to reason with
him. And of all the rivals with whom he might have presented her,
Flora was the only one above suspicion.[8]

Barrie was undoubtedly in love with the Llewelyn Davies boys.

15

Making a Masterpiece

Barrie's *ANON Play* – for some time simply called *Fairy*; eventually to become *Peter and Wendy* – was rapidly progressing. (Several years earlier a mutual bond had sprung up between Barrie and W. E. Henley's small daughter, Margaret. Unable yet to pronounce all her words correctly, in telling Barrie he was her 'friendy', this became 'wendy'. At that time no such name existed, and while a tribute to the little girl, Margaret Henley, who had died at the age of six, it also appealed to Barrie's obsession with the naming of things. In this way the girl of such diversity, Wendy, was given a name as yet untried and open to all possibility.

Its author's custom was to write up a new piece with speed, and *Peter and Wendy* was no exception. The first draft was finished in less than four months. By now a skilled and experienced playwright, Barrie's sense of the theatre was powerful. With this work, however, his famed aptitude for stagecraft was to fall short of his innovations. Much of his experience would prove inadequate, for nothing quite like this play had ever been written, or seen on the stage before.

Between the manuscript draft and the first performance, he would make a vast number of changes, including endless revisions to the plot. Even then, for years to come he continued moulding and remoulding the whole play, while his experiments with the ending went on for years and were never entirely concluded. Barrie didn't see this as failure. Rather, avoiding a definitive end reflected part of the essence of the play itself; a battle with the problem of beginnings and endings, of birth and death and time.

Despite this, the first draft is more or less recognisable as the *Peter Pan* we know, with the five acts and the main *dramatis personae* all there. Some characters were to disappear entirely, others would be renamed: Tinker Bell, for example, at this early stage was called 'Tippy' – a reference to the contemporary fairy spectaculars, in which the little girls of the pantomime danced around in flesh-coloured tights – and Captain Hook was as yet no more than an objectionable schoolmaster.

The reception of any new work naturally generated a degree of edginess and tension in Barrie, but with this particular first draft his feelings were qualitatively different. He knew that what he had done was without precedent and, unusually, he was overcome by a sense of misgiving and unease. A far more radical and experimental playwright than many recognised, in his work Barrie was conscious of his aims. Yet in this play he was putting forward ideas more complex and developed than any he had so far presented. At one level the essential themes of his play came from so deep inside his psyche, he would have found it almost impossible fully to explain their derivation. In gestation for almost his entire life, what he had finally written flowed from his pen like a kind of automatic writing.

A few days after finishing the play, Barrie was the guest of the evening at the Playgoers' Club. Then, on his birthday, 9th May, he gave an important speech to the Royal Literary Fund. On this occasion, for the first time women were invited as equal participants and not simply as guests. Barrie warmly applauded this move in a speech where, as was his custom, he played the part of the man weary of the world. Characteristic of all his art, Barrie injected his speech with forthright little barbs, while simultaneously drawing his audience on to laughter. Equally routinely, in between the slightly unsettling moments of candour, he struck a pose as the unpractised speaker:

> I don't know what it has sounded like to you, but all the time I
> have been speaking I have seemed to hear my own voice trotting
> behind me, like some dreadful beast in a story by Mr Wells. However,
> I am sure you will forgive an unpractised hand . . .[1]

The notion of being an unpractised hand was nonsense; like any good actor Barrie had rehearsed his part to perfection. In keeping with the idea of the speech as performance, he was almost ill with nerves beforehand. He continued by speaking of good fortune: 'I have had too much of the luck, and I want to cut a piece of it off and give it to someone else who has had too little.'

This was heartfelt, but, with the new play constantly on his mind, for the moment he felt as much in need of luck as ever he had done in the past. Perhaps it was this preoccupied frame of mind that generated the blend of energy and melancholy captured so evocatively by William Nicholson, when he painted Barrie that spring. Barrie knew many people and had good friends, but Nicholson's portrait brings out the sense that ultimately he was a remote and lonely man.

Needing reassurance, he took *Peter and Wendy*, for the moment called *The Great White Father*, because it is about origins, to the great actor-manager Beerbohm Tree, and insisted on reading him the whole thing at one sitting. Seeking Tree's professional opinion showed forethought on Barrie's part: Tree was renowned for the extravagance and scale of his productions. But the result of this momentous encounter was not auspicious, and Tree wrote to Charles Frohman in America with a grim warning:

> Barrie has gone out of his mind . . . I am sorry to say it but you ought to know . . . He's just read me a play . . . so I am warning you. I know I have not gone woozy in my mind because I have tested myself since hearing it but Barrie must be mad.[2]

By April Frohman himself had arrived from New York. Barrie, deeply apprehensive, and fearing that Frohman wouldn't want the play, had decided he must offer him something as leverage. Thus, when Frohman dined as Barrie's guest at the Garrick Club, Barrie brought with him two plays. These were *The Great White Father* and another recent work, *Alice Sit by the Fire*. He told Frohman of his misgivings, and said that although he didn't think *The Great White Father* would be a commercial success, it was his 'dream child' and he wanted to see it staged so much he would *give* Frohman *Alice Sit by the Fire* to compensate him for any loss. Barrie need not have worried about the staging of his play. Frohman was not only an outstanding manager, he also believed his friend was a great artist. Having assured Barrie that he would produce not one but both of the plays, Frohman then proceeded to read them.

In his own way Charles Frohman was as unusual as his friend. With regard to work he was a reckless and inveterate gambler, who was also immensely successful. Just as unorthodox as Barrie, in allowing the strangeness of the 'dream child' to envelop him, Frohman was captured – in a way that Beerbohm Tree had failed to be – by the power of its extraordinary vision. He decided immediately that Barrie was to have anything he wanted for the production of his play, and in this Frohman, too, was a visionary. He had only one objection; the title must be changed. Barrie's suggestion was immediately accepted; the play would be called, simply, *Peter Pan*.

It was clear from the start that Barrie's play would consume huge amounts of preparation time and finance if it was ever to reach the stage. Both sets and cast were very large: there were over fifty characters, including twenty-four speaking parts, among them Redskins, pirates, wolves, a jaguar, a lion, an ostrich, a dog, a fairy and a crocodile. Added to this, four of the cast must somehow fly around the stage in a series of unprecedented manoeuvres. And although on the surface the play appeared to be for children, its range of style and moods was an intoxicating mix, with stretches of the dialogue too sophisticated for any child. What was it that had so captivated Frohman in Barrie's manuscript that day? The answer lies in part in the nature of the friendship between these two most curious men; it was based above all on the discovery of a kindred spirit. They shared the problem of how to fully participate in an adult world. Although never truly integrated into it, they had each succeeded in transforming their handicap into a powerful creative force.

Frohman never married, was overweight, well known for his gentle benevolence, and respected and admired as one of the most intelligent and intuitive directors of the time. He would famously sit cross-legged on a low sofa as he read through vast numbers of scripts, while munching his way through even greater piles of sweets. In responding to the accusation of 'commercialism' Frohman commented: '. . . to produce something for the few critical people. That is what I'm trying for. I have to work through the commercial – it is the white heat through which the artistic in me has to come.' George Bernard Shaw said of him:

> There is a prevalent impression that Charles Frohman is a hard-headed American man of business who would not look at anything that is not likely to pay. On the contrary, he is the most wildly romantic and adventurous of men of my acquaintance. As Charles XII became an excellent soldier because of his passion for putting himself in the way of being killed, so Charles Frohman became a famous manager through his passion for putting himself in the way of being ruined . . .

In explaining his dedication his biographers said:

> He left all financial details to his subordinates. All he wanted to do was to produce plays and be left alone. Yet he had an infinite respect for the man to whom he had to pay a large sum. He felt that the actor or author who could command it was invested with peculiar significance. Upon himself he spent little. He once said, 'All I want is a good meal, a good cigar, good clothes, and a good bed to sleep in, and freedom to produce whatever plays I like.' . . .

He was a magnificent loser. Failure never disturbed him. When he saw that a piece was doomed, he indulged in no obituary talk. 'Let's go to the next,' he said and on he went.[3]

Dion Boucicault, who had become Frohman's chief London producer, was to direct *Peter Pan* for the Duke of York's, because it was Frohman's favourite London theatre. Frohman's biographers wrote:

> It required the most stupendous courage and confidence to put on a play that from the manuscript sounded like a combination of circus and extravaganza: a play in which children flew in and out of rooms, crocodiles swallowed alarm clocks, a man exchanged places with a dog in its kennel, and various other seemingly absurd and ridiculous things happened. But Charles believed in Barrie . . . Money was spent lavishly; whole scenes were made and never used. He regarded it as a great and rollicking adventure.[4]

In late October of 1904, rehearsals for *Peter Pan* at last began at the Duke of York's. Barrie had by now read the play to several friends, while Frohman, who had become obsessed, would act out various incidents, whole scenes, to anyone he could persuade to listen. Meanwhile, Barrie's instinct for publicity, plus his wish that the 'creation' of the play should be as a mystery to the actors, made him engender a deliberate air of secrecy about the entire proceedings. This, of course, sent the press into a frenzy of activity. Guards were stationed outside the theatre to prevent anyone stealing in and, frustrated at being kept away, the newspapers resorted to printing a series of wildly inaccurate stories. All this had the effect of whetting the public's appetite even more.

The cast were drawn into the conspiratorial atmosphere in which *Peter Pan* was realised, and a tone of inscrutability was established after the first day's rehearsal. Boucicault called his actors together and said, 'I would like to swear you all to keep everything you see and hear in this play an absolute secret. Nothing must leak out as to what the play is about.' To help enforce this rule not only were the members of the cast not given full texts of the play, they were not even given a script relating to their own words and cues within it. All they had was a script showing the immediate scene or action in which they were to take part. Thus, no actor had any way of knowing where their part fitted into the play as a whole. In this, Barrie was taking his cast beyond mere conspiracy. At some level he was acting as their 'creator'. The only one who knew exactly who and what they were to be was Barrie. He was the puppet-master in control.

Having accepted the part of Wendy, Hilda Trevelyan received a card announcing nothing more than the place of rehearsal. Added to this was a cryptic note that read 'Flying, 10.30'. With no information about the play at all, on arriving at the theatre she was asked if she had a life insurance. Answering 'no', she was immediately sent off to apply for one, and only then was she permitted to don the terrifying flying harness and begin her initiation.

While he was writing *Peter Pan*, Barrie contacted George Kirby of the Flying Ballet Company. He asked Kirby if it was possible to design for him a system so that the actors might fly above the stage and dispense with the very visible harnesses Kirby's company presently used. In addition, Barrie wanted a means of ensuring that the harnesses could be attached and then detached from the flying wires much more rapidly than had so far been possible. Kirby rose to the challenge and invented a completely novel mechanism, which made for much more convincing flying. This system required considerable skill and the cast were made to spend a whole fortnight taking lessons from Kirby in the difficult and dangerous arts of landing and take-off!

Weeks before the actors began their rehearsals, the tireless Boucicault made his own preparations, and these continued evolving virtually until the moment the first curtain rose. A number of cumbersome and elaborate sets had to be manoeuvred on to the narrow stage while retaining space for the flying, and various trapdoors had to be cut and positioned in the stage floor. Virtually all the props were made especially for the production, while Barrie's instructions for the lighting were so innovative that learning how to make them work was a very slow process. There was music to be composed, important dances to be choreographed, and, significantly, Barrie had incorporated more mime than in any of his other works. Meanwhile, the designing, making and fitting of the costumes was a huge task for a company numbering fifty.

The costumes for the Darling children and the Lost Boys were to be based on the Davies boys' own clothes, and Barrie wrote to Sylvia, 'It seems a profanation to turn your pretty ideas to stage account, but I am giving the basketful of them to those people nevertheless, and the pictures too.' Another radical move was Barrie's choice of a painter, William Nicholson, as the designer for many of the players' costumes, which included the outfits for the Eskimos, Redskins, pirates and Captain Hook. Henry J. Ford was chosen as the designer for Peter and Wendy. Although Nicholson's vanity was as great as many of the actors', making it difficult for him to work as part of a team, he was grateful to Barrie for this 'first opportunity of coming to grips with the theatre'. Nicholson's early biographer wrote, 'One of the points on which Barrie was most insistent was that the pirates should be *real* pirates, not Gilbert and Sullivan travesties.'

Nicholson designed for Hook (Sylvia's brother, Gerald du Maurier) a 'superb wig of purple chenille, arranged to look like snakes', and 'darker than the darkest thing imaginable', but Gerald's wife said it made him look like a 'cross between Charles II and a fourteen-year-old schoolgirl', so du Maurier refused to wear it.[5]

Peter Pan was an extraordinary amalgam, not strictly a play, a ballet or a pantomime. In early notes and several of Barrie's manuscript versions of the play, he incorporated much stronger elements of the Harlequinade than were finally in the staged version. What interested, even obsessed him was the transformational element of this earlier feature of theatrical history, which was crucial to the development of English pantomime. In the following description of the Harlequinade one can easily appreciate his fascination.

It evolved from the fusion of the dumbshow of the commedia dell'arte actors at the Paris fairground theatres, where dialogue was forbidden, with the convention which in burlesques of contemporary dramas allowed Arlequin to assume diverse personalities without losing his own identity.[6]

The layers of meaning Barrie was laying down in *Peter Pan* were complex and subtle, yet without some appreciation of it as the distillation of years of thought and experience it might well be considered pretentious, showy and eccentric.

Before the six gruelling weeks of rehearsal began, Dion Boucicault familiarised himself with the play so well that any of its lines was instantly at his command. His dedication to and faith in the venture were absolute. Week after week he and Barrie encouraged, cajoled and inspired the cast (when necessary acting out any and every one of the parts). At the same time he oversaw vast amounts of complex technical detail. Everywhere at once, and in his own way as unconventional as Frohman, Boucicault became the play's lynchpin. Indeed, without two such remarkable and inspired men, Barrie's drama would almost certainly never have reached the stage.

Barrie himself, meanwhile, was expending huge amounts of energy on major revisions to the script (and sometimes even the plot). His fluid approach to a work was never more in evidence, or necessary, than in the making of *Peter Pan*. Day after day he was there at rehearsals, following his usual procedure of flirting with the actresses, watching, listening, revising, and incorporating actors' improvisations. With this play, however, he made so many changes he was later to refer to having 'hacked' at it.

And as the weeks went by and December drew closer, sometimes it was only Barrie and the indefatigable Dion Boucicault who were still able to make out what was really going on.

No one had ever worked with such a strange and experimental work; many had never worked so hard in their lives; none had had to manage such a quantity of mechanical gear and complex props. Somehow, they all struggled on, and became as dedicated to the play as were by now its slightly crazed author and director. Despite the company's dedication, however, as the days passed everyone's doubts increased; epitomised by the 'depressed man in overalls', as Barrie later referred to him, who, while 'carrying a mug of tea or a paint box, used often to appear by my side in the shadowy stalls and say to me, "The gallery boys won't stand it!" He then mysteriously faded away as if he were the theatre ghost.'

Out of the chaos, and always keeping the larger picture in mind, Boucicault valiantly hauled the company towards the opening night. But by this time almost all believed that the play would probably be an unmitigated disaster.

On 15th December an announcement was made in the press: the opening night was to be 22nd December. But with only a week to go before the first night, the depiction of the fairy (now called Tinker Bell and played by an actress in front of a large reducing lens) was too complicated to work, half the mechanical gear was not yet installed or rehearsed, and the stagehands were still protesting at their work. The difficulties appeared never-ending. Then, on 21st December, the night of the dress rehearsal, disaster struck. One of the mechanical lifts suddenly broke, and as it came crashing down brought half of the scenery with it.

Utterly frustrated and disappointed Boucicault realised he had no choice but to postpone the first night. By this stage he, Barrie, the technical staff and the cast were all suffering dangerously from overwork. When it seemed that nothing more could go wrong, matters grew even worse. The stagehands refused to work over Christmas. There was nothing to be done, and with great regret Boucicault was forced to move the launch to 27th December. But he was now grimly determined that nothing would prevent the performance from going ahead. When *Peter Pan* finally opened, Barrie had rewritten the ending for the fifth time. Yet more new technical problems had obliged him to retreat to a dressing room and completely cut the last two and a half scenes (in later performances these were reinserted). Rehearsing all through the night of the 26th, the company struggled home to bed at dawn.

16

'*I'm youth I'm joy . . .*'

O n the evening of 27th December 1904, the curtain finally rose
on the first performance of *Peter Pan*.
        Unwilling as Barrie was to make a conclusive ending, the
numerous manuscript versions of the play mean that no single one is quite
definitive. The first *Peter Pan*, then, was only the first of many. With this in
mind, the resumé that follows is an amalgamation of stage directions from
the printed version of the play and the book Barrie later made of it, called
Peter and Wendy. The book is probably the closest to the play as it was acted
on stage for many years. This is because Barrie could not bring himself to
make a printed, and therefore a conclusive, version until twenty-four years
after that first performance. By this time it was 'charmingly polished and
cut and beautified – and had lost . . . a little of its virility in the process'.[1]

The Darlings have three children, Wendy, John and Michael, whose
conscientious nursemaid, Nana, is a Newfoundland dog.

> The Darlings could not afford to have a nurse . . . Of course Nana
> had been trained by Mrs Darling, but like all treasures she was born
> to it . . .
> No nursery could possibly have been conducted more correctly,
> and Mr Darling knew it, yet he sometimes wondered uneasily
> whether the neighbours talked. He had his position in the city to
> consider. Nana also troubled him in another way. He had some-
> times a feeling that she did not admire him.[2]

The play opens with the children being put to bed by Nana and Mrs
Darling, who is dressed in her evening gown and about to go out to
dinner with her husband.

> She does not often go out to dinner, preferring when the children are
> in bed to sit beside them tidying up their minds, just as if they were

drawers . . . repacking into their proper places the many articles of the mind that have strayed during the day, lingering humorously over some of their contents, wondering where on earth they picked this thing up, making discoveries sweet and not so sweet, pressing this to her cheek and hurriedly stowing that out of sight. When they wake in the morning the naughtinesses with which they went to bed are not, alas, blown away, but they are placed at the bottom of the drawer; and on the top, beautifully aired, are their prettier thoughts ready for the new day.[3]

A young boy named Peter Pan flies in through the nursery window. He teaches the Darling children to fly, and entices them away to Never Land, an island we all seek in childhood but never reach except in our imagination. (In 1902 the playwright Wilson Barrett wrote a play he called *The Never Never Land*, which refers to an Australian Aboriginal area in the Northern Territory. It would be entirely appropriate if this had inspired Barrie's name, when the Australian one derives from a people who gave to the repository of their understanding of themselves the name of the Dream Time.) It is on the island of Never Land that Peter lives with the Lost Boys. They are

the children who fall out of their perambulators when the nurse is looking the other way. If they are not claimed in seven days they are sent far away to the Never Land to defray expenses.[4] The boys on the island vary, of course, in numbers, according as they get killed and so on; and when they seem to be growing up, which is against the rules, Peter thins them out. . .[5]

Peter Pan ran away from home the day he was born because he didn't want to grow up. He has been given the gift of eternal youth. To Wendy he says scornfully: ' "Don't have a mother." . . . Not only had he no mother but he had not the slightest desire to have one. He thought them very over-rated persons.'[6]

Peter often keeps company with fairies, who have taught him how to fly. His assistant is a fairy named Tinker Bell, who

was not all bad; or rather she was all bad just now, but, on the other hand, sometimes she was all good. Fairies have to be one thing or the other, because being so small they unfortunately have room for only one feeling at a time. They are allowed to change but it must be a complete change.[7]

Redskins and animals also live on the island of Never Land, and Captain Hook and his fellow pirates visit periodically. Captain Jas Hook is said to resemble Charles II, and was educated at Eton.

> He still adhered in his walk to the school's distinguished slouch. But above all he retained the passion for good form.
> Good form! However much he may have degenerated, he still knew that this is all that really matters.[8]

Some time ago Peter had cut off the Captain's right hand, now replaced by a hook, and thrown it to a passing crocodile. The hook became a gruesome and fearful weapon:

> Yo ho, yo ho, when I say 'paw',
> By fear they're overtook.
> Naught's left upon your bones when you
> Have shaken hands with Hook!

Unnervingly announced by a ticking clock it swallowed long ago, the crocodile is forever in search of Hook in order to consume the rest of him. Meanwhile, the ruthless yet tortured Hook lives in terror of the crocodile. He is also forever trying to find Peter, to take his revenge upon the cocky boy, who is as vain as Hook himself.

Tiger Lily is a Redskin princess who likes Peter Pan a lot. She is marooned on a rock at Hook's orders, to be drowned by the rising sea. By an ingenious stratagem Peter rescues Tiger Lily, and from then on the Redskins are friends and protectors of the Lost Boys.

On the island Wendy sets up home, and here she mothers her brothers, the Lost Boys and Peter Pan, of whom she has become very fond. At last, after many adventures, and missing their mother, the children feel guilty at their absence from home. There is no mention of missing their father, who meanwhile does penance for indirectly causing the children's escape. He is literally in the doghouse, Nana's kennel, to which *The Times* is delivered, and a taxi carries him to work in his kennel each day.

> The great heart of the public was touched. Crowds followed the cab, cheering it lustily; charming girls scaled it to get his autograph; interviews appeared in the better class of papers, and society invited him to dinner and added, 'Do come in the kennel.'[9]

Peter Pan and the Lost Boys fail to prevent the Darling children from returning to their heartbroken parents. But before they can leave, Hook

and his pirates defeat the Redskins and gleefully take the Darlings and
Lost Boys prisoner.

> By all the unwritten laws of savage warfare it is always the Redskin
> who attacks, and with the wiliness of his race he does it just before
> the dawn, at which time he knows the courage of the whites to be
> at its lowest ebb . . .
> That this was the usual procedure was so well known to Hook
> that in disregarding it he cannot be excused on the plea of igno-
> rance.
> The Piccaninnies, on their part, trusted implicitly to his honour,
> and their whole action of the night stands out in marked contrast
> to his. They left nothing undone that was consistent with the repu-
> tation of the tribe.[10]

Hook attempts to kill Peter by poisoning his medicine, but Peter is saved
by the heroic action of Tinker Bell, his fairy assistant (who jealously vies
with Wendy for his attention). Peter then furiously pursues Hook, and,
dagger at the ready, he swears this terrible oath: 'Hook or me this time.'
Meanwhile Hook paces the deck of the Jolly Roger:

> From far within him he heard a creaking as of rusty portals, and
> through them came a stern tap-tap-tap, like hammering in the night
> when one cannot sleep. 'Have you been good form to-day?' was
> their eternal question.
> 'Fame, fame, that glittering bauble, it is mine,' he cried.
> 'Is it quite good form to be distinguished at anything?' the tap-
> tap from his school replied.
> 'I am the only man whom Barbecue feared,' he urged; 'and Flint
> himself feared Barbecue.'
> 'Barbecue, Flint — what house?' came the cutting retort.
> Most disquieting reflection of all, was it not bad form to think
> about good form?[11]

Hook is about to make the Darlings and Lost Boys walk the plank off
the pirate ship, when Peter arrives to save them. In the ensuing duel
Peter is triumphant, and finally pushes Hook overboard into the jaws of
the waiting crocodile, now even more dangerous because his clock has
at last run down. But Hook secures

> One last triumph . . . As he stood on the bulwark looking over his
> shoulder at Peter gliding through the air, he invited him with a

gesture to use his foot. It made Peter kick instead of stab. At last
Hook had got the boon for which he craved.

'Bad form,' he cried jeeringly, and went content to the crocodile.

Thus perished James Hook.[12]

The Darling children at last return to their overjoyed parents. Wendy
begs Peter to come with them, but he refuses, and so she will wait for
his return once a year. Peter comes back, but only twice. He has no
understanding of time, being outside it and immortal. He forgets Wendy,
until years later he returns and discovers that she has a daughter of her
own, called Jane.

She [Wendy] had risen; and now at last a fear assailed him. 'What
is it?' he cried, shrinking.

'I will turn up the light,' she said, 'and then you can see for yourself.'

For almost the only time in his life that I know of, Peter was
afraid. 'Don't turn up the light,' he cried.

She let her hands play in the hair of the tragic boy. She was not
a little girl heart-broken about him; she was a grown woman smiling
at it all, but they were wet smiles.

Then she turned up the light, and Peter saw. He gave a cry of
pain; and when the tall beautiful creature stooped to lift him in her
arms he drew back sharply.

'What is it?' he cried again.

She had to tell him.

'I am old, Peter. I am ever so much more than twenty. I grew
up long ago.'

'You promised not to!'

'I couldn't help it. I am a married woman, Peter.'

'No you're not.'

'Yes, and the little girl in the bed is my baby.'[13]

Peter goes to stab the child in the bed, but then, in despair, 'He sat down
on the floor . . . and sobbed; and Wendy did not know how to comfort
him, though she could have done it so easily once.'

Peter transfers his attentions to Jane, whom he then carries away with
him to Never Land. And thus the cycle will continue, even with Jane's
daughter, Margaret, and on, by implication, for all time.

One hundred years later, when to most of us Peter Pan appears harmless
and conservative, it is hard to imagine the degree of conviction and optimism

necessary to bring about this most radical piece of theatre. Played and read repeatedly down the generations, the bare bones of the story are so familiar that it requires an imaginative resourcefulness to conjure up the scene on that first night in 1904. London society was there in force, so were the critics, and a glittering West End audience waited expectantly, quite unprepared for the play they were about to see. The occasion was characterised by Barrie's considered ambiguity. And while rehearsals leading up to it might have appeared chaotic, and Barrie himself at times unsure, in fact his play was a distillation of the forces driving the whole of his life and art.

At first sight *Peter Pan* appears to be for children, yet its premiere was played in front of an audience composed of adults, and held in the evening, when Barrie would customarily present a new play to the public. Intuitively he knew that within his play was a set of themes that would speak as much to every adult as they would to any child. Rather than drawing out the distinctions between adults and children, in *Peter Pan* Barrie blurred them and encouraged a mutual suspension of belief, an abandonment of reality. The difference here between adult and child would only be in what kind of reality was being forsaken.

As the curtain went up there was a stunned silence, while a large dog busied itself preparing for a small boy's bedtime bath. The audience's silence was soon replaced by gasps of delight, as one outlandish scene after another demanded that they give themselves up to the fantasy. It appeared that they were only too willing to throw off their adult guise, recapture childhood and pass the rest of the evening enthralled. Barrie had caught them in his spell, and when Peter Pan despairingly attempted to save the fairy Tinker Bell's life by crying out, 'Do you believe in fairies? If you do wave your handkerchiefs and clap your hands,' there was such a joyful roar of assent that Nina Boucicault (sister of the director), playing Peter Pan, was temporarily reduced to tears.

Gerald du Maurier made a superlative Captain Hook, and, just as Barrie intended, he became the personification of all that was most terrifying to the childish imagination. In rehearsal du Maurier had already imbued the part with such inspiration that in response Barrie had changed a number of his lines. Many years later Gerald's daughter, the novelist Daphne du Maurier, would write:

> . . . with his flourish, his poses, his dreadful diabolical smile! That ashen face, those blood red lips, the long, dank, greasy curls. The sardonic laugh, the maniacal scream, the appalling courtesy of his gestures; and that above all most terrible of moments when he descended the stairs and with slow, most merciless cunning poured

the poison into Peter's glass . . . Gerald *was* Hook . . . he was a tragic and rather ghastly creation who knew no peace, and whose soul was in torment; a dark shadow; a sinister dream; a bogey of fear who lives perpetually in the recesses of every small boy's mind. All boys had their Hooks, as Barrie knew; he was the phantom who came by night and stole his way into their murky dreams. He was . . . a lonely spirit that was terror and inspiration in one. And because he had imagination and a spark of genius, Gerald made him alive.[14]

Some years later Barrie wrote to Hilda Trevelyan that she had been an 'incomparable Wendy', while Nina Boucicault seemed perfectly to capture the haunting quality, the enigma that is Peter Pan. One of Barrie's first biographers wrote lines which will cause any devotee of the play much regret that they failed to see her in the role.

Miss Boucicault as Peter Pan . . . The best, as no one has ever questioned, because of this haunting, eerie quality, this magic and this sadness . . . [she] was the Peter of all Peters . . . She was unearthly but she was real. She obtruded neither sex nor sexlessness . . . Above all she had the touch of heart-breaking tragedy that is there in the story from beginning to end; yet she never seemed to know it.[15]

When the final curtain fell, the cast were amazed as they were called back again and again to waves of tumultuous applause.

Meanwhile, across the Atlantic, poor Frohman desperately awaited news of the performance with a friend in his house outside New York. Hours passed, and still there was no word. His biographers wrote:

It was a bitterly cold night, and a snowstorm was raging. Frohman's secretary in the office in New York had arranged to telephone the news of the play's reception, which Lestoque was expected to cable from London. On account of the storm the message was delayed. Frohman was nervous. He kept on saying, 'Will it never come?' His heart was bound up in the fortunes of this beloved fairy play. While he waited with his friend Potter, Frohman acted out the whole play . . . Finally at midnight the telephone rang . . . Frohman jumped up from his chair, saying, eagerly, 'What's the verdict?' Potter listened a moment, then turned, and with beaming face repeated Lestoque's cablegram:

PETER PAN ALRIGHT. LOOKS LIKE A BIG SUCCESS.

This was one of the happiest nights of Frohman's life. Meanwhile, in London, as the curtain calls continued, Barrie, his director, stagehands, the entire company, were left utterly astonished. Against all expectation *Peter Pan* was a triumph.

A year later, Frohman opened the play in New York, where the critics were enthusiastic in their praise. Night after night audiences flocked to the theatre, embracing the play with an enthusiasm that outdid its huge London success. With Maude Adams as the boy, Frohman took *Peter Pan* out across the United States. People everywhere were clamouring to see it and Peter became the most talked-about 'child' in America.

The actress Gladys Cooper, who became a notable and perceptive Peter, wrote, 'I am inclined to hold and maintain that *Peter Pan* is really more of a play for grown-ups than children.' If we accept that the play emerges naturally out of the major preoccupations of Barrie's life and work, then it is also reasonable to accept that Gladys Cooper was right. *Peter Pan* is a remarkably ambitious and profound meditation on the problem of time; on its beginning and end, and on our own beginning and end within it. Yet, at the same time, an essential part of the play's genius lay in its corresponding appeal to children. In the gradual refining of his dramatic methods Barrie had been at pains to speak to as varied an audience as possible, and this led naturally from adults to children. That he had succeeded with this part of his audience is marvellously demonstrated in Eva le Gallienne's comments on her American performances as Peter Pan in the late 1920s and early 1930s:

Nothing ever equals the audience at the free Christmas matinée of *Peter Pan*, which we gave once a year. On this occasion the children are completely uninhibited, for they are almost entirely without the control of grown-ups. Also many of them have never before seen any sort of entertainment and the whole thing is completely real to them.

None of us will ever forget the first of those matinées. The children did not know the ordinary applause, and they simply yelled their approval . . . When Tink is dying and Peter goes to the footlights crying out, 'Don't let Tink die: if you believe in fairies, clap your hands,' etc. Hand clapping was not enough for them. They screamed, 'YES! YES! We believe! We believe!' in a frenzy of anxious excitement. Never has Tink been saved as she was that day. In the ship scene where Peter yelled, 'Down boys and at 'em,' it was pandemonium! The children hopped up and down in their seats, some of them jumped up and ran down the aisles in a wild effort to help us conquer the pirates, and when Peter finally jumped on the barrel and with a mighty blow felled Hook to the ground, the cheers that went up stopped the show for three minutes. I have never heard such a noise inside a theatre. We were all complete wrecks after the performance. It was so hard not to break down and cry, the response was so touchingly genuine.[16]

And Barrie's *Peter Pan* was called back year after year, drawing in so many audiences that it became one of the most successful plays ever staged. For over fifty years a role in the play – any role – was coveted. Noel Coward would write that in 1913 he had 'satisfied a long-cherished desire to be in *Peter Pan*, which was the mecca of all child-actors'. (Coward played Slightly.)

To be offered the part of Pan, or Hook, became a crucial mark of recognition in an actor's career, and the two roles were taken by some of the most famous actors and actresses of the twentieth century. These included: Pauline Chase, Maude Adams, Fay Compton, Gladys Cooper, Jean Forbes-Robertson, Anna Neagle, Margaret Lockwood, Glynis Johns, Mia Farrow and Dorothy Tutin. Chief among the actors who have played Hook are Charles Laughton, Boris Karloff, Donald Wolfitt, Alistair Sim and more recently Dustin Hoffman. For more than fifty years the sense of continuity in production was remarkable. During the course of their careers some actors played an unusual number of characters, while others played one for lengthy periods of time. George Shelton, for example, became so synonymous with the role of the pirate Smee that he called his reminiscences *It's Smee*.

Although a good many reviewers were enthusiastic, as many others were nervous at something they didn't know how to categorise. *The Bookman* was approving and wrote:

> [J.M.B.] has written one of the most exquisite plays of our time. Like all masterpieces of art it is a revelation and an incarnation of things eternal. We see . . . not fictitious adventures for boys, but the actual adventures of the Soul of Boyhood. For 'grown ups' it has an exquisite humour.

Another critic said:

> Peter Pan does not actually resemble any real boy, because in him are summed up all the salient characteristics of all real boys . . . it

is a fantasy which in its own way has become will again . . . the ingenious and direct will of a child; the lyrical phantom comes to life in an epic song of liberation in childishness.[17]

G. K. Chesterton described Barrie as

> The most diffident of men and the most impudent of artists. I mean by impudence a sort of impossibility; a sudden steepness in a story as it winds its way through strange countries, to which I know no parallel, and which I find it difficult to describe . . . There is a perversity of fancy which reacts against fantasy itself; a rebellion in fairyland . . . in Barrie the imagination works in ways which nobody can expect, even if he is expecting the unexpected.[18]

From the beginning, not all children liked *Peter Pan* and the play has always had its adult detractors. As a major work of art it has inevitably provoked strong reactions, and there have always been those who loathe it. One of the first of these, Barrie's friend Anthony Hope, who had created his own fantasy world with *The Prisoner of Zenda*, famously sat unmoved throughout the first performance, and at the end he was heard to groan, 'Oh for an hour of Herod.'

Max Beerbohm, who divined some of the main currents of his time, although feeling uneasy about aspects of Barrie's work, did go some way towards an understanding.

> Undoubtedly *Peter Pan* is the best thing he has done − the thing most directly from within himself. Here, at last, we see his talent in its full maturity . . .
>
> Mr Barrie is that rare creature, a man of genius. He is something even more rare − a child who, by some divine grace, expresses through an artistic medium the childishness that is in him.
>
> Our dreams are nearer to us than our childhood, and it is natural that *Peter Pan* should remind us more instantly of our dreams than of our childish fancies. Our English dramatist, a man of genius, realised a dream for us; but the logic in him prevented him from indulging in that wildness and incoherence which are typical of all but the finest dreams. Credible and orderly are the doings of Puck in comparison with the doings of Peter Pan.[19]

Although Shaw appreciated much of the complexity of Barrie's writing, as an artist he was out of sympathy with everything Barrie stood for. He believed that *Peter Pan* was an artificial freak that completely missed its mark, and was 'foisted on children by the grown-ups'. To show Barrie how a play for children ought to be made Shaw went on to write *Androcles and the Lion*, though it never remotely competed with *Peter Pan*'s success.

Peter Pan has always eluded categorisation, and the majority of critics have traditionally refused, or been unable, to define it. In this way they believed they could write it off as a childish, whimsical and sentimental thing. It is clear, however, that the implications of *Peter Pan* extend beyond the world of the child, speaking with as much force to any adult prepared to listen. The play unites its audience in a shared reservoir of joyfully subversive memory and imagination. But the secret of its power and the reason for its greatness as a work of art, lies in the extraordinary vividness of the symbols with which Barrie has fashioned a modern myth. In this myth two worlds are depicted for us, and in different ways each of them is made to appear equally valid. These worlds are distinguished above all by their contrasting attitudes to time.

In one of these worlds is the Darling household. Here Mrs Darling and Wendy represent the female principle through a combination of beauty, strength and shrewd practicality. Crucially, as mother and potential mother, they also represent the capacity to procreate. Robustly and cheerfully these two accept the power of Time and Memory, but like most characters in the play they also have their ambiguities. Mrs Darling, the nurturing mother, also controls and orders lives; by implication too much. She is both a creative force and one that blocks the creativity – the imagination – of others. Peter Pan wants to be mothered. But at the same time, as the character exemplifying the glory of the imagination, he is in conflict with mother figures, ruthlessly undermining and attacking motherhood, and the order and principle of procreation that at different times Mrs Darling and Wendy represent. Wendy accepts time, she is practical and motherly. At other times the knowing seductress she also indulges in the Never Land world of fantasy and imagination.

Emerging from these ideas, and placed at the heart of the play, is Barrie's decision to have Peter Pan portrayed by a young woman rather than a boy. With Peter played like this, an underlying tension is set up, subliminally pointing to the heart of Peter's tragedy. In denying death he must deny creation, too. Thus, his world, the Never Land, is one without beginning or ending or death. In attempting to deny a beginning Peter *must* deny sexuality, infused as it is with those crucial implications of creation. And with Peter played by a young woman – who has advances made to her (him) by three *other* young women, Tinker Bell, Tiger Lily and Wendy – the possibility of procreation has implicitly been removed:

women cannot procreate with each other. (In rejecting sexuality Peter Pan is a kind of cipher for much at the heart of Barrie's own plight, and almost certainly one of the major reasons for the breakdown of his marriage.)

Peter goes on to reject the figure at the heart of creation: the mother, Mrs Darling – a rejection epitomised in those lines quoted earlier: ' "Don't have a mother." . . . Not only had he [Peter] no mother but he had not the slightest desire to have one. He thought them very over-rated persons.' And with another inspirational leap Barrie has Nana the dog also belonging to the world of Mrs Darling and Wendy. If reality imposes appropriate forms of behaviour, then fantasy completely abolishes such expectations. Dogs would like to be human; this is their fantasy. Thus, Nana is the children's nanny because dogs are utterly reliable. She represents true order; in other words order in the service of life.

Next there is Mr Darling, mercilessly portrayed. In a light-hearted, matter-of-fact way, Barrie reveals contempt for a man who has shirked the challenge of masculinity. George Darling is a most disdainful portrait of a wimp. One who is so terrified of time, he has capitulated before it. He is a fusspot whose pride is in conformity and servility, so that he can't bear to be late for the office, and the stool on which he sits is more powerful than any length of clanking chain. His two sons, John and Michael, are depicted as in-betweens. They haven't as yet been forced to make any choices about time.

In the second world, the Never Land (initially Never Never), the Island of Lost Boys, the ruling principle is the complete denial and near obliteration of time. In this way Peter Pan, whose home is the Never Land, has only a minimal capacity for memory. There is neither any real past nor any real future; there is only an eternal present. And as one who denies time, Peter is ultimately shallow. His passions are intense, but evanescent; he has no emotional endurance.

Captain Hook is a tragic figure, which explains his cadaverous gloominess. His tragedy lies in being unable – unlike Peter – successfully to abolish time. Hook instead is haunted by it, possessing the enduring reminder of the past in his very person: his hook. While the equally enduring reminder of his ominous future lies in the crocodile, who carries time (and death) ticking away in its belly. Indeed, in the ticking crocodile Barrie created one of the most original twentieth-century images of death, and shows it inseparable from its coupling with time. For Hook the ticking clock of time comes to a dreadful halt, in death.

The Redskins, meanwhile, are decent primitives. They belong to an age before our own and are less differentiated as individuals. No anxious choices loom over them. They are fierce and straight; simple, stoic and loyal. They accept fate. Barrie implies that unfortunately we can't go back to that period, which is distant and different from our own.

Although at times charming, the pirates are mostly serviles, who have handed over their freedom to Hook. They are not really much better than George Darling, and are disposed of fairly easily by the Lost Boys.

Finally, the Nurses, who mislay the little boys, are the negatives of Mrs Darling, Wendy and Nana. They are *forgetful*; they have failed to stand up to time, and to watch it sufficiently carefully. Instead, they gossip while their charges fall out of their prams. The Nurses, then, are the female counterparts of George and the pirates. The implication being that in this world, unlike the Never Land, one must be responsible, and remember time, or else one pays a price.

In his writing Barrie reached ahead of his own time. With his novels about Tommy Sandys, despite their brilliance and insight, he had not quite arrived at the heart of the matter. With *Peter Pan,* on the other hand, in his continuing struggle to give up play (the imagination) by growing up, he carried on the battle with time through the inspirational idea of creating an entirely separate world. And herein lies the profound difference between Barrie and the other great writers for children. All of them – Edward Lear, Lewis Carroll, Rudyard Kipling, Kenneth Grahame, Beatrix Potter, Tolkien, C. S. Lewis, Roald Dahl – no matter how subversive or anarchic their worlds, wrote stories that include the idea of negotiating with and becoming adult. No matter how impious or irreverent, they all acknowledge time. By implication these authors are saying: 'How can we make the best of the world as it is?' But in *Peter Pan* it is unavoidably clear that at the deepest level Barrie's little hero refuses to grow up. He fears the very qualities of adulthood, and this is Barrie's dilemma. When he sees that a child is growing up, a part of him mourns. Barrie, for whom time with its implications of mortality was an obsession, is saying to us:

> I wish that the universe were radically different, since the world as it is is not just tragic, it is for me an impossibility. To be completely human – with its full range of both practical and imaginative poten- tialities – and to grow up; these are in a sense contradictories. By growing up, by co-operating in social order, living, one has to curtail the imagination; by doing this one is obliged to give up so much that one becomes an unacceptably diminished person.

Therefore, he is driven to create the glorious immortal Boy. A little god, in whose very name the ideologies of the first disciple, Peter, who exemplifies the Christian Church, collides with Pan, the ancient pre-Christian pagan god of many meanings. Pan, who represents sensuality and nature, started out as a goat and only gradually became half human. Peter Pan, then, is the Boy, who represents beauty, charm and eternal youth. He is the personification of abandonment, of play and of childhood. To achieve this he lives in the Never Land, an alternative to the real world, where growing up never happens and where the glorious imagination is ever alive. Thus when Hook asks Pan who he is, jubilantly he cries out (with variations in different manuscripts.) 'I'm the new world – I'm poets singing . . . I'm youth, I'm joy. I'm a little bird that has broken out of the egg.'

Like almost everything Barrie wrote, *Peter Pan* is deceptively simple. Contrary to its easiest interpretation, in his myth Barrie is *not* simply setting youth against age as an ideal against a lost paradise. He is showing how wonderfully seductive is youth's appeal as an alternative to the human dilemma. A dilemma in which he sees only fickle change and death. But Barrie is entirely aware that his fantasy of endless youth is flawed, profoundly tragic and ultimately impossible. (Thus, the essential message of his play is that we try to eliminate time at our peril.)

At the same time, Barrie is all the characters in *Peter Pan*. He cannot hold together his multiple personalities, cannot make up his mind between them, so he will celebrate and give them all their due, their 'hour upon the stage'. Meanwhile, he carefully specifies the strengths and limitations of his characters, and through them ruthlessly exhibits his own inadequacies. Pan, Mr Darling and Hook are all equivocal male figures, and in them Barrie is experimenting with the idea of masculinity. No character in *Peter Pan* is essentially masculine. As never before, Barrie is making a sincere attempt to interpret himself. It is as if he lets out a cry of pain and says, 'But what about me, the maker?' This maker knows that a supreme work of art requires a new kind of person, Peter Pan, and this new kind of person must have a new kind of society in which to exist, the Never Land, but what is there for him who is its creator and lives in another world?

Play, myth, ritual, art, religion – these overlap and intermix inseparably, and their corresponding expressions and activities spring from the unconscious, the ultimate depths of both person and cosmos. Moreover, it is a far larger unconscious than the Freudian one, no more than a small part of it. By suspending certain common-sense categories, especially in play, Barrie understood that we are able to participate in the truth of the depths, which would otherwise be closed to us. Myth, as the natural expression of the fundamental movements of the spirit, is a shelter wherein our conscious and unconscious harmoniously meet. And serious play is the active feature of myth.

Those less privileged children of New York who responded with such total abandonment to Barrie's play did so because, to their delighted amazement, their actual world was being articulated and represented for them by a master. He spoke their most essential language – not super-ficially, but at the deepest level – far better than they could articulate it themselves. Unsurprisingly, they were enchanted.

As for the adults, as one critic wrote,

> One does not criticise this play, one renews one's youth in it. There are, no doubt, some who curl their lip when it is mentioned, but to do that is to condemn not the play, but themselves. Barrie has here caught the imagination of the world's infancy, and what need he fear if severely-minded persons scowl, so long as children cheer? Consider how many boys and girls have surrendered their terrible sense of fact in order that they might save the life of Tinker Bell . . .[20]

When Max Beerbohm says that Barrie is a child he is, on the face of it, correct. But Beerbohm reveals his own limitations here, since some-times the child has a more accurate and healthy vision, both spiritual and practical, than the adult.

By 1904 Britain had become an industrial society whose underlying doctrine – in practices and beliefs – was that empirical science was the only valid way of thinking. Other modes of 'knowing' and being were by now frowned upon. They were either, like myth, often seen at best as primitive, at worst false; or, like play, merely trivial and to be outgrown and discarded as soon as possible. Charles Dickens's portrait of Thomas Gradgrind, the High Priest of Fact in *Hard Times*, sums up this attitude without too much exaggeration.

As a counterpart to the steady rise of empirical science throughout the Victorian period, there was a steady decline in self-confidence about playing. In 1831 R. S Surtees published the first of the Jorrocks adven-tures. Jorrocks, that robust, shrewd, down-to-earth cockney grocer, was devoted to hunting, fishing and shooting, and any other pastime that came his way. Surtees takes for granted the universal and self-justifying attraction and value of playfulness and active play, as much for adults as for children. Over the last one hundred and fifty years an unmistakable trend is clear: at first everyone played, then it was mostly children, now even many children seldom play, with the hours busily occupied in front of a screen.

The growth of a magnificent body of children's literature in Britain had its negative side: a tendency, as time passed, to put up barriers and build walls between the prosaic, disciplined life of adults and a playful life for children

At the time when the factory system and urbanisation were developing steadily in Britain, many of the world's games were being formalised: association football, rugby football, tennis, golf, the Queensberry Rules for boxing. Although this was remarkable and must have done much to make the constraints of industrialism more acceptable, these were largely spectator sports, overlapping with, but not quite the same as, play. The increasingly large numbers of spectators had become passive; they themselves were not playing.

Peter Pan could neither have been written nor well received much before its time. Barrie doesn't set out to convey his own opinions, something he was deeply against in his work. Instead, he offers up a reflection of the new, industrialised society in which he lived. In living memory society had changed so much that the majority of people were still unclear how to go about their lives. What Barrie does in *Peter Pan* is to transform the nature of the questions facing a people quite suddenly living in an age of doubt.

17

Disquiet

Not far from the Barries' new home at Leinster Corner, the Llewelyn Davies family were coming to a decision. This was set to affect the next phase of their lives as much as Barrie's play was to influence his own. With the growing size of Arthur and Sylvia's family, they had moved from 23 Kensington Park Gardens to a larger house at number 31. But with five boys and a staff of four, their house was once again proving too small. They must also face the pressing question of where the older boys, George and Jack, would be sent to school. Arthur's income had gradually improved through his hard work at the bar, but it was insufficient either to fund a larger London house or to send five boys to boarding school. The decision to move was probably Arthur's. Initially, Sylvia, who had lived in London all her life and loved it, may well have objected. If so her husband won her round, and in the spring of 1904 the Davieses left the city.

In Berkhamsted, a country town, they were able to take a larger house; Arthur could easily commute the twenty-five miles to London each day on the train, while the boys were to attend the day school nearby. Here, they would grow up as their father wished, in healthier rural surroundings. In making this move, was Arthur also attempting to distance his family from the influence of Jim Barrie?

Considering the degree to which Barrie had so insistently made himself part of the Davieses' lives, it seems unlikely that he wouldn't have known of their impending move. Perhaps it was kept from him until the move was imminent. In whatever way he discovered it – his reaction is not recorded – there is no doubt that for the moment a gaping chasm had opened in his life. A letter to little Peter Llewelyn Davies, in November of that year, reveals a hint of the great sense of loss he felt at the Davieses' absence.

My dear Peter
Sometimes when I am walking in the Gardens with Luath I see

a vision and I cry, Hurray, there's Peter, and then Luath barks joyously and we run to the vision and it turns out to be not Peter but just another boy, and then I cry like a water cart and Luath hangs his sorrowful tail.

Oh dear, how I wish you were here, and then it would be London again.

Goodbye.

Write soon.

Your loving godfather

J. M. B.[1]

Barrie was never in any formal way made godfather to the Davies boys.

Shortly after the Davieses' move, Frohman, who like Barrie was a devotee of Paris, persuaded his friend to spend some time with him there. The story is told by Frohman's biographers that he had organised a series of sumptuous Parisian entertainments for Barrie, beginning by taking rooms at one of the city's smartest hotels. His attempts to indulge Barrie royally – from a box at the Théâtre Français, to supper at the Café de Paris – were rejected one by one in favour of far simpler entertainment at a country fair at Neuilly, outside the city. Here the two friends apparently spent the evening playing at 'flinging rings on to pocket knives'. With his extraordinarily accurate eye Barrie of course was a great success and wrote to Peter Davies telling him they had 'won eleven knives and if we go back we shall win some more'.

Returning home early in July, Barrie was soon faced with a situation by contrast alarmingly adult and far removed from the diversion of his and Frohman's childlike games.

Mary had gone ahead to Black Lake and Barrie went down to join her there after his return to London. Their tenth wedding anniversary fell on 9th July, and the next day, in a far larger than normal notebook – given to him by his old school friend Wedd Anderson – Barrie made a series of harrowing notes. These carry such an air of mournful authenticity they can only be the record of an actual event.

Tin Wedding in 10th Year   10th July 1904

Idea – Husband & wife story, scene caused by husband – evidently they don't get on well together – his fault – she violent – interrupted by visitors with Tin Wedding presents (he hasn't remembered it is their wedding day). She immediately in woman's way sort of manner talks as if husband best in world – how he spoils her, & pretends grand present from him, &c. When they're gone, he remorseful & swears to make it happy day yet for her (thinks he's doing finely) then she shows true self – says can quarrel over little things . . . but not over big things. Too late to talk of love & his giving it to her, *she no longer wants it.* Her own love for him has gone from her, spilt, ended, &c . . . She says he can have affairs with other women as he wills. They don't disturb her. *Do as he likes about that.* Wld like to go on pretending to people happy &c, less for his sake (he had thought it all so touching & *all for him*) as [because] it's a woman's way, &c.

He wishes cd do anything for her wedding day and she admits there's one thing he cd do. Sometimes for dif[ferent] reasons – as good mood or [because] he's going off to dinner &c. he paws her & and he keeps old custom of kissing her goodnight. She asks him not to do these things as her Tin Wedding gift. He consents she goes off about business of house leaving him crushed. Curtain . . .

– Audience probably think she is to be sweet long-suffering creature. Her parents, &c, all deceived by her now as always about their married life. She tells him she has borne for long & forgiven & forgiven, and loved but love gone for a year & *he hasn't even seen it gone.*

She doesn't love any other but tired . . . no use – not in her to have these feelings but once.

– She has scunner [revulsion] of him over goodnight kiss & tells how feels at night coming on & has resorted to various artifices to escape kiss. She knows he has gone . . . to bed or out feeling *he has made her better.*

Does she really have a scunner of him now? Perhaps not man she supposed she married.

– She on agonies & years of forgiveness, self-deceptions, clinging to straws, & now all these have gone. Like stick in fire, flaming, red, sparks, now black & cold.

Her original love for him – how he had always . . . such perfect faith in it . . . She might tell how even tried to be like mistress . . . and he hadn't seen what striving after . . . but laughed at [her?] . . .

Her pretty ways (and I did have them) gone . . . so her loving touch in music can't play . . . now – all was done for you. She spoke with sudden passion about scunner of him.

She wished she cd have old (emotions?) . . . love . . . but dead.

He had thought they were getting on so much better of late [because] no rows.

They to go on with this life (. . . in separation) . . . She says he mustn't bother to . . . conceal his 'affairs' from her – she doesn't care whether he has them or not.

But don't let friends [know?].

He points out she embraced him before friends – She how little he knows how horrible it was to her – Best to deceive.

Not so much to deceive parents as old school friends &c à la S.T.'s mother [Jean Sandys in *Sentimental Tommy*].

He thinks she was very generous to him in deceiving guests, but she tells him it wasn't generosity at all but a woman's vanity . . .

– He says can't we pick up the pieces (of our love) & she says no – love not a broken jar but fine wine – contents spilt – can't pick that up.

– She says . . . I'm no grand figure of tragedy – not tall enough – too plain – hands too red – I'm just a woman who made a mistake (twelve years ago), Mary abt us.[2]

This grim document largely speaks for itself. Over the years of the Barries' marriage we catch no more than fleeting glimpses of what it must have been like as Mary persevered in her determination to make things work. But here we are given the full force of her misery and defeat, with its conclusion in emotional exhaustion and disillusionment. By contrast Barrie appears genuinely shocked by his wife's revelations, as if over the years he had gained no real insight into her intentions or her feelings. He still cannot fully emotionally engage with what is happening, and so is driven to distance himself by writing it all down as potential material for his work. From this point onwards, Mary's sense of reality appears to have held sway in their marriage. Having faced her husband with what she saw as the truth of their existence, the private pretence that their marriage still functioned now ceased. In public, meanwhile, they carried on much the same as before.

When Barrie wrote of Hook in the following passage, one knows that not only was Peter Pan created out of himself, but so also was Hook.

Hook trod the deck in thought . . . and knowing as we do how vain a tabernacle is man, could we be surprised [if he was] . . . bellied out by the winds of his success? But there was no elation in his gait, which kept pace with the action of his sombre mind. Hook was profoundly dejected. He was often thus when communing with himself . . . in the quietude of the night. It was because he was so terribly alone.[3]

Barrie could be searingly honest and a cold analyser of the truth. Strange genius that he was, at heart his nature was chameleon. Neither a cold nor a warm person, there is really no adjective that adequately describes him, but he was indeed terribly alone. Shut out from so much, this was emphasised in the lines at the end of *Peter Pan*, when the Darling children finally return to their mother

'George, George,' she cried when she could speak; and Mr Darling woke to share her bliss, and Nana came running in. There could not have been a lovelier sight; but there was none to see it except a strange boy who was staring in at the window. He had ecstasies innumerable that other children can never know; but he was looking through the window at the one joy from which he must be barred forever.[4]

The Davieses' removal from London did not deter Barrie for long and he soon became a frequent visitor to the house in Berkhamsted – 'a mighty nice one', as Peter Davies later said. Barrie must have wilfully ignored the tensions that surely existed between Mary and Sylvia Davies, although whatever he permitted himself to think on the matter was never committed to his notebooks. In the spring of 1905 he invited Sylvia to stay with him and Mary at the fashionable resort of Dives in Normandy. Sylvia accepted the invitation and was accompanied by two of her boys, Jack, and Michael, now aged five. Arthur, meanwhile, took George and Peter to stay with his father in Westmorland. The baby, Nico, remained at home with the nurse, Mary Hodgson. How much Sylvia was aware of the effect of her presence as a third party in the Barries' marriage we can only guess at. For his part Arthur well understood that as a du Maurier his wife craved a glamorous edge to her life; something that Barrie was willing to provide. Arthur's serious-mindedness was tempered by considerable patience, but even a man of monumental composure must at times have felt exasperated by Barrie. Not long after the Davieses' move to Berkhamsted he had made them – or was it really Sylvia? – a present of a pony and cart, about which he wrote Sylvia a typically proprietorial letter.

If K is right I think you should get her. She sounds promising. The thing to do is to have her sent to you on trial, so do that . . . I am writing our friend 'Mart' that you are having a pony, also writing to Windover to hurry the cart . . .[5]

Barrie signs the letter 'Your loving JMB'. Many years later Peter Davies wrote:

I wonder if any sharp words passed between A. and S. before this gift was accepted? One of the many things which conspire to lend a certain unreality to childish recollections is that it is almost impossible to me to conceive a quarrel between these two. But on the other hand it is equally impossible to believe that relations weren't strained, and at pretty frequent intervals, too, by the infiltration of this astounding little Scotch genius . . .[6]

The pony finally chosen was, incidentally, named Crichton.

The little Scotch genius's way of managing life was, at heart, anathema to Arthur. This included an apparent urge to 'acquire' Arthur's wife and his children, with Sylvia a seemingly willing participant. Barrie's was an invasive presence, but would these strange associations – about which there was inevitable gossip – have been possible had Arthur not been so civilised and long-suffering? In Barrie's undoubted oblique reference to aspects of Arthur's life in the creation of Mr Darling, was there an implication that Barrie also thought he was spineless?

While Arthur and Sylvia remained devoted to one another, Arthur was also a dedicated and gentle father to his five boys. Indeed, a thought-provoking comment recorded years later by one of those boys sheds significant light on both parents' personalities.

Sylvia wore her children as other women wear pearls or fox-furs. They were beautiful children, but beautiful as background to her beauty. If one of the boys was ill, it was never Sylvia who held their heads or took their temperatures – it was always Arthur who did that kind of thing.[7]

Once again Dolly Ponsonby's observations are germane here.

I remember a funny sort of conservatory through which you passed to go into the . . . garden – it was filled with plants and flowers by Sylvia. Mary [Hodgson] would put the prams there – and Sylvia said, 'I do wish they wouldn't leave the prams here.' And Arthur said, 'I think the prams are more beautiful than the flowers.'[8]

While playing the part of the contented wife, Mary Barrie was also trying to make for herself a life with some meaning; one that no longer revolved around her husband. Responding to the fashionable Arts and Crafts Movement and its advocacy of hand-made objects, she took a course in enamelling. Then she hired a studio in Kensington and spent a good part of her time making enamelled objects for sale in fashionable shops such as Liberty. She also spent more time with her own friends, and gave dinner parties at Leinster Corner without her husband, who often retreated quietly out of the back door as Mary's friends entered by the front. Mary did still entertain their mutual friends, albeit less frequently, and in the summer of 1905 fulfilled her part as hostess to house parties at Black Lake. The following year she took a motoring holiday in France with a friend, Molly Muir, while for the first time Barrie staged the Allahakbarries' annual cricket matches and festivities at Black Lake without her. A number of friends were boarded out nearby, while others, such as the Lucases and the Hewletts, stayed with Barrie at the cottage. Once again Sylvia was invited, this time for a fortnight, and she came 'accompanied' by little Michael.

All who cared for the Barries observed the development of their increasingly separate lives with feelings of impotence, while on the outer edges of their circle there was, inevitably, rumour and speculation. Barrie's habitual reserve, even on the rare occasions it was breached by a friend, was almost invariably reinforced with one of those devastatingly dismissive looks, effectively silencing even the most intrepid enquirer. Mary, meanwhile, became more confirmed in the slightly challenging air of defensiveness that had long been an aspect of her public persona. In this way, she was able to transform any probing concern into a subtle form of counter-challenge. Both husband and wife made themselves deaf to rumour by busy occupation.

For Barrie the habit of occupation was so ingrained that it had become a sop, a substitute for any real integration of his complex personality – his many personalities – and there was nothing to make him bring a halt to it now. Having kept his warring selves at such a distance from one another, why should he address them now, when by doing so he might have to face things increasingly difficult to bear? After those chilling notes set down on the morning after his wedding anniversary, Barrie, at least, settled into this new phase of his marriage without any outward signs of anguish. For the moment anyway, this new *modus vivendi* permitted him to pursue his fascination with Sylvia and her boys with less complication.

At forty-five, restless as ever, he still kept most conscious anxiety at bay by incessant activity. That summer – with Michael Davies and the Hewletts' and the Lucases' children as catalysts for re-entry into the world of childhood – he worked hard on revisions for *Peter Pan*. At the same time, true to type, Barrie continued his devastating subterranean commentary on himself. Throwing out the excruciating Beautiful Mothers scene, Act III of *Peter Pan* now became the famous Mermaids' Lagoon. Here, Hook and his pirates have a dramatic encounter with Peter and Wendy, who are eventually marooned on a rock to die. Peter acts the hero and succeeds in forcing Wendy to save herself by flying off to safety hanging on to the tail of Michael's kite. Left behind with the waters lapping higher and higher over the rock,

> Peter knows that it will soon be submerged . . . from the coral grot-toes is to be heard a sound, at once the most musical and the most melancholy in the Never Land, the mermaids calling to the moon to rise. Peter is afraid at last, and a tremor runs through him, like a shudder passing over the lagoon . . .[9]

And he says '(with a drum beating in his breast as if he were a real boy at last), "To die will be an awfully big adventure." '[9]

Then, just before it is too late, Peter Pan is saved. He doesn't die; he cannot. For when he chose eternal youth, he was doomed to live for ever. Barrie cannot live for ever. He knows he will grow older, and that one day, unlike Peter, he must die.

Peter Pan proved so immensely successful in London that at the end of its London run in April Frohman announced that it would be brought back the following Christmas. Bookings were to remain open all year. Frohman was also now making great preparation for the play's American launch with Maude Adams as Peter Pan. After its premiere in Washington in October 1905, *Peter Pan* moved on to New York, where it was an immediate and enormous success. After the Empire Theatre's longest ever single engagement, and Frohman's tour of the play across the United States, seen in 'one-horse towns' and in the grandest theatres, Peter had become a figure of iconic status.

In the late autumn of 1905 there was great anticipation as rehearsals began in London for the first revival. With Hilda Trevelyan as Wendy and Sylvia's brother, Gerald, as Hook, the cast remained almost exactly the same, but for one major change. The 'incomparable' Nina Boucicault was dropped as Peter Pan, and Cecilia Loftus took her place. Barrie was a natural autocrat, and his immense success, together with considerable involvement in the staging of his plays, meant that his casting decisions were law. Admittedly his instincts usually led him to the right judge-ment, but if the descriptions of Nina Boucicault's performance are anything like accurate, then her rejection in favour of Cecilia Loftus, who was an apparently mediocre Peter, was a mistake that has never properly been explained.

During its seven-month run in New York *Peter Pan* made over half a million dollars for Barrie and Frohman. This was money that neither of them needed, nor really wanted. For the rest of his life Frohman used it to continue funding an enormous number of theatrical ventures and 'stars'. For the rest of Barrie's life he gave large amounts of it away, sometimes with forethought and at other times on a whim, in the manner of the self-made man, to individuals in need or to charities and other worthy causes.

In this period Barrie wrote two one-act plays, one a political satire and the other a dig at George Bernard Shaw. They were not thought suitable for the major theatres, yet the devoted Frohman had them rehearsed and staged at the Comedy Theatre, where the poor response meant that they were taken off after less than three weeks. Equally capable of a masterly detachment about his work as he was of the most insufferable subjectivity, this time Barrie mistakenly stuck to the conviction that his two plays were good. In the meantime he was negotiating with Frohman over *Alice Sit by the Fire*, the play he had given his friend as a sop when he thought *Peter Pan* might be refused. *Alice Sit by the Fire* was on for the best part of four months, but this was as much because of Ellen Terry's appearance than on account of its merits. Even Ellen Terry, however, couldn't make of it a success.

For years Barrie's notebooks had been filled with ideas, usually as numbered points. He might concentrate a thought into a couple of lines; sometimes a single word was enough. However they were recorded, and a good proportion of them never came to anything, some of the notebooks contain as many as six or seven hundred ideas. From his earliest days in London until virtually the end of his life, Barrie filled these astonishingly small booklets with a streaming succession of thoughts. This year they had titles such as: *A Thousand Nightingales*, *Voices*, *The Stolen Wood*, a play entitled *Father and Son*, more new notes for *Peter Pan*, and another title reading, simply, *Character*, about a man

> who fails to develop normally, whose spirit remains young in an aging body, constantly upset by the painful astonishment known to all of us when some outlawed proof suddenly jars our inward conviction of perpetual youth.[10]

The creative richness of these notebooks, begun more than a quarter of a century earlier, was maintained for some time after Barrie completed the first draft of *Peter Pan*. Looking over the phenomenal surge of literary activity generated in the first years of the new century, however, it is noteworthy that *all* the ideas he would go on to develop in his later plays had by this point been set down. Apart from the numerous one-act plays, the germ of the full-length ones that Barrie was yet to write – *Dear Brutus*, *What Every Woman Knows*, *Mary Rose* and *Shall We Join the Ladies?*

– already existed in the notebooks. After about 1906 or 1907, although the development and refinement of his thought provided some important work, Barrie produced no major new ideas.

In January 1906, feeling he was floundering, he wrote to his old friend Quiller-Couch:

> I am growing into a complete hermit bounded north south east and west by my own petty little notions which I usually abandon in the middle not because they are actually bad but because they work out so dolefully second class. I have been having a bout of this depressing kind lately and little to show for it but a philosophic countenance. The glorious thing is not to know it's second class.[11]

In that same month Mary Barrie was at her mother's deathbed in Hastings, where she died as a result of bronchitis. Mrs Ansell had lived in Hastings since her husband's death in Mary's youth.[12] Barrie makes no mention of his mother-in-law's death in his notebooks.

In early June he once again invited Sylvia to accompany him to Paris, but a dramatic sequence of events was to call a halt to the proposed visit.

Arthur Addison Bright was the agent whom Barrie had taken on years before to negotiate his first successful contract with *The Professor's Love Story*. Bright had confirmed and maintained his position as one of London's busiest and most highly regarded agents, and over the years he and Barrie had become good friends. It was also Bright who had first introduced Barrie and Frohman to one another, and they each felt a keen sense of loyalty to him. Consequently, when it was discovered that he had embezzled several clients' box office returns, Barrie and Frohman at first refused to believe it. For a time Bright managed to cover his tracks, but with an investigation gradually closing in on him, in May 1906 he finally yielded to pressure and confessed. Altogether, he had misappropriated what was, for then, the astoundingly large sum of twenty-eight thousand pounds, and sixteen thousand of those were Barrie's. Bright had no real need of this cache. He had spent none of it, and instead secreted it all away in his bank. The consensus was that he had temporarily gone insane. Barrie's horror mingled uneasily with a sense that the vast sums he was earning were corrupting to some of those who came within his orbit.

Dismay at his friend's actions rapidly turned to forgiveness: he wanted simply to forget everything and continue as before. Barrie's fortune was now such that he hadn't even noticed anything had gone missing, and believed that if he hadn't been so nonchalant about his finances, Bright might never have been tempted. For the others involved, neither so successful nor so magnanimous as Barrie, it wasn't enough to have their capital returned, and, baying for their pound of flesh, there was nothing more Barrie could do to protect his ruined friend from the due process of law. While awaiting his trial, in a terrible state Bright travelled to Switzerland for a brief rest. After a short time there, unable to sleep, to find any rest or face the future, he shot himself.

Barrie was devastated. Grimly he travelled out to Switzerland with Bright's younger brother Golding – who subsequently succeeded his elder brother as Barrie's agent – in order to identify and bring back the body. In that same spirit of partial responsibility and exoneration, Barrie wrote in *The Times*: 'For many years he had been my most loved friend.'

As if this melancholy episode had been a portent, more was soon to follow.

18

'The saddest most terrible night . . .'

A few days before Bright's suicide, Arthur Davies had written to his sister, Margaret, at their father's rectory in Westmorland. His plan to visit them with Michael while Sylvia was away on her Paris trip was abandoned. He was instead 'doomed to spend Whitsuntide less agreeably'. A slight swelling in the side of his face needed removing by a surgeon and would require a few days' recuperation in a nursing home. Afterwards, assuming he was fit to be left alone, Arthur wrote that Sylvia would 'probably leave with her friends for Paris on Tuesday', and Arthur's brother, Crompton, would be his companion on his first day at home. On 1st June, the day Barrie's obituary of Bright appeared in *The Times*, Sylvia wrote to Margaret that Arthur seemed 'pretty well' and that she hoped to get him home soon. The following day, however, the news was less favourable. Sylvia would definitely not be making the trip to Paris with the Barries.

The doctors had discovered that the swelling in Arthur's jaw was not an abscess. Instead, they had found a very serious growth: it was sarcoma. The surgeons decided that they must remove half of Arthur's upper jaw and palate; that he would be 'incapacitated' for six weeks or so, and unable to speak properly for three or four months. Arthur wrote to tell Margaret that there would 'always be an impediment in my speech. I think of our future and the boys.' He asked if she would come and help them through 'this trying time', and told her that the last fourteen years – the years of his marriage – especially, out of his forty-three, had left him with no ground for complaint. He added, 'But this needs fortitude. We both try our best.'

Over the coming months Arthur and Sylvia would indeed need fortitude to do their best. On Whit Monday, 4th June, their friend Dolly Ponsonby confided to her diary:

Got a letter from M.D. [Margaret Davies] to tell me the most *tragic* news about Arthur D. – that he has a terrible disease, sarcoma . . .

It is simply unbelievable & I can think of nothing else. That splendid, selfless, brave Arthur, who has slaved & worked all these years – to have his career absolutely changed if not *wrecked* by this – it is *incomprehensible*.

By 8th June Crompton was writing to their father with the results of Arthur's operation. He told the Reverend Davies that the surgeon – as was apparently intended all along – had removed his cheekbone. When Arthur came round he would be in some pain, and be given morphia as soon as possible. Clearly deeply moved by his brother's plight, Crompton said that Arthur's 'Courage and serenity was so great it gave others courage I felt . . .' Barrie telegraphed to the Reverend Davies the following day that his son was now conscious, and that Sylvia had sat with him for an hour. Barrie had arrived.

It remains unclear the degree to which Arthur was resentful about Barrie's increasing presence in his family over the last few years. Certainly two of his elder sons, Peter and Jack, disagreed about his feelings towards Barrie. Jack apparently thought Arthur kept his irritation barely concealed. Peter, on the other hand, was more charitable in his judgement and believed that though Arthur must have resented Barrie he was given much cause to modify his views in the next few months.

As soon as Barrie received news of the impending operation, he cancelled everything and made himself available to Arthur and Sylvia. Before the operation, Arthur wrote to his father that the kindness of all the family and of many friends was a great support: 'Sylvia, of course, is brave and utterly devoted . . . Barrie has been wonderful to us – we look on him as a brother.'

In the days before a national health service, when hospitals and doctors were paid for directly, it is unlikely that with Arthur's large family to support he possessed anything more than a fraction of the finances a serious operation would involve. The Reverend Davies and Sylvia's mother, Emma du Maurier, came forward with help; so apparently did several of their brothers. But in later years Arthur's son Peter believed it was Barrie who played the leading financial role. This meant that the doctors, and any nursing, would have been of the best. Peter Davies had no proof of Barrie's generosity, but the circumstantial evidence convinced him that he paid for almost everything. Barrie devoted himself untiringly to Arthur and Sylvia's needs. At the patient's bedside in the nursing home every day, he read him the newspaper, maintained a stream of letters to friends and colleagues on his behalf, or simply sat and kept him company.

For most of the time, although overcome by his suffering, in order to sustain and support her husband Sylvia made a huge effort to appear resolute and calm. Her brother, Gerald, soon came to visit Arthur, and outside his room afterwards Sylvia broke down in tears, saying in her misery that the doctors had 'spoilt my darling's face'. On 14th June Dolly Ponsonby wrote in her diary,

> Went to see Arthur Davies in a nursing home. It was very sad but they are both remarkable. He looked very altered but with his usual determination insists upon speaking in spite of having no roof or teeth, both of which he will have later – in spite of this I understood nearly everything he said. He tried to smile & made remark as I left about my being beautiful in his old dry chappy way . . . But to see Sylvia tending this poor maimed creature was something I shall never forget. She seemed a living emblem of love & tenderness & sorrow – stroking his hair & his hand & looking unutterable love at him & so beautiful – it seems to have completed her – She broke down a little outside & we talked about it, but she is brave – it was wonderful to see her.

On a visit to Arthur two weeks later, Dolly lamented,

> It seems sadder than ever & I hate his not being able to use his eye. Sylvia looks better and is more cheerful. Mr Lucas [E.V. Lucas] was there & quite came up to my expectations. Little Barrie was of course there, lurking in the background.[1]

With her use of the word 'lurking', once again Dolly gives us an insight. Here we catch a glimpse of the irritation and sense of oppressiveness that Barrie's embrace of the Davieses must frequently have provoked in their families and friends. More compassionately, we see that he had effectively taken on the role – more recognised and acceptable at the time – of bachelor uncle. What often began as charitable friendliness on the part of certain families might well develop into a relationship of subtly mutual support. Here the Davieses were no exception, and in the final analysis Sylvia herself clearly felt as much sustained by Barrie's presence as he did by hers. Yet, this 'uncle' had not so much been invited as inserted himself into the family. More than that, Barrie was *not* a bachelor: he was a married man.

Nothing he ever did was simple and his relationship with the Davieses was conducted with greater intensity than most other 'uncles' would ever have imposed, or their 'families' have tolerated. Barrie's friendships were at times tinged with an air of possession many found distasteful. This must have irritated Arthur when he was well, but during his illness he appears to have yielded increasingly to Barrie's solicitude, and his son Peter believed that eventually Arthur was not only grateful to Barrie, but found himself returning his affection. Peter's brother Jack, on the other hand, thought that Arthur never appreciably altered his opinion of Barrie. It was simply that their father became reconciled to Sylvia's willingness to accept Barrie's largesse.

Arthur was to be fitted with an artificial jaw. Barrie's apprehension that it was pointless, which he voiced in a letter to Sylvia, was to prove depressingly accurate. The excruciating pain of 'wearing' the clumsy contraption would soon become more than Arthur could bear.

A couple of months after the operation Sylvia's mother took Cudlow House at Rustington for the family's summer holiday. If in the past Barrie was sometimes seen as a self-imposed guest, for Arthur and Sylvia at least this was no longer the case. Whatever others might have concluded, he spent most of August with the Davieses and Mrs du Maurier, as one of the family. Much later, Peter Davies would say he thought Barrie's devotion to Sylvia arose, at least in part, out of *her* devotion to Arthur. Although Barrie had a tendency to slip into the role of champion without whom everything would probably collapse, his concern for Arthur was genuine and unceasing.

Whereas Arthur had previously referred to Barrie as Sylvia's friend, he now called him 'Jimmy'. And while Barrie continued in his role as the boys' chief entertainer, Arthur told his sister that between the sea bathing were 'endless games of cricket and lawn tennis in the garden'. Although Peter Davies would later refer to Barrie's presence at Rustington as 'a queerish business', Arthur wrote to his sister that the holiday had been 'entirely successful'. Staying close by at her parents' seaside house, Dolly Ponsonby saw them several times, and in the middle of August she wrote in her diary:

Went to see Sylvia in the evening. She is an amazing creature – certainly beauty and charm could go no further – and now she is more beautiful with a touch of sadness in her face & in her wonderful blue garments. She talked so naturally of all her hopes and fears regarding Arthur and how Margaret Davies's 'luxury of woe' attitude nearly killed her & M.'s intenseness about everything. I enjoy to think of Sylvia when Margaret says she hates money & rails against it & Sylvia saying 'I should love to have it – I should like to have gold stays & a scented bed & real lace pillows' & Margaret shocked and swallowing it all. Arthur is more pathetic than he was – it gives one a terrible twinge to see his poor maimed face, always escaping from people. Mr Barrie is always with them, a nurse to the children & an extraordinarily tactful and helpful companion to Sylvia and Arthur – though his moods like those of most genius types appear to be a little trying.[2]

On 30th August Dolly 'Went to dine with Sylvia and Arthur alone. He was very silent. Sylvia and I talked & A. seemed to be pretty happy listening.' Next day Dolly's children swam with Peter and Michael, and then they took Sylvia out in the 'motor', across the Sussex Downs. On 1st September, 'The whole Davies family came to tea . . . we sprawled on rugs on the lawn and Matthew [Dolly's two-year-old son] a great favourite with the charming boys.'

Having failed to secure the house for another week Arthur told his sister that they had 'succumbed' to an invitation from Barrie to stay in Scotland at a village called Fortingall, 'among high mountains and surrounded by burns in which the boys will fish'. Arthur said they were 'prodigiously excited'. With no interest at all in field sports he would doubtless have appreciated the grandeur and beauty of the scenery, and also his boys' enjoyment, but one senses, too, that some of Barrie's masterfulness was at work here. He was immensely difficult to refuse, no doubt more so when one was ill.

Several months earlier, his irrepressible friend Alfred Mason, whose range of friendships was always broad, introduced Barrie to the explorer Captain Robert Falcon Scott. In September 1904 Scott and his team had returned aboard their purpose-built ship, the *Discovery*, from that first great British Antarctic expedition. Antarctica was one of the last great wildernesses, and having endured twenty-six months in the world's most inhospitable climate, in territory hitherto unexplored, Scott and his men were hailed as heroes.

Through the recently expanded press, millions of Victorians had been made aware of the exploits of men such as Dr Livingstone, Stanley and Nansen. During the second half of the nineteenth century the British came to look on their explorers as heroic figures. Different social groups were able to interpret their activities in subtly contrasting ways: as Christian evangelism, as the extension of the Empire or as a contribution to the newly popular advancement of science. Added to this was the implicit belief that exploration – journeys to unknown and hazardous places – gave ample scope for the display of strength of character by meeting physical hardship with selflessness and courage.

On his return home, Scott had travelled Britain giving talks in packed lecture theatres, including the Albert Hall, where, flanked by the flags from his sledges, he spoke from the stage to rapt audiences. He wrote up his expedition for the publishers Smith Elder (Smith was another friend of Mason's), and on its publication in October 1905 *The Voyage of the Discovery* sold well, adding to the explorer's prestige.

Barrie's need for heroes meant that he was already predisposed to feel great admiration for this young man of the moment. What could not have been predicted was the particular mutual appreciation that sprang up between these two. Believing Scott to be the manliest sailor in the world, Barrie was inspired by the explorer's unaffected simplicity and charm. Scott was equally impressed by Barrie's position and name, and surrendered to the magical appeal Barrie was still so capable of exerting when he felt inspired. The young captain from the Admiralty was invited to stay at Black Lake Cottage, was entertained by Barrie and his friends, and openly admired this glamorous new world to which his celebrity had now given him access. For a time he was seen with the well-known young actress Pauline Chase, Barrie's and Frohman's protégée, who would take the role of Peter Pan for eight years.

While Barrie was in Scotland with the Davieses, Scott had written saying that he was contemplating another expedition, to the South Pole, and at the same time asked if Barrie knew of any young man who might want to apply for a vacant position at Osborne Naval College. Barrie wrote back by return saying, 'I know the right boy so well that it is as if I had been waiting for your letter . . . from his earliest days he has seemed to all of us cut out for a sailor . . .'

Indeed, Jack, now almost thirteen, was delighted, having indicated for some time that this was his proposed career. (Scott himself had begun as a naval cadet at thirteen.) Barrie was also helping with a plan to get George to Eton, as Arthur felt that this was Sylvia's wish. George sat the scholarship exam, and although he didn't achieve quite high enough marks for it he would none the less be at Eton by the following autumn. Having passed the entrance exams for Osborne College, Jack soon left home to become a naval cadet. There seems little doubt that it was Barrie who provided the wherewithal for the older Davies boys' new lives.

Shortly after their return home Arthur saw his specialist, Roughton, once more. The news could not have been worse. Roughton told him that the tumour had spread; another operation was impossible, and there was nothing more they could do. Arthur wrote and told his sister, Margaret. He said that Roughton didn't know how long he had left, but thought it would be somewhere between six months and a year. With compo-sure and dignity he spoke of his consolations in having a wife and children, of his concern for his wife, and of how it was 'All very terrible for her . . . My burden is far less heavy than Sylvia's.'

Next Arthur wrote to his ailing father, now over eighty, with the hope that he would bear whatever was in store for him in a way that befitted the son of a 'brave and wise man'. He added:

> I am troubled for myself, but much more for Sylvia. She is brave to a degree that I should hardly have thought possible, busy all day with endless activities & kindnesses for me & for the boys & all the time the burden is almost heavier than she can bear . . . she shrinks terribly from the loneliness after I am gone. Barrie's unfailing kindness and tact are a great support to us both . . .[3]

Barrie was given Arthur's prognosis, and wrote immediately to Sylvia saying that he would be there the following day.

> I shall bring a bag, and stay the night or not, just as you like. I am thinking of you and Arthur all the time . . .
> Your loving J. M. B.[4]

Then for a time Arthur's condition stabilised. Everyone relaxed a little and felt there might be a chance. But towards the end of November Arthur wrote to his sister in Cumberland saying that the artificial jaw had become useless. The family were told that hopes for a recovery were now quite groundless, and soon Arthur was forced to take morphine for the pain.

On 1st December Barrie wrote a letter to Dolly Ponsonby that leaves one wincing at his 'masterfulness'. Noticeable also is his shrewd and practical attitude to Arthur's illness; far removed from the unworldly artist he was so often made out to be.

> Leinster Corner
> Lancaster Gate, W.
>
> Dear Mrs Ponsonby
>   I think they would like to see you at Berkhamsted and also think you should write and propose going down, and I know that the best any of us can do for them at the present is to be fairly bright and hopeful . . .
>   There was never very much hope. The one thing in his favour has always been his own courage.
>   However well you know him you can't realise how heroic he has been. He still is.

There is still reason to have a little hope, and I expect you can help them best by showing you are hopeful yourself. I have said more to you than to any other person, and would like it to go no further than your husband. If he could go down that would be a good thing too – and treat the situation as not much worse than when he was at Rustington.

I am going down today till Monday.

Yours very sincerely

J. M. Barrie[5]

Dolly Ponsonby was never a meek or especially biddable woman, but this summons from Barrie may have been the immediate reason for her visit to Sylvia and Arthur very shortly afterwards. The entry in her diary for 5th December reads:

A luncheon party consisting of the Nansens, Herbert Gladstone . . . I left in the middle to go down to Berkhamsted where I spent the saddest most terrible night I can remember. Suffice it to say that Arthur Davies cannot live & told me so – but had not told Sylvia.

Friday 6th

Returned to London after luncheon. It was awful having to leave him & I longed to go down on my knees to him & tell him I thought him the noblest most heroic being that ever lived – but it couldn't be & I had to persist in telling [him] he would live. Sylvia is an example of everything a woman should be – Her care of him & of the children – her patience and lovingness & strength – there is no one like her.

That Christmas *Peter Pan* was once again revived, with Pauline Chase as Peter, and Arthur asked Margaret if she would take the boys to see it. This year *Peter Pan* was receiving double the publicity. Barrie had permitted Hodder & Stoughton to publish the Peter Pan chapters extracted from *The Little White Bird*, which were to be called *Peter Pan in Kensington Gardens* and decorated with Arthur Rackham's now famous illustrations. It was through this book that many more thousands of children came to know *Peter Pan*. Barrie presented a copy to the Davieses with a dedication that read:

To Sylvia and Arthur Llewelyn Davies
and their boys (my boys)

Apparently he didn't appreciate the insensitivity of adding '(my boys)' in the book he presented to their dying father.

Arthur's suffering dragged on mercilessly into the New Year. In February Barrie, who maintained his role of keeping friends informed of Arthur's state of health, wrote to Dolly Ponsonby:

> I don't know whether you have heard lately of Mr Davies's condition. For some weeks now haemorrhages have been frequent and though he has always so far rallied from them he gets weaker and weaker . . . Mentally he is as clear as ever . . . the . . . treatment has apparently had little if any effect, but it was . . . expected . . . It has helped to give Mrs Davies a little hope at times. She still bears up and is with him all the time . . .[6]

Barrie tells Dolly that 'the doctors (and there have been many) all feel the end cannot be far off. Miss Davies [Margaret] also is here and of course the nurse. He clearly understands the gravity of it all but he is serene and undismayed.' Arthur could no longer speak and was only able to communicate by writing down what he wanted to say.

Then, there was a respite, and in early March Barrie told Dolly the doctors thought

> that for some weeks there has not been any increase in the disease. I don't suppose the courageous would find the least hope in this, but foolishly or not I cling to the possibility. Arthur himself has an idea that he is a little better and of course this helps Sylvia. But he is looking wasted. Any day may destroy her hope.[7]

Arthur seems to have understood quite well that there was nothing more to be done, though he probably only communicated this to Sylvia herself towards the very end. Whenever possible Barrie kept vigil at his bedside, and one of Arthur's notes told him, 'I just like to see you.' He wrote that the last six months had been the happiest of his life, and told Barrie that he didn't think that anyone had ever done so much for him. Asking to read to him, he said, 'Give me your hand.' Eventually, in early April, Sylvia sent the boys away to their grandmother du Maurier at Ramsgate for the Easter holidays. Knowing he was dying, Arthur must have agreed to this, even suggested it. At last he was released from pain when, on 19th April 1907, he died.

Throughout this period Barrie kept his own notes, and in those for *A thousand Nightingales* an entry reads:

Dying man's fears to friend that he may break down & blubber at
end – weakness may master him . . . His idea wd have liked to have
children – to live on in them. Speaks to friend (a father) about great
difference in dying if you have children (yourself living on) – if you
haven't you go out completely.[8]

Barrie had been profoundly moved and unsettled by Arthur's, and Sylvia's,
suffering. An entry at the end of January, which begins the new notebook for 1907, revealed his urge to be released from the anxiety and
distress he had been experiencing and observing around him for these
last months.

> The Lovely moment. Finest Dream in the World.
>   That it is early morning & I am out on a Highland road – dew
> &c – it is time before I knew anything of sorrow pain or death.
> Everyone I have loved is still alive – it is the morning of life – of
> the world.[9]

At Arthur's death, his brother Crompton became the Davies boys' official guardian. In addition, there were nine aunts and uncles and two
grandparents to offer assistance. Although none of them was wealthy,
together the relations might well have managed to support Sylvia and
her boys in a modest lifestyle. No doubt, given the opportunity, Crompton
and the other relations would have fulfilled their duty in a kind and
conscientious way, but here we are made aware of Barrie. When Arthur
died, or perhaps beforehand, Barrie made it clear that his wealth was at
Sylvia's and the boys' disposal. If Sylvia accepted his support this would
represent a significantly different life to the one her own and Arthur's
family could provide. There is little record of family discussions, or disagree-
ments, regarding Sylvia's and the boys' future. We can, however, be clear
about the eventual outcome. Barrie made himself financially responsible
for Arthur's wife and his boys.

Both sets of relations ended by having only a limited amount to do
with their welfare. That Barrie appears fairly quickly to have become
the leading, and controlling, player in the situation must have come
about as much as anything because Sylvia was willing to accept his financial support. Arthur's death had been expected for some time, but when
it came there was a numb feeling of loss and sorrow in the household,
and Sylvia was heartbroken. Whatever relations or friends might have
argued to the contrary, Sylvia must have justified to herself the financial security Barrie was prepared to offer as the least she could do for
her fatherless sons.

When the boys' school terms ended that summer, Barrie took them and Sylvia far away from Egerton House in Berkhamsted; the place now redolent with sad memories of Arthur. The party travelled north to Scotland, to Divach Lodge, a house set high amongst the wooded hills overlooking Loch Ness. Here, from late July until well on into September, they fished. Meanwhile, Barrie wrote to a friend, 'I do nothing up here but fish & fish & fish, and we ought all to be fishes to feel at home in this weather.'

Mary had been very much on the periphery of Barrie's association with the Davieses' struggle and bereavement over the last harrowing months. Quite possibly this was because he had made it clear that he, and only he, was the special friend. That Mary went with the party to Scotland and acted as hostess was as much as anything to ensure that a situation, by the standards of the day most unorthodox, might appear less so. For those wet summer holiday weeks the Barries entertained a succession of guests, including the playwright Harley Granville Barker and his wife the actress Lillah McCarthy, the boys' uncle Crompton and the explorer Captain Scott.

The boys were kept busy fishing, chasing after butterflies or being entertained by Barrie's cheerful young niece Madge Murray. Barrie, meanwhile, still found time to work on two new plays. Years later, Peter Davies would comment that, although he and his brothers enjoyed themselves, it must have appeared an odd ménage to the visiting adults. He added that the whole pattern of the holiday 'seemed to have something deplorable about it'.[10]

No public statements were ever made about Barrie's role in the Davies family, but it wasn't long after their return from Scotland before Egerton House in Berkhamsted was sold, and with financial help from Barrie Sylvia was able to return with the boys to London. Peter Davies later recorded that their large new house in Campden Hill Square, not far from their old home at Kensington Gardens, and the Barries' house at Leinster Corner, was a better address. He remembered too, how conscious he had been that the sale of Egerton House was the end of something, a halcyon period never to be retrieved. Of the three older boys, Jack viewed Barrie with a degree of resentment and suspicion, perceiving him as attempting to usurp his father's position. As for the younger boys, it was simply that Mr Barrie, or Uncle Jim, had always been around and continued in the same way now. To their delight he soon played the 'stamp game', in which, with the help of a coin, he deftly attached a stamp to the ceiling of one of the rooms. Barrie had yet again marked a house and its occupants as his own.

★

In the autumn, with Jack already away at naval college, George now left home for Eton. He quickly settled in, writing cheerful letters home in which he thrilled to his new-found knowledge of that 'secret society' public-schoolboy slang. Sylvia meanwhile, went with the smaller boys to stay with her mother at Ramsgate while awaiting the renovation of Campden Hill Square.

During that first year of widowhood, she did her best to create for the three younger boys a home life with a semblance of normality, rather than one in which she revealed the daily misery of her loss. The irrepressible cheerfulness and vitality of her sons, combined with regular visits from friends and relations, gradually helped to revive something of her appetite for life. This more buoyant frame of mind, growing slowly as the year wore on, would have been severely undermined if Sylvia had understood how her second son, Jack, was faring at Osborne College. He was suffering from merciless bullying, but said nothing. Feeling passionately that it would be intolerable for his mother if he imposed on her more worries than she had already experienced, Jack kept his loathing of the college to himself. Neither would his distance from Barrie ever have permitted any admission of vulnerability. At fourteen, Sylvia's son must have felt very much alone.

19

The End of a Marriage

By November Barrie had become involved in a very public campaign
that would soon take up a considerable amount of his time. Since
1904, with J. F. Vedrenne, young Granville Barker had, determinedly
and brilliantly, been managing the Royal Court Theatre. Staging Shakespeare
and forgotten classics, such as *Euripides*, they also consistently introduced
the work of as yet uncommercial modern dramatists. These included
Galsworthy, Maeterlink and Bernard Shaw – whom Granville Barker did
much to promote. For some time Barrie had been attending rehearsals
and speaking to the younger playwrights. He was flattered at their
recognition of him, and in turn found their rebelliousness attractive and
commendable.

The Royal Court's ethos was essentially one where the play came first,
and popular appeal and the box office second. In addition, Granville
Barker and a group of other writers and directors increasingly believed
that the Official Censor of Plays should be abolished. With this in mind,
when Granville Barker's new play, *Waste* – in which a talented politician's
prospects are permanently ruined by the scandal of a divorce – was refused
a performing licence by the Lord Chamberlain's Examiner of Plays, the
playwrights were up in arms. They had half expected the ban but its
implementation galvanised them into action.

John Galsworthy, and Gilbert Murray, the great Greek scholar and
populariser of Greek drama, organised a committee seeking the aboli-
tion of the Censor's Office, and Barrie became one of the campaign's
staunchest supporters. Henry James, Thomas Hardy, Bernard Shaw and
George Meredith joined the cause, and Galsworthy drafted a letter to
The Times, which was signed by seventy dramatists. While trying to write
his current play, *What Every Woman Knows*, Barrie made time to host
numerous committee meetings at Leinster Corner, send out circular
letters and draft a petition to be put before the Prime Minister. Soon he
was writing to Sylvia saying:

I am having a life of it over this censorship business. Receiving committees, telephones, telegrams, &c all day and every day. I've done more business this week or two than in all the rest of my life . . . It was stupid of me to be pushed into it but now that I am I've got to do my best. There is just a shadow of a chance of its having any practical results.

(Granville Barker's play had to wait until 1936 for its first public performance, when Nina Boucicault, 'the Peter of all Peters', would make her last stage appearance as the Countess Mortimer.)

In recognition of the long hours Barrie was putting into the campaign the committee found him a secretary, Gilbert Cannan, a young man not long down from Cambridge, who had recently given up reading for the Bar. Cannan's aspirations no longer lay with the law, and he was already writing. He had also met and fallen in love with a striking young painter-sculptress, Kathleen Bruce. Kathleen Bruce's life revolved around artists and writers, and to her numerous admirers she responded, above all, to the reflection of herself she saw in their eyes. Gilbert Cannan was tall, slim, with a fine profile, shaggy blond hair, a 'crooked smile', and an aura of sadness that made his undoubted beauty yet more compelling; people turned when he entered a room. His looks, his immense vitality and his passionate admiration for her in turn kept Kathleen Bruce beguiled.

Some time earlier, at a lunch given by Aubrey Beardsley's sister, Mabel, while seated between Barrie and Max Beerbohm, Kathleen had noticed a particular guest who appeared somehow out of place in this august artistic gathering.

Far down the other side of the table was a naval officer, Captain Scott. He was not very young, perhaps forty, not very good looking; but he looked very healthy and alert, and I glowed rather foolishly and suddenly when I clearly saw him ask his neighbour who I was.[1]

After a second meeting, once again at Mabel Beardsley's, with Henry James and the traveller Ernest Thesiger amongst the company, Kathleen Bruce and Scott's courtship began in earnest. For several months, though, finding her two suitors' interest in her a stimulating confirmation of her magnetism, she was torn, unable to make up her mind between the young Gilbert Cannan and the more celebrated Robert Scott. Unwilling to commit herself, Kathleen procrastinated and continued to see them both. For many weeks she received up to four extravagantly poetic letters a day from Cannan, while Scott consolidated his position with greater dignity and restraint. The three parties even had a meeting together to discuss the 'problem'.

Eventually, despite Scott's lack of means, and his familial responsibilities – his father and brother were dead and he was presently responsible for his mother and several sisters – Kathleen agreed to marry him. Her decision was largely based on his proven strength of character and the likelihood that he would be the right man to father her son. Although regarded by her contemporaries as a Bohemian, Kathleen Bruce had determinedly maintained her chastity for the man she would marry. Her prime concern was his qualifications as a prospective father, rather than his possible qualities as a husband. She was also convinced – rightly as things turned out – that she was to have a son.

Gilbert Cannan, at twenty-three almost painfully idealistic and naïve, nevertheless sensed correctly that Kathleen wasn't in love with his older rival. While Cannan's letters continued arriving, Kathleen was not without regret.

> With his tall thin frame, his shock of corn-coloured hair, it seemed woefully hard to throw it all away; and his constantly repeated, 'With you I can conquer the world' clanged through my mind with a tiresome insistence of conviction.[2]

Gradually, however, she became more convinced of her decision and Cannan, having quoted lines to her from Granville Barker's play, 'It's the waste of a good man. Oh the waste!', began to seek solace for his wounded heart elsewhere. He was now often at Leinster Corner working for the Censorship Committee. The Barries liked him, Mary was always a good listener, and soon Gilbert was confiding his present sorrows to her. He had a strong need to be mothered, and Mary was a nurturing figure. Cannan now sometimes accompanied her to social events, but to Kathleen he wrote, 'What does she want of me?' Gradually the friendship developed, and in another letter to Kathleen he said,

> Yesterday Lillah and Mrs Barrie came and had tea – Mrs Barrie suddenly began to talk to me like a mother. She really is a dear thing, and she seemed to need a good deal of me – I feel the need and give – gladly.[3]

Barrie and his wife were often at Black Lake Cottage with friends. They had also developed the habit of having companions to stay without the other being present. And, in company with her female friends Mary now invited Cannan too. Set deep in the countryside with the soughing pinewoods nearby, Black Lake Cottage was indeed idyllic, far away from the strains of city life, and gossip and prying eyes.

In the summer Kathleen announced her forthcoming marriage to Scott. Barrie, who always retained a penchant for matchmaking, took offence that he hadn't been informed before the public announcement, moving Kathleen to write urgently to her fiancé, 'We must not hurt so sensitive and dear a person. Please write to him [quite] by return of post . . . as nice a letter as ever you can think of.'

Although Sylvia and Arthur had attracted many friends during their marriage, that summer must have been a forceful reminder to Sylvia of her ultimate solitude, when she took the boys to stay at a farmhouse in the New Forest. One of her chief sources of comfort, and the boys' entertainer, Barrie, was conspicuously absent for most of their holiday. Rehearsals for *What Every Woman Knows* meant that it was difficult for him to leave London for any length of time. On his way down for a brief visit to Sylvia and the boys, Barrie was asked to stay with Dolly and Arthur Ponsonby at Shulbrede Priory. Dolly wrote in her diary:

> Mr Barrie arrived in the evening. He was quite talkative at dinner, discussed Galsworthy whom he admires tremendously both as a man and a writer . . . He thinks he is a man of very strong passions kept well under control. He was good about L. Granville B. too [Lillah, the wife of Harley Granville Barker] – said she had no sense of humour – but was a genuine sort of creature. We talked a great deal about Sylvia's boys & it is extraordinary to see how they fill his life and supply all his human interest. Of course J. M. B. does alarm me, I feel he absolutely sees through one & just how stupid I am – but I hope also he sees my good intentions. The things he says about people so absolutely knock the nail on the head that though they are not in the least unkind they are almost cruel.[4]

Arthur Ponsonby's diary entry for the same occasion is no less well observed than Dolly's for being more succinct. At the same time, as a man of sophistication and high politics, his commendation of their visitor reveals the effect Barrie could have upon those who spent any time in his company.

> J. M. Barrie stayed here for the night coming down from the rehearsal of his new play. I have never met a man with a more just discernment, he sees everything, gives everything its right proportion and in his very quiet modest way expresses the result of his

perceptions so perfectly and so humorously that one becomes completely captivated. . . I feel he has a great nobility and simplicity of character.[5]

With customary extravagance Frohman was staging *What Every Woman Knows* at the Duke of York's. (In one scene describing an election, one hundred extras were crowded on to the stage.) All the main actors were familiar names, except Barrie's niece, Madge Murray. The play was a success; Max Beerbohm wrote that the characters 'are creatures of real flesh and blood, winged by Mr Barrie's whim; an immense relief from the sawdust stuffed figures that the average playwright dresses up'.

On 2nd September, the day before the launch of the play, Kathleen Bruce and Captain Scott were married at Hampton Court Palace. Gilbert Cannan was constrained to accept defeat, but Scott's final conquest of Kathleen troubled Cannan less as the autumn wore on. He now had a number of literary contacts; he was writing a novel, and some thought he was showing considerable potential. Both Cannan's literary and social lives were developing, helped considerably by association with the Barries.

Peter Pan's huge success over three Christmases meant that it was now an established annual theatrical event. With every year the popularity of the play grew, until fifty years after its first performance an actor who played in it on a number of occasions would write,

> And behind all this was the magic of the play itself, the well-known lines still springing out in new and spontaneous perfection, the humour and the leavening of tragedy never growing stale. Added to this there was, for the actors, the intangible, indescribable 'pull of the house': the house was with us as in no other play, with us heart and soul, inarticulately loud with delight and appreciation, culminating in the roar of ecstatic abandon – so admirably matched by the incomparable music – as Peter, Wendy, John, and Michael fly out of the nursery window. Night after night one tasted of that overwhelming communion between actor and audience, one experienced the touch of Barrie's supreme genius, one knew why Shelton and Kelt and English and Trevor had returned to their parts year after year . . .[6]

Barrie's involvement in his first full-length play since *Peter Pan*, plus the Censorship Committee work, had kept him busy in his study or the theatre for several months, so now he suggested a plan. As recompense for seeing much less of the Davieses that summer and autumn of 1908, after Christmas and the opening of *Peter Pan* he would take them all on a three-week skiing holiday to Switzerland. The party would be made up of himself and Mary, Sylvia and the boys, and Gilbert Cannan. Not having skied before, George wrote to his mother from Eton in great anticipation.

> I have asked my tutor about clothes for Switzerland . . . The journey will be pretty exciting, I expect. I expect to be ill going from Dover to Calais, or wherever you cross the Channel. It will be glorious fun at St Moritz . . .
>
> Is Mrs Barrie coming? Perhaps she'll prefer it to Motor Touring . . . we shall be a whacking party. It is kind of uncle Jim to do it all.[7]

The boys enjoyed themselves skiing. They also had the added interest of Gilbert Cannan, an entertaining and amusing companion. Moving in a sphere somewhere between the boys and the adults, Cannan's position was, however, oddly ambiguous.

What was unambiguous was the mutual attraction between Cannan and Mary Barrie: Mary was radiant and Cannan captivated. Peter Llewelyn Davies later commented that it wasn't actually at St Moritz they had stayed but at 'the slightly less fashionable Caux'. He wondered was this because it was a 'more suitable place for the oddly constituted party', and added that 'it must have been a queer quarter of adults that conversed together after the boys had gone to bed'.[8]

Did Barrie see the attraction between his wife and this most appealing and intelligent young man? With the capacity to close his eyes to uncomfortable subjects, perhaps also it didn't suit him to observe what was blindingly obvious. Outwardly, as well as delighting in the company of Sylvia and her boys, Barrie was enjoying a new flirtation with the Duchess of Sutherland and was sending letters to her in England.

Barrie's wife and Sylvia fulfilled his need for mother figures, yet he also craved 'the chase'. Here for a time he could play the role of the robust, masterful man. In many ways Barrie was masterful. Although it is virtually certain that he never consummated any of his numerous flirtations, he doesn't appear to have been essentially different from other trophy-hunting males. He never ceased to need the thrill of collecting a succession of women. To Barrie's ego this was crucial, but to his heart it meant far less. Meanwhile, his letters to each current flirtation ranged nonchalantly from the idiotic – almost infantile – to that of the astute, interesting and knowing man of the world. To penetrate through the games and subtle digs to Barrie's real thoughts, supposing he knew what they were himself, was a near impossibility.

What was also impossible was that Sylvia, a sensitive and subtle woman, should fail to notice the relationship developing between Mary Barrie and Gilbert Cannan. (It was said by some later that she encouraged it.) Sylvia's position in regard to the Barries was an ambiguous one. While her devotion to her husband had never been in question, she none the less cared for Barrie and enjoyed his company. She also laughed at him and teased him. Presumably at times she felt sorry for him. It was also true that Sylvia's most unorthodox position, as a widow placed somewhere between husband and wife, would be much simpler if husband and wife were no longer together.

Towards the end of the Swiss holiday Sylvia suddenly became unwell, alarmingly so, with great pain near her heart. A doctor at the hotel refused to treat her, saying he was on holiday, and fortunately the episode passed. After her return to London, however, she was never fully to recover her health.

Cannan worked hard with Barrie on the Censorship Committee. Having brought together so many playwrights, it was decided to form a dramatists' club, with Arthur Wing Pinero as its first president. Cannan's literary promise meant that he was also invited to join. Meanwhile, in April Barrie made a journey to Edinburgh, where, at his old university, he received another honorary degree. Accepting his doctorate of literature with a characteristic speech, he then wrote to Sylvia saying 'I am slowly recovering from the functions, which continued for about six solid hours. [Edinburgh] Must be about the most romantic city on earth. But it strikes cold on me nowadays, for the familiar faces have long gone and there are only buildings left.'

In 1909 Barrie was forty-nine. Increasingly at the centre of things, he received daily proof that his success had made him welcome in society. And yet, as each new honour confirmed that success, he was torn. Knowing in his heart that the centre of the establishment was not the place for a real artist, someone inevitably, almost by definition, an outsider, it was a place where he neither belonged nor with any consistency wanted to be. In the early summer the establishment held out another enticement when it offered him a knighthood. Arthur Pinero and Herbert Tree were each offered one, too, and let their names be duly printed in the Birthday Honours lists. Despite Sylvia's attempts at persuading him otherwise, without offering any reasons, Barrie declined.

In that same month he commissioned the sculptor George Frampton to make a statue of Peter Pan – eventually to be put up in Kensington Gardens. Frampton was given a dynamic set of photographs of a beautiful and passionate little Michael Davies, fighting stick in hand. Taken two summers earlier by Barrie – as Michael's father lay dying at

(*Above left*) Starkey; (*below left*) Eskimo; (*below right*) Tiger Lily; William Nicholson's watercolour costume designs for the first *Peter Pan*. (*Above right*) Peter Pan was so popular that by 1907 publications such as *The Peter Pan Picture Book* (ill. Alice Woodward) were being produced.

William Nicholson's perceptive study of Barrie, 1904

One of the minute books (*c.* 2" x 3") in which
all Barrie's numbered notes were kept

Nina Boucicault, 'the Peter of all Peters'

Hilda Trevelyan, whom Barrie called
'my incomparable Wendy'

(*Top left*) Gladys Cooper, a notable Peter Pan, said that '*Peter Pan* is really more of a play for grown-ups than children'. (*Top right*) Eva le Gallienne wrote of the New York children's audience, 'Hand clapping was not enough for them. They screamed YES! YES! We believe!… Never has Tink been saved as she was that day.'

(*Bottom left*) Eileen Vanbrugh, the lead in many Barrie plays, including his first success, *Ibsen's Ghost*. (*Bottom right*) Sir George Frampton's statue of Peter Pan, on Barrie's instruction secretly installed in Kensington Gardens overnight for May morning, 1912.

Back row: George and Peter Llewelyn Davies, the Duchess of Sutherland. Front row: Nico, Barrie and Michael in 1911; Barrie was now the boys 'guardian'.

Sir John Lavery's portrait of Barrie, who is shown still holding the pen in his right hand

The London apartment at Adelphi Terrace House, where Barrie lived for the last twenty-seven years of his life

Captain Scott. One of
his last letters was to Barrie.

Lady Cynthia Wemyss' wedding
to the former Prime Minister
Herbert Asquith's son 'Beb'

Lady Cynthia Asquith,
one of the beauties of her day,
secretary and friend from 1917

Sir Arthur Quiller-Couch, Professor of
English at Cambridge and the editor
of *The Oxford Book of English Verse*

(*Above left*) George Meredith, the first major literary figure Barrie came to know
(*Above right*) Thomas Hardy, whose quiet searching after truth gave him, for Barrie,
a heroic dignity

(*Below left*) Charles Turley Smith, of unfailing sympathy and humour; as obsessed with cricket
as was Barrie. (*Below right*) Arthur Conan Doyle, friend and early literary collaborator.

Ellen Terry, whose partnership with
Henry Irving was one of the triumphs
of the English stage

H.G. Wells, who urged Mary Barrie
not to marry her lover, Gilbert Cannan

Captain Scott's son Peter's portrait of Barrie
in his Lutyens inglenook

E.V. Lucas, journalist, publisher, authority on Lamb,
with his wife Elizabeth and daughter Audrey

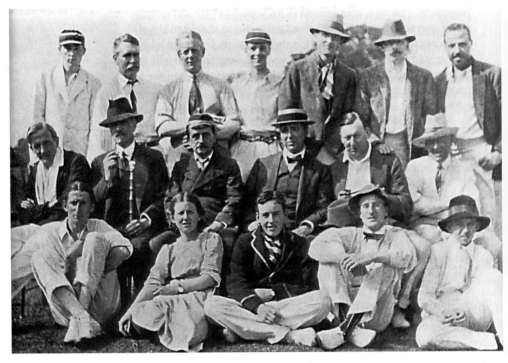

The last of the Allahakbarries' cricket matches, 1913. Back row, left to right: George Llewelyn Davies, Thomas Gilmour, Will Meredith, George Meredith Jnr, Denis Mackail, Harry Graham, Dr Goffe. Centre: A.A. Milne, Maurice Hewlett, Barrie, George Morrow, E.V. Lucas, Walter Frith. Front row: Percy Lucas, Audrey Lucas, T. Wrigley, Charles Tennyson, Willie Winter.

Barrie in old age dwarfed by his desk (now at his birthplace). The leather top is scuffed by his cuff links on left and right from writing with both hands.

Egerton House – while fixing the camera with a fiery intensity, the boy wears the romantic Peter Pan costume Barrie had asked William Nicholson to design.

Then in May his old friend George Meredith died. Barrie was deeply saddened at the passing of this great figure, for whom he felt much affection and respect, but Meredith's death was at the same time a drama in which Barrie was driven to take a leading part. As chief assistant and mourner, he joined in organising the request that Meredith's ashes should be buried at Poets' Corner. To the dismay of many, the Dean of Westminster refused – largely because of his objection to Meredith's view that no marriage should last for more than five years. Denied Westminster, Meredith's ashes were taken in a coach to rest in Dorking Cemetery, beside his second wife.

Barrie was flattered to be asked by Meredith's executor, the biographer and politician Lord Morley, if he would write the life of their mutual friend. But after shuffling about with the papers and letters for part of that summer, he had self-knowledge enough to admit, 'there is no one less qualified than I to write the Life of anyone'. As one of the greatest fantasists of his generation, thankfully, for posterity, Barrie thought it best to refuse.

Busily occupied, he wrote to Sylvia, presently staying at her mother's house in Ramsgate with the two smallest boys. Sylvia must have asked Barrie to fulfil some duty for Peter, at school in London, and in his reply he makes an avowal of intent. He also gives us another glimpse of self-knowledge – this one concerns his moods.

Dearest Jocelyn [Barrie had always enjoyed using her second name, almost in opposition to her husband.]

I shall try to get to the school tomorrow at ½ past 4 and see Peter off. At three I am going to see about Meredith's letters and don't know how long it will take.

How I wish I were going down to see Michael and Nicholas . . . I feel they are growing up without my looking on, when I grudge any blank day without them. I can't picture a summer day that does not have Michael skipping in front. That is summer to me. And all the five know me as nobody else does. The bland indifference with which they accept my tantrums is the most engaging thing in the world to me. They are quite sure that, despite appearances, they are all right. To be able to help them and you, that is my dear ambition, to do the best I can always and always, and my greatest pride is that you let me do it. I wish I did it so much better.

It is always such a glad thought to me to find you even a little finer woman than I had thought. I am sorry about the pains in your head.[9]

It was now July, and the official Censorship Committee had finally been appointed to examine forty-nine witnesses, after which they were to issue a report. There was now great interest from the press. With that urge to be at the centre of things, Barrie would remain at Black Lake Cottage for the summer rather than going further away from London – the Committee was to sit on throughout August. Sylvia and the boys were once again to spend their summer holiday without Barrie, this time in a rectory on Dartmoor. The last performance of *What Every Woman Knows* would take place on 28th July, and the following morning the Censorship Committee was to sit to take its evidence. Barrie was preparing his own evidence to put before them.

In a state of some agitation Hunt, the gardener at Black Lake Cottage, asked to speak with Mr Barrie. Hunt was set to blight Barrie's life by forcing his hand with the truth. His resentment at Mary's criticism of his gardening had been fermenting for several months, and he could no longer hold back. It was his duty to tell Mr Barrie that Mr Barrie's wife and Mr Cannan were having an affair. Barrie was so shocked he was unable to ask the gardener any questions, and simply took his hat and coat and caught the train up to London. When Mary arrived back at Leinster Corner from her studio, he asked her if she would deny what the gardener had told him. On the contrary, Mary was relieved finally to tell the truth. Adding to Barrie's agony, not only did she refuse to deny her year-long affair with Gilbert, but she also said that he was the most important person in her life. Now that her husband at last knew · the truth, Mary asked for a divorce. She could no longer struggle on with a marriage that was only half a life.

In a state of turmoil Barrie insisted they take themselves to see their friend and lawyer, George Lewis. Calmly and sympathetically the urbane Lewis did his best to encourage Mary to 'see reason', while Barrie entreated her to think again. He would forgive everything, no one need ever know about the affair, and he would never mention it again if she only promised to cut Cannan out of her life. But Mary was not to be swayed, even by the final suggestion that her husband would offer her a deed of separation on any reasonable terms she might suggest. Despite warnings that the path of separation was one leading to scandal, ostracism and the uncertainty of a relationship with a man only just over half her age, Mary remained implacable. Once her secret relationship was revealed, she became determined to accept nothing less than a complete break. Her gradual loss of hope had at last been replaced by the possibility of a happier future, and having glimpsed it she refused to give it up. Mary insisted on a divorce.

She retreated to Black Lake Cottage, while Barrie hid himself at his friend Mason's flat. Here, distraught, unable to sleep at night, he paced the floor for hour after hour, keeping everyone nearby awake. More painful meetings took place. Cannan, increasingly a believer in 'free love', and in part aware that the publication of this affair would do little good for his own reputation, naïvely suggested that he and Barrie should 'share' Mary. At this stage it appears that Cannan's thoughts were not of marriage.

Barrie, meanwhile, was blind to the effect that his own flirtations, his ongoing obsession with Sylvia Llewelyn Davies, and his long-term neglect might have had on his wife. He was afraid of the scandal but also deeply distressed at the thought of losing Mary. She wrote to their friend H. G. Wells:

> I must promise never to think of the past or long for it but give myself up to loving J. and accepting his loving advances . . . He seems to have developed the most ardent passion for me now that he has lost me; that frightens me. I must go back to what I was . . . Poor thing, he is distracted and I am dreadfully sorry; he says he knows that I would be happier with G. C. and that we ought to marry one moment, and the next clamours for me . . . You have been a dear friend, I shall never forget it. Don't mention a word, will you, to anyone.[10]

Sir George Lewis no doubt advised Barrie that for the present it would be unwise if he saw much of Sylvia Davies; it was possible that Mary might put Sylvia's name forward in the divorce. But in all the discussions, and the court hearing, Mary appears not once to have mentioned Barrie's relationship with Sylvia. Neither did she seek to absolve herself of her infidelity. Wells had written to her that she and Cannan were 'sillies' and that they should 'go and live together and get babies as soon as you can like two sensible people'.

Disillusioned with his own current marriage, Wells tells her not to marry, because

> It gives you both amazing powers of making Hell for one another. So take an old Sinner's advice & *tell* them you are married when the time comes, & don't marry unless there is a child to legitimate. I'll always say I know you & declare that I was a witness at the registry office if you want confirmation.[11]

But Mary was not Wells, and needed legitimisation of her relationship. She both admitted her adultery and, regardless of the consequences, now believed that the right thing to do was to marry the man she loved. The Barries' friend Maurice Hewlett wrote to her, 'I think J. is behaving very badly . . . I envy Cannan the chance he has of making life good for you. I don't see how I can meet J. after this. It amazes me that Mason hasn't made him more of a gentleman.'

Barrie blamed Mary's friends, and some of his own, for supporting her. Knowing that he was at fault, he went through agonies of self-censure. This didn't mean that anyone who agreed with him wasn't resented. Indeed, those who criticised Mary were more often than not rebuffed. Barrie was suffused with an all-pervading sense of failure, and embarrassment at the thought that this failure was so public. He rejected almost all attempts at sympathy, and was unable to face his plight with any distance or real composure. As always, the real experience of life was dramatised, and Barrie must suffer histrionically.

With a loyalty that went beyond mere good nature, Mason not only had him to stay in his flat, but also, after they had both given their evidence at the Censorship Committee in August, took him away to Switzerland. Before leaving Barrie wrote to Sylvia:

> Mason and I are going off on Saturday morning. I've managed not to see anybody, have no heart for it, but I do a little work and feel quite well. I've just been to Leinster Corner to collect lots of warm things in case it's cold at Zermatt. It is always so painful to me to go to the house now.[12]

Another very old and always faithful friend, Gilmour, went with them. It was thought that walking in the clear mountain air would provide distraction for Barrie; that the exercise would help him to sleep at night. However, when it was suggested that he learn to climb, he resented the guide's instruction, refusing to be told what to do. Only Mason climbed, then, while Barrie and Gilmour walked, edged all round by the extravagant, clarifying beauty of the mountains.

Mason's and Gilmour's selflessness was occasionally rewarded, when Barrie briefly surfaced, animated, from his dismal mood. A little further respite from his anguish and self-absorption was given his friends in the periods he spent away from them writing notes. These, however, were more than notes. Using the old habit of distancing himself from himself through working, Barrie was writing a short play, which he called *The Twelve-Pound Look*. As was his custom he diagnosed at least a part of his present malady.

Regarded by many as his best one-act play, in *The Twelve-Pound Look* Barrie drags important elements out of his own experience, and transforms them into art. The characters here are not exactly Barrie and his wife, but through them he gropes his way towards a partial truth. Unable to refer to any sexual inadequacy, likely to have been a major element in the failure of his marriage, Barrie describes his distaste for his success. The play also shows how the wife, Kate – her attributes are those of the archetypal Barrie heroine; with a superior mentality, maturity and depth of character – is so much more worthwhile a person than her husband, the ambitious Harry Sims.

Harry Sims is about to be rewarded for his success with a knighthood. In order to deal with the many letters of congratulation he anticipates, he employs a typist. Shocked to discover the new typist is his ex-wife, Kate, Sims wants to know the identity of her lover, who brought about the destruction of their marriage. 'Surely a man has the right to know with whom his wife bolted?' But Sims's overblown ego is given a serious knock when she tells him:

There was no one Harry; no one at all.
Sir Harry: It is unbelievable.
Kate: I suppose so; but it is true.
Sir Harry: Then what mad impulse?—
Kate: You were a good husband according to your lights.
Sir Harry (stoutly): I think so . . . all women envied you.
Kate: How you loved me to be envied.
Sir Harry: I swaddled you in luxury.
Kate (making her great revelation): That was it.
Sir Harry (blankly): What?
Kate: How you beamed at me when I sat at the head of your fat
    dinners in my fat jewellery, surrounded by our fat friends.
Sir Harry: . . . We had all the most interesting society of the day.
    It wasn't only businessmen. There were politicians, painters,
    writers—
Kate: Only the dazzling glorious successes. Oh the fat talk while
    we ate too much – about who had made a hit and who was slip-
    ping back, and what the noo house cost and the noo motor and
    the gold soup plates, and who was to be the noo knight . . .
    One's religion is whatever he is most interested in, and yours is
    in Success . . . I couldn't endure it. If failure had come now and
    then – but your success was suffocating me . . . the passionate
    craving I had to be done with it, to find myself with people who
    had not got on.
Sir Harry (with proper spirit): There are plenty of them.

Kate: There were none in our set. When they began to roll down-
hill they rolled out of our sight.
Sir Harry (clinching it): I tell you I am worth a quarter of a million.
Kate (unabashed): That is what you are worth to yourself. I'll tell
you what you are worth to me: exactly twelve pounds . . . (She
presses her hand on to the typewriter as lovingly as any woman
has pressed a rose.) I learned this. I hired it and taught myself
. . . and with my first twelve pounds I paid for my machine. Then
I considered I was free to go, and I went.[13]

Having learnt to type in the last year of her marriage, Mary Barrie had
offered her secretarial skills to Barrie and Cannan in their work for the
Censorship Committee.
A reviewer observed of the play:

Barrie has never contributed anything more incisive, more capa-
cious . . . than this short stinging satire on male illusions . . . With
a few strokes of characterisation and reminiscence, we have before
us three complete persons, the woman who rejected the egoist, the
woman who accepted the egoist [Harry Sims's second wife], and
the egoist.[14]

In spite of what must have been an exhausting few weeks in Switzerland
for Barrie's two friends, on their return to London at the end of September,
Mason returned to his work as an MP while allowing Barrie to share
his flat. Barrie, meanwhile, was seeing much less of Sylvia and the boys,
though he did take Michael to his first day at Wilkinson's prep school
in Orme Square.
By now all of the Barries' friends had heard the news. In 1909,
whatever affairs a small section of society might have indulged in,
and whatever private accommodations they arrived at when their relationships foundered, to formalise them in divorce was still extremely rare.
Without question, it was a colossal stigma. Aware of the dramatic effect
the publicity would have upon the Barries' lives, and in an attempt to
stem the great tide of gossip sure to arise, a group of their friends sent
a private letter to the editors of all the leading newspapers hoping for
their discretion. The letter was signed by, amongst others, Lord Esher,
William Archer, Edmund Gosse, Maurice Hewlett, Henry James, A. E. W.
Mason, Arthur Pinero, Beerbohm Tree and H. G. Wells.
Not all the newspapers cooperated, and less than two weeks after
Barrie's return from Switzerland, on 13th October 1909, his divorce
proceedings were reported. Mary didn't defend the case that on the

grounds of adultery their marriage had broken down, but her evidence included the claim that Barrie had failed to consummate the marriage. Rumours circulating more or less humorously for years now appeared confirmed.

Barrie's self-consciousness was so fine-tuned that even genuine emotion was quickly overtaken by an unrelenting habit of observing himself. This was almost a reflex reaction, affecting all his thoughts and feelings, and leaving him quite incapable of the abandonment of self, the relinquishment of self-consciousness necessary to experience real passion. One can go further and say that Barrie's marriage was almost certainly not consummated. Indeed it would seem reasonable to assume that it was an impossibility.

Traditionally it has always been said that Mary wanted children, and that the lack of them was one of the reasons for the breakdown of the Barries' marriage. If this was true, the comment Mary subsequently made in one of her books may have been an attempt to conceal her disappointment at what would remain her childlessness. 'The sight of babies rouses mixed feelings in me. I am not quite happy with them. Something about them puts me off, their humanness to tell the truth. They are little people. I have never been really happy with people. Some constraint tightens me up when I am with them.'[15] She goes on to describe how she felt much happier with animals.

Shortly after the Barries' divorce case George Meredith's son, Will, wrote to Charles Scribner in the United States saying:

I want to write to you so that you, as his true friend, as you are, may contradict false rumours on your side & save our friends from the scandalmongers.

The whole truth is that Mrs B. is a woman – with a woman's desires – which for many years she had controlled (& she had no children which made it harder) . . . & [Barrie] as so often is the case – with genius [has] but little virility . . . Barrie urged her to return to him & give up the other – she, having at length after battling against it, given in to the longing of her heart after a virile man, & no doubt the secret woman's longing for . . . a child, would not.

That is the story & one may say, with truth, that there is no sort of vice on her part & only the most generous behaviour. Nevertheless, it is deeply to be regretted and I hardly know how Barrie will fare – left to himself without some woman.[16]

On his enquiring after her, Mary Barrie wrote to Wells that her husband 'came out badly in court. 3 lies. First, never said it was the only time. 2ⁿᵈ. It is *my* cottage, lease is in my name and I bought it with my money. 3ʳᵈ. It is seven years since we separated and that does not spell happiness until 18 months ago. This has damaged us a lot in the eyes of the public but with our friends, well, they all know better.'

For a time Mary lived on her own at Black Lake with Luath as company. She refused any alimony from Barrie, but asked for the car, the chauffeur and the dog. She and Cannan were to marry, but not until April, and for propriety's sake they were advised to spend little time in each other's company. Mary wrote:

> . . . at the time my first marriage came to an end . . . I was living alone at the cottage with Luath. He became dearer to me than ever. He was hardly ever away from me. He slept in my room, he ate with me, he walked with me, he talked to me. I busied myself with my beloved garden; he lay nearby watching. He knew something strange was happening, that things were not as they used to be.[17]

On this sad note the Barries' fifteen-year marriage was brought to a close.

On the day of his divorce Barrie managed to drag himself round to Robert and Kathleen Scott's flat to wish them well – he was to be a godfather to their son. Afterwards he returned to Mason's flat, where he remained in retreat, until finally permitting a small number of friends to see him. His reluctance to return to his own now wife-less home appeared permanent.

When Granville Barker advised that a flat was being vacated in Adelphi Terrace House, Sir George Lewis's wife, Elizabeth, immediately went to look it over. She decided that Barrie should take it on and set to work at once. Having arranged for him to sign the new lease, Leinster Corner was disposed of, and a married couple, Harry Brown and his wife, were brought in to take care of Barrie. Elizabeth Lewis organised and chose the decoration, and by the end of November the new incumbent, still uninterested and most of the time immersed in a welter of misery, was installed in his new home.

In Robert Street, set just back from the busyness and roar of the Strand, Barrie's flat on the third floor of Adelphi Terrace House was absolutely central, and yet in those days it felt like a pleasant backwater. Through its leaded windows there were striking views out over the Embankment Gardens and the Thames beyond. To the east one could see as far as St Paul's, and to the west the Houses of Parliament. Gradually, friends were permitted to visit, while it was immediately clear that in Mr and Mrs Brown, Lady Lewis had chosen well.

Harry Brown, a North-countryman who combined bright cheerfulness with an astute sensitivity, was a calming and genial spirit in the flat. He soon became devoted to Barrie, and cared for him unfailingly for the next twelve years. His introspective, moody and erratic employer would in turn greatly appreciate this man (and his equally calm wife, the cook) as one of the few still, sure points in a life of inner turbulence.

In time Barrie was to feel such attachment to Adelphi Terrace House that he chose to live there for the remainder of his life.

20

A Kind of Family

Sylvia Davies was again unwell. Only two days after Barrie's divorce was finalised, she collapsed at home in Campden Hill Square. Her son Peter, who was there at the time, recalled that as an agitated Mary Hodgson told him to make himself scarce he was overcome by a 'feeling of direness and fatality, and a sense of shocked misery and half-comprehending desolation, which has remained with me ever since'.[1]

The family doctor was called, and recognising the gravity of the situation in turn summoned a specialist. Whatever the suspected cause for Sylvia's previous ill health had been, during the summer she appeared to have recovered much of her energy and spirits. The news the specialist now gave Mary Hodgson and Barrie could not, then, have been worse. Sylvia was suffering from cancer. Since the tumour was too close to her heart to operate, the specialist told them there was nothing he could do. The truth was kept from Sylvia herself, while the boys were told simply that their mother would need to rest, for a long time. A nurse, Miss Loosemore, was employed to look after her, and for a time the Llewelyn Davieses and the du Mauriers were unaware of the gravity of Sylvia's illness.

During the last months their Davies relations had seen less of Sylvia and the boys. Peter later wrote that this was a consequence of a 'slow drift apart' between Sylvia and Arthur's relatives. Arthur's sister, Margaret, was much occupied with caring for their father, now eighty-four, while the brothers were all busy with their own families. Even though Crompton, the boys' guardian, had with great tact done as much as he could, in the face of Barrie's insistent presence it was difficult for the Davieses to make any significant contribution. Certainly they couldn't offer the financial support that Barrie had been only too willing to give. But as Peter Davies wrote: 'The curious position of J. M. B. was something that, however thankfully they may have recognised the value of it, they found rather hard to swallow.' He goes on to say that inevitable though the 'drawing apart' may have been, he believed it was a great misfortune for himself and his brothers. 'Had it been possible to instil into us, in our impressionable years, more of the balanced, able, essentially sound Davies characteristics, we should have benefited accordingly.'[2]

By the time George returned home from Eton and Jack from naval college for Christmas, their mother was often too weak to leave her room. With Mary Hodgson now running the house, Nurse Loosemore was there to care for Sylvia. The awful confirmation of her illness, and Barrie's final, slow emergence from the shock of his divorce, meant that despite an increasingly full social calendar he was regularly at Campden Hill Square. He did what he could for Sylvia and frequently saw Michael and Nico. As an honorary member of the family, it seemed only natural that with the onset of Sylvia's illness Barrie was permitted to manage many details of their lives. Peter wrote that he 'was closer by far to us, as well as directing our destinies, than any of our real uncles'.

Into the spring of 1910, with a few days' respite here or there, Sylvia's illness progressed on its slow but deadly course. After a time she could no longer walk any distance and had to be wheeled from place to place in a bath chair. Kept ignorant of the seriousness of her condition, she must have told herself that things would get better. Despite knowing the truth, did Barrie tell himself the same thing? In April Sylvia wrote to Nico, taken away for a few days' holidays by the seaside with Mary Hodgson.

> Darling
>
> Today Peter, Michael & Nurse & I went twice to Kensington Gardens. Michael sometimes sits at the end of the bath chair & guides it while the man pushes it behind. Will you guide it when you get back?
>
> It is very hot . . .
> Goodnight my dear little boy.
> Loving & loving,
> Mother[3]

And Barrie wrote to amuse Sylvia by telling her of an evening engagement, the Academy dinner, full of pomposity: 'In all the world there cannot be a much more solemnly dull festivity . . . no one would like it so well if it were less dull.' He also kept abreast of George's academic and sporting progress at Eton. This was clearly something that George wanted, and in early July he wrote to his mother, 'I have written to ask Uncle Jim to fulfil his telephone promise and come down tomorrow.' How much he was aware of her illness is not clear, but his delightfully cheerful letters, full of an apparently uncomplicated *joie de vivre*, may in part have been an attempt to bolster her morale.

Shortly after receiving George's letter, and clearly feeling unwell, Sylvia wrote telling Barrie that she wouldn't be able to get down to Eton. Peter was sitting for a scholarship, and Sylvia asked Barrie to buy some non-scholarship collars for him, like those George had already. No doubt Barrie bought the collars, but they were not needed. Peter won his scholarship.

Although no one would tell her the truth, Sylvia was now convinced that she was seriously ill. For the summer holiday she chose a remote farmhouse in Devon, on Exmoor, not far from the Doone valley. To her surprise both Barrie and the doctor agreed to the venture, although Sylvia's mother was horrified at the idea. Did Sylvia believe for a little that her fears were unfounded? The journey was exhausting: five hours by train and then a fifteen-mile car ride to Ashton Farm. Her friend Dolly Ponsonby came to Campden Hill Square to say goodbye before they all set off. She went home to her husband that evening and wept, telling him that seeing Sylvia made her realise she was going to die and that Dolly would probably never see her again.

Once the Davieses and Barrie were settled in at the farmhouse, Mary Hodgson was kept at a distance from Sylvia. Everyone knew Mary's devotion was absolute, but they also recognised that her emotions were so intense and erratic that she couldn't be relied upon to help foster an atmosphere of calm. For a time Sylvia seemed stronger, and Barrie was encouraged. The doctors had said an operation was out of the question, but they didn't rule out the possibility that the disease might go into remission. Sylvia's improvement meant that Barrie was confident enough to leave her in Devon, returning for a couple of weekends. On one of these he brought Maude Adams to meet her. Crompton Davies came for a few days, too.

Quite suddenly Sylvia grew worse. Emma du Maurier arrived to help take care of her daughter and was put in the one spare room in the house. This meant Barrie was obliged to stay at rooms in the village nearby. From there he arrived each day to take up his post at Sylvia's bedside, just as he had done for Arthur. Mrs du Maurier wrote regularly to her daughter May of Sylvia's deteriorating condition, and indicated how appalled she was at their distance from medical help. Nurse Loosemore stayed to care for Sylvia, while the inept local doctor was dispensed with and another one called from London to remain in constant attendance. At this new development Sylvia became angry, and then broke down and wept, saying, 'I believe I am very ill.' Her nights were painful and only partially relieved by painkillers: she had become very pale and thin, and her mother wrote: 'It breaks my heart to look at her.'

The boys understood that their mother was rather ill, and were encouraged to go off each day to lose themselves in physical activity: fishing, golfing, walking expeditions, and the consumption of huge Devon cream teas. In the evenings Sylvia had a little more energy and for a short time luxuriated in their cheerful company as they reported on their day. Everyone – except the boys, who were still kept ignorant of the gravity of Sylvia's condition – knew they could no longer hold out any hope. No matter what was said to the contrary, Sylvia also knew that she was dying, and wrote out a will. Unbeknown to her sons, with the passing of each long summer's day, her life was ebbing away. Finally, on 27th August, while the boys were out on an expedition, with their grandmother, Barrie, Nurse Loosemore and the doctor at her side, Sylvia quietly died. She was forty-four.

Peter later said that he didn't believe any of his brothers, including seventeen-year-old George, had actually understood that their mother was going to die. He recalled walking back from fishing to the farmhouse ahead of George.

> It was a grey, lowering, drizzly sort of day . . . As I walked in at the gate; it struck me that there was something peculiar . . . in every window the blinds had been drawn. Somehow or other the dreadful significance of this sombre convention conveyed itself to my shocked understanding, and with heart in boots and unsteady knees I covered the remaining thirty or forty yards to the front door. There J. M. B. awaited me: a distraught figure, arms hanging limp, hair dishevelled, wild-eyed.[4]

Barrie now told Peter what Peter already knew, 'brokenly, despairingly, without pretence of philosophy or resignation or the stiff upper lip. He must have been sunk in depths far below all that, poor Jimmy . . .'[4] Barrie's suffering was terrible. He was unutterably miserable: heartbroken at the loss of the beautiful creature whom he had worshipped as a woman and a mother for over twelve years of his life.

When Jack returned to the farmhouse in the car from a day's golf with a friend, he was solemnly ushered into a room alone with Barrie, who informed him of his mother's death. At some point Jack was incensed by Barrie telling him that if his mother had lived she and Barrie were to have been married. Neither the du Mauriers nor the Davieses knew of this engagement, and no mention of it exists in the surviving correspondence. Years later, when Nico came to marry, Barrie presented Nico's bride with some of Sylvia's jewellery. In giving a sapphire and diamond ring he said it was the engagement ring from himself to Sylvia, because they were to have been married.[5]

As an adult Peter was sceptical about this engagement. He believed that Barrie had the capacity to imagine such a thing because he wanted it, and then gradually came to believe it. In addition, Peter thought that if his mother had given Barrie any encouragement in these thoughts it could only have been to humour him, particularly when she realised that she was dying. Further than that, in his own complex way, in the knowledge of Sylvia's imminent death Barrie could have constructed a fantasy engagement. Its very impossibility led him in time to believe it was real.

Michael and Nico were to stay on at the farmhouse with Mary Hodgson, while George, Jack, Peter and Barrie returned to London with Sylvia's coffin on the train. The amnesia brought on by emotional distress meant that Peter could later remember virtually nothing of the journey. Jack, however, deeply embarrassed at what he saw as the intemperance of Barrie's behaviour, recalled a 'hideous five-hour train journey'. Each time they pulled into a station Barrie would get out and stand, head bowed, beside the guard's van as if on 'sentry-duty' for the draped coffin inside.

Sylvia was buried in Hampstead Cemetery with 'my Arthur', and beside her beloved father, George du Maurier. And so, in the space of just three years, Arthur and Sylvia's five sons were faced with the death of not one, but both of their parents. The question now was where and with whom the boys would live. Various members of the family would have taken some of them on, but none could take on all five. And Sylvia had been adamant she wanted them to remain together at Campden Hill Square. Several meetings took place between Barrie, the uncles and Emma du Maurier, who had never warmed to him, despite his generosity and kindness.

According to Barrie, the will Sylvia had written at the farmhouse on Exmoor was not found until several months after her death. Barrie copied it out and sent it to Mrs du Maurier, saying that it was an 'exact copy of Sylvia's will'. This was presumably done because both the Llewelyn Davies and du Maurier families were dissatisfied with the position into which Barrie had manoeuvred himself. We don't know exactly what passed between him and the boys' relations, but the tenor of their discussions comes down to us. The anger and frustration of Sylvia's family must have placed Barrie under an obligation to justify himself, hence he sent the copy of Sylvia's will. One of the sentences in Barrie's copy read: 'What I would like would be if Jimmy would come to Mary, and that the two together would be looking after the boys and the house and helping each other, and it would be nice for Mary.' What Sylvia had actually, quite clearly, written, was not 'if Jimmy would come to Mary', but rather: 'What I would like would be if Jenny [Mary Hodgson's sister] would come to Mary and . . . be looking after the boys.'

In this document, Sylvia named her mother, J. M. B., her brother Guy and Arthur's brother Crompton to be trustees and guardians to her sons. Faced with the absolute determination of the one person who was prepared to take on all five of the boys, and who had the resources to do so, both sides of the family appear to have been forced into a retreat. Not only was Barrie prepared to look after Sylvia's sons, he saw it almost as his right. Besides, in his lifetime Arthur had accepted, however reluctantly, the value Sylvia placed on Barrie's wealth.

Shortly after Arthur's death Sylvia had begun to draft a will – Barrie called this 'notes for a will' – in which she said that she wanted her 'dear one's letters to me burnt unread' and buried with her. She added that 'of one thing I am certain – that J. M. Barrie (the best of friends in the whole world) will always be ready to advise out of his care for . . .' and here Sylvia stopped and wrote no more, until three years later on her deathbed, when she wrote the second will on Exmoor. Despite having said in the earlier document that she hoped her sons would be 'content to be poor if it should have to be', Sylvia's family knew that she also wanted 'the best' for her children. No one except Barrie could, financially at least, offer them as much.

Accordingly, Campden Hill Square and the staff to run it were kept on, with Mary Hodgson, the boys' passionately devoted nursemaid, in charge. Mary's and Barrie's long-standing antipathy to one another asserted itself now and again, at which point the boys would, more often than not, take on the role of adults and broker between them a kind of peace. Meanwhile, although Barrie now divided his time between the house in Campden Hill Square and his flat in Adelphi Terrace House, he insisted to the boys that his *home* was with them. His yearning for the children he was unable to give his wife had been uncannily and spectacularly fulfilled. In October of that year, 1910, he wrote in his notebook, 'Beware or you may get what you want.'

A few pages later we find the boys' birth dates jotted down:

George July 20 1893
Jack Sept 11 1894
Peter Feb 25 1897
Michael June 16 1900
Nicholas Nov 24 1903

And in the following year's notebook Barrie wrote, 'Play. Man who brings up 4 girls as guardian (better than boys?).'

At fifty, despite a large number of friends and many acquaintances, Barrie's fame and huge wealth frequently accentuated the isolation he was already inclined to feel. A note reads, 'Play. On man who wants to be loved for his worth alone (amazed when finds is loved for himself).'

For thirteen years the Davies family had taken an increasingly central role in Barrie's life, but now he had placed himself *in loco parentis* for the five boys. He acted as their father, and wanted also to be their mother. As their self-appointed guardian this made it both easier and more difficult, for him and the boys. He loved them, he nurtured them, never let them want for anything, did everything he could to protect them, and made them the centre of his emotional life. But at times he also wanted more from them than they were prepared or able to give. He did not in fact love them equally, but his expectations of them, and his corresponding disappointments, too, were more intense than any well-balanced parent would have thought wise. At various times Barrie felt extremes of pride, possessiveness, protectiveness and a desire for gratitude. A healthier parent might have concealed or tempered these qualities, but this he could never do.

Over the next ten years he would see four of the Davieses through Eton, take them on numerous holidays where expense was no object, send them to the best outfitters, entertain them to the theatre and at the most expensive restaurants. Materially they would want for nothing. Their unorthodox guardian loved them dearly as if they were his own, but in many ways he was deeply unsuited to their care. This, ultimately, was the cause of clashes between Barrie and Mary Hodgson. Their intense personalities were equally unfitted for their respective roles, and each wanted these young people for their own.

Family and friends were sometimes perturbed at the luxurious life to which they felt Barrie, a man of largely abstemious habits, had introduced the Davieses. It was a life that everyone saw as the complete antithesis to their father's restrained style. None the less, the boys were not mercenary and the attachment and loyalty they felt for their guardian (Jack was the exception here) didn't spring from the fact that he gave them all his money could buy. Despite Barrie's moods, and the great silences that accompanied them, he was not only a doting 'parent' but also someone the Davieses appreciated for his humour and warmth. Over the years, however, several others would find it impossible to deal with the notorious silences.

The future poet laureate, Cecil Day Lewis, who became a friend of Nico's at their prep school, was introduced to Barrie one day. Day Lewis remembered a large dark room with a small dark man sitting in it. He showed 'no perceptible enthusiasm – indeed I don't think he uttered a single word. After this negative encounter, we went up to an attic and fired with an air gun at pedestrians in the Square.' Unsettling encounters such as this were common for visitors. A friend of Michael's later recalled, 'I was terrified, and didn't dare utter a word in his presence. He never said a word, just sat there like a tombstone. I viewed him with the utmost dislike, and I think that went for most of Michael's friends, though they never would have told Michael.' Sylvia's sister May could never overcome her tendency to freeze up in Barrie's presence and wrote to her mother after one visit, 'He paralyses me as much as ever.'

By the spring of 1911, Barrie was beginning to emerge from his mourning for Sylvia. After his divorce from Mary, one of the first visitors he permitted at Adelphi Terrace was E. V. Lucas. Lucas was a man of diverse, sometimes eccentric interests, who had friends in a number of quite different circles, and to some of these he introduced Barrie. This complex and sometimes dark personality included an infectious sense of humour, which Barrie particularly appreciated. Across the way from Barrie lived George Bernard Shaw. Always a little wary of one another, the two playwrights none the less socialised together, while on the upper floor of Adelphi Terrace was Harley Granville Barker and his wife, Lillah McCarthy.

In Barrie's new role as a bachelor, living at the very heart of this prodigious city, he came to relish the proximity of the Savoy Grill to Adelphi Terrace, and was often seen there with Lucas. Another friend regularly at the Savoy in Barrie's early days as a newly single man was Alfred Mason. When Charles Frohman was over from the United States Barrie took him to the Grill without fail. Expensive restaurants were one of the few luxuries in which he indulged, though it wasn't really for the food, or wine, that they gave him pleasure. It was hardly likely that the son of an Auld Licht would become a gourmet. What Barrie savoured was the theatre of the whole event. Never forgetting or hiding his humble origins, he always remained fascinated by the idea of himself, the boy from a two-up two-down weaver's cottage, being fêted by the grand maîtres d'hotels in these most opulent of Edwardian establishments.

Despite beginning to enjoy his bachelor existence, when Barrie informed Quiller-Couch that 'mostly I am with them [the Davies boys]', he dramatises his role and implies that he does little but care for them.

I have in a sense a larger family than you now. Five boys whose father died four years ago and now their mother last summer, and

I look after them, and it is my main reason for going on. The Llewelyn Davies boys . . . Couldn't you get up to town for a day or two – preferably not a weekend as I am rather tied up with the boys then.[6]

That year, 1911, there was to be a great Shakespeare Ball at the Albert Hall in aid of the founding of the National Theatre, and Barrie's friend the Duchess of Sutherland asked him to suggest a design for her costume. The fancy dress ball was a conspicuous social event, and although torn between his relish of society and contempt for the extravagance of the occasion, Barrie did put in an appearance. Predictably, he didn't dress up.

Not long afterwards he wrote and asked the duchess if she might suggest somewhere in Sutherland where he could take the boys for August and September. He said:

What they yearn for is to be remote from Man and plenty of burn trout fishing, of which they never tire from the rising to the setting of the sun. The rate would not so much matter but there should be space for about ten of us including maids.[7]

Did the Davieses – who were sustained by a large number of friends – really yearn for somewhere 'remote from Man'? Alternatively, Barrie may have been saying that what he wanted was to spend time with them in a place where he could enjoy their company without the interruption of their friends. He wrote to Nurse Loosemore, who had attended Sylvia in her last months, saying that the boys 'are all happy I think'. No doubt, in their own way, they were making the best of their circumstances. Certainly the traumas they had experienced, plus their consideration for Barrie, appear to have made them accommodating. Creating discord at this time would most likely have encouraged them to feel even more insecure; if they threatened the flimsy structure that now represented their family life, this, too, might fall apart. Barrie had made himself their family.

The Duchess of Sutherland suggested Barrie might like to take the remote Scourie Lodge. Barrie told his friend Charles Turley Smith that their journey would be 630 miles by train, by car another 44, and that the nearest small town was as far from London as was Paris. While Barrie and the boys were holidaying with their entourage in these far-off regions, he wrote to Dolly Ponsonby. An equivocal letter, it appears oblivious to the response his taking charge of the Davieses might have provoked in their parents' friends.

I brought up Michael and Nicholas and the household a few days ago & Peter follows on Tuesday and George a week later . . . Jack is on his cruises and won't be able to join us. It is a beautiful place, I think, on the west coast with the wildest mountains right to the sea and . . . fishing which is what the boys like to do for ever. Michael has just counted on the map 50 lochs within 9 miles of us . . . I think it is the kind of place Sylvia would have liked them to be at. It was on 25th July we went to Exmoor and on 26th August she died. The place they were at on Dartmoor a year before is not very far from the Galsworthys [where Dolly and her husband were due to pay a visit] . . .

Up here the air is so fresh and keen that a fire is good at night and the heady London is a memory. It is solitary when the children have gone to bed but George and Peter will liven up the house of an evening. Don't ever think that they have so many friends that you don't matter. In any case I shld like you to matter, and indeed it is rather sad to see how many old friends of Sylvia's and Arthur's have drifted out of all personal contact with the boys. Of course very few of them knew the boys. She had a large room for friends but you were among the very few who knew the other room.

Yours always

J. M. Barrie[8]

Many years later Peter Llewelyn Davies decided to put together a family record. Using letters and papers connected by an occasional commentary, he recorded their history from 1812 until 1915. This included his parents' marriage, their lives with their sons and friends and the family's relationship with Barrie. Referring to his record as the *Family Mausoleum*, more often than not Peter called it the *Morgue*. He wrote asking Dolly Ponsonby if she would recall her memories of his parents, which she continued to do for several years. Replying to an early letter from her Peter wrote:

You are of course perfectly right about our being spirited away, as children, from our mother's and father's friends. It would not be easy to say to what extent, if any, the process was deliberate, and to what extent in the peculiar circumstances inevitable; the whole business as I look back on it was almost unbelievably queer . . . but at all events it was a bad thing, among some things that were good, for the children concerned; and I can well imagine what the thoughts of old friends of Sylvia's and Arthur's must have been.[9]

A few days after Barrie's letter to Dolly she recorded a visit made to her at Shulbrede by Margaret Davies, the boys' aunt.

> She looked very worn and tired and beautiful. How she takes out of herself with her ardent sympathy & her loves and hates. I listened to her putting her case to Arthur against the Suffrage Conciliation Bill & it was very interesting & so extraordinarily well put . . . But even if the practical things can't be carried out to the letter – she leads the way . . . and no scheme of reform is too large for her . . .

And two days later Dolly wrote:

> M. & I talked all morning of Sylvia and Arthur's boys – and Jimmie Barrie. M. is very desperate at moments about them & I have felt too the pity of their easy luxurious lives. In fact it has been on the tip of my tongue to say to J.M.B. does he want George to be a fashionable gentleman? Of course in principle he doesn't. In principle he is all for the ragged ragamuffins & says he wants the boys to be for them too – but in his desire to make up to the boys for all they have lost, he gives them every material pleasure. Nothing is denied them in the way of amusement, clothes, toys etc. It is very disheartening and when one thinks of Arthur, their Father – almost unbearable.[10]

Barrie had been working on a novel of *Peter Pan*. He called it *Peter and Wendy* and it was brought out in London and New York in October 1911, with illustrations by F. D. Bedford. Like *Peter Pan in Kensington Gardens, Peter and Wendy* would become a standard children's present for many years to come. They may well have seen the play, but it was through *Peter and Wendy* or abridged versions of the play that most children in the first half of the twentieth century became so familiar with the story of *Peter Pan*. And still Barrie had not allowed publication of the play's text.

He spent Christmas in bed with bronchitis, an illness to feature more prominently in the record of his health from now on. His frequent colds more often than not developed into a cough, which in turn usually became bronchitis. Sometimes he stopped smoking his pipe for a few days but it was always resumed, and he now had a chronic incipient cough.

At the end of January 1912 he was elected to the committee of the Royal Society of Literature – proposed by Austin Dobson, man of letters, biographer, and friend of Edmund Gosse. The proposal was seconded by

Bernard Shaw. A week later Barrie's one-act skit on the theatre, *A Slice of Life*, was launched, and the following week Frohman opened it in New York. The play didn't do too badly, but on the whole Frohman's fortunes were in decline. The repertory theatre in London, into which he had valiantly poured so much money on behalf of the English avant-garde, was not a commercial success. In America tastes were changing in favour of burlesque, vaudeville and cinema, and away from the kind of expensive theatrical productions in which Frohman specialised. He became very ill with a form of rheumatism, leaving him bedridden for most of the following six months. Although afterwards he remained unable to walk without a stick, struggling with pain Frohman remained his buoyant and smiling self.

Peter Pan continued its hugely popular annual revival, but for the moment Barrie appeared unable to come to Frohman's rescue with another success. Barrie's own life, with each of its many and varied social facets kept apart from one another, continued at such speed it is surprising that during this period he wrote anything at all. Yet, always the notebooks were filled, at greater length now than for some time. At present he was also at work on three different plays, *Rosalind*, *Half an Hour* and *The Adored One*.

Then, in April, the largest, and supposedly the safest ship in the world, *Titanic*, struck an iceberg on her maiden voyage to America. Of more than two thousand passengers on board, over fifteen hundred went to their deaths with the ship. The world was deeply shocked at *Titanic*'s loss, and Barrie was not left immune. Two of his friends died. The loss of one of these, W. T. Stead, gave Barrie good cause to dwell once more on beginnings and endings, for it was this old rogue who had had the initiative to publish Barrie's very first articles in the *Pall Mall Gazette*. A few weeks after *Titanic*'s sinking another aspect of Barrie's writing life was to be marked in quite a different way.

George Frampton had at last completed his statue of Peter Pan, and with the permission of the Commissioner of Works, and the support of King Edward VII, the eternal boy was secretly prepared for display at Barrie's instructions. Throughout the night of 30th April, not far from the Serpentine in Kensington Gardens, workmen laboured, and very early in the morning removed the screens behind which they had been working. The statue's overnight appearance, 'as if by magic', caused a great stir, and its existence provoked as much controversy as delight. While a large number sprang to its defence, others demanded to know how an author could put up a statue of one of his own characters in a public place without public permission. Questions were asked in the House of Commons, articles were written for and against, but Frampton's statue of Peter Pan remains to this day in Kensington Gardens in the place where it first 'sprang up'.

The summer of 1912 was George's last half at Eton. He was in Hugh Macnaghten's house, considered to be the best of all. Macnaghten had long ago been Arthur's colleague, then he became a good friend of Barrie's. Peter recalled that in his way Macnaghten was as odd as Barrie, and 'too good to be wise'. With Macnaghten as his tutor, George had flourished. He was in the first XI, was captain of football, Treasurer of Pop – the school's elite social club – and had also won the coveted Essay Prize. His years at Eton had seen the development of his beautiful looks and that natural sense of poise inherited from both his parents. With this he combined a personality that made him one of the most admired and well-liked boys in the school. Elected early to Pop, normally barred to all but those in their final year, a contemporary later recalled that George had 'absolutely no vanity'.

> No conceit whatsoever. It was quite extraordinary . . . for someone quite so successful . . . He wasn't a great talker, but he had great charm. He was rather shy, rather reserved, but his sense of humour was exquisite.[11]

Barrie felt for him a deep sense of devotion and had become tremendously proud of this 'gallant', as he called him, and over the last few years visiting him at Eton whenever an opportunity arose. For many boys, the frequency of this strange little man's presence – taking George out for the day, watching him play cricket from the side – would have caused much embarrassment, but George's composure and quiet self-assurance meant that instead he welcomed 'Uncle Jim's visits as something simply to be enjoyed.

Now overseeing two boys at Eton – Peter had arrived in 1910 – Barrie was familiar with the school. His fascination with the whole institution grew so much that he would even incorporate it into the published version of *Peter Pan*, so that Captain Hook's last words as he fell to his death in the crocodile's jaws became '*Floreat Etona*'.

When Barrie decided he liked something, or someone, he usually strove to know more about them than anyone else, implying a greater familiarity, and therefore sense of 'ownership'. With Eton it was different, and Barrie explained this in 1924 when he gave a speech to a girls' school – his niece was then headmistress – in which he said,

> Your great public schools: I never feel myself a foreigner in England except when trying to understand them. I have a great affection for

one at least of them. They will bewilder me to the end: I am like a dog looking up wistfully at its owner, wondering what the noble face means, or if it does have a meaning. To look at, these schools are the fairest things in England . . . they draw from their sons a devotion that is deeper and more lasting than almost any other love . . . Those schools must be great, and yet I don't quite see how it comes about . . . It is not scholarship – pooh – it is not even physical prowess, it is not an awakened soul or any exclusive manliness not even a superior way of wearing waistcoats. They describe it briefly and unanswerably as a something, and perhaps wisely leave it at that, putting us in our place forever . . .[12]

In George's last summer at school, prior to going up to Trinity, Cambridge, Barrie wrote words of encouragement to him, saying that if his father and mother were alive they would be very pleased with their 'eldest born'. And George was certainly to bow out of Eton with a flourish. At the great annual Eton v. Harrow cricket match at Lord's he not only made a record for Eton that day, he also bowled the top Harrovian batsman and took a sensational catch, recorded in the broadsheets next day. Barrie was immensely proud, while George's little brother Nico, now almost nine, walked round all day as if he had been given a magnificent present.

For their holiday that summer Barrie took the boys to a Scottish mansion on the isle of Harris, called Amhuinnsuidhe Castle. Peter said, 'the cost must have been fabulous . . . the fishing was to match'. A succession of friends arrived to stay with Barrie, the boys, and their retinue of maids. This year, in addition to such old friends as E. V. Lucas, his wife and daughter, Audrey, the writer Anthony Hope, his wife and children, and two recent friends, Lord Lucas (Auberon 'Bron' Herbert) and his sister, Nan, made up the party. These two would be close friends of Barrie for the remainder of their lives. Bron Herbert was a tall, intelligent man with an infectious vitality, who had lost a leg while a correspondent for *The Times* in the Boer War and sported a wooden one in its place. As the youngest and most likely to make a *faux pas*, Nico had been given instructions that under no circumstances should he mention this disability. On Bron Herbert's arrival Nico promptly asked if he could see the wooden leg, to which the cheerful reply was, 'Yes. Where's my bedroom? Come upstairs and I'll take it off and show it to you.'

This was the summer from which Barrie would later extract a significant event and incorporate it into the Dedication to the first printing of *Peter Pan*, in 1928.

The rebuffs I have got from all of you! They were especially crushing in those early days when one by one you came out of your belief in fairies and lowered on me as the deceiver. My grandest triumph . . . is that long after No. 4 [Michael] had ceased to believe, I brought him back to the faith for at least two minutes. We were on our way in a boat to fish the Outer Hebrides (where we caught Mary Rose) . . . His one pain was the absence of Johnny Mackay . . . the loved gillie of the previous summer who had taught him everything that is worth knowing . . . but could not be with us this time . . . As the boat drew near the Kyle of Lochalsh pier I told Nos. 4 and 5 [Michael and Nico] it was such a famous wishing pier that they had now but to wish and they should have . . . No. 4 thought it more of my untimely nonsense and doggedly declined to humour me.

Barrie asked Michael whom he would most like to see there and, after saying that wishing was 'rot', Michael finally relented and contemptuously wished for 'Johnny Mackay'. At considerable cost Barrie had arranged for the gillie to be there, '. . . waiting for him, loaded with fishing paraphernalia. I know no one less like a fairy than Johnny Mackay, but for two minutes No. 4 was quivering in another world than ours. When he came to he gave me a smile, which meant that we understood each other, and thereafter neglected me for a month, always being with Johnny.'[13]

An intensely sensitive boy, in appearance much like his mother, Michael already had that insouciant du Maurier charm, while his younger brother Nico would later say of him that he was always 'the cleverest of us five'. Barrie adored Michael; they were very close. Michael was a more complex child than George at the same age, and it seems to have been accepted without resentment that he touched Barrie's heart a little more than his brothers. He still looked up to his 'guardian' as to no one else, but Michael was no longer quite the malleable little boy he had been at his mother's death, and his awareness and maturity meant that it wasn't always Barrie who guided or took control.

Three years earlier, in 1909, Barrie's friend Captain Scott had published plans for his British Antarctic Expedition. Although the public response was at first slow, appeals to patriotism and civic pride raised the profile of the venture and donations rose to £10,000. With sponsorship, a government grant of £20,000 and further funds from various sources, the expedition had bought and equipped the wooden whaling ship *Terra Nova* and set sail for the Antarctic in June 1910. The aims of the explorer were changing, and scientific experiment and exploration were now major motivating forces. Thus, at a farewell lunch for Scott's officers in London, the President of the Royal Geographical Society said that the twin aims were for the glory of science and the nation: 'I have not the slightest doubt that a rich harvest of facts will be reaped.' A secondary aim – though some would argue otherwise – was that Scott wanted his party to be the first ever to reach the South Pole.

This is not the place to retell the well-known story in any detail, but its sad outcome was to have particular relevance for Barrie. By one of those coincidences of history, it was in a little house on the edge of Glen Prosen, just outside Kirriemuir, and lent them by the publisher Smith, that Scott and Wilson planned their fateful journey to the South Pole. Early in 1913, over two years after her husband had left for the Antarctic, Kathleen Scott set sail for New Zealand, where it was expected that the *Terra Nova* would soon return. On 10th February, the ship did indeed return, but with only part of the original expeditionary force. The news in the evening papers that day shocked the nation. It told not of Scott's triumphant return, but of his death, almost a year before. It was a major coup for the British press, who were the first to tell the story.

> Christchurch (N.Z.) – Monday – Captain Scott reached the South Pole on January 18 of last year, and there found the Norwegian tent.

Amundsen had reached the Pole before them and left his tent, records and flag as proof. Much criticised in some British quarters, before he left Norway Amundsen had kept secret his intended attempt on the Pole. Scott wrote, 'It is a terrible disappointment and I am sorry for my loyal companions.'

Still on the ship bound for New Zealand when she received news of his death, Kathleen was also sent Scott's journals, with their now famous record of his last days. These spurred his wife to write in her diary, 'that was a glorious courageous note & a great inspiration to me. If he in his agony-wracked condition could face it with such sublime fortitude, how dare I possibly whine.'

Barrie, like most of the nation, was deeply affected by Scott's words. As more information about the Antarctic expedition was given to the press it produced an almost unprecedented response. In Britain and around the world, newspapers were filled with comment on the event – seen as an heroic struggle to compare with the greatest in world history – while unprecedented numbers of newspapers covering the story were sold. Lord Curzon wrote to the press that he believed public feeling 'had been quickened by this tale of mingled heroism and disaster as by no other event in my time'. Messages of sympathy poured in from presidents, governments and civic bodies from across the globe. Memorial services were held throughout Britain, and attendance swelled to match that following the sinking of *Titanic*. A special service was held at St Paul's, with huge numbers of mourners, led by the King.

Barrie had additional cause for sadness and regret. Before Scott's departure, a misunderstanding of some kind had occurred between the two men (the most likely explanation for which is that Barrie understood Scott to have made comments about Barrie's relationship with Sylvia Llewelyn Davies), and Barrie was now haunted by what might otherwise have been said or done. Then, on 11th April he received a letter addressed to him from Scott, and sent on from New Zealand by Kathleen. Whatever had happened between them was quickly forgotten. How could it be otherwise when, though dying, one of the greatest of contemporary heroes was at pains to heal their rift? Putting aside the disputes over Scott's management of the expedition that have continued until the present day, under the terrible conditions of the frozen wastes his emotional and physical endurance, shown till the end, were everything that Barrie admired. Scott wrote,

My dear Barrie

We are pegging out in a very comfortless spot – Hoping this letter may be found and sent to you I write a word of farewell – it hurt me grievously when you partially withdrew your friendship or seemed to do so – I want to tell you that I never gave you cause – If you thought or heard ill of me it was unjust – Calumny is ever to the fore. My attitude towards you and everyone connected with you was always one of respect and admiration – Under these circumstances I want you to think well of me and my end and more practically I want you to help my widow and my boy your godson – We are showing that Englishmen can still die with a bold spirit fighting it out to the end. It will be known that we have accomplished our object in reaching the Pole and that we have done everything possible even to sacrificing ourselves in order to save sick companions. I think this makes an example for Englishmen of the future and that the country ought to help those who are left behind to mourn us – I leave my poor girl and your godson . . . do what you can to get their claims recognised.

Goodbye. I am not at all afraid of the end but sad to miss many a simple pleasure which I had planned . . . I may not have proved a great explorer, but we have done the greatest march ever made and come very near to great success. Goodbye my dear friend.

Yours ever

R. Scott[14]

The effect of this letter on Barrie was profound. He wrote by return to Kathleen — now Lady Scott, her husband having been given a post-humous knighthood — saying that he was very proud of the wishes expressed by his friend. He would do everything he could for the Scotts' little boy, Peter, and wanted to be the friend to her that her husband had wished for. Kathleen possessed as strong and stubborn a personality as Barrie, and over the years she would manage, with a fair amount of adroitness, to ensure that he remained a friend to herself and her boy, while never permitting him to 'own' them.

It was proposed that Scott's journals should be prepared for publica-tion, and Kathleen asked Barrie if he would compose a piece describing 'The Last Scene'. This famous passage concerning the explorers' deaths would make its own significant contribution to the formation of Scott's posthumous image.

Barrie's complex attitude to privacy and his own celebrity was set aside when it came to one of the greatest heroic figures of the age writing to him near death that 'I never met a man in my life whom I loved and admired more than you.' Excluding the references to the rift between them, Barrie willingly gave Scott's now famous letter for publication. In doing so, he felt himself less bookish and by association more the man of action that part of him hankered after being. He also subtly interwove himself with the heroes' legend. The book in which the letter was published, *Scott's Last Expedition*, was arranged by Leonard Huxley and published in November that year. It was an immediate and huge success, one news-paper even calling it 'a great book, perhaps the greatest ever written'.

Over time Barrie would incorporate Scott into his own pantheon of youthful heroes. Heroes as much as anything because they had died young. He would solemnise this in a famous post-First World War speech in which he said,

When I think of Scott I remember the strange Alpine story of the youth who fell down a glacier and was lost, and of how a scien-tific companion computed how the body would again appear . . . many years afterwards . . . Some of the survivors returned to the glacier to see if the prediction would be fulfilled; all old men now; and the body reappeared as young as on the day he left them. So Scott and his comrades emerge out of the white immensities, always young.[15]

21

War

Michael Davies's years at prep school were at an end, and in April he left London and Campden Hill Square to begin his first half at Eton. A few days later Barrie wrote to his old friend Charles Turley Smith. A diffident, sensitive man, Turley Smith was one of the very few to whom Barrie felt able to reveal a part of his essential self, and the plea for his friend's company was heartfelt.

> Many thanks for the bluebells and a squeeze of the hand for every one you plucked. Still more for the affection that made you know how sad I would be about Michael gone to school. He is very lonely there at present, and I am foolishly taken up about it. It rather broke me up seeing him crying and trying to whistle at the same time.
>
> I wish you could manage to come to us in Scotland this year – August and September. Few things could now give me so much pleasure as to know you mean to do this. *I would rather have you than anyone.*[1]

While George Davies had loved Eton, his brother Peter at least discovered how to protect himself from those aspects of boarding school life he found threatening. Despite these precedents, Michael, both sensitive and intelligent to a degree, was for a long time less capable of mastering his vulnerability. Unlike George, who found his feet within days, Michael cried himself to sleep every night and had great difficulty at first in making friends. He was desperately homesick, missing the two most constant and stabilising, if unorthodox, influences since his mother's death – Barrie and Mary Hodgson. As Barrie gently persisted in trying to allay Michael's fears and loneliness, he tried also to conceal his own gloom, for his pain at Michael's departure was consuming.

This boy's unusual presence had absorbed Barrie's emotions increasingly over the last few years, and their relationship had developed into one of great sympathy and closeness. Barrie was anxious for him, telling friends he believed that Michael had proved the least able to incorporate his mother's death into his own life. Barrie once remarked to a member of the family that on being told his mother had died the ten-year-old Michael's first reaction was fury. Alert to the child's sensibilities, Barrie tended him with a solicitude not quite reserved for the other boys. In this way he had made a habit, for as many days each week as he was able, of either walking Michael home from school or playing games with him when he arrived back at Campden Hill Square. This devotion extended to sitting up many times through Michael's terrifying and recurring nightmare, in which sleepwalking frequently took him on a desperate search for something he was forever unable to find.

In an attempt to calm Michael's fears about leaving home, it was decided that rather than the customary weekly correspondence, they would write to one another each day. Although Michael did finally settle at school, he and Barrie continued their daily communication, and by the time Michael left Eton they had together written at least two thousand letters. Aware that these might be misinterpreted, Peter later said they were 'too much' and decided they should be destroyed.

Like any over-attached parent, Barrie had as much need of these letters as did the boy he was writing to. Again, like the parent who cannot let go, as Michael grew and learnt more independence, often unconsciously Barrie employed a hundred subtle ways to prevent him from moving on. The tenor of most of Barrie's conversation was that the Davies boys must strive to become men worthy of their parents and their family, and he believed it. But at the same time his deep antipathy to growing up, his love affair with the imagination, the Never Land, was always there as an undertow, and at times it overwhelmed him. This was the powerful and driven man who had written, 'Nothing that happens after we are twelve matters very much.' This was the self that wanted only to live in the imagination. The self that recalled with such triumph Michael's momentary joy at his fairy-granted wish, to have the gillie Johnny Mackay with them at Amhuinnsuidhe Castle. Barrie was triumphant, because for those few moments he had halted Michael's progress towards the real world of the adult.

In June of 1914 Barrie's name appeared in the Birthday Honours List as 'Baronet'. Having refused a knighthood in 1909, he was apparently unable to resist the flattery of the hereditary title. For a while the three older Davies boys were at a loss as to how they should address him, and in the process oscillated between pride and a cheerful derision at Barrie's heightened status. To George, Peter and Jack, in those more formal times, their 'guardian' had always remained Mr Barrie, but that was no longer possible. They tried Sir Jas, but Barrie clearly didn't like it. For a while the younger boys called him Sir Jazz Band Barrie. Jack, who was never close to him, called him 'The Bart' or, in a more irritated frame of mind, 'The Little Baronet'. Unable to refer to him by his formal title, Sir James, the boys eventually fell back on Michael and Nico's longstanding name for him, 'Uncle Jim'. Even Jack sometimes felt obliged to do the same. Faced with this problem of naming, Barrie's old friends continued calling him Jamie or Jimmy, while for many others he gradually became known simply as J. M. B.

Why did Barrie accept the title? In the unrecorded speech of thanks he made at the dinner given by his friends, he apparently gave no clue. It was said by detractors that he had become a snob. He did enjoy spanning several different worlds, and those of high politics and high society were two with which his status had increasingly brought him into contact. And, in between seeing old friends, when outside London, if he wasn't visiting George at Cambridge, or Peter and Michael at Eton, Barrie might well be found at one country house party or another.

At the same time as enjoying his extensive social contacts, in part under E. V. Lucas's influence, he had become fascinated by the increasingly popular forms of mass entertainment, in particular the revue and the cinema. Indeed, in 1913 he took the Davies boys many times to see the immensely successful American revue *Hullo Ragtime*. Perhaps related to these new interests, none of the plays Barrie wrote during this period was more than one act, and several of them were staged in the new variety theatres.

Since 1910, Barrie had become less prolific. In large part this must have been due to the time, and above all emotional energy, taken up first with his divorce and then with accommodating himself to caring for the Davies boys after their mother's death in the summer of 1910. By 1913, at fifty-three, Barrie's colossal imaginative and physical energy was finally a little reduced. Even so, of the four one-act plays he had running in 1913, three of them were successful. The fourth, *The Adored One* – starring the beautiful and tempestuous Mrs Campbell, for whom Shaw wrote *Pygmalion* in the same year – was definitely *not* a success. For the first time in Barrie's theatrical career some of the first-night audience loudly voiced their disapproval, and a popular newspaper signalled Barrie's failure with the headline 'Baronet Booed'.

His subtle and thoughtful vision had never been more than half understood – even by a critic as perceptive as Max Beerbohm. More often than not Barrie had taken on the extremely difficult task of looking at fundamental questions in works aimed at a large audience; in other words he had tried to be both profound and popular. Of course, he was constrained to attempt popularity – he would otherwise have made a poor living as a writer. But he also had little patience with the rarified atmosphere of small elitist groups professing various social and artistic ideologies. For Barrie the necessity of popularity was not a burden. He accepted it willingly as a challenge, while still admiring other writers, for example George Meredith, whose failure with the majority meant that their sales never amounted to more than a fraction of his own.

Years before, when he was already a rich man, Barrie could have left his popular audience behind and written avant-garde plays for a small and uncommercial stage. His antagonists would argue that he didn't do this because popular writing was all he was capable of. However, antipathetic as he was to the subtle elitism that had crept into judgements about what was good or bad literature and drama over the previous twenty or thirty years, Barrie's consistent aim was to reach as many people as he could. He was trying to ask questions about the plight of man in the modern world. Difficult questions, he hid them under layers of apparently uncontroversial artifice and humour. These could, however, be understood by anyone who was prepared to think. Instinctively, Barrie was quite aware that the value of what was popular was the robust core of every culture; one of the people himself, he understood them. This was one of the reasons why, unlike many of his contemporary dramatists, Barrie was interested in the new mass entertainments. And of all the recently developing forms, it was the essential ability of film to experiment with and question ideas about reality and fantasy – what is real and what is not – that made it the most miraculous and exciting invention to this man whose artistic life had been dedicated to discovering this very same thing.

At the end of the year he had taken the older Davies boys to see Gaby Deslys, the exotic French music-hall star, in her revue about nothing more serious than undisguised and joyful 'entertainment'. Called the pocket Venus, with her huge 'wondering eyes, pearl pink complexion' and provocative stage performances, in fantastic, suggestive costumes Gaby Deslys also had a well-publicised and scandalous private life, and was one of the most venerated, and richest, sex symbols of the period. Barrie and the Davieses were just as smitten as any of the other thousands, including the young poet Rupert Brooke, who went over and over again to see her perform in London, Paris and New York. Barrie's pre-eminent position in the theatre meant he could procure a meeting with Mlle Deslys. Succumbing to her warmth and flirtatiousness, he found that her inability to speak anything but the most limited English only added to her allure.

Determined to engage with the cinema, Barrie decided he would make a film and incorporate this into Gaby Deslys's revue. He became so taken up with the idea that many thought he had lost all sense of proportion. Whether this event represented Barrie at his most arcane and obscure, or was simply an indication of the lunacy of which he was capable, and the status he now possessed, he decided he would host what he called a 'Cinema Supper' with entertainments. He would have the evening filmed and use it for Gaby's revue. Expense was not one of the evening's constraints. That year, from a mixture of plays, revues, sales of books, and investments, Barrie made over forty-five thousand pounds, in 1913 a vast sum. About one hundred and fifty luminaries of the theatre, society and politics were invited to the cinema supper. So, on 3rd July many of the figures of the day – headed by the Prime Minister and Mrs Asquith – arrived at the Savoy Theatre for a banquet with an entertainment to follow.

Voted one of the society events of the year, the evening was a great success. But as word got out that Barrie intended showing to the world at large his illustrious guests entertaining themselves, in a period when private and public occasions had much clearer boundaries and celebrity was not yet an obsession, the response was very unfavourable. Prime Minister Asquith, at the time unaware that his unguarded gestures at a private evening were to be shown to the public, sent a letter from 10 Downing Street forbidding that any such thing should happen.

Undaunted, with Granville Barker as joint director, Barrie went down to the Hertfordshire countryside, where he had persuaded a most unlikely cast of friends, dressed as cowboys, to perform for him a burlesque of the Western. H. G. Wells and the writer and society figure Maurice Baring had been suspicious and refused to join in, but Bernard Shaw, Lord Howard de Walden, G. K. Chesterton and William Archer were prepared to play in front of the cameras. When Shaw found out that not only was the film to be shown in public, but that it was also designed, amongst other things, to send him up, he wrote to Barrie saying that if it was shown he would sue.

The revue Barrie eventually wrote, called *Rosy Rapture*, was launched in March 1915. He may have been interested in this new mass entertainment medium, but that didn't mean he had the ability to master it. In many ways he wasn't brash enough. *Rosy Rapture* was definitely not a success, and after a few weeks it was taken off.

At the end of June 1914 Barrie wrote to George, holidaying in Italy with two Eton–Cambridge friends. While encouraging him not to forget his first introduction to the country, 'a little heaven below', Barrie envied him his 'roof garden and fireflies'. A couple of weeks later he told George that in the 'stress of going to the opera' with Peter they had forgotten to wire him the results of the Eton and Harrow cricket match. He said that Peter had dragged him to the opera two nights running, and 'neither he nor Michael patronised the match'. Peter later commented on Barrie's 'only faintly humorous' references to his misguided preference for such things as opera, and the ballet, which was even more frowned upon. He came to feel strongly that

> A little more encouragement in the artistic way would have been very good for us all . . . The fact is that music, painting, poetry, and the part they may be supposed to play in the making of a civilised being, had a curiously small place in JMB's view of things.[2]

At pains to be fair, Peter adds the backhanded compliment that Barrie did introduce the boys to 'the lighter side of life', and 'what we didn't know about revue was scarcely worth knowing'. He also generously gives Barrie credit for guiding them, 'with much wise criticism', down a number of literary paths.

A glimpse of the exalted nature of Barrie's social life shows him, towards the end of July, at a supper at Maurice Baring's, from which he walked back with Lloyd George to number 11 Downing Street in the early hours of the morning, the two men talking all the way. Then, Barrie was off on a train bound for Auch Lodge in Scotland – a shooting lodge near the Bridge of Orchy in Argyllshire – for fishing with Nico, Michael and George. On 31st July Barrie wrote to his friend Bron Herbert (Lord Lucas) that 'Nicholas is riding about on an absurdly fat pony which necessitates his legs being at right angles to his body. The others are fishing.'

Suddenly, as if a presage of the catastrophic events about to be unleashed upon the world, news came that Barrie's brother Alick had died. Alick left behind a wife, two sons and four daughters. What were Barrie's thoughts as he walked once again in a funeral procession behind the last but one of his siblings? Alick's kindness and generosity to him as a boy and young man had been crucial to his development. At the same time Alick represented much of what his brother had reacted against in his attempts to articulate his own strange and original vision. As someone whose apprehension of the world was at such variance to his brother's, could Barrie ever properly voice his gratitude to him? His debt was perhaps repaid in part via Alick's wife and children after his death. In Barrie's notebooks there is an entry: 'The dying. Friends around talk of other things. Wonder about dying, when silent really making preparations for dying – for the journey.'

After burying his brother, Barrie returned to the Davies boys and the fishing lodge in Argyllshire. Auch Lodge was remote, and for a day they remained ignorant of the fact that on 4th August the Germans invaded Belgium, and Britain immediately declared war. Barrie wrote on the 14th,

> We are so isolated from news here, that when I wrote last I was quite ignorant that Europe was in a blaze. We occasionally get the morning papers in the evening, and there may be big news today. I don't see myself how we can keep out of it long in any case, and if so, probably the sooner the better . . . It seems awful to be up here at such a time catching fish . . . and all the world is spate and bog.[3]

On 5th August Peter arrived at Auch Lodge from London bringing a letter from the Adjutant of the Cambridge OTC, which said that it was the duty of all undergraduates to offer themselves for service. Peter had just left Eton and was due to go up to Cambridge in the autumn. He wasn't keen to join up but assumed that the appeal also included him. He and George travelled down to London, leaving Barrie and Mary Hodgson with the two younger boys in Scotland. By early September George and Peter had been enlisted in the army as junior officers, while Jack was already mobilised as a sub-lieutenant in the navy. On 2nd September Barrie and several other high-profile writers, including Thomas Hardy, Galsworthy, H. G. Wells, Arnold Bennett, John Masefield and Robert Bridges, had received letters from Downing Street. They met with the Chancellor of the Duchy of Lancaster, who asked them to write as much as they could to disseminate the British point of view. The government soon recognised, however, it had underestimated the unpredictability and waywardness of writers, and the proposition was dropped.

In the meantime, Barrie decided that he should go to America and drum up support for the Allies. Having said to a friend, 'we must all try to do something', he persuaded Gilmour and Mason to go with him. In utmost secrecy about their rather amorphous mission they set off aboard the *Lusitania*. Before they had arrived in the United States word had got out, and the clandestine ambassadors were met by letters from the Consul-General and the British Ambassador begging Barrie to call off his 'mission', in case it should offend the Americans and embarrass the British government. The *New York Tribune* meanwhile published banner headlines saying, SIR J. M. BARRIE CAUGHT TRYING TO SURPRISE NEW YORK.

On 22nd September Barrie wrote to Lord Lucas's sister Nan Herbert saying,

> We dine in a garden restaurant 20 floors up . . . There are inviting targets here for the German siege guns . . .
>
> Our 'mission' here has been bungled somehow . . . I have therefore pretended to interviewers etc. that I came here to attend to my private affairs . . . which degrades me in my own eyes and doubtless in those of other people, for it sounds a contemptible reason for coming to America at such a time. However, it suits those in authority.
>
> I think I could have done some useful work if they had just left me alone, but it is not greatly needed, as I find America is quite splendidly on our side.[4]

He told George that he was going to stay with ex-President Theodore Roosevelt, and was soon back in Britain. By the end of November Barrie had completed what he called his 'war play', *Der Tag*. Meanwhile, George and Peter were in training camp at Sheerness, where, Peter later recalled, on their first night George declared that for the first time in their lives they were up against something really serious. For the last two years George had been seeing a young girl, Josephine Mitchell-Innes, met at a dance given by his aunt May. The young couple were now unofficially engaged, and George wrote to Josephine of his misgivings. Unlike Josephine's brother, who thought the whole business was going to be rather fun, George was fatalistic; he had no illusions about what the future might bring.

Underneath his air of light-heartedness, and what Peter referred to as George's 'unorthodox attitude', unlike many of his youthful colleagues George appears to have understood with unusual prescience the terrible significance of this war. His thoughts chimed with the comment Sir Edward Grey would later make of 1914; it was, he said, 'the year in which the lamps went out all over Europe'. Familiar as we are with the statements heard repeatedly since the First World War, this makes them no less true: with the death of millions of men, life in Britain was set to alter, and would never be the same again.

Although at the beginning Barrie had written to a friend that he believed 'our young men . . . are to be as right as rain', three months into the war, when there had already been appalling loss of life, he was more apprehensive. He wrote frequently that he was longing to see George and Peter, and by mid-November a note of desperation had crept into his letters. For the first time in George's life, instead of signing himself 'affectionately', Barrie signed his letters 'your loving J. M. B.'.

At the onset of hostilities, Bron Herbert immediately offered his country house, Wrest Park in Bedfordshire, as a hospital. After vacillation by the authorities as to its precise use, by November Wrest was receiving wounded soldiers. Bron and Nan Herbert were organising their home as a hospital with considerable skill, and Barrie felt great warmth and respect for them, donating £1,000 to the venture. Feeling restless, sometimes useless, and that he should be making a contribution towards the war effort, he began making regular visits to Wrest Park. Working tirelessly, the Herberts impressed him with their conviction and personal involvement, and Barrie was thus inspired to organise entertainments and games for the invalids. He became a sensitive arbiter of the sometimes difficult relations between staff, when he wasn't talking and listening to the wounded men.

Writing to George at the end of November, Barrie thanked him for sending a letter on what would have been Sylvia's birthday. He told the young man that he yearned to have him by his side at all times, and that George probably didn't realise what help he had been to him, 'and become more and far more as these few years have passed. There is nothing I would not confide in you or trust to you . . .'

As the war progressed Barrie worried constantly about the boys' prospects at the Front. Sending George his *Eton Chronicle* he noted that eight per cent of ex-Etonians had been killed. In his preoccupied state he also did what he could to keep the boys informed of each other's progress. He told George that Jack had wired saying he might be able to get up for a brief visit. Away at sea, it was a long time since Jack had seen any of them. Early in December George was posted to his battalion in the Rifle Brigade and told Barrie he was permitted a short leave prior to setting out for the Western Front. By mid-December he was gone.

Barrie would soon begin writing a short, uncomfortable play, *The New Word*, whose central idea is the difficulty felt by men – here a father and son – in demonstrating their affection for one another. In this connection his friend Alfred Mason would later refer to 'the emotional frankness with which Barrie could always write but never speak'. Barrie told George how shocking he found it that he was really gone and said, 'I shall have many anxious days and nights too, but I only fall into line with many mothers. The Orea cigarettes will be sent weekly, and anything else I can think of to cheer you . . .'

In loving and caring for the Davies boys, Barrie often revealed the nurturing, mothering side of his nature. In truth, he was as much Wendy as he was any of the Lost Boys, Peter Pan or the tortured Captain Hook. With the Davieses Barrie was able to become more of his many selves, and several that had no outlet anywhere else. He was in part mother, father, brother, sister, adoring friend, guardian, entertainer and guide.

George wrote from France at the beginning of January that the fear of death wasn't as prevalent as he had expected, rather it was the hardships that had to be overcome. But he added, 'One gets very soon into the way of taking them as they come . . . Don't you get worried about me, I take every precaution I can and shall do very well.' At every opportunity Barrie sent provisions and extra clothing or footwear. After a bout of illness that prevented him from re-entering the trenches, George thanked him for the 'the Burberry and boots . . . As to the ski boots, I don't know what I should do without them. I put little slippers inside them and keep as warm as possible.' This year, and for the duration, the famous phrase 'To die will be an awfully big adventure' was removed from the annual revivals of *Peter Pan*.

Like thousands of other young men in the same position, George was resolutely cheerful so as to protect those back home. He sought to shield Barrie, Mary Hodgson and his younger brothers from the horrors of the trenches and the carnage everywhere around him. Meanwhile, his uncle Guy du Maurier, a lieutenant-colonel in the Royal Fusiliers, was sending back chilling details of the war to his wife – or as much anyway as the censor would allow through. Positioned only a few miles down the line from George, du Maurier talked of trenches full of dead Frenchmen, because each one killed was left 'in the squelching mud at the bottom'. When soldiers then tried digging or draining, the bodies were unearthed 'in an advanced state of decomposition'. Du Maurier wrote of the dreadful stink everywhere, and that there were 'many Highlanders just in front – killed in December I think – and they aren't pleasant'. That day he was obliged to send two hundred of his men to hospital with frost-bite or, worse still, gangrene, sometimes with their toes dropping off. He told his wife he would try and see George, whom he thought was nearby, and that he hadn't seen anyone else he knew lately, because 'I fancy most of the Army I know are killed or wounded.'

At the end of February Barrie told George that he had been 'reading and re-reading' a new letter from him, when he was delighted to have Peter unexpectedly arrive on short leave. Having commented on Peter's increased maturity – he was just eighteen – Barrie reminded George that

Life, sir, is odd, as you have been seeing these last two months, but it is even odder than that. Such a queer comedy of tears and grimness and the inexplicable – as your Du Maurier blood will make you understand sooner than most.[5]

On 7th March, clearly much affected, George apologised to Barrie, but felt the need to unburden himself. He had been within a few yards of a soldier who was killed when the top of his head was blown off. George added, 'it was a dreadful sight . . . it made an impression'. Then on the 11th Barrie wrote to him with the painful news that his uncle Guy had been killed. Barrie told George that Guy had possessed the du Maurier charm at its best; a charm underscored by sadness. 'He had lots of stern stuff in him, and yet always the mournful smile of one who could pretend that life was gay but knew it wasn't. One of the most attractive personalities I have ever known.'

Horribly aware of the constant danger he says he knows George finds himself in, Barrie tells him he doesn't care 'a farthing' for any kind of military glory. He fervently hopes that the knowledge of all George is to him will make him take great care of himself.

> It was terrible that man being killed next to you, but don't be afraid to tell me of such things. You see it is at night I fear with painful vividness. I have lost all sense I ever had of war being glorious, it is just unspeakably monstrous to me now.[6]

To this moving letter George replied that it was very bad about Uncle Guy. He wondered how he was killed, and said that 'this war is a dreadful show'. Surrounded by death, George none the less tried to give comfort, bravely exhorting 'dear Uncle Jim' to keep up his courage. He assured him, 'I take every care of myself that can decently be taken. And if I am going to stop a bullet, why should it be in a vital place?'

According to a fellow officer, George had a premonition that these were hollow words. A few hours later, sitting with other officers on a bank listening to instructions from their colonel, he did 'stop a bullet'. Shot through the head, his death was apparently immediate. A few days later Aubrey, Tennyson's son, wrote Peter a poignant letter giving him as many details of George's death as he had managed to collect together. He told him that the men had taken much trouble with George's grave, and planted it with violets. He went on:

> When I got here, I was told by an officer who has been in the battalion for some years that he had never known any officer . . . who after so short a time had won the love of everyone, so much so that all his brother officers felt when he was killed that . . . they had lost one of their best friends. As regards myself I don't think anyone can ever take his place, as there is no one whom I have ever loved more.[7]

When the news arrived in London, utterly convulsed in his wretched-ness, Barrie wailed to Mary Hodgson, 'This dreadful war will get them all in the end!' He sent word to Peter at Sheerness. With stark simplicity the telegram read: GEORGE IS KILLED. HOPE YOU CAN COME TO ME.

It wasn't George alone who had foreseen his death. Barrie, too, had had a premonition, and said later that he knew George was killed before he heard the news.

Peter responded to Barrie's desperate plea without delay, and asked for compassionate leave. There was little, however, that he or his three surviving brothers – all back at Campden Hill Square by the end of the week – could do for Barrie. Plunged into blackness, he paced up and down, or wrote letters telling of the misery that had befallen them. To his friend Charles Turley Smith, who had written commiserating with him, Barrie wrote back in a flat tone, 'Just a word to say what you will like to know, that George was killed instantaneously. It was a night attack. I had a letter from him two days after I knew he was dead. This is now the common lot.'[8]

Peter would later say of George that it wasn't only the awful fact that their older brother had died, but that with his death something irre-placeable had gone out of all their lives. He described George as having in him so much that was good, without being in any way prim. He said he was fun and so tolerant, and would have been 'such value always'. Aside from his own sorrow, Peter felt pity and compassion for Barrie, prostrated with grief for the young man 'whom he had loved with such a deep, strange, complicated, increasing love, and who as he knew well would have been such a pillar to him . . .'

Peter said that George had combined the famed du Maurier charm with

a good leavening of sound, kind, sterling Davies in him too. I think he had that simplicity which J. M. B. . . . saw in Arthur, and which . . . I dimly perceive to be perhaps the best of all characteristics . . . This much is certain, that when he died, some essential virtue went out of us as a family. The combination of George, who as eldest brother exercised a sort of constitutional, tacitly accepted authority over us . . . with the infinitely generous, fanciful, solicitous, hopelessly unau-thoritative J. M. B. was a good one and would have kept us together . . . As it was circumstances were too much for J. M. B. left solitary, as well as for us, and we became gradually . . . individuals with little of the invaluable, cohesive strength of the united family.[9]

Not long before Barrie had written in a notebook,

The Last Cricket Match One or two days before war declared – my anxiety and premonition – boys gaily playing cricket at Auch, seen from my window – I know they're to suffer – I see them dropping out one by one, fewer and fewer.[10]

A week after George's death, *Rosy Rapture* opened with *The New Word* as a curtain raiser, but the author wasn't present at the first night. He had taken Michael and Nico to stay with the Herberts, believing that at Wrest Park his and the boys' pain would be counterbalanced by the Herberts' quietly practical and constructive response to the war-inflicted suffering. Any respite for Barrie was to be shortlived.

Charles Frohman was due to travel over from the United States for his spring visit, and Barrie had asked him to bring forward his departure to the beginning rather than the end of May. *Rosy Rapture* was doing badly, and even with a number of revisions the response had not improved. Barrie found it hard to accept that something had been a failure, and that his accustomed rapport with his audience might have broken down. He was convinced that the remarkable Frohman was the only person who could turn the play around.

Ignoring the warnings of his American friends about German U-boats, on 1st May the obliging Frohman boarded ship for Britain. Six days later, within sight of the Irish coast, a German submarine torpedoed the *Lusitania*. Heeling over immediately, the great ship plunged to the bottom of the sea in barely twenty minutes with the loss of over eight hundred of the eighteen hundred passengers on board. The next day Frohman's body was washed ashore. Apparently unruffled at the prospect of death, he had refused a place on one of the few lifeboats. Echoing the famous phrase from *Peter Pan*, Frohman is reputed to have said, 'Why fear death? It is the most beautiful adventure in life.'

His body was taken back to America, where he was widely mourned. Memorial services commemorated the reckless and joyful abandon with which this utterly focused, odd and unceasingly good-natured man had devoted himself to bringing hundreds of plays and players to the attention of the public. Entirely modest, his understanding of his contribution was none the less revealed in the response to his friend Paul Potter, who once picked up a theatrical paper and said, 'Shall I read you the theatrical news?'

'No,' said Frohman. 'I *make* theatrical news.'

When once asked how he would like to be remembered he said, 'He gave Peter Pan to the world . . . it is enough for any man.'

In Frohman Barrie had lost not only one of his most significant friends, but also the man who, above all others, had asserted his faith in his art.

It is not an exaggeration to say that without Frohman's instinct, generosity and willingness to gamble, Barrie's masterpiece, *Peter Pan*, would never have reached the stage. In writing a tribute to his friend, Barrie praised Frohman's great 'humour and charity and gentle chivalry, and his most romantic mind'. Barrie was painfully aware that another vital and sustaining element in his life had disappeared.

22

'Something in ourselves . . .'

At the end of May 1915, Asquith's Liberal government gave way under trenchant criticism of such failures as the shortage of muni- tions and the position in Gallipoli. A coalition government was formed. Bron Herbert resigned his parliamentary secretaryship and joined the Royal Flying Corps. Less than three months later he would ask Barrie to consider stepping in and helping his sister, Nan, run the hospital. Still restless, grieving and missing George terribly, Barrie agreed, and in mid- September wrote to Bron:

> I am very . . . proud that you have sufficient faith in me to make this proposal . . . I have seen enough of the soldier's life in city hospitals to know how fortunate those are who have a Wrest to go to . . . However stupidly I may do it I feel sure I won't enrage Nan as a Committee would do.[1]

He also launched into another project. For some time he had followed the reports of French children, wounded, separated from their parents or orphaned, and discussed with Elizabeth Lucas (E. V.'s wife) a plan he had in mind. He asked if she would go out to France, and set up, at his expense, some kind of refuge-hospital for these youngest casualties of the war. Elizabeth willingly agreed to Barrie's scheme and set off almost imme- diately, with a letter from Sir Edward Grey to the British ambassador, and an initial two thousand pounds from Barrie.

With help from the Society of Friends Elizabeth was offered the château Bettancourt, previously occupied by the Germans. The château and its gardens were neglected and chaotic, but after a period of stren- uous work Elizabeth set up a clearing-house and hospital for the chil- dren of Rheims and its environs. With only a matron, one nurse, a small group of untrained girls from the Barrie-Lucas circle drafted in to help, plus the gentle Charles Turley Smith as orderly, Elizabeth's and Barrie's refuge was quickly established. Singly or in groups, the traumatised and wounded children began to arrive, and soon there would be as many as sixty in the château at any one time. By late July Barrie was making his first visit. He talked with the children and the staff, listened, did his best to entertain, and a few weeks later wrote to Nan Herbert,

> I went to France to see that little hospital I told you of. It is in a desolate château . . . and is on the Marne. The guns are to be heard in the distance all day, and I was usually wakened in the morning by aeroplanes. In the stillness they fill the world with sound. The patients are women and children, either extremely wounded or destitute and ill. One little boy had his leg blown off by a shell . . . The villages in that part are in a dreadful condition, some of them about one house standing in fifity . . . There are thousands of Germans buried thereabout, and a grim notice has been issued on the Marne ordering all people to chain up their dogs at night. The dogs have taken to wandering and digging.[2]

Back in England he wrote telling Elizabeth Lucas how touching and impressive it had been to see her huge efforts at Bettancourt. He told her 'what a difference knowing you has made to my life . . . [it] would have been so much gloomier without you. I would go off feeling happy, really happy if I could be sure that all was well at Bettancourt.'

A few days later, in early August, he set off with Michael and Nico for their annual fishing holiday in Scotland. This year they were such a small party there seemed little point in taking a house and instead Barrie booked them into a hotel at Glengarry, Inverness-shire. From there he told a friend,

> It has been rather grim in Scotland this year. The highlands in many glens are as bare of population owing to this war as if this were the month before Creation. I have just Michael and Nico with me and they feel it too, but they climb about, fishing mostly, and if you were to search the bogs you would find me in one of them loaded with waterproofs and ginger beer . . .[3]

The war dragged on, and Barrie struggled to manage his increasing horror of it and virtually everything it represented. As always, he kept himself occupied. He looked after and worried over the Davies boys, carried on his hospital visiting, at Wrest and in London, saw friends and tried to cope with his increasingly large correspondence. At various times over the past few years he had enlisted Elizabeth Lucas's aid in small amounts of secretarial work for him, but she was no longer available to help.

Barrie's fame meant that, for years, apart from a large number of admiring letters he had regularly received others making requests of one kind or another, from pleas for money to literary assistance and favours. Striving to manage his correspondence he was less and less successful. The loyal Gilmour still helped with his tax and investments, and although Barrie's plays were performed consistently and brought him large sums throughout the war, his everyday literary affairs were slowly but steadily descending into confusion.

For the duration of the war, while his notebooks were slimmer than previously, he continued writing. Dissatisfied with much of this production, he did nothing with it and wrote to a friend, 'I either work too much or not at all, and of late I've been slinging off heaven knows how many short plays, once I think six in a week.' A number of these pieces, one-act plays for the war effort or dramatists' appeals, were performed. Three of the full-length works, *A Kiss for Cinderella, The Old Lady Shows her Medals* and *Dear Brutus,* were great successes.

When he had finished *A Kiss for Cinderella* Barrie gave the manuscript to Gerald du Maurier, who had added the role of distinguished producer to his acclaim as an actor. Gerald and Barrie's relationship was one of critical mutual respect, and was never particularly easy. After demanding from Barrie, and achieving, many changes to the text, Gerald took it on and opened the play in March 1916.

During the spring, interspersed with visits to Wrest Park, Barrie also watched a star-filled cast – with contemporary luminaries such as Arthur Bourchier, John Drinkwater, Gerald du Maurier, Vesta Tilley, Ellen Terry, Hilda Trevelyan and Gladys Cooper – rehearse a revival of *The Admirable Crichton*. Even during the war, when his work was staged Barrie persisted in his old habit of sitting in on rehearsals. *Crichton* was once again a great success and remained on the London stage for over seven months. In the midst of all this theatre, a week before the Battle of Jutland, and the sinking of the *Hampshire* with Kitchener aboard, Peter Davies left to join George's old regiment at the Western Front. Now a tall, thin, increasingly quiet and withdrawn young man, Peter was capable of silences almost as lengthy as Barrie's own. Communication between them had become more strained of late, leading Barrie to fret even more over Peter's well-being on the battlefields of France.

That autumn there followed what appeared to Barrie as a never-ending catalogue of death. His nephew Charlie was killed on the very first day of the Battle of the Somme, though the family wouldn't know for certain for nearly four months. Leaving a young wife and three children, Alick's eldest son had become a journalist, gone against Barrie's wishes and married the girl of his choice. According to the family, although Barrie helped financially, albeit erratically, having little to do with them, from a distance he continued in his urge to control. The war next took E. V. Lucas's brother, Percy, then Charlie Barrie's younger brother and Gilmour's eldest son. Meanwhile, Barrie was sometimes overwhelmed by anxiety and unease at the thought of Peter on the battlefields of the Somme. In all, there would be over half a million British deaths.

That September the last of the boys left prep school and Barrie said his farewells as Nico joined Michael at Eton. More robust than Michael, with a cheerful disposition, Nico settled in well at the school from the start. With his departure, however, one of the most intense and emotionally satisfying periods of Barrie's life came to an end. Since their mother's death six years earlier, Barrie had taken responsibility for almost every detail of the Davies boys' lives, until one by one they left him for the adulthood of which he was so very much afraid.

Shortly before Nico's departure for Eton, a telegram reached Barrie from Nan Herbert at Wrest Park. Fire had broken out in one of the wings, and though two hundred men were courageously helped to safety, and no lives lost, the damage to the house was serious. Bron Herbert was about to leave for France in command of a squadron, and together with Barrie he decided that reconstruction of the house would be too lengthy and expensive. The staff wanted to carry on, so did an exhausted Nan, but Bron and Barrie believed it was impossible. Bron Herbert made the decision to sell up his family house, together with all its contents, and then he left for France.

A few days later, after two months on the Somme, and the worst slaughter of the war, Peter was invalided back to hospital in England suffering from shell-shock and eczema. Leaving hospital, he went to live quietly at Campden Hill Square for several months, where he remained very withdrawn and difficult to reach. Peter's experience was now utterly different from Barrie's and he must literally have felt in a world apart. Barrie decided that in order to assist his recovery the younger boys should come to him at Adelphi Terrace after their holidays, rather than returning to Campden Hill Square.

At Bettancourt, meanwhile, worn out and ill from unceasing work, Elizabeth Lucas was no longer able to carry on. Barrie was immensely disappointed, but understood that while his friend could do no more there were now other organisations that would take over their work. They agreed that the hospital would have to close down. More bad news. On 4th November Bron Herbert was reported missing, last heard of flying over the German lines. A month later, when his death was officially announced, Barrie celebrated his life in an obituary in *The Times*, whilst privately grieving that another close friend, a good and kind man, had been lost to this terrible war.

A few weeks later Barrie was introduced by Kathleen Scott to a young New Zealander, Bernard Freyberg, who was recovering from battle wounds in hospital. Originally a dentist, Freyberg would be mentioned six times in dispatches before the war had ended. His almost absurd valour had already won him a VC and a DSO, and he later became the youngest brigadier-general in the British army. The flattery and fame this brought him appeared to have no effect on his charm and simplicity of character. A friend wrote in her diary, 'I love his lack of humour, his frank passion for fighting . . . There is a sort of directness, bluntness, and inter-personal finesse . . . there is a distinct grimness about him at times . . .' Enjoying Freyberg's open avowal of intent to lead, she commented, 'All this sounds melodramatic and vainglorious, but it is completely inoffensive, so unself-conscious and simple is he in his complete self-confidence.'[4]

After commanding the Allied Forces in Crete before the German invasion in the Second World War, Freyberg became Governor of New Zealand in 1946. Barrie was quickly drawn to this young man, who, like Captain Scott before him, felt great admiration for the playwright, so utterly different from himself. From their first meeting the liking, admiration and eventually protectiveness these two felt for one another, despite thirty years' difference in age, would continue for the rest of Barrie's life.

Of the many short plays Barrie wrote during the war, that autumn he only produced one. *The Fight for Mr Lapraik* is a Jekyll-and-Hyde piece revealing something of the darkness in his mind at the time. It is also an insight into one of the most consistent and troubling themes running through his life. Inspired by a nightmare he had recorded in his note-book, the story is a chilling study of the blackness and horror created by a divided mind. In the play a ghostly young Mr Lapraik returns to his elderly wife. When asked who the man is who poses as her husband, he replies, 'He is what I have grown into, my dear, I am what he used to be.' He tells her that he had been woken by 'something bending over me, pushing me stealthily . . . I know that the degenerate thing I had become was trying to push me out of this shell that is called me, and to take my place.' In Barrie's nightmare, at this point he runs to his long-dead mother for protection but to no avail, for the next day his two selves have reversed their roles.

Characteristically turning all personal material to good use, he trans-formed his nightmare into something yet unimagined for the stage. In this play Barrie expanded on one of the most important themes concerning, even obsessing him, in an exploration and a portrayal of the human psyche. Needless to say, *The Fight for Mr Lapraik* or *The House of Fear*, was far too disturbing for any theatre to consider staging at the time.

In early January 1917, while staying in Brighton with Michael and Nico for the end of their Christmas holiday, Barrie worked on *The Old Lady Shows her Medals*. Before they could return to Eton, first Nico then Michael caught chicken pox. At Campden Hill Square Barrie devoted himself to their care as much as any protective mother. The death of the boys' parents, and now the war, first taking their brother, then continuing unrelentingly to consume family and friends, had heightened Barrie's sense that death was never far away. Easily alarmed, his growing fear that Michael would soon have to go into the army sometimes overwhelmed him.

At seventeen Michael was now a gracious, quick and intelligent young man, capable of the dark moods that provoked Barrie to call him 'Michael, the dark and dour and impenetrable'. Over the years at Eton he had learnt to conceal his feelings, and as protection had developed a veneer of imperturbability. His du Maurier looks and charm, his reserve, his highly developed sense of wit and his unconcern about being popular conspired to make his friendship all the more desirable. Although a friend later said he was 'wholly un-Etonian', Michael was in Pop, that most select of clubs, and had become one of the swells of the school.

Neil and Tintinabulum, a highly personal story written at around this time, describes Barrie's sense of loss at a child's movement towards adulthood. The story is a kind of elegy to Michael's boyhood, and his withdrawal from the unselfconscious childish attachment to his 'guardian'. The young Neil grows into Tintinabulum.

> I never know him quite so well again. He seems henceforth to be running to me on a road that is moving still more rapidly in the opposite direction . . . He [Tintinabulum] had to refashion himself on a harsher model, and he set his teeth and won, blaming me for not having broken to him the ugly world we can make it . . . By that time my visits [to Eton] were being suffered rather than acclaimed. It was done with an exquisite politeness certainly . . . Gladly, for his sake I knew my place.[5]

The author says that this is written down so that he can see more clearly whether Tintinabulum 'really does like me still. That he should do so is very important to me as he recedes farther from my ken down that road which hurries him from me.' Extending the idea of a child being lost to a parent as it grows to adulthood he continues, 'he no longer needs me,

of course, as Neil did, and he will go on needing me less. When I think
of Neil I know that those were the last days in which I was alive.'

Barrie had recently been told that his ex-wife, Mary, was alone, impoverished and working in a hospital depot rolling bandages and packing
medical supplies. Mary had married her lover, Gilbert Cannan, in 1910,
and for the next six years they were sometimes at the centre, sometimes
more on the periphery of the avant-garde literary and artistic circles of
the period. Cannan had been taken up by Ottoline Morrell and Bertrand
Russell, and was a friend of luminaries such as Lawrence, Compton
Mackenzie and John Middleton Murry. Working enormously hard to
make his name through translating, and writing novels and poetry, he
was constantly short of money. The great literary promise some thought
he showed was epitomised in an article by Henry James, in 1914. James
singled out four young authors for praise: Hugh Walpole, Compton
Mackenzie, D. H. Lawrence and Gilbert Cannan, and compared them to
Conrad, Galsworthy, Wells and Bennett.

Cannan and Mary had remained childless, and Cannan became increasingly claustrophobic at what he now interpreted as Mary's mothering.
Having first seduced Mary's maid, he then fled from both his wife and
the pregnant maid to a third woman. His growing periods of mental
instability were eventually to overwhelm him, and in 1917 Kathleen Scott
told Barrie that he had already spent short periods in mental homes. In
1923 Cannan was finally placed in an asylum, where he was to remain
until he died, a much calmer man, in 1952.

Knowing that Mary was too proud to ask for help, Barrie wrote to
her in March 1917.

My dear Mary
    It would be silly of us not to meet, and indeed I wanted to go
to you all day yesterday. I thought perhaps you would rather come
here, and of course whichever you prefer is what I prefer, but that
is your only option as I mean to see you whether the idea scares
you or not. Painful in a way the first time but surely it need not
be so afterwards. How about coming here on Wednesday to lunch
at 1.30? . . . All personal troubles outside the war seem so small
nowadays. But just one thing I should like to say, because no one
can know it as well as I, that never in this world could a young
literary man have started with better chances than Mr Cannan when
he had you . . .
    Yours affectionately
    J.M.B.[6]

There is no record of their meeting, but according to Elizabeth Lucas Mary misunderstood Barrie's intention and thought he was once again offering her marriage. Barrie believed that almost invariably people repeated their mistakes, and knowing that it was he who had blighted Mary's life, he didn't make the mistake of thinking there was any possibility of going back. As a result of their meeting, he arranged for an annual allowance to be paid to Mary. For much of the rest of her life, she lived in France, eventually dying in Biarritz in 1950. Barrie family legend has it that he also paid for her to keep a little apartment in London to which she briefly returned each year.

At the end of Easter 1917 Peter was judged fit to return to the horrors of the Somme, and early that summer Barrie went to France to find George's grave. He asked Thomas Hardy to accompany him, but Hardy replied, 'I have come to the conclusion that old men cannot be young men, and that I must content myself with the past battles of our country if I want to feel military.' Having received official permission, and instructions for finding the grave, Barrie set off alone. On the boat crossing the Channel he met the architect Edwin Lutyens, also on his way to France (with fellow architect Herbert Baker and the director of the Tate Gallery, Charles Aitken), to advise on military cemeteries and their memorials. Lutyens and Barrie had been friendly for several years and Barrie now joined their party. They stayed at a château near Montreuil, from where Barrie set out with a military escort in and out of the lines to find George's grave. On his return he semed unable to write or speak about the experience. In a letter to his wife, Lutyens, however, tried to express his own distress:

> What humanity can endure and suffer is beyond belief. The battlefields − the obliteration of all human endeavour and achievement and the human achievement of destruction is bettered by the poppies and wild flowers that are as friendly to an exploded shell as they are to the leg of a garden seat in Surrey.[7]

After his return from France, Barrie moved from his flat on the third floor to another much larger one on the fourth and top floor of Adelphi Terrace. The flat had recently been vacated by the American Joseph Pennell and his wife, the adversarial biographers of the painter James McNeill Whistler. The new flat required a fair degree of remodelling and redecoration, and Lutyens persuaded Barrie to let him do the work. From the largest room, which Barrie chose for his study because of the handsome inglenook fireplace Lutyens designed for him, there were even more striking views over the Thames than in the flat downstairs. In October Barrie wrote to Elizabeth Lucas telling her of

> the wonderful view of the river, especially when the searchlights sweep the sky. Hardy was staying with me lately and he and Wells and Shaw and Arnold Bennett and I sat one night watching the strange spectacle. It is an exposed spot, tho', and after air raids I always find shrapnel on the roof.[8]

On more than one occasion that winter, after joining Barrie for dinner, Lutyens and William Nicholson watched with him from the great heights of the Adelphi Terrace roof the searchlights criss-crossing a sky turned red by the burning Zeppelins.

Barrie quickly became very attached to his prodigious Lutyens fireplace and wrote to Elizabeth early in 1918,

> I emerge out of my big chimney to write to you. I was sitting there with a Charlotte Brontë (when I read her I mostly think of Emily) and there was a gale on the roof; it is probably not windy at all down below but with the slightest provocation the chimneys overhead in their whirring cowls go as devilish as the witches in *Macbeth*, whom they also resemble in appearance. I hope, however, it is a sufficiently dirty night as the sailors say to keep the air raiders at bay.
>
> My fire behaves handsomely now and the logs – three footers – do go a-roaring; the smell of them ushers you into the room like a nice farm-hand . . . Sometimes as I sit there I have a queer feeling that I am downstairs . . . and this is somewhere else up here. Downstairs seems to belong to those Victorian days before the war and it is queer to have lived in them without knowing what was coming.[9]

In September 1917, Jack married his young fiancée, Geraldine Gibb, the daughter of a Scottish banker. The first of the Davies boys to marry, Jack had upset Barrie by becoming engaged without asking his advice or permission. At the same time Geraldine's mother was concerned at the thought of having such a strange man as Barrie connected to their family. The young couple had reluctantly waited, because Jack wanted to secure the allowance from Barrie he knew might be withheld if he contravened his wishes. Geraldine felt no particular sympathy for Barrie, and it would take some years before she, her husband and Barrie were able to accommodate themselves more successfully to one another.

That autumn Barrie wrote Kathleen Scott a series of letters in which he proposed himself, instead of Lord Knutsford, as her son Peter's guardian in case of her death. Lord Knutsford, who also wrote making his case, was a widower whose adult daughter lived at home. He had known Peter Scott since the boy's earliest childhood, and was an eccentric and sympathetic figure. The image of these two ageing men not so subtly battling it out for the guardianship of this delightful seven-year-old boy is both a poignant and amusing one. As it turned out, with good sense and tact Kathleen chose Lord Knutsford as Peter's guardian, while maintaining her friendship with Barrie.

Early in 1917, Alfred Mason had arrived to stay with Barrie for a week. Barrie became ill with bronchitis then pneumonia, and was eventually taken off to Douglas Shield's nursing home to recover. But before he became significantly ill, he confided to Mason his fear that he was drained of all new ideas. Mason suggested Barrie look out the outline of the story he had described to him years before. Called *The Second Chance*, it described a group of people who are granted the second chance in life they long for, only to decide that for most of us there is no such thing. Barrie searched out his notes and read them to Mason. Before he had finished, they both knew he had found his new play. And in hardly more than a fortnight he had written the first draft of what would become *Dear Brutus*.

Dear Brutus – the title taken from *Julius Caesar* – charts the journey of several characters who each long for that second chance. Barrie would say in a later edition of his plays that his subject was the struggle between the darkness and the light; the struggle between the dark of illusion and self-delusion and the light of self-knowledge and understanding. Gerald du Maurier directed and took the lead part, Will Dearth. He evoked Dearth's grief, tinged with a final hint of optimism, with such pathos that it came to be regarded as one of the greatest roles of his career.

On Midsummer's Eve the eight members of a house party enter an enchanted wood, where they each find their wishes have been fulfilled. With echoes of *A Midsummer Night's Dream*, *Julius Caesar* and *The Tempest* running throughout the play, via each of his protagonists Barrie mercilessly comments on himself. Purdie, for example, spends much of his time paying court to other women and not his wife. The figure symbolising Barrie is, however, as much as any of the others, Lob, the mischievous, elusive, silent Puck-like master of ceremonies, who sends his guests into the wood of self-knowledge. Then there is Will Dearth, the childless man whose marriage is falling apart.

Purdie describes Lob as 'an old ruffian' but Dearth says that he is 'rather fond of him. Our lonely little host. Lob, I thank thee for that hour.' That hour was the fulfilment of his wish for a 'dream-child', the little girl whose heartbreaking final plea is one of the most memorable lines in the play.

> (She tries dutifully to count her hundred, but the wood grows dark and soon she is afraid again. She runs from tree to tree calling to her Daddy. We begin to lose her among the shadows.)
> Margaret (out of the impalpable that is carrying her away): Daddy, come back; I don't want to be a might-have-been.[10]

Dear Brutus, like Barrie's next full-length play, *Mary Rose*, returns in part to his Scottish roots and folklore traditions, where people are transformed by enchanted places. What this enchanted place, Lob's wood, really does is to make the characters look into themselves, and here lies the potential for change. The ultimate message of the play, however, is that for most of us, no matter how many chances we are given, the challenge of altering ourselves is beyond us. Thus, the compulsive philanderer, Purdie, admits to Joanna,

> It isn't accident that shapes our lives.
> Joanna: No, it's Fate.
> Purdie: . . . It's not Fate, Joanna, Fate is something outside us. What really plays the dickens with us is something in ourselves. Something that makes us go on doing the same sort of fool things, however many chances we get . . . Something we are born with . . . I haven't the stuff in me to take warning. My whole being is corroded. Shakespeare knew what he was talking about –
>
> > The fault, Dear Brutus, is not in our stars,
> > But in ourselves, that we are underlings.[11]

And yet, Barrie's final note of optimism has Will Dearth and his wife making a gentle and tentative reconciliation

Just as the theatres were never short of audiences, craving distraction from the struggle and anxiety of daily life in wartime, so Barrie continued to socialise. In December, for example, after an early-morning air raid, he was at a dinner with literary friends: the Galsworthys, E. V. Lucas, the classicist Gilbert Murray with one of his daughters, H. W. Massingham and Joseph Conrad, now sixty and three years older than Barrie.

On the domestic front, a vexing question, which had rumbled on for years, was about to surface and finally reach its conclusion. Over the last few years Mary Hodgson's role at Campden Hill had changed from that

of the Davieses devoted nursemaid to their housekeeper. Deeply attached
to them as she was, her opinion of Barrie had never altered since those
early days in Kensington Gardens, when he had fought her for the boys'
allegiance. Each half of this odd and entirely mismatched couple was as
stubborn and possessive as the other. In addition, Mary's capacity for
unrestrained emotion had at times an almost manic quality to it. True to
Barrie's dictum, neither of them had really changed very much. Instead,
they were more confirmed in their habits of personality.

The Davieses, particularly Michael and Nico, for whom Mary was as
close to a mother as they possessed, would hear nothing said against her.
Whatever Barrie privately thought, he was not prepared to risk his reputation by voicing criticism of her in front of them. So it was that on
occasions when something might well have been said to curb Mary's
outbursts, Barrie did nothing. Equally there was no one there to curb
his own excesses of temperament. For years Mary had privately fumed
over what she saw as his lack of authority and overindulgence of the
Davieses, who were now only at Campden Hill on holiday or leave. With
little to do, Mary felt that her promise to Sylvia to care for her sons was
fulfilled, and in 1916 she handed Barrie her notice. He was unprepared,
and aware that no one could replace her in the lives of the two younger
boys, he asked her to stay on longer. But Mary's offer of resignation may
have set him thinking.

Over Christmas the following year, whether out of thoughtlessness or
as a tactical move to precipitate change, Barrie told Geraldine that she
and Jack should move into Campden Hill Square, where Geraldine would
take over the running of the house. This provoked a violent reaction from
Mary, whose possessiveness had made her refuse to speak to Jack's bride
at their wedding. For several weeks Mary's jealousy created enormous
emotional tension in the house. Eventually, after a series of dramatic incidents, Geraldine felt that nothing more could be done, and in great distress
decided that she and Jack must leave for a hotel. Having done so, that
night she was taken to a nursing home with a miscarriage. Knowing that
she was helpless to do anything about the strength of her emotions, Mary
blamed herself for what had happened and once again handed in her
notice. Peter, Michael and Nico tried to dissuade her, but she was adamant
that she must go. After more than twenty years of antipathy towards one
another, before Mary's departure she and Barrie both relented a little and
a rapprochement of sorts took place. Barrie wrote to Elizabeth Lucas,

I had begun to feel in my bones tho' that it was all too fine a flat
for me and that for my lonely purposes all I really needed was this
and the bedroom . . . However, the way has been cleared by troubles

at Campden Hill. Mary is going sometime in February. This means Michael and Nicholas making this their home, as my idea is to put caretakers into Campden Hill for a little and then store the furniture and dispose of the lease.[12]

With Mary Hodgson's departure a crucial stage in the boys' lives was over. At the conclusion of the school year of 1918 Michael was due to leave Eton, and Barrie's panic grew at the thought of his approaching enlistment. They decided that he would join most of his friends in the Scots Guards, and return to Eton after the summer to await his call-up to the army. At eighteen Michael had become a more restless and melancholic young man, whose aloofness and inscrutability Barrie was unable to comprehend. At the same time Michael was still very close to him, trusting his guardian, although now less consistently, with some of his deepest concerns. Barrie was in turn utterly devoted to Michael, whose tutor at Eton, Hugh Macnaghten, described him as probably the most intelligent and sensitive boy who had passed through the school in his time. Michael read much and wrote, co-editing the *Eton College Chronicle*; he was in Pop, and was also good at sports: this included membership of the Football XI. E. V. Lucas would write of him,

> He seemed to have everything at his feet, and one used to look at him and wonder what walk of life he would choose; but he gave few signs, being, for all his vivid interest in the moment, more in the world than of it, an elvish spectator rather than a participant.

Barrie's respect and admiration for this unusual boy was such that – however advisedly – he sought Michael's opinion as his chief literary counsel. Michael's rejection of an idea or a piece of writing meant that Barrie would almost invariably stop working on it. In the *Dedication to Peter Pan* – a crucial document, because so filled with overt and covert information – Barrie says that No. 4 (Michael) was,

> while still a schoolchild, the sternest of my critics. Anything he shook his head at I abandoned and conceivably the world had thus been deprived of masterpieces. There was for instance an unfortunate little tragedy which I liked until I foolishly told No. 4 its subject, when he frowned and said he had better have a look at it. He read it, and then, patting me on the back, as only he and No. 1 [George] could touch me, said, 'You know you can't do this sort of thing' ... Sometimes, however, No. 4 liked my efforts, and I walked in the azure that day when he returned *Dear Brutus* with the comment 'Not bad'.

In early November 1918, when Barrie set off with Gilmour for another visit to the Front, it was becoming clear that the war was nearing its close. Everyone seemed to know that Germany was about to collapse, and the companions were taken up and down the lines in a staff car. On Armistice night Barrie was in Paris. After dining with Kathleen Scott, then working in Paris, they went out into the streets, and were caught up in the celebrations as people danced and sang and cried out, 'C'est fini! C'est fini!' Michael would not have to go to war.

Despite his closeness to Barrie, Michael's increasing maturity meant that he was searching for more independence, more room to discover who he was and what he might be. Barrie, however, would never have much conception of emotional restraint. Michael suggested spending some time in Paris, or travelling, before going up to Oxford. But with Hugh Macnaghten's help Barrie dissuaded him from fulfilling his bid for independence. Michael's affection for Barrie always made it difficult for him to go against his wishes, and with mixed feelings he went up to Oxford in January 1919.

23

Cynthia and Michael

Barrie's renown meant that his postbag was now unmanageable, and in that last summer of the war he finally employed a secretary to help him overcome the mounting disorder of his correspondence. Lacking any shorthand or typing skills, Barrie's new assistant was by no means a conventional secretary. No matter, Barrie made it clear he intensely disliked the idea of 'efficiency', typewriters, shorthand and filing systems. With his life-long abhorrence of facts and all their relations, this was only to be expected. In keeping with this unorthodox approach Barrie's new secretary was not found through an advertisement, but at a dinner party of mutual aristocratic friends. On their first meeting Barrie had succeeded in making even this sophisticated young woman feel ill at ease, and in her diary, kept during the war years, Lady Cynthia Asquith would write: 'He destroyed my nerve for ages, so great a bore did he convince me of being. I could *not* make him smile . . . I was even reduced to commenting on objects on the table – luckily there were some red bananas.'[1]

Despite her feeling of utter ineffectualness Lady Cynthia had been struck by Barrie's 'sad, sunken eyes, the huge domed forehead, the mournful strangely deep – almost hoarse voice'. She felt his melancholy so strongly that it seemed 'a sadness which might have come from aeons of experience, or from the death of innumerable dreams'.

Meeting again, her impression was the same, but on their third meeting Lady Cynthia wrote in her diary that Barrie was

scarcely recognisable. For the first time I saw, not once, but repeatedly that famous smile, which irradiating his face, made you feel you had 'rung the bell'. I saw too that amusement and kindness . . . as well as sadness could look out of those seared, but strangely beautiful eyes . . . No longer did I want to go and drown myself. Not only did he amuse me and put me on the best of terms with myself, he had become a fellow of infinite jest. How could I have labelled him *shy*! He held the table.[2]

Barrie was at last more forthcoming, and on discovering that Lady Cynthia was looking for work, he told her he needed help with his papers and invited her to tea. Over the teacups he described how he would like her to deal with the large correspondence, exercise her discretion as to what needed answering or called for his opinion, and encourage him to bank his cheques. His secretary later found a large quantity of these stuffed into a drawer. From the moment he finished detailing her duties Barrie appeared to assume she had accepted the position.

Lady Cynthia Asquith was the third of seven children born to the 11th Earl and Countess of Wemyss. Growing up at the family's Gloucestershire seat, Stanway House, Cynthia's upbringing involved the typical English upper-class mix of the grand, the frugal and the austere. She would later write of her family's substance,

> Since we lived in a large house, amply staffed and almost continu-ally full of visitors, there must, according to present day standards, have been a considerable amount of money, yet I cannot remember a time when finance was not an ever-present worry to my parents. There was always talk of the necessity for 'retrenchment' – some-times even, desecrating thought, of the letting of Stanway, and in most ways we were brought up most unluxuriously.[3]

In 1910 Cynthia had married the former Prime Minister Asquith's eldest surviving son, Herbert – called Beb. With such differing political view-points, neither family had approved of the match. This was not helped by the fact that in the same year as the young couple's marriage the Prime Minister, Beb's father, had done his utmost to break the power of the House of Lords. Meanwhile, having trained as a barrister, Beb gave it up in order to write, proving unable to support his wife with the ease her family would have preferred. Money was a perpetual problem. At present Beb was away at the Front, and, combined with voluntary war work, Cynthia's financial contribution was vital.

Cynthia Asquith was one of the beauties of her day, but contempo-rary artists – Sargent, Tonks, Augustus John, McEvoy, Lavery and others – were hard put to capture her particular fascination. Her friend, the novelist L. P. Hartley, wrote after Cynthia's death, in 1960

> She was a complex personality, and the aspect of her that dazzled and enchanted was only one of many. To meet she seemed all fire and air ... She could think deeply, but she spoke lightly ... Laughter, above all laughter at herself, was outwardly an essential expression

of her spirit . . . Her face often showed that she had had more than her share of sorrows, but she made light of them . . .

One cannot think of her apart from her physical presence and the beauty . . . that was as various and unpredictable as her talk . . . You could truly say of her, in the words of Shakespeare, whose plays she knew almost by heart, that a star danced when she was born and went on dancing till she died.

But underlying these gossamer qualities . . . the mercurial emanations of her temperament, was a stable bedrock of character and a strong practical sense that made her . . . the most reliable and dependable of friends. To them she gave of herself, and her time, unstintingly.[4]

Some instinct perhaps told Barrie that in this young woman he had discovered something singular, and his offer of a very reasonable salary left her feeling unable to decline. Still uncertain, Cynthia wrote to her friend the critic Desmond MacCarthy for advice. He replied:

I am glad you have taken the situation . . . It seems to me . . . you like being adored – in that being no exception. A Dulcinea is a necessity to Barrie. Sentiment is only irritating to an onlooker, and when it is combined with playfulness and real kindness and springs from a cold detached heart, it is a delicate thing, delightful to receive. Barrie, as I read him, is part mother, part hero-worshipping maiden, part grandfather, and part pixie with no man in him at all. His genius is a coquettish thing, with just a drop of benevolent acid in it sometimes.[5]

For the most part an astute analysis, none the less, like so many of his contemporaries, MacCarthy also misreads, and therefore underestimates, the unsettling force of Barrie's brilliance, hidden rather too successfully under his humour as a 'coquettish thing'.

The secretarial arrangement began with Barrie vague as to the days and hours when he required Cynthia's help. However, under the pseudonym they conjured up for her, during the following nineteen years, as C. Greene, she would prove herself an indispensable right hand. Her intelligence, clear-sightedness and ability to organise soon proved not the least of Cynthia Asquith's attractions to her new employer. Beautiful, entertaining and well-connected, too, sandwiching her time with Barrie between her family and the demands of a hectic social calendar, Cynthia not only showed herself competent to deal with Barrie's chaotic administration, she also became adept at managing his fluctuating moods. In a short space of time she would realise, too, that despite Barrie's great fame and many friends he was really intimate with very few. Indeed he appeared to her rather lonely. Her own personality, and her young son, Michael, quickly endeared Cynthia to Barrie, and he was soon inviting her to join his guests at Adelphi Terrace suppers, or escorting her to his favourite restaurants.

While learning to manoeuvre the seesaw of Barrie's moods and silences, and his 'immensely strong personality', Cynthia would come to recognise that there were many occasions on which it was impossible to reach beyond what seemed 'an impenetrable shell of sadness and preoccupation'. When sunk in one of his silences, to Cynthia Barrie appeared 'all grey ashes and devastatingly depressing'. She astutely described him in a letter to her husband as 'an extraordinary plural personality'. She had perceived correctly that Barrie's self was a shifting thing. Nearing sixty, he was still no nearer to reconciling his many warring selves.

His new secretary noted that despite Barrie's haphazardness he was capable of an unerring shrewdness. After many years of familiarity with both the man and his work she would say,

> To my mind the essential Barrie is not sentimental. The real sentimentalist refuses to face hard facts. Barrie does not. For all his reputed 'softness', he is no escapist. He faces the most painful truths. The silver coating of his writing covers a core of hard truth, not to be found in the work of many self-styled realists, who for all their brilliant cynicism seem yet naively to suppose that by derision or scolding they can alter human nature.[6]

Cynthia asks what could be more realist than the message of *Dear Brutus*, where no matter a person's chances and resolves they cannot escape their own nature. Far from finding Barrie the embodiment of his great creation Peter Pan – who refused to grow up – with typical perception and understanding Cynthia thought him 'more than old, in fact I don't know whether he was ever a boy'. The 'poignant haunting little figure' intrigued her as much as she intrigued Barrie, and their relationship would soon recast itself from one of business to one of complex friendship. A friendship in which Barrie would come to depend upon Cynthia more and more, and she, too, in less obvious ways would also rely upon him.

One evening Barrie kept her highly amused while he acted out passages from a typescript he had from a publisher, who described it as the 'unaided' work of a girl of nine. The sparkling and misspelt view of 'High Life', and the adventures of Ethel Monticue and her admirer, Mr Salteena, tell how King Edward appears 'rather sumshiously in a small but costly crown and slips away to tuck into ices'. And Mr Salteena grows 'jellus' of his successful rival Bernard Clark, 'a rather presumshious man'. In addition Mr Salteena is 'fond of digging in the garden and I am parshal to ladies – I suppose it's my nature. I am not quite a gentleman but you would hardly notice and it can't be helped anyhow.'

Barrie found the little book so amusing he agreed to write a preface for it. When Daisy Ashford's *The Young Visitors* duly came out that May, its huge success became a considerable trouble to Barrie when both letters and children's manuscripts poured in to Adelphi Terrace. No matter what he and his secretary did to contradict the idea, there were always many who believed that it was Barrie himself who had written Daisy Ashford's little book.

That year his fame became even more widespread when one of Hollywood's most famous directors, Cecil B. De Mille, made a film of *The Admirable Crichton*. De Mille's film, *Male and Female* (Barrie hated the name), had as its female star Gloria Swanson, one of the most sought-after Hollywood actresses of the time. This exposure to Hollywood was, however, by no means Barrie's first encounter with the silver screen. As early as 1912 he was writing to his agent, Golding Bright, about a Mr Pinker offering him '£2000 in advance of royalties for P Pan in cinematograph. This can't be, but it has struck me since – what about certain of my other things? Suppose you communicate with him.'[7] When we recall that today the value of this offer is worth approximately fifty times that amount, it was a large sum. By 1918 Barrie was writing to Bright, 'As for filming *Sentimental Tommy* and *Tommy and Grizel* . . . only a big offer would tempt me, but if one is made I'd consider it.' Clearly a large enough offer was eventually made, for in 1921 *Sentimental Tommy* was filmed by Paramount. Throughout the twenties and into the thirties Barrie's works were regularly being adapted for film, starring some of the screen's most celebrated stars. He complained 'I get grand cables for a film play from Mary Pickford', and in 1930, for example, Gary Cooper played the title role in the film of *The Old Lady Shows her Medals*, called *Medals*. In all, from the first silent production of *The Little Minister* in 1915, during Barrie's lifetime there were fourteen screen adaptations of his work. These continued after his death up to the present day, with the most recent an adaptation of *Peter Pan* made in 2003. As this book goes to print a film adaptation of his life, *Finding Neverland*, is on release.

In 1918 Barrie had written to Bright, 'P Pan film I'm not having done at present. Was offered £20,000 in Paris the other day, advance sum!' At the end of 1920 he had written to Maude Adams in the States revealing his clear perception that what theatre and film could achieve must not be confused with one another. He sent her

> my idea of how Peter Pan might be filmed . . . I think it's only worth doing if one can have the many things shown that can't be done on the stage, for we may be sure that what *can* be done on the stage can be done much better than on the screen.[8]

The film that was eventually made in 1924 didn't use Barrie's carefully crafted 15,000-word scenario. Excited by the possibilities of projecting his play still further into the world of illusion, through a medium he understood to have such imaginative power, with customary thoroughness Barrie's scenario had

> all the sub-titles, and a mass of fresh visual detail which, to anyone but a film producer and his attendant experts, must surely have seemed like a gift from Heaven. It's authentic, it comes from the one and only source of the saga, who took enormous trouble over it, and never forgot for a moment the special medium for which it was meant.[9]

But in its wisdom Hollywood rejected this scenario in favour of simply filming the play, thereby failing to make the crucial adjustments that Barrie had appreciated were necessary. His disillusioned comment about Hollywood's *Peter Pan* – 'It is only repeating what is done on the stage . . . and the only reason for a film should be that it does the things the stage can't do' – echoed precisely what he had said to Maude Adams should not happen.

In addition to the huge promotion of Barrie's name through film, in his lifetime his plays and novels were translated and performed in countries across the world. At different times he could write to Bright: 'All right they can adapt *Half an Hour* to the French stage if they wish to and you can guard against its being properly produced'; 'All right about *Quality Street* in Yugoslavia and *Dear Brutus* in Holland'; '*The Old Lady* at the Comédie Française is very interesting'; 'Yes, I think that's an excellent idea about Charles Laughton for Crichton.'

In the summer of 1919 Cynthia left London for a few months. Barrie was tetchy at her departure. Although she continued with a small amount of work, he must, for a time, manage largely without her help. Just as importantly, while Cynthia awaited the birth of another child Barrie had to do without her company. Cynthia and Beb had been lent a friend's house in Suffolk, and in one of the many – sometimes daily – letters that passed between Barrie and his secretary he told her that 'the Oxford term ends in about a week and unyokes Michael, but he won't be here long if he can get off on a contemplated reading party. He will be 19 then (everything seems to be going wrong with me).'

Struggle though he did to overcome them, Barrie's conflicts found little accommodation; despite the great contribution he made in his art, he remained absorbed by the idea that it was a lamentable thing to grow up. He was torn. The quintessence of his understanding was represented in *Peter Pan*, where on the one hand he understood and respected aspects of time, while on the other hand he abhorred it and was terrified.

Cynthia appreciated the sense of isolation she understood Barrie felt, and invited him to stay with them in Suffolk. Barrie's reply was telling.

> I don't suppose I shall be able to get down. I want to come but I shd have done it before Michael got back. They shrink, these boys, from going anywhere, the death of their parents is really at the root of it, and down in my soul I know myself to be so poor a substitute that I try to make some sort of amends by hanging on here when there is any chance of my being a little use to them. Even in admitting this I am saying more to you than I do to most.[10]

It is hard to believe Barrie managed to deceive himself that this was true. The fact was, he wished it were. Neither Michael nor his cheerful younger brother shrank from seeing people, and neither of them had any shortage of friends or invitations. More to the point, Michael was reaching an age when Barrie's possessiveness was becoming a burden. In confirmation of this, when Michael brought friends back to Adelphi Terrace it was rarely a success. The fierceness of Barrie's love and his high expectations weighed upon Michael, leaving him with a sense of responsibility he may well have felt unable to fulfil. Beyond Adelphi Terrace his life was, though, becoming his own, and he began to discover other social circles than those in which Barrie moved. Michael stayed, for example, at the literary socialite Ottoline Morrell's Garsington Manor, where her Bloomsburyite friends, such as Dora Carrington and her lover Lytton Strachey, thought highly of this obviously gifted young man.

During the summer, a problem troubling Barrie for some time reached a point of crisis. A small lump that had developed on his right hand became painful, leaving his dreadful writing more illegible than ever. Not only his right hand but now his whole right arm was excruciatingly painful and he was unable to use his hand at all. In the midst of a renewed burst of activity, he desperately wanted to write the play that was now falling into scenes and acts. The only solution was for him to write with his left hand.

His anxiety that this might impede the recent flow of ideas proved unfounded. When a child Barrie had naturally been left-handed, and as he progressed with his new play, although at first the writing was uneven, he discovered it wasn't difficult. Indeed, to the great relief of his correspondents his writing quickly became far more legible.

Although he underwent treatment that autumn, the result of which is uncertain, Barrie continued to write mostly with his left hand for the rest of his life. He soon voiced the idea that the writing from his two hands emerged from different people, the left-handed one more sinister than the right. Talking about the other, left-handed person, in his typically indirect way, gave him the opportunity of discussing himself at some length, something he had never indulged in before. Through McConnachie, as he dubbed his alter ego, Barrie did reveal more, but he also used this new form of expression to obscure and tell riddles with as much spirit as he ever had before. Anyone who believed that through McConnachie they might gain more insight into the pathways of Barrie's mind was frequently mistaken. It was always dangerous to take him too literally.

When Michael returned from a trip to Paris with friends he found Barrie hard at work on his new play, to be called *Mary Rose*. His first thoughts on its theme had been taken down as long ago as 1892: 'Play – The haunted House – on all ghosts really mothers come back to see their children.' In *The Little White Bird* he had expanded this to 'the only ghosts, I believe, who creep into this world, are dead young mothers, returned to see how their children fare'. Writing to his friend Quiller-Couch in 1906, he said he was convinced that 'the return from the dead is a strong dramatic motive'. In another letter to Quiller-Couch, in 1911, Barrie developed his ideas further and said that 'No one should come back, however much he was loved.' During the summer holiday of 1912, at Amhuinnsuidhe Castle in the Outer Hebrides, while fishing near Loch Voshimid Barrie had pointed out to Nico a tiny island. Recalling something he had put in his notebook, he described it as the island that 'likes to be visited', and said that people vanished from such islands. Years later they would suddenly reappear, and while they remained exactly the same as on the day of their disappearance, in the intervening years everyone else had grown old.

Barrie's notebook for 1905 has '[James] Hogg's *Queen's Wake* a sort of Rip Van Winkle' jotted down. In the 'Kilmeny' section of Hogg's poem, the queen falls asleep in the woods and disappears for seven years. After briefly returning, she once more disappears, never to be seen again. Barrie drew the disparate elements of his plot together, and was finally writing his play. Here, the troubled ghost of a happily married young mother, Mary Rose, who had vanished from a Hebridean island years before, returns from another world. In this one, unaware that she is unchanged after twenty-five years, Mary Rose searches through the family's abandoned house for her lost baby son. She fails to recognise him when as a prodigal – he ran away to sea at twelve – Harry returns a grown man to the empty and bleak house that was his parents' home. There Mary Rose discovers him, not realising he is her son. Harry's kindness allows her to find some tranquillity, he 'lays the ghost' and she appears to return to the island – it remains unclear whether this is heaven or the fairy world – to die.

Barrie's mysterious and at times frightening play was much altered between manuscript and production. In the process it grew shorter, his vision grew darker and, in combination with Norman O'Neill's music, including the 'wordless singing of the "Island Voices" played on a carpenter's saw', the play grew increasingly poignant.

In the trajectory of his plays Barrie has written his life story. In the early period one could say he is talking about himself and the world, and refusing to make up his mind. He sees himself in part as Sentimental Tommy. In *The Admirable Crichton* and *Quality Street* he is grappling with the idea that a multiple personality might be a prelude to decision. Then, at the peak of his powers with *Peter Pan*, Barrie lets out that cry of pain; he still can't make up his mind. Therefore, specifying all their strengths and weaknesses, he will give all the different characters their due. And, flawed though he knows it is, this – *Peter Pan* – is something like a conclusion. He admires Phoebe Throssel in *Quality Street*, he admires the Admirable Crichton, but then with *Dear Brutus* he begins another, less optimistic and darker phase. Life is now something more grim, it is all about 'might have been', and there are no second chances.

In *Mary Rose* Barrie appears to be saying that the world of eerie, misty highland glens, the world of faery that captures Mary Rose, is one that is old, obsolete and bankrupt. Although Mary's husband, Simon, is a decent enough man, he can only half cope. He suffers some of the narrowness of the British ruling class, and although he has tried to grow up he has achieved this at the cost of sympathy and spontaneity. Cameron, the servant, is more robust, and so is Harry, Simon and Mary Rose's son. He has returned from a new world, Australia. Although less subtle, he is likeable, courageous and masculine. Harry is able to face danger because he hasn't subjected himself to the psychic surgery his father had felt obliged to carry out. Thus, neither has Harry felt the need to obliterate the feminine element within him.

A new incarnation of the world, for which Barrie had been searching all his life, is articulated in *Peter Pan*. But that new world is one of symbol and myth. Here, in *Mary Rose*, Barrie attempts to say that what Harry represents is a real not a fantasy new world. A world released from the worst aspects of the past. And with this Barrie leaves behind islands, to him of such symbolic importance: places which represent both good and evil, and also the means of leaving this world in order to discover something crucial about ourselves.

Barrie's own life, meanwhile, was becoming more intertwined with Cynthia Asquith's, and his tendency to domination and ownership was once again beginning to make itself felt. Oblivious to the irritation his open admiration of Cynthia might cause her young husband, he also found it difficult to understand why there might be any objection to her attendance at Adelphi Terrace almost every day, and a number of evenings, each week. Cynthia kept her difficulties with Beb from Barrie, but Beb was not as forbearing as Arthur Davies had been. Like the Davieses' marriage the Asquiths' was a secure one, and Beb accepted that numerous men adored his wife. He also knew that she enjoyed – needed – this admiration, but he refused to accept that Sir James should have need of so very much of her time. After the birth of their son, Simon, Beb was annoyed that Cynthia agreed to return to work for Barrie at all. Cynthia reasoned, however, that as Beb's earnings as a literary adviser were not sufficient to keep them, how otherwise were they to survive?

This was unquestionably true, but Cynthia and Barrie's relationship was already more complicated than that. Of course, with great tact and skill, and always that engaging presence, she had imposed order on Barrie's papers where before there had been only chaos, but Cynthia had done more than that. Her full and interesting social life meant that she was never short of company, and yet she chose to spend good parts of her time with this strange little man. Aside from the friends they had discovered in common, as Cynthia and Barrie introduced each other to more friends, their social lives were becoming interconnected, and this now included Cynthia's family. Barrie was weaving the old spell around this new friend and companion, someone whose mind was often as nimble and sharp as his own. But the admiration and interest was not on his side alone, and a subtle interdependency was developing between the two.

In the summer of 1920 Barrie hired an entire island, Eilean Shona, off the north-west coast of Argyll, for Michael and Nico's summer holiday. Nico brought two friends from Eton, while Michael asked others from Oxford, including Roger Senhouse, who had been with him at Eton. Barrie invited Elizabeth Lucas and her daughter Audrey, whom the boys had known since they were small children. At first the weather was fine and Barrie wrote to Cynthia about

> so perfectly appointed a retreat on these wild shores . . . Superb as is the scene from the door, Michael, who has already been to the top of things, says it's nought to what is revealed there – all the western isles of Scotland lying at our feet. A good spying ground for discovering what really happened to Mary Rose.[11]

The play had been staged that spring with Fay Compton in the title role and giving probably the best performance of her career. *Mary Rose's* success led some critics to say it was the best of Barrie's works.

A few days after his enthusiastic letter the weather changed, leading him to complain of 'about 60 hours of it so wet that you get soaked if you dart across the lawn'. Michael drew Barrie several times, provoking him to write to Cynthia,

> Michael has been drawing more sketches of me and they are more than enough. He has a diabolical aptitude for finding my worst attributes, so bad that I indignantly deny them, then furtively examine myself in the privacy of my chamber, and lo, they are there.[12]

Barrie complained it was a very Etonian household and that he felt left out by the endless 'shop talk' and the capacity of the young to make him almost feel an intruder. He asked Cynthia did his letters seem aged, because he certainly felt it on the island. Commenting acidly on the English habit of tennis, he called it 'an extraordinarily polite game', whose chief word he believed is 'sorry', and decided that this is what is imparted at public schools 'and can't be got anywhere else'. 'I feel sure that when any English public school boy shot a Boche he called out "sorry". If he was hit himself he cried out, "Oh well shot."'[13]

In the previous year, 1919, Barrie had accepted the post of Rector at St Andrews University. (He had felt most gratified at the appointment because it is a post chosen not by the professors or vice-chancellor, but by the students.) While on Eilean Shona his thoughts were turning to a potential topic for the rectorial address he was soon obliged to give. On this Michael and his friends were more willing to join Barrie in discussion. His notes give a powerful glimpse of what must have been the tenor of their conversations. We see Barrie, disillusioned with himself, his generation, authority, and displaying an open-mindedness about the frustrations of an alienated postwar youth. It is as if his conversations with these young people were confirmation of his lifelong fear, and final disenchantment with what age represents.

> Age and youth the two great enemies . . . age (wisdom) failed – Now let us see what youth (audacity) can do. The two great partners in state shouldn't be Tory, Liberal or Labour – but age and youth. . .
>
> Rectors all advise work, labour sublime outlook . . . This not really in touch with the young men they used to be . . . Youth already knows nearly as much as old and feel far more. Old advising young . . . rather a mockery just after war which young men died for . . . They shd put statesmen, who make war in front line. They shd be convicting me in dock (instead of my addressing) & condemning.
>
> The two sides (really old & young – i.e. before and after war) don't understand (admit) that they have different views of what constitutes immorality . . . (This really the great result of war which at first didn't seem to show itself. It isn't those who fought agst their elders, but those who have been growing up *since* the war agst outlook of others (the soldiers are merely discontented). In short, there has arisen a new morality, which seeks to go its own way . . . agst the . . . protests of the old morality. This sentimentality is . . . the flag of the old (at least in new's opinion). From art the two seek different things. In the old's play, novels &c, what public wanted was to be made to like characters so much that the work *had* to have happy endings – to be *sympathetic* was the one aim of the artist . . . all must end happily at any cost . . . The New no longer ask for this. They don't care tho' characters end miserable or not – they don't want to be sympathetic with them, they enjoy seeing them stripped of their qualities as much as the Old liked these to be emphasised. They are out for dissection, exposure, they have lost simple faith – probably the war is main cause of it – they query everything. Perhaps they accept too little & we accepted too much &c. In a play they cd be shown in action as things will be a few years hence, when by the passing away of the old (or a revolution) they have established their new morality and new laws of the land. The Sentimental-Sympathetic may be illegal. – the old put out of way and little statuettes of them kept instead . . .[14]

Despite these thought-provoking notes, Barrie found it quite another thing to act upon them when his heart was involved. Hiring Eilean Shona was a dramatic gesture intended above all to please Michael. It was an attempt to divert him from his intention of leaving Oxford and making for Paris to learn to paint, as his du Maurier grandfather, George, had done before him. Michael was no longer so amenable. His moods fluctuated dramatically and he was uncharacteristically argumentative. That spring Dora Carrington had written to Strachey talking of this and saying, 'Perhaps that is just the gloom of finding Barrie one's keeper for life.'

Michael was deeply attached to his guardian and had no wish to hurt him, but his desire for greater independence was constantly frustrated when Barrie met his essays in this direction with what amounted to an emotional blockade. With this an underlying theme of the holiday, it was not in the end a great success. The days when Barrie was still the centre around which the Davies boys' lives revolved were past, but he was reluctant to see that out of the change a different kind of relationship might emerge and grow. In theory Barrie wanted the boys to grow up; he wanted all the benefits that this brought with it. At the same time he battled with his old instinct: that growing up was something forever to be regretted.

Back in adult mode, he enlisted Hugh Macnaghten and Elizabeth Lucas's help in persuading Michael to stay at Oxford until he had finished his degree. To Barrie and his friends it appeared the most responsible thing to do. Michael no doubt ultimately saw their success as another failure on his part to break away. Returning for his final year at Oxford, however, brought him no closer to resolving his considerable inner turmoil. As Michael struggled to come to terms with who he might be, Barrie was holding on, still weaving the web of need and support. And, while Michael tried to disengage himself, painfully connected to one another their almost daily letters continued to pass back and forth.

In the autumn Barrie wrote to Elizabeth Lucas thanking her for having had 'a steadying effect'. He went on to say,

> All sorts of things do set him 'furiously to think', and they seem to burn out like a piece of paper. He is at present I think working really well . . . and has at any rate spasms of happiness out of it, but one never knows of the morrow . . .
>
> He has the oddest way of alternating between extraordinary reserve and surprising intimacy. No medium. In his room at Oxford lately he suddenly unbosomed himself marvellously. One has to wait for these times, but they are worth while when they come.[15]

That Christmas the Davieses were staying in Paris with Elizabeth and Audrey Lucas. *Peter Pan* was having its sixteenth consecutive revival, and as always Barrie attended rehearsals and continued making changes to the script. *Peter Pan* had become a play without end.

In the notebook for that period, interspersed with notes for *Peter Pan* are ongoing thoughts on Barrie's rectorial address at St Andrews, plus some revealing comments on himself.

– T. Hardy great when political swells are dead, rotten & forgotten. So far as self is concerned, neither school nor university of any [importance to me] . . . Nothing disgusts me more than people beslavering me with praise, but I think an individual may have done me harm by thinking too little of me.

Good subject for Rectorial address might be the mess the Rector himself has made of life . . . first piece of advice, don't copy me.

– Great thing to form own opinion, don't accept hearsay . . . Question authority. Question accepted views, values, reputations. Don't be afraid to be among rebels.

. . . Speak scornfully of the Victorian age. Of Edwardian age. Of last year. Of old-fashioned writers like Barrie, who accept old-fangled ideas.[16]

This 'old-fashioned writer' was invited to spend that Easter with Cynthia and her family at Stanway. He next went on to Corfe Castle in Dorset, where Michael was staying at a pub, reading for his finals with Rupert Buxton, now his closest friend. On 9th May, Barrie's sixty-first birthday, Cynthia celebrated with him at the Ritz, a custom that would continue until the end of his life. Two days later she travelled with him down to Dorset to visit Thomas Hardy at Max Gate. Cynthia wrote of the visit in her diary, adding that Hardy and his wife were 'owned' by a dog whose presence she found most eccentric and irritating.

Throughout dinner, which he spent not under but on the table, walking about quite unchecked, and contesting with me every forkful of food . . . Undistracted by the snarling and scrunching of his dog, Hardy . . . talked more than I had heard him yet.[17]

The old man took them to see the cottage where he was born, and Barrie

refusing to be thwarted in his intention to enter the hallowed precincts, made me hold together two decayed ladders while . . .

he precariously climbed up to the window and contrived to open it. He scrambled through, and shortly afterwards, with a bow opened the door, to Hardy, who, returning the bow, re-entered the home in which, eighty-one years before he had first cried because – to quote words so much after his own heart – he had 'come to this great stage of fools'.[18]

Back in London Barrie was working hard on the murder play he had written for Michael, *Shall We Join the Ladies?*. It was to have its premiere at the opening of the Royal Academy of Dramatic Art's new theatre on 27th May. The cast included some of the greatest theatrical names of the day: Marie Lohr, Irene Vanbrugh, Fay Compton, Charles Hawtry, Dion Boucicault, Sybil Thorndike, Lillah McCarthy, Leon Quartermain, Cyril Maude, Madge Titheridge, Hilda Trevelyan, Norman Forbes, Johnston Forbes-Robertson and Gerald du Maurier.

On 19th May Cynthia worked at Adelphi Terrace until six, then left to have supper with a friend. Barrie was writing to Michael. At about eleven o'clock, on leaving the flat to post his letter, a man approached him, introduced himself as a reporter from a London newspaper, and asked could Sir James give him any more details about the drowning. Barrie asked what drowning he was referring to and the reporter realised he knew nothing of the news just in from Oxford. Two undergraduates, Rupert Buxton and Michael Llewelyn Davies, had been drowned that day while swimming in Sandford Pool. Barrie knew that Michael had been unable to overcome his fear of water, and never learnt to swim. Some time later Cynthia was woken by the telephone and Barrie's almost unrecognisable voice saying, 'I have had the most terrible news. Michael has been drowned at Oxford.'

24

Beyond the Reach of Time

When Cynthia and Beb arrived at Adelphi Terrace, Peter Davies and Gerald du Maurier were already there. Barrie looked appalling. They tried, without success, to persuade him to go to bed. Eventually Cynthia and Beb left. Cynthia returned early next morning to find that Barrie had been pacing the floor all night. He was inconsolable. Cynthia phoned Gilmour, who came, made arrangements for Michael's body to be brought back to London and organised the funeral. The morning papers had spread the news, and all through that grim day the phone rang at Adelphi Terrace.

Peter went down to Eton and brought back Nico, who remained very quiet. When Barrie saw him he cried out, 'Oh take him away.' Years later Nico would say he understood how his closeness to Michael had meant that for Barrie his presence was simply unbearable. Nico felt that he must tell Mary Hodgson, then working in Queen Charlotte's Hospital. From the top of a bus he caught sight of her, and ran back down the street. When she saw Nico's face Mary knew, and they stood together in a doorway and sobbed.[1]

For two days and nights Barrie didn't sleep. In her diary Cynthia wrote that he looked like a man in a nightmare. She rang his friend and doctor Sir Douglas Shields and begged him to come and give Barrie something to make him sleep. At this point Barrie was so dazed he hardly knew those around him. Cynthia had sent her children to Margate with their nurse, and spent most of each day at Adelphi Terrace. She made Barrie eat, stayed late, made him go to bed. She answered the phone, kept friends and sympathisers informed and at bay.

Following the inquest Michael's body was brought back to Adelphi Terrace, where it remained until the funeral two days later. Barrie stayed in his bedroom and would see no one; there was great anxiety that he might take his life. Then, on 23rd May, Michael was buried in Hampstead Cemetery, close by his parents, Sylvia and Arthur, and his grandfather, George du Maurier. He was deeply mourned by all those who knew him. Even those who had known him little were affected. Lytton Strachey wrote to Ottoline Morrell saying, 'I am sure that if he had lived he would have been one of the remarkable people of his generation.' Quite a few believed that Michael's and Rupert Buxton's deaths were not an accident but suicide. If so, one of the underlying causes might have been that Michael was wrestling with the possibility of his homosexuality.

After the funeral, despite his own misery, Peter Davies continued coming in and doing what he could for Barrie, who was bereft and remained virtually unreachable. It was said of Cynthia at this time that 'it was she who preserved his reason', and Barrie now turned to her for almost everything. In the days following Michael's death his friendship with her had taken on a new significance.

After discussion with Beb, in order to try and lift a little the utter misery into which Barrie had descended, Cynthia took him and Nico to join her sons at Margate. Little Michael and Simon played carelessly for hours on the seashore, and although much older, now seventeen, Nico often joined in, prompting Cynthia to confide to her diary that he was 'a great wag and entrances them'. Watching the children's endless play on the sands, sometimes even himself persuaded to take part, as one long summer's day passed into another, Barrie's spirits were gradually imbued with a hint of something lighter. He grew calmer, began to sleep a little more.

Some weeks after he had returned to London he wrote to Cynthia, still at Margate,

> I hope you are having a quiet happy time with the children . . . Yesterday being Michael's birthday seemed specially sad to me as it wore on but it passed as everything passes and I had quite a good night. I won't ever attempt to thank you for the loveliness of mind and heart with which you have helped and encouraged me at this time. Any courage I have got seems to come from your example.[2]

The intensity and magnitude of Barrie's loss was revealed in a letter to his old friend Elizabeth Lucas when, seven months later, he wrote, 'All is different to me now; Michael was pretty much my world.'

A year later, in a letter to Michael's college tutor at Christ Church, Robin Dundas, Barrie said,

> It may seem strange to you that I didn't write long ago, but what happened was in a way the end of me, and practically anything may be forgiven me now. He had been the one great thing in my life for many years, and though there are little things to do they are trivial.[3]

All Barrie's letters to Michael came back to him, and since he was unable either to read or destroy them they were stored away in his desk. With Cynthia's enduring support in the bleak aftermath of Michael's death, seeing only the very closest of friends, in a desultory kind of way, Barrie carried on.

A summer holiday must be arranged for Nico, and Barrie suggested that Cynthia, Beb and their boys should accompany them to France. At this point Beb finally demurred. Cynthia had been with Barrie at his flat almost daily since Michael's death. She lunched with him, and if he asked her to she stayed on late. Beb had said little, but now he refused Barrie's offer of a holiday, and he didn't want Cynthia and the boys to go either. Disagreement between Cynthia and Beb over the holiday rumbled on, occasionally flaring up into blazing argument. Meanwhile, Barrie refused to understand why it might not be possible. He said he was distressed, and without them didn't know what he would do with poor Nico for the summer.

Although Cynthia thought Beb foolish for refusing to accept a holiday they couldn't themselves afford, her final loyalty lay with her husband. She was, all the same, torn. She felt great concern for Barrie, who was also adept at emotional manoeuvring. He didn't scruple to put himself in a pathetic light when he wanted something to happen.

Sylvia Llewelyn Davies's and Cynthia Asquith's relationships with Barrie involved two important differences. First, Cynthia clearly looked after Barrie, whereas *he* had looked after Sylvia. Second, Beb Asquith was less reticent about his feelings concerning Barrie's monopoly of his wife than Arthur Davies had been. The problem was still unresolved in early July. In some desperation, Cynthia wondered if Barrie might like to take her parents' house as tenant for the month of August, as they would probably be away staying at their other house in Scotland. Cynthia felt that spending a companionable period at Stanway might help to ease a little for Barrie the gnawing pain of the first summer without Michael.

Barrie was encouraged, and grew more enthusiastic. Yes, he would be pleased to take Stanway for August. He knew and liked the area from years ago when the Allahakbarries had played cricket nearby at Broadway. He and Cynthia had friends in common and could each invite others, too, while the plan also enabled Cynthia and her children to spend time in the house she loved above all others.

Once the summer residence of the medieval abbots of Tewkesbury, Stanway had passed, via the Traceys, into Lord Wemyss's family in the eighteenth century. Set just below the Cotswold hills and built of that golden Cotswold stone, Stanway's beauty is heightened by the lovely three-storey arched gatehouse, in 1921 attributed (erroneously) to Inigo

Jones. With its gabled roofs and its high hall, from which the great stone-mullioned bay window overlooks the village church, the house is encompassed by lawns and terraces. One of these is 'skirted by a wood of yew trees', another, a wide grass terrace, leads up a steep bank to the stone summer house, called the pyramid, giving the hill its name. Just beyond lies the vast and stately tithe barn.

Barrie had already fallen under Stanway's quintessentially English spell, but on this visit, as tenant and host, he came to know its history and surroundings better. Being Barrie, he must begin to conjure his own magic, add his own interpretations. And as he became more familiar with this beautiful house, just as he did with his friends, so Barrie came to feel a touch of propriety. Reflecting these aspects of his will to 'ownership', those Barrie trademarks, the stamps, were soon thrown up on the pennies to stick upon the ceiling. The old habit had never died. Indeed, as he had made his ascent in society, Barrie had now 'stamped' the ceilings of many of the great houses of Britain. Contrary to some of the gossip, however, none of his increasingly illustrious friendships made him into a snob. He was something grander and more complex than that. It was true that he was pleased he had made of himself a success. At the same time he *knew* that he was special, and judged himself in his own way the equal of anyone.

To the Cotswold paradise of Stanway that summer Barrie invited a succession of friends and family. This included his sister, Maggie, with her husband and their rather odd son, an expert at chess; Nico with Eton friends; Jack with his wife Gerrie and their new baby, Timothy; the critic Charles Whibley and E.V. Lucas; the distinguished academic Walter Raleigh; the socialite Violet Bonham-Carter and Barrie's American friends, the publisher Charles Scribner and his wife. The entire Australian cricket team, then in England, were invited for the day and created a great stir in the village. And still the visitors came. Cynthia was worked almost to breaking point keeping the endless round of guests organised and provided with meals, acting as Barrie's hostess and simultaneously functioning as his secretary most mornings. On several occasions it was clear that Barrie had overreached himself and he became irritable, morose, and would hide away in the library. And yet, removed from his accustomed surroundings for that month, with such distraction each day, sometimes momentarily forgetting, his broken spirit was a little soothed. The feeling of permanence, an enduring past, lent by Stanway itself, contributed immeasurably to this. Cynthia would write that at times he could be found 'contentedly gazing at the house, which, he said, varied like a living face; or he would wander into the tithe barn and stare up at the great timber rafters of its roof'.[4]

Barrie wrote to Elizabeth Lucas saying,

Our time at Stanway was the best I think we could have had, and there was so much for Nicholas to do that he was mostly happy. He is overwhelmed at times by what he has lost and is a touching boy at such times.[5]

With great reluctance Barrie returned to London to resume a life without Michael. The only response to distress he knew was retreat or occupation with busyness. Therefore he wrote, and was socially in constant demand.

That autumn Charlie Chaplin was on a visit to England and E. V. Lucas entertained him at the Garrick Club. Along with a small party of other guests, Chaplin had said he would like to meet J. M. Barrie. Once again in the land of his birth, Chaplin, who had recently made his masterpiece, *The Kid*, was now the most popular actor in the world. On his arrival central London almost came to a standstill, as traffic was blocked all the way from Waterloo station to the Ritz on Piccadilly, where he was staying. Everywhere Chaplin went he was mobbed by adoring crowds.

He later made it clear in *My Trip Abroad* that the person he wanted to meet above all others was the man who had created *Peter Pan*. Sitting side by side at the Garrick Club dinner that evening, it was immediately apparent these two strange men had discovered a rapport. Their mutual fascination meant that Chaplin was invited back to Adelphi Terrace with one of the other guests. The talk continued until three in the morning, when Gerald du Maurier, who had arrived earlier, finally took Chaplin away to his hotel, walking back down the Strand. The meeting of the small Jewish boy from the East End and the small linen weaver's son from Kirriemuir had been a notable success. Barrie wrote to Cynthia, 'He has a rather charming speaking voice, and a brain withal. A very forceful creature and likeable. The police who are put on to guard him all produce their autograph books for him to sign. The ordinary stage drama he called the 'Speakies'.'[6] Chaplin himself wrote: 'I notice that Barrie looks rather tired and worn . . . Du Maurier tells us that [he] is not himself since his nephew has drowned, that he has aged considerably.'

It was true. Although on occasions such as this Barrie could rouse himself, become genuinely animated and exert that vital sparkling self, in reality his spirit was partially spent. He was threadbare and lost. Fate had dealt him a deadly blow, striking at the very heart of the question which had consumed his life, the problem of growing up. As in an ancient Greek tragedy it was given to Barrie that with his two best beloveds – the brothers George and Michael – the problem would be solved, but at a terrible price. As the five brothers were 'thinned out' by Fate, so the two who had died before their time would remain in his memory forever young. They were beyond the reach of time now, and nothing could ever harm them, or make them grow old.

Although the pain of George's death had driven Barrie into the depths of sorrow, somehow, out of this suffering, the artist in him had been able to create, transforming that suffering first into *Dear Brutus* and then *Mary Rose*. But with Michael's death, though his imagination grew no less fertile, he aged almost overnight. No longer young, though he was still only sixty-one, his drive and willpower were finally diminished. Although Barrie's success was still such that in 1923 he had no fewer than five plays running concurrently on the London stage, the man whose energy had always been so prodigious found that the high level of stamina required to fashion ideas into great art was no longer available to him. He continued putting thoughts in his notebooks, and small pieces of work were produced, but they were no longer converted into any major new work.

Peter Pan continued with its annual revival and was still the high point of London's theatre at Christmas. Maintaining the theme of his play as never-ending, Barrie was always present at rehearsals, adding and taking away. That year, however, a bad bout of bronchitis obliged him to remain at Adelphi Terrace. Cynthia failed in persuading him to recuperate at a nursing home, but she did manage to get him down to Stanway for Christmas.

On Boxing Day Barrie received a letter of commendation; he had been appointed to the Order of Merit. He was elated. His mentors, Meredith and Hardy, had preceded him in receiving the honour, and he accepted with pride the public affection and approval showered upon him at the news. An article in *The Times* said there was no epithet that could describe him so well as the 'etcetera' which frequently replaced a list of the academic honours he had by now received. (These would soon include honorary degrees from both Oxford and Cambridge.) The writer continued, 'therein lies all the unknown, the possible, the incredible, the impossible, and therefore probable, that make up so much of Sir James Barrie, Bt. Etc, as the world has been allowed to see'.

His artistic productivity may have been slowing down, but one way in which Barrie's deep urge to communicate found an outlet in these later years was as an orator. His rectorship of St Andrews University would soon come to an end, and, with its culmination, he was preparing to give his address. The project had been concerning him for months, and early into the new year of 1922 he was hard at work. Having at last decided on the subject, courage, draft after draft was thrown out as Barrie struggled with the grandeur of his theme. How was he to find a way of talking meaningfully and without presumption about such a subject to hundreds of young students, a good number of whom had served in the recent war? As the weeks passed he grew more anxious, and relied heavily upon Cynthia's support.

But Cynthia was emotionally exhausted from overwork, and a ceaseless round of social engagements she appeared unable to curtail. Unusually, for the moment she was forced to retreat and take a rest. Through a combination of necessity and inclination she led an extraordinarily full and busy life. In between devoting herself to a husband, three sons and countless friends, she spent hours with Barrie each week. Through lack of income (and inclination) for some time now she had also been contributing regular pieces of journalism to various magazines.

Although capable of colossal self-absorption, Barrie was also a kind and sympathetic friend. In an attempt to alleviate Cynthia's exhaustion and depression he wrote,

> It is just a cloud hanging over you because you have lost the physical power for the moment to blow it away. Matter and spirit are not only allied but may be practically the same thing, and I think this is especially so with you. When rundownness makes you despondent you fall into the way of accusing yourself of all the faults that you are so peculiarly without. Just because you are naturally the most brave person that I know, if you falter for an instant you turn on yourself for a poltroon . . . You are the sunshine of this flat as much as of your own home and you never come into it that you are not a blessing to me.[7]

As the date of Barrie's address drew nearer, he wrote, revised, obsessively rewrote, and with each day grew still more anxious. His position as rector permitted him to suggest a list of honorary doctors of literature for the university. This list, although a deserving one, was unorthodox; it included Thomas Hardy, William Nicholl, Sidney Colvin (the Keeper of Prints and Drawings at the British Museum, and friend and editor of R. L. Stevenson), the soldier Bernard Freyberg, John Galsworthy, E. V. Lucas, Charles Whibley and the actress Ellen Terry.

By the time Barrie arrived at St Andrews, he was already exhausted through lack of sleep and strained nerves. Following an evening of festivities he slept little and in the morning, in spite of Cynthia's efforts to prevent him, insisted on making further changes to his endlessly reworked speech. When the moment finally arrived he stood before the large crowd of boisterous students, visibly unsettled at the prospect of subduing them. Having paid virtually no attention to the previous speaker, the students were in an uproar. Barrie was introduced, and the uproar died down. Standing very small and alone before the huge audience, his anticipation of the event had been so intense Barrie was now powerless to begin. As the moments passed the hush that had overtaken the hall grew heavy until, sensing the mounting antagonism in the air, Barrie at last began to speak. Even then, his voice was inaudible, and in agitation he absently fiddled with a paper knife lying before him on the table. Suddenly a voice called out from the audience, 'Put it down, Jamie, you'll cut your throat.'

As the roar of laughter died away a spell was broken, and, with this, Jamie Barrie began to work that other magic once more. In a voice now become firm and clear he soon held his audience in rapt attention, and, launching into confessional mode, he confided in them apparently some of his innermost thoughts and fears. He made them laugh and cheer, and he hushed them into awed silence when, exhorting Youth to demand its fair share in the building of the future, he told them,

> We were not meaning to deceive, most of us were as honourable and as ignorant as the youth themselves; but that does not acquit us . . . If you prefer to leave things as they are we shall probably fail you again. Do not be too sure that we have learned our lesson, and are not at this very moment doddering down some brimstone path . . . but if you must be in the struggle, the more reason you should know why, before it begins, and have a say in the decision whether it is to begin. The youth who went to war had no such knowledge, no such say . . .
>
> Even without striking out in the way I suggest, you are already disturbing your betters considerably . . . the war and other happenings have shown you that age is not necessarily another name for sapience; that our avoidance of frankness in life and in the arts is often, but not so often as you think, a cowardly way of shirking unpalatable truths, and that you have taken us off our pedestals because we look more natural on the ground . . .
>
> In so far as this attitude of yours is merely passive, sullen, negative, as it mainly is, despairing of our capacity and anticipating a future of gloom, it is no game for man or woman. It is certainly the opposite of that for which I plead. Do not stand aloof, despairing, disbelieving, but come in and help – insist on coming in and helping . . . Learn as a beginning how world-shaking situations arise and

how they may be countered. Doubt all your betters who would deny you that right of partnership.

The war has done at least one big thing: it has taken spring out of the year. The spring of the year lies buried in the fields of France. By the time the next eruption comes it may be you who are responsible for it and your sons who are in the lava. All because this year you let things slide . . . seeking cushions for our old bones rather than attempting to build a fairer future . . . Look around and see how much share Youth has now the war is over. You got a handsome share of it while it lasted.

I expect we shall beat you: unless your fortitude be doubly girded by a desire to send a message of cheer to your brothers who fell, the only message, I believe, for which they crave . . . they want to know if you have learned wisely from what befell them . . . you who still hear their cries being blown across the links . . . they call to you to find out in time the truth about this great game, which your elders play for stakes and Youth plays for its life.

Are you equal to your job, you young men? If not, I call upon the red-gowned women to lead the way. I sound to myself as if I were advocating a rebellion, though I am really asking for a larger friendship. You will have to work harder than ever . . .

Izaak Walton quotes the saying that the Almighty could have created a finer fruit than the strawberry, but that doubtless He never did. Doubtless also He could have provided us with better fun than hard work, but I don't know what it is. To be born poor is probably the next best thing. The greatest glory that has ever come to me was to be swallowed up in London not knowing a soul, with no means of subsistence, and the fun of working till the stars went out. To have known any one would have spoilt it. I did not even know the language. I rang for my boots, and they thought I said a glass of water, so I drank the water and worked on. There was no food in the cupboard, so I did not waste time in eating. The pangs and agonies when the proofs came. How courteously tolerant was I of the postman without a proof for us; how M'Connachie, on the other hand, wanted to punch his head. The magic days when our articles appeared in an evening paper. The promptitude with which I counted the lines to see how much we should get for it. Then M'connachie's superb air of dropping it in the gutter . . .[8]

First referred to in this speech, from now on Barrie's alter ego, McConnachie, became a public projection of his many selves. He told the students he had been fortunate in doing something that he loved, and that writing for him was as marvellous as 'playing hide and seek with angels'. (This thought was first voiced in a letter of encouragement to A. A. Milne, in 1910, when Barrie said: 'Hide and seek with the angels is good enough for anyone'.)[9] Nevertheless, he wondered if the unbounded enjoyment he derived from it might mean it had not really been work.

> You will all fall into one of those two callings, the joyous or the uncongenial; and one wishes you into the first, though our sympathy, our esteem, must go rather to the less fortunate . . . who turn their necessity to glorious gain after they have put away their dreams . . .

The students were told that when they grew old he was sure they would cheerfully realise 'we are all failures, at least all the best of us', and he urged them, 'Hanker not too much after worldly prosperity – that corpulent cigar; if you become a millionaire you would probably go swimming around for more like a diseased goldfish.' In addition to work he reminded them that

> Courage is the thing. All goes if courage goes . . . We should thank our Creator three times daily for courage instead of for our daily bread, which, if we work, is surely the one thing we have a right to claim of Him. This courage is proof of our immortality . . . Pray for it.

The best way to achieve this, he suggested, was with light-heartedness. And as an example of this, fumbling in his pocket he drew out the treasured letter from Captain Scott telling of 'their songs and cheery conversation', written as Scott and his companions lay dying in that bleak terrain. Thus, remembering his own terrible dream, whose 'creature' he had now given a name, Barrie warned the students to beware of M'Connachie, for

> When I look in the mirror now it is his face I see. I speak with his voice. Once I had a voice of my own, but nowadays I hear it from far away only, a melancholy, lonely, lost pipe . . . You will all have your M'Connachies luring you off the road. Unless you are constantly on the watch you will find that he has slowly pushed you out of yourself and taken your place.

He read the sonnet Michael had written on Eilean Shona in the previous summer, the last of his life, telling them it was 'by the lad that will never be old'. And after one hour and twenty-seven minutes, Barrie finally reached the end of this astounding performance. For a moment the great hall was silent. Then, all rising to their feet, the young people erupted into a thunderous applause. Later, Barrie was carried triumphantly on their shoulders to the waiting crowds outside.

The papers held columns of praise, and Barrie's publishers quickly answered the huge number of calls for *Courage* to be put into print, while the letters – many simply addressed to McConnachie, c/o Sir James Barrie – continued pouring in to Adelphi Terrace for weeks. Although he returned to London ill with exhaustion, Barrie knew he had triumphed. One unexpected result of this was that for the rest of his life he was besieged with requests to speak. He may caustically have noted that 'there was no surer sign of mediocrity than being accepted as a successful after dinner speaker', but in the decade after *Courage* Barrie became renowned for his oration. His name was now so esteemed that almost anything he said – and he had remained careful to say very little publicly – was instant front-page news, reported in full in *The Times*.

During this period he wrote no plays of note, yet in oratory he discovered a medium through which, at first, both the multiple aspects of his nature and his need to engage were expressed. Much time was spent perfecting his speeches until they became, like *Courage*, small masterpieces of communication. It was as if Barrie had returned to the stage of his schooldays, except now he was master of his audience. He groaned at the prospect of public speaking, and usually suffered from severe nerves, but he also told Cynthia that he enjoyed the thrill of knowing his audience was responding. On each new occasion the showman's mask was exploited to perfection, and when he began to speak, 'So much of the enchantment was the beautiful hoarse voice, and the poignancy of the mournful figure with the weary wrung face, majestic brow and large cigar.'[10]

Barrie often reminisced, and if many listeners were entranced, others were embarrassed, while most were also baffled. For even those who knew him well were unsure how much Barrie meant what he said, how much he fabricated, indeed who exactly this man before them might really be. He never set out to deceive, but since childhood his temptation was, like the prodigious hero of *Sentimental Tommy*, to 'step into other people's shoes and remain there until he became someone else'. Inclined as Barrie was to spend so much of his life in this way, reality and fiction were easily interchangeable so that he could, like Tommy, pass 'between dreams and reality as through tissue paper'. After his death Hugh Walpole wrote of him,

He was an actor. He knew that his accent although honest was bewitching. He knew just when to pause, when to be sad, when to be gay. And although he meant what he said he meant a great deal more than he said . . . And so Barrie tricked nine tenths of us, and knew well that he was tricking us.[11]

Cynthia Asquith would add to this that 'sometimes his face, even while he was delivering a speech, wore a perceptible look of faint disgust, almost as though he felt himself to be performing a rather shabby trick'. When one day she congratulated him on another successful talk, in which he had appeared to enjoy himself as much as the audience, Barrie's comment was a desolating one: 'Looking back on my effusion, it makes me rather ill.' This prompts one to remember that the same man had written, in *Sentimental Tommy*, 'To trick people so simply is not satisfying to an artist.' As an artist who was truthful to himself, who had risen to the apogee of *Peter Pan*, Barrie gradually realised that writing and performing these speeches was for him a poor susbstitute for true creativity.

On 18th May, not long after his St Andrews address, Barrie wrote in sombre mood to Elizabeth Lucas,

> I wish you were here now and often wish it . . . I am glad you found me at a time when I was working. I seem to work so little nowadays and am much happier when I do . . .
>
> Do you know that this day a year ago Michael was alive and that next day he was dead? . . . I feel that he is at Oxford today in his rooms and that tomorrow he is going out to be drowned, and doesn't know it. I spoke about courage as you know at St Andrews, but it does seem to me often as if there was something rather monstrous in my still being here. Peter is coming tomorrow to stay the night and will be everything that is kind.

In their joint sorrow at the loss of Michael, Peter and Barrie had drawn closer together than they had been for a number of years.

As the months passed Barrie continued with his notebooks, and to them he confided some heartrending revelations. One night he had a most potent and disquieting dream about Michael, who was never long from his thoughts.

> I dreamt that he came back to me, not knowing that he was drowned and that I kept this knowledge from him, and we went on for another year in old way till the fatal 19th approached again & he

became very sad not knowing why, and I feared what was to happen but never let on – and as the day drew nearer he understood more and thought I didn't . . . and when the day came I devised schemes to make it impossible for him to leave me yet doubted they could help – and he rose in the night and put on old clothes and came to look at me as he thought I was asleep. I tried to prevent him going but he had to go and I knew it . . .

The above was the dream and the notes to follow come out of thinking about it, all except this that I knew from the moment of his return I must never let him know that anything had happened to him – that this so to speak was vital to his life . . .

I do some things that he had wanted before and that then I had not done . . .

– He can't get past the fatal date . . .

– fatal night coming to me light pressed lips says going to bathe . . .

– Trying to lock in, guarded by others – he is in so much agony of mind tht have to let him go. He goes to pool . . .

– must be clear there is nothing suicidal about it

– when he reappears it is as suddenly from the next room, and in a matter-of-fact way. He never knows he has been away . . .

It is as if long after writing *Peter Pan* its true meaning came to me – Desperate attempt to grow up but can't.[12]

With old age and exhaustion Barrie would be overwhelmed and ultimately defeated by his valiant struggle to come to terms with his deepest emotional conflicts. Long years ago, when his brother David had died, little Jamie had tried to repair his mother's loss by becoming that dead brother. At first, he had done this in a childlike way, by simply wearing his brother's clothes and copying his mannerisms. Over time these efforts at rehabilitating his mother meant that somewhere in his psyche Jamie took on 'being' David more profoundly. Indeed, in order to realise the hopes his mother had harboured for David, Jamie had borne his brother's very soul. At the deepest level, the gargantuan efforts he made effectively saved him from what might otherwise have been a tragic fate. He must work hard, always harder, to achieve the worldly success that his mother had wanted for David. This both kept Jamie going, and also took time. Years. And during those long years it was as if he was living on behalf of his brother.

Jamie had the good fortune to have inherited from his father a strand of immense Scottish toughness and resilience. Without these qualities, his life – which was so intense, so potentially manic, and had such difficult work to complete – might well have burnt itself out by the time he reached adolescence, or at least his twenties. So much of his own childhood was 'lost' in this way that as he became a young adult Barrie attempted to recapture it through playing with children. Years later still, he relived childhood more fully through another little boy, called Michael. His love for Michael developed, above all, because, in that peculiar shelter between the conscious and the unconscious, Barrie *became* that little boy. Finally, with the intervention of the actual world the real Michael first grew apart, and then he died. And the dreadful force of his death shattered for Barrie the Myth. It is not an exaggeration to say that with Michael's death a large part of Barrie died, too.

With the all-consuming nature of his struggle, the work Barrie had set himself to complete in his early life, no matter what happened to him later, took on its own momentum. As was early his custom, he reached down and dragged up from the depths of himself his lost memory, the knowledge of his own history. Hence his conviction that there were no second chances. When you are fairly young you are already so ineradicably yourself that only in the rarest of cases, and with the most heroic efforts, can you do much to alter. And Barrie's personality and drives had been forged by means of such struggle that nothing on this earth could have changed him very much.

After Michael's death, the black moods, for long an integral part of Barrie's life, struck him with greater regularity and sometimes appalling ferocity. What he was unable to comprehend, however, was that these depressions, this despondency, were all quite inevitable. What had nourished him for those past years, his enriching and life-enhancing relationship with Michael, was simply an interlude. An interlude slowing down for a time the inevitable progression towards an unquiet old age. Understandably, Barrie was unable to see this, and so the loss of Michael appeared to him as an absolute tragedy. No doubt he had forgotten that two years *before* Michael's death he was writing to Maude Adams amongst others, with intimations of his plight:

> The days pass, the weeks, the months, and I am in a sort of dead-alive condition . . . Perhaps I am now played out. A well a day! But I have had these horrible squalls before now, and hope to get past this one. I think the chief thing against me is that I seem to have ceased to believe in my knowledge of human nature. I find people so different from what I had thought them that it brings me to the ground. I am too lonely (I wrote the word as if it were 'lively', oh that it were!). I have Thomas Hardy staying with me just now and he is much more lively then he used to be . . . perhaps there is hope for me in my old age.[13]

With this, the dark burden of Barrie's unresolved past now threatened to settle upon him more permanently. His physical health, too, finally began to show real signs of decline. The dreadful cough – he was rarely without either a cigarette or his pipe – plaguing him for more than half his life was grown harsher with the years, and the bouts of insomnia were now routine. Yet, even though these afflictions frequently conspired together and confined him to bed, fortified with his father's stamina and extraordinary resilience, time and again he recovered and went on.

25

Release

Complex and many-sided though he was, Barrie's conflicts did not make the remainder of his life unrelentingly sombre. Critical here, was the constant support and affection given him by Cynthia Asquith. She had long ago ceased simply to be his secretary; she had opened up her life to Barrie and invited him into her family.

A bond of sympathy had arisen between Barrie and Cynthia's spontaneous and unceasingly hospitable mother, Lady Wemyss (née Wyndham). With the languid Arthur Balfour – who remained the love of her life – and Lady Desborough, Lady Wemyss had been a leading member of the set nicknamed the Souls, the coterie that terrified some by its worldly sophistication. (In Sargent's famed portrait, *The Wyndham Sisters*, Mary and her two sisters epitomise the privileged, elegant and social lives led by most of the Souls.) Highly cultivated and determinedly light-hearted, this group of aristocrats – and others whom they drew to their beautiful houses – were something of an oasis in upper-class Philistia.

For many years, as Lady Wemyss drew to her home a sometimes startling assortment of guests, they were encouraged by her kindness, open-mindedness and interest to make house parties memorable occasions at Stanway. One of those who returned many times to Stanway was Barrie, invited for Christmas, Easter, and many of the significant Wemyss family occasions for the remainder of his life.

He also continued for ten years to take the house in the summer, with Cynthia as his tireless hostess organising hordes of people, while her husband Beb travelled down from London every weekend. A number of guests returned each year, to which were added a succession of other less regular visitors. In all they sometimes amounted to forty or fifty in the few weeks that Barrie was the tenant of Stanway.

Apart from the numerous child visitors – Barrie had grown fond of Cynthia's sons, Michael and Simon – and old friends and family, such as Barrie's sister, Maggie, with her husband and their chess-champion son, Willie, Bernard Freyberg, Charles Whibley, E. V. Lucas, Cynthia's brother,

Guy Charteris (future father-in-law of Ian Fleming) and the eccentric and sympathetic local vicar, called by the Wemysses 'The Priest', many other friends came to Stanway on a number of occasions. These included Augustine Birrell, H. G. Wells, G. K. Chesterton, Edith Wharton, John Galsworthy, Lady David Cecil, the first chair of English at Oxford, Walter Raleigh, the critic Desmond MacCarthy, the Russian dancer Kasarvina, Lord and Lady Dufferin, Arthur Quiller-Couch and his family, the indomitable Margot Asquith, Lord and Lady Desborough (the greatest hostess of her day, who said of Barrie, 'You don't know what charm is until you've met that little man'), Anne Charteris, Priscilla Bibesco, Mary, Duchess of Devonshire, Thomas Hardy's widow, Florence, the writer Stephen Gwynne, A. P. Herbert, Lady Gwendoline Churchill, Arthur Conan Doyle, Edward Marsh, L. P. Hartley, and many, many more.

One of the guests who returned several times was the poet Walter de la Mare. He described his first meeting with Barrie to his friend W. H. Hamilton.

I met Barrie for the first time at dinner . . . and brought away an extremely vivid and, in a sort of way, massive impression. There are some men who remind one of quite rich and tastefully decorated shop windows. You are less conscious of what may be in the warehouse, so to speak. In others, the exhibits are fewer, and the ghostly warehouse with its contents is very clearly brought to mind.[1]

Writing to Hamilton in 1928, after another stay at Stanway, it is clear that de la Mare fits Barrie into the latter category.

Apart from the qualities of his writing which no one disputes, I have sometimes wondered whether Barrie has ever set down his innermost feelings and conclusions about this complicated existence of ours. There is that opening act to *Brutus* – which suggests that if he really tackled a tragedy there would be some deadly clouds in it whatever silver linings might appear. Being in his company one feels that – his steady listening and the little he says. Not that an artist is bound to tell everything, or that he should not definitely choose to hold his tongue when he thinks that loosening it will be of no service in what he is most intent on. Still – I wonder what you feel?[2]

Meanwhile, Cynthia wrote that she and Barrie agreed that de la Mare must be 'the most undisappointing poet that's ever been. He enchanted every man, woman, and child . . . I love his questing, marvelling mind, and his refusal – or rather inability – to waste one second's time on small talk.' By the time de la Mare visited Stanway in the summer of 1932, when G. K. Chesterton was also staying, he wrote to a friend that, aside from his head,

> Barrie is a sort of Chesterton *in parvo*, of all but the same angle of rotundity, and to watch them together gladdens the eye. I love talking to Barrie. He is always full of the crispest and most sagacious reminiscences, and I always feel that he has never yet written his *own* book.[3]

Like Barrie, de la Mare fell under the spell of Stanway; it was here – on seeing in the churchyard close by a little woman in black scrubbing her husband's tombstone – that he was inspired to write 'Beneath a Motionless Yew'.

When Barrie took Stanway for the summer of 1922, in addition to his hostess Cynthia and her family, he was accompanied by his new butler, Frank Thurston. The smiling Harry Brown, who had looked after Barrie so devotedly for twelve years, had recently been obliged to leave London as a result of his wife's ill health. Brown bought a small farm in Lincolnshire, and such was his affection for Barrie that every year parcels of fruit and other produce were sent up to brighten his old employer's London table.

Barrie missed Brown, but the new butler-valet-doorkeeper was soon to prove himself, in his own way, as loyal and devoted as his predecessor. Apart from a period in the trenches, Frank Thurston had apparently always worked as a butler, though he could not have been a more different character from the cheerful Harry Brown. Thurston's ability to enter and leave a room with absolute silence was a reflection of his enigmatic and, some thought, slightly sinister personality. To compound the mystery he had somehow familiarised himself not only with Spanish and French, but also with Latin and Greek. In addition to admirably fulfilling his role as skilled and urbane butler, it soon became clear that Thurston was a man of startling learning. Cynthia wrote of him:

> Dictionaries and various learned tomes soon cluttered up the pantry, where I would constantly find him reading Latin or Greek while he polished the silver.
>
> Thurston had an astonishing memory for other things besides living and dead languages. He could supply any forgotten date or quotation. One day Barrie remarked that the only line in an Oxford quotation that survived was 'A rose red city half as old as Time'.

Though we all knew this line, no one of us could remember the name of the poet.'⁴

When Cynthia's husband, Beb, confessed that he couldn't remember the name of the 'rose red city' and no one else at the table could either, Thurston, passing around the meat, finally said, 'Was it not Petra, Sir?'

Thurston's erudition was a permanent source of delight to Barrie and he enjoyed comparing his butler's exalted choice of reading matter with the light literature enjoyed by most distinguished authors. He took to advising guests that if they were thinking of reading a thriller in bed they would be advised 'to hide it between a Pliny and the latest theory of Ethics'.

Contact with children, in this case the Asquiths' sons, Michael and Simon, once again acted as catalyst, and through the mid to late twenties Barrie wrote several short pieces performed at Stanway at Christmas and other holidays. Though the company was made up of children – the Asquith boys and Wemyss cousins – and the plays were in some sense elaborate jokes, Barrie threw himself into their production with as much fervour as if they were performances on the West End stage. In lengthy rehearsals he coaxed, cajoled and at times grew exasperated with the children for not being professionals. They remained dedicated, grew tired, and were sometimes baffled under the tutelage of this small tyrant. And yet Barrie's intensity and enthusiasm spread an excitement amongst them so that when family and friends sat hushed to watch in the great hall, an atmosphere at times both haunting and touching infused the performances of little plays, with titles such as *Where Was Simon* and *The Wheel*.

At Stanway, as well as the possibilities for good conversation over lunch and dinner, for Barrie an integral part of the weeks of holiday were the games. These included croquet, lawn cricket, throwing stamps on to the ceiling, shuffles and charades. As Cynthia noted of Barrie, he was possessed of 'that mysterious asset, a good eye'. She continued, 'How good it was I never fully realised until I saw his almost demonic skill at golf croquet. From the furthest possible distance he would let fly at an adversary's ball and hit it.' But the game to which Barrie became positively addicted was the Stanway version of shuffleboard, and this he played like a demon.

Barrie's craze for shuffles proved even more lasting than I'd hoped. Night after night he would scuttle from the dining table to the board for practice shots; then sides would be picked – usually he captained one, I the other – after which for an hour or so the hall would resound with the clang of the misdirected disks hurtling onto the stone floor, whoops of triumph, yells of derision.

Nearly all the guests caught their host's passion for the game. They snatched what practice they could during the day, and lined up tense with anxiety for the evening's contest.[5]

One of the most enthusiastic Barrie initiates into the game of shuffle-board was the then Lord Chancellor, Lord Cave, who became so obsessed he had a miniature version of it made for his London house.

In keeping with Barrie's accustomed behaviour in most situations, as host he was fluctuating and unpredictable. And although escalating over time, with luck a low period might sometimes lift for weeks. In one of these phases, for days on end he was the most dazzling and exhilarating of companions, and no one could ask for a more charming, considerate, funny and entertaining host.

At Stanway Barrie enjoyed spending time with some of the Stanway characters almost as much as with his grand and illustrious guests. He said, 'the atmosphere around Stanway fosters idiosyncrasy', and would sit for hours with the gamekeeper, Harry Last, or the old ex-coachman, James Prew, listening sympathetically as Prew condemned 'progress'. Cynthia wrote that he would tell Barrie 'how in the early days of "them motor cars" – contraptions which he still hoped, and I think believed, would prove no more than passing follies – he had constantly been summoned to drive the old mare to the rescue of stranded motorists. "Osses is best. Osses is best," he would scornfully chuckle.'[6]

In Barrie's later years, it wasn't only Cynthia who generated the hospitality and support. Although Barrie often gave large cheques to Cynthia as presents, she and Beb remained short of money and were obliged during most summers to let their London house. When they weren't at Stanway, the Asquiths were invited to stay at Adelphi Terrace with Barrie.

He was quite aware that Cynthia needed his money, but he also under-stood that this was not the only thing that tied her to him. Like Sylvia Davies before her, the manner in which Cynthia squared up to Barrie's financial generosity to her wasn't a simple matter. He exasperated Cynthia, annoyed her – at times she lashed out at him – but she also felt for him a particular sense of care and responsibility. Their relationship had become one of reciprocal need. Again, like Sylvia, Cynthia was not in love with Barrie, but at the same time his complex personality never ceased to fascinate her. In turn he paid court to her, respected her, leant on her, and increasingly needed her to care for him and soothe his sometimes raw emotional state. For her part Cynthia gave him a number of her confidences, and, as the years passed, grew more fond of him too. This was altogether safer, less emotionally taxing and less subterranean than his relationship with Sylvia had been

With Lord Tennyson, George Meredith and Thomas Hardy as his illustrious predecessors, in 1928 Barrie was invited to become the fourth President of the Society of Authors. In his acceptance he was conscious of the tribute being paid him, and made himself a conscientious and generous president of this curiously august society. A kind of professional trades union for writers, from its inception in 1884 the Society included amongst its highly individualist members virtually all of the most distinguished writers of the day.

The presidency became vacant with the death of Barrie's old hero Thomas Hardy in January of that year. On the day following Hardy's death Barrie telephoned the Dean of Westminster to request Hardy's burial in Poets' Corner. Unlike his request for this honour for Meredith, in Hardy's case it was granted at once. After much telephoning and letter writing, Barrie then negotiated a compromise of a very literary kind. Hardy's wish to be buried in his beloved Stinsford churchyard, beside his family and first wife, was fulfilled. But it was done with a modification. His heart was buried in a casket at Stinsford, while his body was brought to London for its very public interment at Westminster Abbey.

The abbey was crowded to overflowing as the pallbearers solemnly bore their prize up the long nave aisle. Their number included two prime ministers, Baldwin and Ramsay MacDonald, Barrie, Kipling, Bernard Shaw, Galsworthy and A. E. Housman. By far the tallest and most impressive-looking figure, Shaw, later declared with irritation that 'I looked very well myself, but Barrie, blast him! looked far the most effective. He made himself look specially small.' Barrie understood how to hold centre stage more subtly than Shaw ever did.

He was by now an institution, a kind of national icon, and, whatever the critics might say, the British public had long since taken him to their hearts. He could meet anyone he chose, anything he did was news, and the honours continued to be awarded. When Barrie was appointed to the Order of Merit for his contribution to literature, he wore the court livery for the occasion, but with reluctance. This irksome duty provoked a letter to a friend in which he complained, 'Yes, I had to go to Buckingham Palace and in *knee-britches* (closed car and sneaked to and fro like a burglar). My stockings misbehaved and creased like a concertina.'

Remembering his origins, at his inauguration as chancellor of Edinburgh University, in 1930, Barrie made an impassioned plea for the right of all social classes to a full education. His identification with the poor had remained throughout his life: as he wrote to Cynthia Asquith in December 1920,

> You are right about the two friends of yours I met. The poor one sounds more interesting. I like poor people best. They are so much more human if they don't get bitter, and they can also be human in bitterness. The poor are at their best (and easiest) when they are all poor together, and not flung among the other kind.[7]

While retaining a number of his old literary friends, Barrie was sought after by many others too. His position enabled him to socialise with some of the most absorbing and engaging figures of his time. Amongst these were of course the actresses, including Ellen Terry, Mrs Patrick Campbell and the great Sybil Thorndike. Barrie also enjoyed entertaining the Archbishop of Canterbury, and by contrast the Irish freedom fighter Michael Collins, who became a friend. Barrie's was an intuitive rather than an analytical approach to politics. None the less he liked to feel that his finger was on its pulse, maintaining friendships with the most senior of politicians, including prime ministers from Ramsey MacDonald to Asquith, Lloyd George and Stanley Baldwin.

With regard to his writing, despite his resilient attitude to editorial rejection as a young man, Barrie never grew quite such thick skin about his later work. A younger generation of postwar writers was busy forging new ways of speaking, and in the late 1920s and 30s many of them thought Barrie a whimsical old has-been. Barrie himself remained in touch with much that was going on. His friendship with A. P. Herbert, the young J. B. Priestley, who in 1930 he called '*the* man of those knocking at the door', and his appreciation of D. H. Lawrence's writing, are cases in point. In 1914, less than a year after the publication of Lawrence's *Sons and Lovers*, Barrie was recommending it to friends with a proselytising zeal. In 1924 he wrote to Cynthia (who had earlier befriended Lawrence), that

> I am reading *Kangaroo* . . . In chunks I don't follow him, but it is very vivid, and the coarsenesses − as if those of an ugly youth creeping out of him like ghosts − are really a very small affair. There are power and poetry in him as in few. A . . . man with such a passionate interest in himself, roaming the world in search of that self and finding it everywhere. But he is big, and, I should think, in some ways lovable.[8]

At the same time as keeping abreast of the work of new writers, Barrie's acute sensitivity and awareness of the critics' perception of his own made him say in a speech to the Critics' Circle,

> Your word for me would probably be fantastic. I was quite prepared to hear it from your chairman, because I felt he could not be so shabby as to say whimsical, and that he might forget to say elusive. If you knew how dejected these terms have often made me. I am quite serious. I never believed I was any of these things until you dinned them into me. Few have tried harder to be simple and direct. I have always thought that I was rather realistic.[9]

In 1937 Hugh Walpole wrote that in 1922 there had been the fashion

> of Noel Coward, of the early Arlen. Life was so nasty that we must laugh at it and show that, though it might trample us down, we could snigger to the very end . . .
>
> And still more in 1935, how different! To believe in the Good and the True . . . in 1935 was to declare yourself a catchpenny hypocrite. You *could* not believe in such things the world being what it was. One or two men of letters did so believe – Conrad, Robert Bridges, Masefield, but didn't they get it in the neck if they said so![10]

As time passed, despite Barrie's honours and status, with age and loss he was able to communicate well with only a few. He was slowing down, and frenetic activity and socialising no longer suited him. Yet the old ambivalence remained. Writing to one friend he recognised that he needed to spend time alone. 'It seems to be a law of my nature that I must be a good deal by myself.' While to another he lamented, 'I am alone and lonely.'

To avoid the hours of lying awake he often read into the night. He wrote to Cynthia, 'I feel Trollope and I are living here together, for I seem to spend so much of my time with him, especially in the long hours after midnight.'

Barrie's dark moods were now always close at hand, while the insomnia grew worse. There were official occasions, but most of the time it was only a small group of intimates who really mattered. Amongst these were E. V. Lucas, Freyberg, Turley Smith, Elizabeth Lucas, Cynthia, Peter, Nico, while for friends outside London there was Lady Wemyss at Stanway, and for some time now Frances Horner at Mells, another of the Souls, painted by Burne-Jones. At times even these friends couldn't get through, and Barrie wrote, 'No wonder I sometimes shudder at myself. I do, and then

I get really afraid of the future. To keep oneself at arm's length becomes almost a profession with me.'

In 1933 he returned to Scotland and stayed in a large old white-walled house, Balnaboth, up beyond Kirriemuir in Glen Prosen. Amongst his companions were Cynthia, Beb, their two sons, Michael and Simon, Peter and his wife, Algernon Cecil, Stephen Gwynne, Lady Wemyss and Elizabeth Lucas. Barrie needed to pay this visit to his homeland, though he was unsettled at being mobbed by journalists on the way from Kirriemuir to Balnaboth. He was enthusiastic about having visitors in from Kirriemuir, and then felt exhausted and regretted it when they overstayed. In this way the holiday passed with corresponding swings between what Cynthia called 'gloom and glory' days.

Others might have spent time in laying ghosts but predictably Barrie went in search of reliving his past. Yet, finding its contrast with the present too great for him to bear, he grew distressed. Housman's lines repeatedly came into Cynthia's head:

> That is the land of lost content,
> I see it shining plain,
> The happy highways where I went
> And cannot come again.

Amongst the visitors to Balnaboth was the prime minister, Ramsay MacDonald. Like Barrie, MacDonald suffered from insomnia, and the two men sat up in animated talk into the early-morning hours. The Duke and Duchess of York were staying nearby at Glamis Castle and brought their two little daughters, Elizabeth and Margaret, to tea. The following day a small party was asked in return to Glamis. It was Princess Margaret's third birthday and Barrie sat beside her. Soon after this occasion the little princess heard Barrie's name mentioned and said immediately, 'I know that man. He is my greatest friend, and I am his greatest friend.'

Whatever difficulties the holiday near Kirriemuir presented at the time, afterwards Barrie felt revived by it and wrote to Cynthia,

I am so glad you did enjoy Glen Prosen . . . fain would I have lingered. For the first time perhaps I was 'sweir' to return to London that eternally thrills me and has been to me all the bright hopes of my youth conceived . . . I do love my native region with almost a ferocity of attachment. The houses and its hills and little bridges over the burns had a steadying effect on me.[11]

In the succeeding years, with the progressive bouts of illness and depression Barrie became subject to the most dramatic reversals of mood, and his insomnia grew worse. As once before – after Michael's death – the doctor now prescribed heroin to calm Barrie and help him to sleep. Instead of tranquillising him the drug had the opposite effect. Repeatedly, he failed to sleep, became intensely agitated, and then euphoric. The next morning he would suffer terribly the after-effects of such a 'high'. Miserable, irascible, clamorous, he was frequently confined to bed. Regularly demanding more heroin, no matter how Cynthia reasoned with him, Barrie obstinately forgot its lethal after-effects in favour of the temporary release it gave from his mental and physical anguish. He had to be monitored with care.

For some time the doctors had thought his illness was as much psychological as physical, but they discovered that in fact Barrie's physical problems were real. Although they failed to find their source, cancer was suspected, and Barrie was now often in much pain.

In between the death of old friends, there were beginnings, too. Jack, Peter and Nico were all now married and would provide Barrie with 'grandchildren'. Somehow, though, their marriages conspired, like much else connected with the passage of time, to make him feel superfluous. When Peter had married, in 1932, the last of the Davieses to do so, Barrie had written to Elizabeth Lucas,

I like her very much and they are both very happy. The event is one I have long hoped for and when it is accomplished I suppose I shall feel that my task is over and, as Henley wrote, the long day is done.[12]

But Barrie's long day was not yet done. Despite regular bouts of ill health – in the following year, 1933, he was so ill that for weeks it seemed he would probably not survive – he managed a number of social events. One of the most impressive was the lunch party he organised, in May 1932, for the seventieth birthday of his politician friend Lord Grey of Falloden. To the large book-lined study high up in Adelphi Terrace came some of the most distinguished men of the day. These included the American and French ambassadors, the Archbishop of Canterbury, Neville Chamberlain, Sir Herbert Samuel (leader of the parliamentary Liberal Party), the prime minister, Stanley Baldwin, the ex-politician, essayist and wit Augustine Birrell, Lord Salisbury, Lord Snowden, J. R. Clynes, the editor and biographer J. A. Spender (father of the poet Stephen Spender), Lord Londonderry, Walter Runciman, Lord Macmillan, Winston Churchill, Sir Donald

Maclean, Barrie's old friend Thomas Gilmour, the writer John Buchan, and Bernard Freyberg.

Barrie spent much of his last two years working on a play, *The Boy David*. Once again he was enchanted by a young actress, a German called Elizabeth Bergner, and their friendship spurred him on to a concluding bout of artistic activity. Elizabeth Bergner had asked him to write for her a play on the biblical theme of the young King David and Jonathan. Inevitably one finds echos of a familiar theme: the death of the boy David in childhood, the little boy David in *The Little White Bird* and the lost boy, Peter Pan. But the play also uses visions and dreams to explore the inherent tragedy in the relationship between David and Saul, here a profoundly tormented and divided figure.

After numerous and dispiriting delays *The Boy David* was given a trial run in Edinburgh at the end of November 1936. On the morning of the premiere, with Barrie by now really unwell, Cynthia felt obliged to tell him that his old friend Gilmour had just died. Illness had prevented Barrie from attending many rehearsals, and thus his usual practice of revising as rehearsals progressed was impossible. In addition, Augustus John's sets for the production were quite inappropriate. Despite this, although uneven, complemented by music from the young William Walton, the play was well received in Edinburgh. Several London reviewers, however, travelled up to see it, and preceded its move to London with critical assessments. In a staunch defence Granville Barker wrote that the critics 'wanted to know why an author who had become famous for his power to create characters should go to the Bible for a theme and then distort the story, and in any case have a woman, and a foreign woman at that?' Barker, however, said he 'couldn't understand how anyone with a sense of dramatic dialogue could fail to appreciate the play'. Despite having been seen by 60,000 people, it was taken off after only seven weeks.

The failure of *The Boy David* was said by some to have hastened Barrie's end. Even if it did, he was by now also severely weakened through illness. Coinciding with this literary disappointment was the knowledge that his beloved Adelphi Terrace was soon to be demolished, and he would have to find somewhere else to live. He wrote with regret, 'I have seldom seen the outlook here so lovely as it is after sunsets these nights. All the world a trembling light blue except for the lamps. Sad if one has to say goodbye to it.' And to another friend he said

> Even the light will be taken from me soon as I suppose another monster building will soon be going up. They are debating about it (the demolition of Adelphi Terrace) in the House of Lords

tomorrow, but it is hardly conceivable that commerce will not carry the day . . . I am not really depressed these days, or at any rate it is just over my faults. I gloat many a time over my long unfair good fortune.[13]

Erratic though Barrie's friendship could be, one of the qualities he maintained throughout his life was the capacity to console others when they were truly in need. Though himself ill and worn out, when Lady Wemyss, Cynthia's mother, died early in 1937 Cynthia was able to write of Barrie,

> I shall never forget the gentleness and skill with which, seemingly forgetting all his own sorrow, deep-down tiredness and pains, he set himself, as he alone could, to comfort and support; nor how deeply one could draw on that to some perhaps surprising fund of practical wisdom always available when needed.[14]

As his own health declined still more, his moods could oscillate with a terrible force from impotent fury to abject misery and dejection. This was followed by periods of elation, after which he sometimes recognised almost no one. For years Barrie had found solace in Cynthia reading to him, and in this last phase he repeatedly asked for Shakespeare. This included the passage from *Lear* in which fall the lines:

> Vex not his ghost. O, let him pass! He hates him
> That would upon the rack of this tough world
> Stretch him out longer.

And always there was still the capacity to amuse. Only two weeks before his death Barrie and H. G. Wells were invited to a small dinner at Cynthia and Beb's house in Regent's Park. Cynthia wrote that the two men – who were in the habit of mutually inspiring each other's humour – 'Made us laugh all the way through dinner, especially by their jokes about the startling new symptoms they had invented to tell their doctor, Lord Horder, whom they were shortly to meet for dinner at the Garrick Club.'

The following day Barrie appeared to remember little of the previous evening's entertainment. Cynthia was exhausted, but then thinking he had improved a little she travelled down to stay in Cornwall for a few days with Beb and Simon. Two days later, on 13th June, Peter Davies rang to say that Barrie was suddenly very ill. Cynthia left immediately and drove back to London through the night, arriving at the nursing home early the following morning. Freyberg, Peter and Nico had been sitting out four-hour shifts with Barrie, who looked dreadful, and in the ensuing days was only intermittently conscious. Mary Cannan travelled from France, and stood for a time by the bedside of the man who had been her husband a quarter of a century before.

The end came on Saturday 19th June 1937, with Peter, Nico and Cynthia at his side. For all Barrie's fear in the preceding years Nico would say that in this last period 'He was tired. He wanted to go.' Yet still troubled, at the end the last words he was heard to murmur were, 'I can't sleep.'

The messages of condolence to the Davieses poured in, including one from the King, which read,

WINDSOR CASTLE
PETER DAVIES ESQ 8 BRUNSWICK GARDENS W8
THE QUEEN AND I ARE SO GRIEVED AT THE DEATH OF OUR OLD FRIEND SIR JAMES BARRIE. HIS LOSS WILL BE UNIVERSALLY MOURNED FOR HIS WRITING HAS BROUGHT JOY AND INSPIRATION TO YOUNG AND OLD ALIKE. WE SINCERELY SYMPATHISE WITH YOU IN YOUR SORROW = GEORGE R I[15]

The funeral was an occasion for national mourning. Crowds gathered; reporters and newsreel men came to record the day, and many well-known figures followed the coffin to the cemetery on Kirriemuir Hill. Barrie had made it clear that it was here, with his own kind, that he wanted his final resting place to be. Thus, his name can be found inscribed – as he insisted, 'with no embellishment of any kind' – at the foot of the plain granite gravestone set high on the hill looking out over the rolling farm-land of Strathmore, with its back to the wildness of the glens. The grave-stone already bore the names of his parents, of two sisters who had died in infancy, of his sister Jenann, and of his brother David, whose death long ago had coloured so much of Barrie's own extraordinary and unquiet life.

In Kirriemuir on the day of his funeral the shops and factories remained closed. After the service the streets were lined with people, as the funeral procession made its way along Brechin Road past the tiny cottage where he was born and on up to the cemetery on the hill. In Edinburgh at the same time an open-air service for six hundred was held in the Old College quad of Barrie's university. A month later a memorial service took place at St Paul's Cathedral. With the cathedral full, the Archbishop of Canterbury gave the address.

★   ★   ★

Although Barrie had made a will several times, and had hinted to Cynthia that good provision would be made for her, his struggle with the idea of death meant that whenever she encouraged him to finalise and sign this last will, he refused to talk about it and withdrew. Periodically it would worry him but still he did nothing. Then, on his deathbed, when his doctor, Lord Horder, had been sent for by the nursing-home doctors, so also was Barrie's solicitor, Sir Reginald Poole, the man who had succeeded George Lewis. Cynthia spoke at length to Poole. He consulted with Lord Horder, and some time later Barrie was given medication, which brought him round from what appeared to be a coma. With Poole and Horder as witnesses he finally signed his will. Its dispositions were to shock his relations and others close to him.

Barrie left just under £173,500. In February 1929 Great Ormond Street Hospital for Sick Children, under the chairmanship of Lord Wemyss, had written asking if Barrie would lead the hospital's appeal. Asking them to excuse him, Barrie said he wasn't the right person, that he had 'grown stale through trying to do other not dissimilar things . . . at some future time I might find a way'[16]. He soon relented, however, and in April made national headlines when he presented them with the lucrative rights to *Peter Pan*, *The Little White Bird*, *Peter Pan in Kensington Gardens* and *Peter and Wendy*. Apart from this bequest the lion's share of his estate went not to the Llewelyn Davies family nor to any of his blood relations, but instead to Cynthia Asquith.

Cynthia and Peter were to be Barrie's executors and literary executors. Apart from bequests to friends and relations, such as Elizabeth Lucas, Bernard Freyberg, Charles Turley Smith, his butler, Frank Thurston, the cook, Mrs Stanley, and family members, he bequeathed one thousand pounds and an annuity of six hundred pounds to his ex-wife Mary, 'my dear Mary Cannan with my affectionate regards', to Jack Llewelyn Davies he left six thousand pounds, to Nico three, while Peter was to share Barrie's furniture, manuscripts, letters and other papers, and his real and personal estate, with Cynthia. In addition, Barrie left to Cynthia not only the sum of thirty thousand pounds, but also the rights to *all* his plays and books, with the exception of *Peter Pan* and associated works. Sir Reginald Poole had told Cynthia that she was to share Barrie's rights with Peter Davies, but as it turned out Poole was mistaken, and Peter had inherited none of them. Clearly Barrie was rewarding Cynthia for her devoted care and friendship in the last years of his life. His will was also a message to the Davies brothers, Peter, Jack and Nico. He appeared to be telling them they had failed to include him enough. This may have been correct, though the fault would have been as much Barrie's as theirs. His devotion had become qualified. The heart of the problem was no doubt Jack's, Peter's and Nico's wives. However hard they may have tried to include him, Barrie could never really accept that he was no longer the centre of the boys' lives, and their focus was now turned to their wives and children. At the last, it was growing up that once again appeared to have blighted Barrie's life. As a result he felt that the one person in his last years who had invited him into her life with little reserve was Cynthia Asquith. Jack, Peter and Nico were in a sense Barrie's children, so it was easier for Cynthia, an outsider, to have a more straightforward relationship with him.

Peter had seen earlier drafts of Barrie's will, which differed from the final one, and for a time he and Nico considered contesting it. Unwilling, however, to go through the unpleasantness of challenging Cynthia in the courts, they decided against making formal objection.

For the remainder of the Davieses' working lives Jack was in the navy, while Peter and Nico would both spend theirs involved with books. Peter had launched a successful publishing firm, Peter Davies Ltd, and after a few years Nico joined him there. But the story was not yet quite ended. Mingled with the family papers and material wealth Peter inherited from Barrie, was a complex and often painful emotional legacy. Both his parents had died before he was fourteen, then four years later his older brother, George, was killed in France. In the following year Peter experienced a gruesome period on the Somme, a nervous breakdown, return to the battlefield, and, after the war, Michael's almost certain suicide. At the time Peter was still only twenty-four. With this mournful inheritance in mind, after visiting George's grave in 1945 he wrote to Mary Hodgson saying, 'how I wish I could think more of the happy beginnings and less of the melancholy end'. A year later when writing to Dolly Ponsonby regarding the compilation of his family *Morgue*, in referring to his upbringing Peter said, 'I am only now . . . after thirty years or more, beginning to uncoil myself from the various complexes . . . "all that" twisted me up in.'[17]

To compound the sadness, a letter from Peter to Mary Hodgson in 1950 said he didn't see Jack now. Jack, of whom their cousin, Daphne du Maurier, would say he was 'very bitter about life though not a melancholic', died in 1959. In 1960 Peter wrote a final letter to Dolly in which he thanked her for hers that he 'so loved getting', and said that for him 'writing has become a fearful effort'. He told Dolly she had given him 'treasured glimpses' of his mother and 'of my splendid father'. Concluding, he said that '"melancholy has marked me for her own"'. No more photographs please. We leave here soon, I don't know where for. Thank you so very much for writing.'[18] Dogged by depression, suffering badly from emphysema, and knowing that his three sons, like his wife, were all ill with Huntington's Chorea, shortly afterwards Peter threw himself under a train at Sloane Square underground station. In the same year Cynthia Asquith also died.

Nico lived on for another twenty years. As the youngest and possibly the least damaged by the weight of his heritage, throughout his life he retained that same essentially blithe attitude that had made Michael say of him, 'My tutor told me he wished I was like Nico; he says he's the heart and soul of the house.' Leaving behind a daughter Laura, Barrie's god-daughter and one of the last of the Llewelyn Davies line, Nico died in 1980.

Epilogue

Barrie died honoured with a Baronetcy, and had made more money from writing than any other writer on record. By far the most popular playwright of his day, he nevertheless always had his detractors. As a result, their voice had gained such momentum that by the 1950s and 60s his work was rejected by the greater part of the critical establishment. Regardless of this critical mauling, Barrie's best works remained successful with the public. Apart from those made into Hollywood films in his lifetime, in the sixty-eight years since his death in 1937, his writing continued intermittently to inspire radio and television adaptations, and performance in numerous amateur theatre productions across the English-speaking world.

Despite his hugely successful literary output in his lifetime, since his death *Peter Pan* has so eclipsed Barrie's other writing that many people today know this alone of all his varied works.

Endlessly changed, recast and reworked, hundreds of storybook retellings, Christmas pantomimes, films, and novels have been inspired by Peter Pan's dilemma. The play has twice been made into a Disney cartoon, first in 1952 by Disney himself, and in recent years the National Theatre has staged it. With *Hook,* in 1991, Hollywood reinterpreted it, while in 2003 yet another adaptation of *Peter Pan* was filmed. Here, although the plot is gratuitously altered and the crucially veiled sexual chemistry between Peter and Wendy is made crassly explicit, somehow, even in its gross simplification, Barrie's message is not entirely lost.

In 2004, to mark the one-hundredth anniversary of the play's launch, Hollywood attempted a 'bio-pic' of Barrie himself, interwoven with his creation of *Peter Pan*. *Finding Neverland* mocks history through its wanton (although admittedly Barrie-like) disregard for the facts, and its wholesale reworking of the lives of the writer and those around him. It avoids the darker, more subtle possibilities of the play, including Hook's seductive supplanting of Wendy's father in her emotions, and also the idea of Wendy as Peter's fantasy lover/mother. Even though it crudely simplifies

Peter Pan's profoundly layered and complex significance, what the film does attempt to look at – through Barrie himself – is the sources and consolations of creativity.

Like other outstanding works of art, *Peter Pan* is able to withstand its refashioning for succeeding generations. Yet, what is it about the play that continues, across genres and ages, to exert such strong, universal appeal? Though nominally written for children, *Peter Pan's* implications extend far beyond the world of any child. The force of the myth is elemental, its characters perfectly symbolising aspects of eternal themes: the relentlessness of time, and the problem of growing up. As in all his writing, in *Peter Pan* Barrie neither gives us answers, nor tells us what to think. Instead, he poses questions in an original and subtly expanding way, so that the play opens up possibilities of thought beyond the apparently simple and immediate plot being acted out for us on the stage. To argue that *Peter Pan* is Barrie's personal artistic fantasy, created to relieve the pain or inadequacy he felt in his own private life, doesn't go nearly far enough towards explaining its extraordinary endurance, and its distinction as a major work of art independent of the life of its creator.

Barrie may not have been quite as convinced as Nietzsche that 'God is dead', but he certainly had misgivings. If he held up to his contemporaries a mirror of their anxieties at the dawn of an age of doubt, he also voiced their hesitation at becoming adults in a world where a sense of emptiness and isolation were increasingly familiar experiences. At the same time, he understood that essential aspects of his work were probably unacceptable, unless presented within the context of ostensibly light-hearted fairy-tales. The message of *Peter Pan*, in particular, would otherwise be unacceptable because it is etched with despair. The world in which Peter Pan and Barrie's contemporaries were asked to become adults was coloured by what they saw as the arid practicalities of industrialism, and its fundamental rejection of the joyful and nurturing aspects of play. This world was ruled by rationality and the belief that nothing whatever exists beyond the bounds of human cognition and thought. Many intuitively felt that transition to adulthood here was at the cost of the crushing of their spirit.

As the personification of childhood, Peter Pan represents the sovereign power of the imagination as experienced through play. His whole being is devoted to revealing for us the utterly crucial value of this to the growth of the human spirit. This then must surely be at the heart of the child's, and our own, powerful 'recognition' of the Glorious Boy, who cries out to Hook so triumphantly, 'I'm youth, I'm joy'.

In all Barrie's greatest plays, when the protagonists are taken out of themselves and temporarily escape from their real world, they return to discover a deeper, often disquieting understanding of what they had left behind. Peter's tragedy is that he – unlike Wendy and the boys – has chosen never to return. But his Never Land is only possible by inhabiting an eternal present. By obliterating time, Peter can never move on and grow. Believing that in giving up play a part of him will die, he fails to make the transition from his world to adulthood and informed reality. Here, all being well, carrying with us from childhood an imagination intact, we experience more profoundly and learn to acknowledge suffering, and ultimately our own death.

Contrary to the way in which his play has often been interpreted, Barrie understood perfectly well the tension and the tragic limitations at the heart of his world of fantasy. He was aware that a fantasy inhabited for too long must be a disappointing and inadequate substitute for the real, however fearful and lacking in direction that reality may be.

Peter Pan has become an instantly recognizable symbol of our own time. We could say he has come of age. Life at the start of the twenty-first century identifies easily with his desire for escape; he speaks to our sense of isolation, and the conviction that there is nothing more than man. For the first time in human history, it is possible to be removed from the dominion of brute necessity, and to play all day. As well as the well-publicised celebrity Peter Pans, who retreat into fragile modern Never Lands, thousands of others spend a good parts of their lives inhabiting the fantasy creations of virtual reality; worlds of mechanised imagination and pleasure 'better' than the real world out there.

Superficially colourful and exciting, and yet essentially second-hand, such worlds may have little of the punishing drabness or harshness of the old-fashioned and direct world of our perceptions, but they also avoid the possibility and profundity of either emotional revelation or intellectual illumination. A world such as ours, so rich in opportunities for barren escape, needs more than ever to attend the message at the heart of Barrie's masterwork: that the immortality of the glorious little god Peter Pan was bought at the cost of his humanity. We reject adulthood at our peril.

J. M. Barrie remains one of the most complex and enigmatic figures in twentieth century literature. Accused of failing to penetrate below the 'surface of life', he was also seen as exploiting his public's emotions 'with steady and skilful perversity'. In his favour, it was recognised that he was 'a master-contriver'. Confusing his critics by disguising the profound significance of his work, at his most powerful Barrie presented feeling, while for those prepared to explore, his flights into fantasy served to reveal more lucidly the realities he saw.

Notes

Editions of Barrie's works used are given at the first instance. For other works see the Bibliography. Unless otherwise attributed, references to Andrew Birkin's *J. M. Barrie and The Lost Boys* refer to the original Constable edition, not the new edition published by Yale in 2003.

1. 'It's no' him, it's just me . . .'

1. Margaret Ogilvy Sweeton draft biography (M.O.S.)
2. Barrie's biography of his mother, *Margaret Ogilvy* p. 13, Hodder & Stoughton
3. *Margaret Ogilvy* p. 18
4. Ibid p. 19
5. Ibid p. 37

2. The Happiest Years of His Life

1. *Margaret Ogilvy* p. 32
2. Ibid p. 30
3. Ibid p. 33
4. *Sentimental Tommy* Vol. I, p. 230, Barrie, British Authors, Tauchnitz Edition, Leipzig
5. *Margaret Ogilvy* pp. 26–8
6. Ibid p. 100
7. Ibid p. 169
8. Hammerton, *The Story of a Genius*, p. 36
9. *Margaret Ogilvy* p. 48
10. Ibid p. 49
11. Ibid p. 26
12. Ibid p. 49

13. Ibid pp. 50–1
14. *The Greenwood Hat* p. 88, Barrie, Peter Davies
15. *McConnachie and J. M.B.: Speeches of J. M. Barrie* p. 83, Peter Davies (here-after called *Speeches*.)
16. *Speeches* pp. 5 and 89
17. *The Greenwood Hat* p. 64
18. *Auld Licht Idylls* pp. 14, 42, 43 Barrie, Hodder & Stoughton
19. *The Greenwood Hat* p. 58
20. *Speeches* p. 86
21. Ibid p. 83

3. 'Literature was my game . . .'

1. *An Edinburgh Eleven* p. 2, Barrie, published by *The British Weekly*
2. Hammerton p. 71
3. *The Entrancing Life* p. 10, Barrie, Hodder and Stoughton
4. Hammerton p. 74
5. *Definitive Edition of the Plays (Collected Plays)*, Barrie, ed. A.E. Wilson, Act III p. 251
6. *Speeches* p. 248
7. *When a Man's Single* p. 33, Barrie, George Newnes
8. Ibid p. 34
9. Ibid p. 35
10. *Home Chimes*, November 1884
11. *When a Man's Single* p. 75
12. *Margaret Ogilvy* p. 63

4. 'To be forever known . . .'

1. *The Greenwood Hat.* p. 8
2. Ibid p. 16
3. Ibid p. 17
4. *Margaret Ogilvy* p. 52
5. Ibid p. 53
6. *Courage*, Barrie, Hodder & Stoughton
7. *The Greenwood Hat* p. 271
8. Ibid p. 29
9. Ibid p. 37
10. *Contemporary Review*, June 1890
11. *The Greenwood Hat* p. 281

12. Ibid p. 281
13. Ibid p. 281
14. Ibid p. 178
15. *Letters of J. M. Barrie* p. 138, ed. Viola Meynell, Peter Davies (hereafter called *Letters*)
16. *The Greenwood Hat* p. 132
17. 'Thomas Hardy: The Historian of Wessex', *Contemporary Review*, July 1889

5. *A Serious Purpose*

1. *When a Man's Single* p. 284
2. *Letters* p. 29
3. *Collected American Edition* of Barrie's Works, Introduction
4. *Speeches* p. vii
5. 'Mr B Gould's Novels', *Contemporary Review*, February 1890

6. *'Genius in him . . .'*

1. *Letters* p. 23
2. *Margaret Ogilvy* pp. 68–9
3. *The Little Minister* p. 34, Barrie, Cassell & Company
4. Ibid p. 190
5. *The Greenwood Hat* p. 145
6. Birkin, *J. M. Barrie and The Lost Boys* p. 22, Constable 1979, also Beinecke Library, Barrie Mss, A2/12
7. Ibid p. 22, also Beinecke Library, Barrie Mss, A2/13
8. *Illustrated London News*, 5 December 1891, also Markgraf, *J. M. Barrie: An Annotated Secondary Bibliography*, 1989
9. *Saturday Review*, 13 November 1897
10. *Letters of Robert Louis Stevenson*, December 1892, Vol. 4 p. 273 Tusitala edn.
11. Ibid, November 1892, Vol. 4 p. 257
12. Hammerton p. 159
13. *The Greenwood Hat* p. 261
14. Ibid p. 266
15. Ormond, *Barrie* p. 44
16. *The Greenwood Hat* p. 267
17. Ibid p. 266
18. Moult, *Barrie* p. 104

7. Mary

1. Jerome, *My Life and Times* p. 133
2. Vanbrugh, *To Tell My Story* p. 29
3. *A Window in Thrums* p. 41, Barrie, Hodder & Stoughton
4. 'Barrie as Dramatist: A Divided Mind', *TLS,* June 1937, see Markgraf p. 3
5. Chalmers, *The Barrie Inspiration* p. 185
6. Hammerton p. 172
7. *Margaret Ogilvy* p. 140
8. Birkin p. 23, also Beinecke Library, Barrie Mss, A2/12
9. *Letters* p. 10
10. Ibid p. 29
11. *Margaret Ogilvy* p. 143

8. 'You must decide . . .'

1. Birkin, p. 25, also Beinecke Library, Barrie Mss, A2/14
2. *The British Weekly,* 19 May 1892.
3. Beinecke Library, Barrie Mss, A2/14
4. Ibid
5. Beinecke Library, Barrie Mss, A2/14, also Birkin, p. 25
6. Irving, *Henry Irving* p. 565
7. *Letters* p. 26
8. Ibid p. 10
9. Ibid p. 21
10. Ansell, *Dogs and Men* p. 11
11. Stashower, *The Life of Arthur Conan Doyle* p. 138
12. Ibid p. 139
13. *The Greenwood Hat* p. 184
14. Beinecke Library, Barrie Mss, A2/14, also Birkin, p. 26
15. *Sentimental Tommy* Vol. II p. 186
16. With the cultural imperative such that any woman, and certainly any actress, over the age of thirty was regarded as beyond her prime, Barrie was probably never told his wife's true age. I am indebted to Robert Greenham for this information, described at greater length in *It Might Have Been Raining,* 2005, his study of his grandmother, housekeeper to the Barries at Black Lake Cottage.
17. *Sentimental Tommy* Vol. I p. 84
18. *Letters* p. 6

19. Birkin p. 29
20. *Letters* p. 7
21. Ansell, *Dogs and Men* p. 12
22. Pamela Maude, *Worlds Away* pp. 137–45
23. *Letters* p. 21
24. See *Letters* of Robert Louis Stevenson
25. Ibid
26. *Letters* Barrie p. 8

9. *Dreams and Reality*

1. *Margaret Ogilvy* p. 175
2. *Sentimental Tommy* Vol. I p. 240
3. Ibid p. 121
4. Ibid pp. 1–4
5. Ibid p. 21
6. Worthen, *D.H. Lawrence: The Early Years* p. 264
7. *Sentimental Tommy* Vol. I p. 214
8. Ibid p. 82
9. Ibid Vol. II p. 44
10. Ibid Vol. I p. 206
11. Ibid p. 209
12. Ibid Vol. II p. 185
13. *Critic*, New York, December 1896, see also Markgraf p. 327
14. *Good Words* 40, Douglas, 1899, see also Markgraf p. 328
15. *Letters* p. 10
16. *Atheneum*, January 1897
17. *British Weekly* and *The Critic*, December 1896, see also Markgraf p. 327
18. George Blake, *Barrie and the Kailyard School*
19. *Margaret Ogilvy* p. 148

10. *America and Fame*

1. Walkley *Drama and Life* p. 9
2. Mackail *The Story of J.M.B.* p. 254
3. Marcosson and Frohman *Charles Frohman* (in introduction, by Barrie)

11. *Sylvia*

1. Dolly Ponsonby, *Diaries*, 13 October 1891
2. *Tommy and Grizel* pp. 43–4
3. Birkin p. 47
4. Ibid p. 48
5. Sylvia du Maurier to Mary Ll D, Birkin p. 50
6. Dolly Ponsonby to Peter Ll D, Birkin p. 49
7. Mary Ll D to Sylvia du Maurier, Birkin p. 50
8. Dolly Ponsonby, *Diaries*, 11 October 1891
9. Ibid, 14 October 1892
10. Dolly Ponsonby to Peter Ll D, Birkin p. 53
11. Dolly Ponsonby, *Diaries*, 21 June 1891
12. *Peter Pan* Act I
13. Beinecke Library, Barrie Mss, A3
14. Ibid
15. Ibid
16. Pamela Maude *Worlds Away*
17. Birkin p. 56, also Beinecke Library, Barrie Mss, A2/20
18. *Tommy and Grizel* p. 399, Cassell and Company
19. Ibid p. 101
20. Ibid p. 41
21. Ibid p. 117
22. Ibid p. 158
23. Ibid p. 411
24. Ibid p. 168
25. Ibid p. 179
26. Ibid p. 191
27. Ibid p. 395
28. *Speeches* p. 110
29. Beinecke Library, Barrie Mss, A2/2
30. *Letters* p. 15
31. Ibid
32. Birkin p. 66
33. *Letters* p. 17
34. Ibid p. 11

12. *The Boy Castaways*

1. Humphrey House, Talk for the BBC in 1948, 'Ideas and Beliefs of the Victorians'

2. Ansell, *Dogs and Men* p. 46
3. Walbrook *J. M. Barrie and the Theatre* p. 60
4. *The Times*, 18 September 1902
5. *Sewanee Review*, January 1901, see also Markgraf p. 348
6. *Blackwoods Edinburgh Magazine*, November 1900, see also Markgraf p. 344
7. *The Boy Castaways of Black Lake Island*, Beinecke Library, Barrie Collection
8. Birkin p. 88
9. *Peter Pan* Dedication p. xxvii

13. A Second Chance

1. *The World*, September 1902
2. Walbrook p. 84
3. *Dictionary of National Biography*
4. Mackail p. 288
5. *Collected Plays* p. 390
6. Audrey Lucas, *E. V. Lucas* p. 1
7. Asquith, *Portrait of Barrie* p. 112
8. *Letters* p. 87
9. Ansell, *Dogs and Men* p. 44
10. Ibid p. 46
11. Ibid p. 57
12. *Letters* p. 156
13. Vanbrugh p. 67
14. *The World*, November 1902, see also Markgraf p. 78
15. *The Little White Bird* (*LWB*) pp. 18–19, Uniform Edition, Hodder and Stoughton
16. Ibid p. 20
17. Ibid p. 118
18. Ibid p. 123
19. Ibid p. 122
20. Ibid p. 129
21. Ibid p. 157
22. Ibid p. 160
23. Ibid p. 162
24. Birkin p. 96
25. Dolly Ponsonby, *Diaries*

14. *Origins*

1. *Peter Pan* Dedication p. vii
2. Beinecke Library, Barrie Mss, A2/20, also Birkin p. 95
3. Green, *Fifty Years of Peter Pan* p. 13
4. *LWB* pp. 199–204
5. Nico Llewelyn Davies in interview with Birkin, Introduction, *J. M. Barrie and The Lost Boys*, Constable 1979
6. Nico Llewelyn Davies in interview with Birkin, Introduction, *J. M. Barrie and The Lost Boys*, New Edition, Yale 2003
7. *Civilization and Its Discontents* pp. 102–3, Vol. 21 Standard Edition of Complete Works, Freud
8. Anita Brookner, *Latecomers* pp. 244–5

15. *Making a Masterpiece*

1. *Speeches* p. 20
2. Phyllis Robbins, *Maude Adams: An Intimate Portrait* p. 90
3. Marcosson and Frohman, *Charles Frohman* p. 362
4. Ibid
5. Steen, *William Nicholson* p. 68
6. Hartnoll, *Oxford Companion to the Theatre* p. 236
7. Green p. 84

16. *'I'm youth I'm joy . . .'*

1. Green p. 115
2. *Peter Pan* p. 5, Uniform Edition, Hodder and Stoughton, 1928
3. *Peter Pan* p. 7
4. *Peter and Wendy* p. 46, Hodder and Stoughton, 1911
5. Ibid p. 76
6. Ibid p. 38
7. Ibid p. 73
8. Ibid p. 203
9. Ibid p. 238
10. Ibid pp. 176–7
11. Ibid pp. 203–4
12. Ibid p. 230
13. Ibid p. 264
14. du Maurier, *Gerald* p. 104
15. Mackail p. 347

16. Green p. 161
17. Markgraf p. 258
18. *Bookman*, December 1920
19. See *Living Age* and *Around Theatres*
20. Green p. 156

17. *Disquiet*

1. Birkin, p. 110
2. Beinecke Library, Barrie Mss, A2/5, also Birkin p. 107–8
3. *Peter and Wendy* pp. 202–3
4. Ibid p. 247
5. Dunbar, *J.M. Barrie: The Man Behind the Image* p. 143
6. Ibid
7. Birkin p. 122
8. Ibid
9. *Peter Pan* p. 91
10. Beinecke Library, Barrie Mss, A2/29
11. *Letters* p. 18
12. I am indebted to Robert Greenham for this information, following his discovery of Mrs Ansell's death certificate.

18. 'The saddest most terrible night . . .'

1. Dolly Ponsonby, *Diaries*, 27 June 1906
2. Ibid, August 1906
3. Birkin p. 145
4. Ibid p. 145
5. Barrie letter to Dolly Ponsonby, Shulbrede
6. Ibid
7. Ibid
8. Birkin p. 150, also Beinecke Library, Barrie Mss, A2/30
9. Beinecke Library, Barrie Mss, A2/30
10. Dunbar p. 162

19. *The End of a Marriage*

1. Kennet, *Self-Portrait of an Artist* p. 76
2. Ibid p. 87
3. Farr, *Gilbert Cannan* p. 30

4. Dolly Ponsonby, *Diaries*, 12 August 1908
5. Arthur Ponsonby, *Diaries*, August 1908
6. Green p. 144
7. Dunbar p. 170
8. Ibid p. 171
9. Ibid p. 174
10. Ibid p. 179
11. Beinecke Library, Barrie Mss, A3 Wells
12. Beinecke Library, Barrie Mss, A3 Sylvia LlD
13. *Complete Plays* p. 775
14. Frances Hackett, *Horizons,* New York, 1919, see also Markgraf p. 353
15. Ansell, *Dogs and Men,* p. 10
16. Dunbar p. 180
17. Ansell, *Dogs and Men* p. 95

20. *A Kind of Family*

1. Birkin p. 181
2. Dunbar p. 172
3. Birkin p. 184
4. Ibid p. 190
5. Ibid p. 191
6. *Letters* p. 2
7. Dunbar p. 197
8. Barrie letter to Dolly Ponsonby, July 1911
9. Peter Ll D letter to Dolly Ponsonby, February 1946
10. Dolly Ponsonby, *Diaries*, August 1911
11. Mrs Norma Douglas Henry in interview with Birkin, see p. 185; available in audio form on his website, www.jmbarrie.co.uk
12. *Speeches* p. 64
13. *Peter Pan* p. xxxiii
14. Scott Polar Research Institute, Ms 1453/163D
15. Speech, *Courage* p. 32 pub. Hodder and Stoughton

21. *War*

1. *Letters* p. 68
2. Dunbar p. 205
3. To Lady Lucas, Nan Herbert, *Letters* p. 109
4. *Letters* p. 110

5. Birkin p. 239
6. Ibid p. 242
7. Ibid p. 244
8. *Letters* p. 70
9. Birkin p. 245
10. Beinecke Library, Barrie Mss, A2/35, also Birkin p. 231

22. 'Something in ourselves . . .'

1. *Letters* p. 112
2. Ibid p. 111
3. Ibid p. 112
4. Cynthia Asquith, *Diaries* p. 262
5. Beinecke Library, Barrie Mss, N4/3 *Neil and Tintinabulum*, also Birkin p. 250
6. Beinecke Library, Barrie Mss, A3 and Dunbar p. 218
7. Jane Ridley, *A Life of Edwyn Lutyens* p. 278
8. *Letters* p. 65
9. Ibid p. 89
10. *Collected Plays* p. 1040
11. Ibid pp. 1045 and 1046
12. *Letters* p. 87

23. Cynthia and Michael

1. Asquith, *Diaries* p. 153
2. Asquith, *Portrait of Barrie* p. 4
3. Asquith, *Haply I May Remember*
4. Asquith, *Diaries,* Foreword
5. Dunbar p. 231
6. Asquith, *Portrait of Barrie,* p. 218
7. *Letters* p. 60
8. Beinecke Library, Barrie Mss, A3, Maude Adams, November 1920
9. Green p. 170.
10. *Letters* p. 170
11. Ibid p. 179
12. Ibid p. 180
13. Ibid p. 184
14. Birkin pp. 286–7; also Beinecke Library, Barrie Mss, A2/40
15. Letters p. 96

16. Birkin p. 289
17. Asquith, *Portrait of Barrie* p. 108
18. Ibid p. 110

24. Beyond the Reach of Time

1. Letter from Nico LI D to Birkin, quoted from *J. M. Barrie and The Lost Boys* p. 291
2. *Letters* p. 190
3. Birkin, p. 295
4. Asquith, *Portrait of Barrie*
5. *Letters*, p. 99
6. Ibid p. 194
7. Ibid p. 195
8. *Courage* extracts
9. *Letters* p. 110
10. Asquith, *Portrait of Barrie* p. 76
11. *Speeches*, Preface
12. Birkin p. 297; also Beinecke Library, Barrie Mss, A2/40
13. Beinecke Library, Barrie Mss, A3, May 1919

25. Release

1. Theresa Whistler's well-considered and sympathetic life of de la Mare, *Imagination of the Heart*, p. 324
2. Ibid
3. Ibid p. 356
4. Asquith, *Portrait of Barrie* p. 49
5. Ibid p. 139
6. Ibid p. 143
7. *Letters* p. 188
8. Ibid p. 200
9. *Speeches*, p. 54
10. Ibid, p. viii
11. *Letters* p. 230
12. Ibid p. 138
13. Ibid p. 227
14. Asquith, *Portrait of Barrie* p. 215
15. Beinecke Barrie Mss, A3, telegram to Peter LI D from King George VI
16. Gt. Ormond St. Hospital for Children Archive, February 1929
17. Peter LI D letter to Dolly Ponsonby, February, 1946, Shulbrede
18. Peter LI D letter to Dolly Ponsonby, February, 1960, Shulbrede

Select Bibliography

Crucial to an understanding of Barrie are his own notebooks, forty-eight in all. Kept throughout his life they are not only notes for projected novels and plays, but are also a kind of autobiography, an unsettling combination of self-knowledge and unconscious revelation. Uninterested in facts as Barrie was, one must, however, be wary of reading his notebooks too literally. These tiny books, many measuring no more than c.2"x3", are held in the *Walter Beineke Jnr. Collection,* housed in The Beinecke Rare Book and Manuscript Library at Yale University. As well as the notebooks, the Beinecke holds the majority of original Barrie material: letters, manuscripts, and some photographs. These include Barrie's notes for *Peter Pan,* entitled *Fairy,* plus the typescripts of the early three-act version of *Peter Pan*, notes on *The Acting of a Fairy Play* – Barrie's instructions to actors – the five-act typescript of *Peter Pan*, and the *Epilogue.* Other material, including quite a number of Barrie letters, are in libraries such as the Bodleian, the British Library, the National Library of Scotland, the Scott Polar Research Institute, and the Houghton Library, Harvard University.

Amongst other unpublished sources are: the *Letters and Diaries* of Lord and Lady Ponsonby, Sylvia Llewelyn Davies' close friends. These are invaluable for their perceptive and intelligent observations on Sylvia, her husband Arthur, and Barrie. Dolly Ponsonby's granddaughters, Laura Ponsonby and Mrs Ian Russell, hold these at Shulbrede Priory with important letters from Peter Llewelyn Davies, Barrie etc. *The Barrie Birthplace,* administered by the National Trust for Scotland, contains some drafts of Barrie's work plus early photographs, while the *Lilly Library* at Indiana University holds the original and much annotated draft of *Peter Pan.* Barrie falsely implied it had been lost. He had in fact given it to Maude Adams, one of his favourite actresses. Only the second actress to take the title role, Adams played to packed houses across America and gave her copy of the play to the library. Tanya Sweeton, a great-great-granddaughter of Barrie's brother, Alick, has letters, photographs and papers relating to the Ogilvy and Barrie families, including drafts for a family biography by Alick's granddaughter Margaret Ogilvy Sweeton. Tanya Sweeton also owns the cradle in which Barrie was put as a baby.

Barrie's Published Works

Barrie's major British publisher was Hodder & Stoughton, who did not, however, produce *Better Dead; the Little Minister; Sentimental Tommy; Tommy and Grizel; Neil and Tintinabulum; The Greenwood Hat; The Boy David; the Letters of J.M.Barrie; and McConnachie and J.M.B: Speeches of J.M. Barrie.* In *A Bibliography of the Writings of Sir James Matthew Barrie Bart., O.M.* and *Sir J. M. Barrie: A Bibliography*, by Herbert Garland and Bradley D. Cutler respectively, there are incomplete lists of Barrie's periodical/newspaper articles. Several hundred of these are in the Periodicals Division of the British Library at Colindale. There are many articles in publications such as *The St James's Gazette, Home Chimes, The Pall Mall Gazette,* and *The British Weekly.* A more up-to-date work, *J.M. Barrie: An annotated Secondary bibliography,* by Carl Markgraf, FLT Press 1989, is extremely thorough and useful.

Typically, irrespective of their having been printed, with Barrie's unerring tendency to revise, he left no definitive edition of his plays. Each of three versions cover most of them. Samuel French Ltd publish an acting edition; Between 1913–37 Hodder and Stoughton, Cassell, and Peter Davies published a 23-volume *Uniform Edition of the Works and Plays of J.M. Barrie;* and Hodder brought out *The Definitive Edition of the Plays of J.M. Barrie* in 1942. (Quotations are taken from the Definitive Edition.) *The Letters of J.M. Barrie* by Viola Meynell is essential reading.

Books on Barrie

These include W.A. Darlington's *J.M. Barrie,* Blackie 1938; J.A. Hammerton's *Barrie, The Story of a Genius,* Sampson Low 1929; *James Matthew Barrie: An Appreciation* by J.A. Roy, Jarrolds 1937; Denis Mackail's anecdotal and encyclopaedic *The Story of J.M.B.,* Peter Davies 1941. Mackail, who knew Barrie and many of his friends, and would have been able to interview them, wrote the first full biography. Though politic and essentially accumulative rather than evaluative, it contains useful insights into Barrie's strange character. *Barrie and the Kailyard School,* by George Blake, Barker 1951, is important for its critical stance, while Cynthia Asquith's memoir, *A Portrait of Barrie* (published by Barrie's nephew, James Barrie, in 1954), is a perceptive, sometimes moving account of the last twenty years of Barrie's life. Her *Diaries 1915–1918* are a fascinating insight. Roger Lancelyn

Green's *Fifty Years of Peter Pan*, Peter Davies 1954, is a marvellous study and a compelling read. Janet Dunbar's *The Man Behind the Image*, Reader's Union 1970, is also very useful. Humphrey Carpenter's essay in *Secret Gardens*, Allen and Unwin 1985, is an astute analysis.

Andrew Birkin's *J. M. Barrie and The Lost Boys*, Constable 1979, and the revised (Yale) edition of 2003 are indispensable. *The Lost Boys* is above all a history of Barrie's relationship with the Llewelyn-Davies family. Birkin included material from interviews with those still living who had connection with Barrie, and was the first to publish extensively from Barrie's notebooks. Nico Llewelyn Davies made over to Birkin a large collection of his family papers and photographs, including the volumes of family chronicle Peter Llewelyn Davies had put together and called *The Morgue*. Birkin has put a selection of this archive, his interviews, and some of Barrie's notes, on his Barrie website: www.jmbarrie.co.uk. He sold the greater part of this archive at Sothebys in 2004, making the proceeds over to The Great Ormond Street Hospital for Children's Charity.

For many years after his death, despite the general biographies, Barrie's writing received little critical notice. Two of the best, and most recent studies, Leonee Ormond's 'J. M. Barrie', in the *Scottish Writers* series, 1986, and R. S. D. Jack's *The Road to Never Land; A Reassessment of J. M. Barrie's Dramatic Art*, Aberdeen University Press 1991, give extensive and challenging analyses of Barrie's writing. These works, plus an article by Lynette Hunter for the *Scottish Literary Journal*, 'J. M. Barrie: The Rejection of Fantasy', have proved constantly thought-provoking and stimulating.

In the last thirty or so years psychoanalysis has discovered Barrie. A number of these studies, plus a greater part of the rash of sophisticated literary criticism on Barrie's work, are often narrowly specialist, biased, tautological, or downright hostile. Harry Geduld's *James Barrie*, 1981, and David Daiches' 'The Sexless Sentimentalist', *The Listener*, 12 May 1960, are cases in point. Jacqueline Rose's *The Case of Peter Pan or the Impossibility of Children's Fiction*, Macmillan 1984, is, however, a more balanced and searching psychoanalytical study.

Other Works:

Eleanor Adlard, ed. *Dear Turley*, Frederick Muller 1942
Sandra Affleck, *The Little Red Town and J.M. Barrie*, Kirriemuir 1990
James Agate, *Those were the Nights*, Hutchinson 1946
James Agate, *The Selective Ego*, Harrap 1976
John Allen, *A History of Theatre in Europe*, Heinemann 1983
Mary Ansell, *Happy Houses*, Cassell 1912
— *The Happy Garden*, Cassell 1912

— *Dogs and Men,* Duckworth 1923

Cynthia Asquith, *Haply I May Remember,* Barrie 1950

— *Portrait of Barrie,* Barrie, 1954

— *Diaries 1915–1918,* Hutchinson 1968

William Archer, *The Old Drama and the New,* Heinemann 1923

Max Beerbohm, *Last Theatres,* Hart-Davis 1970

George Blake, *Barrie and the Kailyard School,* Barker 1951

John Boardman, *The Great God Pan,* Thames and Hudson 1997

Robert Boothby, *My Yesterday, Your Tomorrow,* Hutchinson 1962

J. H. Buckley, *William Ernest Henley,* Princeton, 1945

Thomas Carlyle, *On Heroes and Hero-Worship,* ed. Niemeyer, Nebraska, 1966

Dora Carrington, *Letters and Diaries,* ed. David Garnett, Cape 1975

Patrick Chalmers, *The Barrie Inspiration,* Peter Davies, 1938

Pauline Chase, *Peter Pan's Postbag,* Heinemann, 1909

Fay Compton, *Rosemary: Some Remembrances,* Rivers, 1926

Theresa Whistler, *The Life of Walter de la Mare,* Duckworth 1993

Angela du Maurier, *I'm Only the Sister,* Peter Davies, 1949

Daphne du Maurier, *Gerald: A Portrait,* Gollancz, 1934

— *The du Mauriers,* Gollancz, 1937

Guy du Maurier, *Letters From Lieut. Col. G.L.B. Du Maurier . . . To His Wife,* Bumpus 1915

Diana Farr, *Gilbert Cannan,* Chatto 1978

A. D. S. Fowler, *A History of English Literature,* Blackwell 1987

Morris Fraser, *The Death of Narcissus,* Secker and Warburg 1976

Harry M. Geduld, *James Barrie,* New York, Twayne, New York 1971

Roger Lancelyn Green, *Fifty Years of Peter Pan,* Peter Davies 1954

—*J.M. Barrie,* Peter Davies 1960

Joseph Harker, *Studio and Stage,* Nisbet and Co. 1924

Seymour Hicks, *Between Ourselves,* Cassell 1930

Michael Holroyd, *Lytton Strachey: A Biography,* Penguin 1971

Laurence Irving, *Henry Irving* 1951

Jerome K. Jerome, *My Life and Times,* Hodder and Stoughton

John Kennedy, *Thrums and the Barrie Country,* Cranton 1930

Lady Kennet, Kathleen Scott, *Self-Portrait of an Artist,* Murray 1949

C. Day Lewis, *The Buried Day,* Chatto 1960

Marie Lowndes, *Diaries and Letters,* ed. Susan Lowndes, Chatto 1971

Audrey Lucas, *E. V. Lucas: A Portrait,* Methuen 1939

Desmond MacCarthy, *Theatre,* Kee 1954

Isaac Marcosson and Daniel Frohman, *Charles Frohman,* Bodley Head 1915

A.E.W. Mason, 'James Barrie', *Dictionary of National Biography,* 1949

Cyril Maude, *Behind the Scenes With Cyril Maude*, Murray 1927

Pamela Maude, *Worlds Away*, Heinemann 1964

Meredith, *Letters of George Meredith ed. by His Son*, Constable 1912

Thomas Moult, *Barrie*, Cape 1928

Allardyce Nicoll, *A History of English Drama, 1660–1930*, vols V and VI (1959 and 1973) Cambridge University Press

Alan Reid, *The Regality of Kirriemuir*, John Grant 1909

Phyllis Robbins, *Maude Adams: An Intimate Portrait*, Putnam, New York 1956

Bertrand Russell, *The Autobiography of Bertrand Russell, 1872–1914*, Unwin 1967

Peter Scott, *The Eye of the Wind*, Hodder and Stoughton 1961

Robert Falcon Scott, *Scott's Last Expedition*, Murray 1923

George Shelton, *It's Smee*, Ernest Benn 1928

Daniel Stashower, *Teller of Tales, the Life of Arthur Conan Doyle*, Allen Lane 1999

Robert Louis Stevenson, *The Letters of Robert Louis Stevenson*, ed. Sir Sidney Colvin, Heinemann 1924

Ellen Terry, *Memoirs*, Gollancz 1933

Irene Vanbrugh, *To Tell My Story*, Hutchinson 1948

H. M. Walbrook, *J.M. Barrie and the Theatre*, F.V. White 1922

A. B. Walkley, *Drama and Life*, Methuen 1922

Stanley Weintraub, *Whistler*, Collins 1974

Theresa Whistler, *Imagination of the Heart: The Life of Walter de la Mare*, Duckworth, 1993

John Worthen, *D.H. Lawrence: the Early Years*, Cambridge University Press 1992

Index